Emily Post's

Wedding Etiquette

FIFTH EDITION

ALSO FROM THE EMILY POST INSTITUTE

Emily Post's Etiquette, 17th Edition

Emily Post's The Gift of Good Manners

Emily Post's Wedding Planner, Fourth Edition

Emily Post's Entertaining

Emily Post's The Etiquette Advantage in Business, Second Edition

Essential Manners for Men

Essential Manners for Couples

Emily Post's The Guide to Good Manners for Kids

Emily Post's Favorite Party and Dining Tips

Wedding Etiquette

FIFTH EDITION

PEGGY POST

Collins
An Imprint of HarperCollinsPublishers

EMILY POST'S® WEDDING ETIQUETTE (FIFTH EDITION). Copyright © 2006
by The Emily Post Institute, Inc. All rights reserved. Printed in the United States of America.
No part of this book may be used or reproduced in any manner whatsoever without written permission
except in the case of brief quotations embodied in critical articles and reviews. For information,
address HarperCollins Publishers Inc., 10 East 53rd Street, New York, NY 10022.

HarperCollins books may be purchased for educational, business, or sales promotional use.
For information, please write: Special Markets Department, HarperCollins Publishers Inc.,
10 East 53rd Street, New York, NY 10022.

Designed by Joel Avirom and Jason Snyder
Illustrations by Jewell Johnson

Library of Congress Cataloging-in-Publication Data is available upon request.

ISBN-10: 0-06-074504-5
ISBN-13: 978-0-06-074504-2

06 07 08 09 10 /RRD 10 9 8 7 6 5 4 3 2 1

I dedicate this book to every bride and groom:
May you have a joyous wedding day
and a lifetime of happiness!

Acknowledgments

I T IS WITH DEEP APPRECIATION that I acknowledge the following for their contributions to this book.

First, I thank the many brides and grooms who have shared their wedding quandaries and experiences with me, showing that they really do care about being respectful and kind to each other and to those involved in their weddings.

A special thank-you goes to Elizabeth Howell for her tireless work and fresh ideas from start to finish, making sure that this book is up to date for today's brides and grooms.

Many thanks go to Toni Sciarra, my editor at HarperCollins, who has steadily and cheerfully overseen the book's editing and production; and to her teammates, Greg Chaput, Nick Darrell, Donna Ruvituso, Diane Aronson, Leah Carlson-Stanisic, and Karen Lumley for all of their help.

For their invaluable insights and ongoing encouragement, I thank the Emily Post Institute team, Cindy Post Senning and Peter Post, and our agent, Katherine Cowles.

The creative talents of Martha Hailey, Alexis Flippin, and Royce Flippin are tremendous additions to the book, and to them, too, I offer my gratitude.

With appreciation for giving me the opportunity to assist their readers with their wedding questions, I wish to recognize Ellen Levine, Judy Coyne, and Margaret Magnarelli of *Good Housekeeping;* Rosanna McCollough and Marilyn Oliviera of WeddingChannel.com; and Clare McHugh and Lauren Lipton of *InStyle Weddings*; and Sarah Stebbins.

There are professional wedding consultants who have shared their expertise with me, and it is with pleasure that I thank them: Mark Kingsdorf, Lee Minarczik, Ann Nola, and David Michael Schmidt.

Finally, I acknowledge the fantastic legacy of Emily Post, my great-grandmother-in-law, whose compassionate spirit and timeless wisdom still serve as relevant foundations for today's weddings.

Contents

CHAPTER 7

Invitation Etiquette

103

Timing for Ordering and Mailing · Invitation Styles · Invitation Wording ·
Sample Invitations · Wedding Announcements · All About Envelopes · Insertions ·
Stuffing the Envelopes · A Change in Plans · Invitation Do's · Invitation Don'ts ·
Miscellaneous Stationery Items · Newspaper Wedding Notice

CHAPTER 8

Gifts of Love

147

Gift Registries · All About Wedding Gifts · Wedding-Celebration Gifts ·
Monogramming Gifts · Displaying Wedding Gifts · Exchanging and Returning Gifts ·
The Importance of "Thank You"

CHAPTER 9

The New Wedding Helper: Technology

167

The Etiquette of E-Mail · When *Not* to Use E-Mail · When E-Mail Is Appropriate ·
Assembling Your E-Mailing List · On-line Gift Registries · Creating Your Own
Wedding Web Site

CHAPTER 10

Wedding Celebrations

175

Wedding Showers · Bridesmaids' Luncheon · Bachelor and Bachelorette Parties ·
And the Party Never Ends . . . · The Wedding Rehearsal · The Rehearsal Dinner ·
Wedding-Night Afterglow · Morning-After Gathering · Another Wedding Celebration:
A Belated Reception

people marrying for the second time (or more)—has changed the way remarriages are celebrated. The old rules that said an encore bride may have only a small ceremony or should not wear white simply don't hold true today. Finally, the changes in family structure pose a host of complicated questions of their own: When parents are divorced and remarry and family trees branch out in all directions, who is responsible for what and who is seated with whom—and who keeps track of it all while making sure everybody stays happy?

Whatever questions and challenges come your way, I hope this book will give you the guidance relevant to today. Most important, I hope you'll have fun, whether your wedding is small and informal or grand and traditional. Really, all that's needed for the "perfect" wedding is the love the bride and groom feel for each other, the confidence to make decisions, and the consideration to make sure that everyone involved is treated with courtesy. A sense of humor comes in handy, too, to help you negotiate any unexpected bumps along the way.

The date is set, the time is nigh, and it's time to get busy. As the two of you approach one of the most important days of your lives, just remember to keep the details in perspective and your happiness and joy in the forefront. May it all turn out beautifully—the perfect wedding for *you*.

Peggy Post
December 2005

The Wedding That's Just Right for You

For my own wedding, my husband and I put on a casual clambake reception—complete with seafood and corn on the cob—because we decided it just felt right for us. But what, you might wonder, would my great-grandmother-in-law Emily Post have made of our decision? That's easy: She'd have been there with bells on! Emily Post was one to change with the times, understanding that "etiquette" is first and foremost about making people feel comfortable with one another, whether they're going about the business of their daily lives or readying a wedding ceremony. Also, she knew that the magic of a wedding lay less in the details than in the tender quality of the occasion and the radiance of the couple. "The radiance of a truly happy bride is so beautifying that even a plain girl is made pretty, and a pretty one, divine," she wrote in *Etiquette* in 1922. "She and the groom both look as though there is sunlight behind their eyes, as though their mouths irresistibly turned to smiles."

While that sentiment has stayed the same, weddings themselves haven't. Changes in society, from a more culturally diverse population to the redefinition of the family, have revolutionized the rite, giving rise to more informal ceremonies, a revival of ethnic customs, and a more active role for the groom. Beyond that, weddings have become more adventurous and imaginative, with destination and theme weddings part of the evolution.

Sometimes these changes can be confusing and stressful to sort through—a truth that is constantly driven home to me whenever I'm working on my monthly etiquette column in *Good Housekeeping* magazine, on the WeddingChannel.com Web site, or on my articles in *InStyle Weddings*. I find that wedding questions come from all quarters—brides, grooms, parents, attendants, guests, wedding professionals—and that the queries reflect changing family structures and the relaxing of traditional rules. One future bride wonders, "Which of my fathers can walk me down the aisle? And can my mother?" Another, deciding on gift registries, asks, "Is it okay for us to register at a camping goods store?"

The flood of questions points out the differences in weddings today. First, they are more personal, with brides and grooms bending tradition to suit their backgrounds, preferences, and tastes. Multicultural customs are playing a big role in celebrations: African Americans brides are "jumping the broom" into wedded bliss, Irish American couples are dancing to spirited Celtic folk tunes, and Chinese American women are donning traditional red cheongsams (for good luck) at their wedding banquets. Second, today's two-career couples take a different attitude about how expenses should be divided and who will foot the bills. Third, the groom, and sometimes his parents, are more involved in the planning and organization than ever before. (Happily, the old saying "A man never knows how unimportant he is until he attends his own wedding" has mostly fallen by the wayside.) Fourth, the phenomenon of encore marriages—

- Anticipate and take steps to avoid potential problems that may lead to discord.

The same attention and care applies to your relationship with suppliers and contractors, be they the caterers and musicians serving an elaborate event, or the florist and stationer who satisfy the needs of a smaller informal wedding.

Keeping the Joy in the Process

An engagement and planning a wedding is a time of joy and community that can bring people together in the most wonderful of ways. This closeness can breed friction, however, and the land mines involved in making deeply emotional decisions can detonate unexpectedly. These are highly charged times, indeed, and you'll need to be on your toes to make sure that feelings are not hurt, that your family and close friends feel included in the planning, and that niggling old problems and past grudges don't cause wedding-planning gridlock. Most important, you'll want to find ways to take good care of yourself and your fiancé, to maximize your coping skills, and to minimize worries about petty matters. There's also *Emily Post's Wedding Planner,* the companion to this book, to help keep you organized along the way. Here is some savvy advice to ensure that your planning process is smooth:

You're a Twosome: The two of you need to be a solid front—a team—and, most important, each other's support amid a barrage of wedding advice as you make the big decisions. Although such advice is well meant, it can also be confusing and tiresome. As you sift through it, your fortitude will have to come from yourselves and each other.

Remember the Three C's: Always keep your focus on the three C's of wedding planning:

- Consideration

- Communication

- Compromise

How you handle your wedding plans can foretell how you will handle the other major decisions of your life together. This is the time to develop a way of reaching accord with each other in the future. But remember that along with the stress that can accompany both the big decisions and the little details, there should be a sense of adventure and fun. You are celebrating one of the most joyous milestones in your lives.

Before You Begin:
The Heart of Your Wedding

You're engaged! As the couple of the moment, it's likely that you're in the throes of rejoicing with your parents and friends, picturing a life of married bliss. With all the excitement comes another wish—that of a perfect wedding. But what does "perfect" mean? For one thing, it no longer describes only the storybook formal event with six bridesmaids and yards of white tulle. (Indeed, simple weddings are some of the most beautiful.) In truth, the ideal wedding personalizes style and surroundings to reflect who you are, where you have been, and the direction you intend to go. The goal is a celebration wherein the interests of all concerned—you, your family, your wedding party, your guests—are given utmost care and attention. It is about planning your wedding celebration with the following tenets in mind:

- Let consideration be your guide. Make decisions based on preserving and enhancing the important relationships in your lives.

- Give thought to the kind of occasion that you, your family, and friends will feel comfortable with.

- Forgo a tradition if you think it threatens to cause a family rift. Or try to include a tradition that means a great deal to someone important to you.

- Rely on tact and sensitivity when involving others—even stepparents and extended family members.

- Be considerate of the needs of the elderly or infirm guest. And find ways to give children special roles if they're included.

Weddings and high tech. The Internet plays a growing role in registries, gift selection, and shopping for wedding supplies and vendors; wedding-oriented chat rooms and bulletin boards enable couples around the world to share information and advice. Couples can create their own wedding Web sites and use on-line wedding-planning companies, though e-mailing invitations and thank-you notes is still an etiquette no-no.

Encore and family weddings. Nearly 45 percent of today's weddings are "encore" events, meaning that the bride, the groom, or both have been married before. More remarrying couples with children are hosting "family weddings" that actively involve their children in the ceremony.

Involved grooms. Grooms are now as likely as brides to be active participants in wedding planning and decision making. Couples often take mutual responsibility for everything from financing to writing thank-you notes.

Celebrating different religious traditions. Interfaith marriage services often combine elements from both faiths. Couples of different faiths—or the same faith—may ask several officiants to perform the service.

Including parents. Mothers as well as fathers can escort their daughters in the processional, and more brides are asking both parents to accompany them on the walk down the aisle.

Honor attendants. It's not unheard of anymore for a bride to have a male friend as one of her attendants or a groom to include a female as one of his. When these friends fill the roles of "best woman" and "man of honor," they are known as "honor attendants."

More wedding attire choices. Modern brides increasingly express their individual taste and style in their attire. Wedding dresses and accessories can include colors, designs, and fabrics that reflect the bride's culture or ethnic heritage. Attendants' outfits are often chosen with consideration for future use, and many brides have their bridesmaids select dresses in the same or coordinating colors but in different cuts to flatter them. Black is no longer "out" for bridesmaids or women guests, and white can be acceptable for guests as well.

Variations in color. Traditional white still reigns, but color is blooming not only in bouquets and floral arrangements but also in brides' and grooms' attire, invitations and announcements, reception decorations and table linens, wedding cakes, and gift wrappings.

Destination weddings. More couples and their guests are traveling to distant locations for their big day. Guests often turn the trip into a longer vacation.

Family Matters

If your family or families are complicated by divorce, remarriage, step relationships, or family feuding, give serious thought to these issues as early in the planning process as possible. Your marriage is highly unlikely to heal rifts among family members, but with forethought and tact, you can prepare yourself to head off serious difficulties.

Unfortunately, divorced parents are not always on friendly terms. Although well-mannered adults will lay their differences aside for a wedding, you should avoid putting them in awkward and uncomfortable situations. Seating divorced parents together at the ceremony or reception isn't necessary (see also Chapter 20, page 352: "Seating parents who are divorced"; and Chapter 15, page 284: "Seating parents"). Asking divorced parents and their spouses to the same social events can be stressful for everyone, including other guests. Most parents will do everything in their power to make your wedding special, but you have responsibilities to them as well, which may mean adjusting what you want to what others *need*.

The traditional wedding vows include the words *for better* and *for worse*. Couples would be wise to apply these words to their families. Will your plans make difficult family relationships better or at least keep them on an even keel? Or will having everything your way cause pain and lingering resentment? When you look back on your wedding in ten or fifteen years, will you be proud of everything you did and remember a day that was happy for everyone?

21st-Century Wedding Trends

Trends don't always become traditions, but the following current wedding customs seem to have real staying power:

Personalized weddings. Today's marriage ceremonies often blend elements that have special meaning for couples—and perhaps their families—with traditional religious and secular vows. Many couples make a concerted effort to "fight the hype" of the wedding industry by planning their weddings as expressions of their interests. Lavish might be in, but so is intimate and individualized.

Sharing the costs. Wedding expenses are no longer the exclusive responsibility of the bride's parents but are frequently shared by the couple, as well as by the bride's and sometimes the groom's parents. More and more couples pay most or all of the expenses. With wedding costs so high, it's no wonder that "who pays" is one of the first conversations that engaged couples have.

Stay Calm: Don't let stress and anxiety send you into an emotional tailspin. It is an emotional time; you are going through a rite of passage—even if you've lived together or are an older couple with grown children. Don't let the details bog you down. When things get tough, keep reminding yourself that it is the marriage, not the wedding, that is important. To help keep things on an even keel:

1. **Include, don't exclude.** Even if you're doing everything yourselves, keep others—your mothers, children, or friends—in the loop. Don't let them feel left out. You see yourself as adding to your family with this wedding, but your family may feel they are losing you. Give them extra attention. Ask their advice periodically—but not about things you have already decided on, or you will have to either reject their advice or change your plans and give up something you really want to do.

2. **Be forgiving.** When things get touchy between you and your family, be the first to apologize. Remember, pride goes before a fall. In other words, what possible difference does it make to you to apologize first?

3. **Stop reacting.** Take a deep breath and think about what might be motivating someone to be so difficult. Is he feeling left out of your life? Is she worried about what your relationship will be with her once you're married? If you can't figure it out, take another deep breath.

Take Care of Your Relationship with Your Fiancé or Fiancée: Throughout your engagement, remember to make time to enjoy each other. Don't let the planning and the stress it will bring keep you from truly savoring this special time together as a couple. Immerse yourselves in the fun and happiness your engagement brings.

Take Care of Yourselves: To keep yourselves intact and calm as all around you lose their heads:

- Eat right—you need the energy.

- Exercise—you need the release.

- Get enough sleep—you can cope much better when you're rested.

- Go on dates—the two of you need time alone together.

- Find beauty in everything—and where you can't, find humor.

Delegate Duties: Others will want to help. And what bride and groom couldn't use some assistance—especially if you don't plan to use a bridal consultant? You may discover how fortunate you are to have friends and family willing to help out. If yours is an elaborate wedding and you have a hectic personal schedule, delegate certain tasks and even major responsibilities to those who have generously offered to take them on. Your wedding day may be the most important time to delegate tasks. It is the time for you to focus on your ceremony and enjoy the reception afterward.

Once you have relinquished a responsibility, don't dwell on it, second-guess yourself or others, or micromanage. When you've put someone in charge, let others know. Tell the florist your sister is in charge of flowers and to contact her and not you. Let the tent supplier know that your fiancé is overseeing tent details—and give the groom's telephone number.

Stay Organized: It doesn't take long for chaos to reign if you don't begin with a system of organization. Whether you use the *Emily Post Wedding Planner,* set up computer files, or devote a briefcase just to wedding-related papers, you'll find everything is easier to manage when you can locate it in a snap. Here are a few tips from the most efficient brides and grooms:

- Create a master to-do list, preferably in time sequence.

- Carry fabric swatches, photos of gowns, photos of locations, and table measurements at all times.

- Design a contact list with the names of everyone you're working with, including telephone and fax numbers business and e-mail addresses.

- Carry a calendar with all your appointments highlighted.

- Create a folder for all contracts; staple copies of contracts to the appropriate pages in your organizer and don't leave home without them, in case you have to check details from one supplier when working with another.

- Keep copies of important papers you will need (birth certificates, any divorce papers, driver's licenses) in one envelope or folder.

- Check off completed to-do's as you accomplish them. You'll feel great as you see the number of check marks grow.

CHAPTER 1

ENGAGEMENT ETIQUETTE

PERHAPS ONE OF YOU popped the question in the most romantic or surprising way imaginable. Or the decision just sort of evolved. However it happened, you've decided to get married and now you're engaged.

Couples often ask how long an engagement should be. The simplest answer is, "As long as it takes." Do you want to marry at a specific time of the year or on a certain date, such as your parents' anniversary? Do you have a special location in mind? If so, you may need to reserve wedding and reception sites as much as a year to eighteen months in advance. Religious requirements can be a factor in the equation. And sometimes an engagement is shortened or prolonged by events beyond a couple's control, such as military service or a business relocation.

An engagement may last only a few days or weeks or extend over a number of years. The average period is about fourteen months. Your engagement should be a time for contemplation and mutual consideration of the monumental step you're preparing to take. You are two individuals who have pledged to become a couple, and during the engagement, you will begin to sort out what it means to act in tandem. Parties, presents, and pretty clothes may come to mind first, but they're only symbols. The essence lies in ideals of commitment, mutual respect, fidelity, compromise, ongoing communication, and enduring love.

Your engagement is also a time of overwhelming detail—and enough stress to test the most solid of unions. Don't give in to pressures to stage a celebration that is more about the festivities and less about you. Stay focused on your vision. Delegate chores to others who have offered to help. Stick to the day-to-day routine activities of your life. And, whether the time between your engagement and your wedding is six weeks or six months, remember to take time off from organizing every now and then to enjoy each other, and to immerse yourself in the fun and happiness your engagement brings.

Making It Official

The term officially engaged is a misnomer. There is no official validation for an engagement—no tests to take, papers to sign, or fees to pay. What is generally considered an official engagement is one that has been announced to family and friends, and if the couple wishes, in a public forum such as the newspaper.

If you were previously married, do not become officially engaged until you are divorced. It's deemed inconsiderate and in poor taste to announce an engagement when a divorce is still in progress. Even if an annulment or divorce is imminent, an engagement should not be announced until it's final.

Sharing the Good News

Usually people know when romance is in the air and marriage is a possibility, but family and good friends deserve your special attention and there is an order to the telling. The guidelines of when and whom to tell have to do with people's feelings. Certain family members and close friends should hear the news first.

Children. If one or both of the engaged couple have children, they must be told before anyone else. This is critically important for young children, and for teens whose lives will be dramatically changed by the addition of a stepparent and perhaps stepsiblings. They may be thrilled, but they are just as likely to be doubtful, reluctant, and even frightened and resentful. It takes love, honesty, and infinite patience to transform individuals into a family, so respect every child's need to question your decision and seek your reassurance. You should also tell an ex-spouse, if for no other reason than to smooth the way for your children's involvement.

It's just as important to inform adult children before publicly announcing an engagement. No matter how far away they may live or how independent they are, children of any age should be uppermost in the couple's concerns.

Parents. After children, parents deserve priority. You can each inform your own parents or speak as a couple with both sets of parents. If your parents don't know your fiancée or fiancé, it's your responsibility to arrange a meeting. If your parents live at a distance, you can make introductions by phone, but also plan to visit as soon as you can. Nothing is better than getting together in person.

When parents are separated or divorced, the news is conveyed to each—in person, if possible, or by the most convenient means. Even if a parent and child are somewhat estranged, a parent should not hear the news of his or her child's marriage plans from outsiders.

In the event that the announcement will be a total surprise, each member of the couple should be considerate of his or her own parents and talk privately with them first. This allows parents to ask questions that they may be hesitant to ask with their future son- or daughter-in-law present. Couples who are mature enough for marriage should understand that parents have perfectly normal worries and should be allowed to express their concerns. Openness at this stage may prevent difficulties later.

The old custom was for a suitor to speak first with the father of the young woman, declaring his intentions and getting the father's consent before proposing to the daughter. Although this tradition is obsolete, it's still a sign of respect for a prospective groom to meet with his future in-laws and discuss his career and life plans. This conversation might take place before the engagement, when the couple tells their parents of their engagement, or soon thereafter—whenever seems most appropriate.

Relatives and close friends. Depending on your family structure, there are probably some relatives—siblings, grandparents, close aunts, uncles, and cousins—and good friends whom you will want to inform soon after you tell your parents. Always include them as special people in the know before the rest of the world finds out. When and how you spread the word is up to you, so long as you're sensitive to people's feelings and thoughtful of what is going on in their lives.

Don't make promises before you have planned the wedding. Some couples find themselves with a much larger wedding party than they want, or can afford, because in the euphoria of becoming engaged, they ask too many people to be bridesmaids and groomsmen. Others risk hurting the feelings of people they care about by having to rescind such invitations.

If you become engaged during a time of difficulty—when a family member or close friend is seriously ill or recently deceased, for example—share your good news, but keep it low key and don't expect everyone to react as they would under happier circumstances. Depending on the situation, a couple may have to delay parties and newspaper announcements.

Colleagues and coworkers. A newly engaged employee may want to inform a boss or supervisor first as a matter of courtesy. The easiest way to spread the news among your colleagues is to tell one or two people and ask them to tell the others. At some point, you should discuss your impending change in status with the person in charge of employee compensation and make necessary alterations in benefit, insurance, and retirement plans.

Getting Families Together

A wedding is not just the joining together of two people, it's also the joining together of two—and sometimes more—families. When the families of engaged couples don't know one another or are only slightly acquainted, the couple has an obligation to arrange a gathering of some sort.

Parents meeting parents. The parents of a newly engaged couple may live too far apart for a face-to-face meeting. The conventional etiquette calls for the parents of the future groom to contact the bride's family. But nowadays, it matters very little who makes the first move, though a bride's parents might want to wait a bit to give the groom's family a chance to honor custom. A phone call is the easiest route; if the couple live near one set of parents, they might all get together for a conference call to distant relatives. Handwritten notes are always nice. E-mail is possible, and some people may find its casual tone an easier way to introduce themselves and express their pleasure at the engagement. Both sets of parents should act with spontaneity and in the spirit of friendship, regardless of who makes the first contact. If it is impossible for them to meet, they should at least attempt to call or write so that an initial introduction is established.

Who hosts? Organizing the first meeting is traditionally the responsibility of the groom's parents, but the diversity of today's family structure, not to mention hectic work and travel schedules, often makes it difficult to follow custom. The bride- and groom-to-be are best positioned to know when a meeting will be convenient for everyone and what kind of gathering is most likely to put everyone at ease. Who actually hosts the occasion is a matter of preference more than tradition. If the bride's mother is a homemaker who loves to entertain, why stand on custom? A casual event, such as a barbecue or weeknight supper, is often most

A QUESTION FOR PEGGY:

WHAT TO CALL THE IN-LAWS?

Q: *I'm unsure what to call my future in-laws. Up until our engagement, I've been addressing them as Mr. and Mrs. Jenkins.*

A: Continue to call them exactly what you have been calling them. Since you have addressed them as Mr. and Mrs., just keep doing so until they suggest otherwise. Most married couples refer to their in-laws by their first names. If after you are married, your in-laws have not suggested a less formal address, ask them what they would like you to call them. If they want you to call them "Mom" and "Dad," it's fine to—if you feel comfortable. Or you could opt to use their first names.

comfortable. But if one set of parents has a more formal lifestyle than the other, a good compromise might be a dinner or weekend brunch at a nice mid-range restaurant.

When parents are divorced. When parents are divorced and when there are stepfamilies to consider, a couple will often have to organize several get-togethers. Engaged couples should think carefully about their family structures and have realistic expectations. Separate meetings should be arranged with each set of parents so that everyone involved has a chance to meet.

Under no circumstances should divorced parents be forced into social situations that have the potential to make them—and others—feel uncomfortable. As much as you may want to have your parents reunite as an intact family in honor of your own wedding, it is too much to hope that your engagement and marriage will heal old wounds caused by divorce, remarriage, and other complicated family arrangements.

Newspaper Announcements

In addition to calling and writing family members and friends, a couple often decides to submit an engagement announcement to newspapers. Because it is inappropriate to send printed engagement announcements, some couples make their announcement public through the newspaper. An engagement announcement should never be made if either member is still legally married to someone else. Nor is a public announcement appropriate when there has recently been a death in either family or when a member of the immediate family is desperately ill.

If you want to announce your engagement in print, the first step is to contact the appropriate department of the newspaper(s) in which you would like the announcement to appear. Most newspapers provide information forms to complete. If you submit your own announcement, the newspaper will check with you personally to ensure that the information is accurate. Before contacting a paper, study its engagement section, especially if you want the announcement in a paper that you aren't familiar with. This will tell you what kind of details the paper normally reports and whether they use photographs.

Generally, an engagement announcement appears two to three months before the wedding date, though this isn't a hard-and-fast rule. Information is submitted several weeks in advance. Couples often haven't set the wedding date when an announcement appears. If you delay contacting the publication until the last minute, however, the paper may not be able to accommodate you.

Most announcements are brief and follow a format similar to the one below. But some papers use an informal style, include more information, and may ask to interview couples about details of their courtship and engagement.

Traditionally, the parents of the bride-to-be make the announcement. The basic wording includes full names with courtesy or professional titles; city and state of residence if not the same as the hometown of the newspaper; highest level of education of the couple; and their current employment.

BASIC WORDING

Mr. and Mrs. Allen Perry of Fairview, Maryland, announce the engagement of their daughter, Jane Ellen Perry, to William Paul Kruger, Jr., son of Dr. and Mrs. William Paul Kruger of Newcastle, Missouri. A September wedding is planned.

Miss Perry, a graduate of Richmond Nursing College, is a physical therapist with Bonaventure Hospital in Baltimore, Maryland. Mr. Kruger was graduated from Monroe University and is employed as loan manager with First Bank of Baltimore.

Engagement and wedding announcements are a public service of the newspapers—though many papers now charge fees—and you cannot dictate or edit the contents. Using or dropping courtesy titles, for example, is determined by a publication's overall style, not the preference of people whose names appear in the paper. Larger newspapers tend to have a more concise announcement style than suburban and rural publications, and virtually all publications give some precedence to prominent community members.

The following samples indicate how a number of different situations may be treated in print:

WHEN PARENTS ARE DIVORCED . . .

Divorced parents are listed as individuals, by their current legal names and places of residence, and never as a couple. If the bride's parents are divorced, the mother usually makes the announcement, though the father may do so if he is the custodial parent.

Ms. Martine Cousins of Hartsville, Colorado, announces the engagement of her daughter, Sarah Louise Baker, to . . . Miss Baker is also the daughter of Mr. Albert Baker of Boulder.

When the groom's parents are divorced, the announcement follows this pattern:

Mr. and Mrs. Lamar Hughes announce the engagement of their daughter, Caroline Hughes, to Justin Marc DuBois, son of Mrs. Thomas Shelton of Centerville, Ohio, and Mr. Jean Marc DuBois of Brighton, Michigan.

When the parents of both the bride and the groom are divorced, the usual form is:

Mrs. Walter Murray announces the engagement of her daughter, Elizabeth Leigh Considine, to John Carter Lowndes, son of Mrs. Harriett Lowndes of Seattle and Mr. Houston Lowndes of Palmetto, California. Miss Considine is also the daughter of Mr. Horace Considine of Melbourne, Australia.

A stepparent is not usually included in a formal announcement unless he or she is an adoptive parent or the natural parent is not a part of the bride or groom's life, but stepparents might be mentioned in a lengthier or more informal announcement.

WHEN DIVORCED PARENTS MAKE A JOINT ANNOUNCEMENT . . .

Divorced parents of the bride-to-be may want to make the announcement together. Both are listed by their current legal names (whether or not they have married again) and places of residence:

Mrs. Walter Murray of Gladstone, Washington, and Mr. Horace Considine of Melbourne, Australia, announce the engagement of their daughter, Elizabeth Leigh Considine, to . . .

WHEN A PARENT IS DECEASED . . .

When one of the bride's parents is deceased, the surviving parent makes the announcement:

Mr. Gerald MacKenzie Brown announces the engagement of his daughter, Leslie Brown, to . . . Miss Brown is also the daughter of the late Marie Compton Brown.

When a parent of the groom is deceased, this form is generally followed:

Mr. and Mrs. Gerald MacKenzie Brown announce the engagement of their daughter, Leslie Brown, to Peter Carelli, son of Mrs. Benjamin Carelli and the late Mr. Carelli [or when the mother is deceased: Mr. Benjamin Carelli and the late Mrs. Carelli or the late Katherine Boyd Carelli].

If both the bride's parents are deceased, a close family member (or members) may make the announcement:

Mr. and Mrs. Seth Sheridan announce the engagement of their granddaughter, Cynthia Sheridan, to . . . Miss Sheridan is the daughter of the late Mr. and Mrs. Frederick Sheridan [or the late Frederick and Margaret James Sheridan].

WHEN THE BRIDE IS A DIVORCÉE . . .

When the bride is a young divorcée, it's still traditional for her parents to announce her engagement, using the name she has adopted since the divorce:

Mr. and Mrs. Joseph Crane announce the engagement of their daughter, Portia Crane Bowman, to . . .

An older woman or one who is independent of her family might want to announce her own engagement, following the basic format below. When the groom-to-be is divorced, there's usually no indication of his status in an announcement. However, some papers now mention previous marriages and the children of engaged couples in informal announcement stories.

WHEN THE COUPLE MAKES THE ANNOUNCEMENT . . .

It's not uncommon for older couples and those who do not have close family to make their own announcements. The wording is simple:

Ms. Gayle Ann Parker and Mr. James Newsom [or Gayle Ann Parker and James Newsom] are pleased to announce their engagement. [This may be followed by information about their parents or simply about the couple and their planned wedding date.]

WHEN THE GROOM'S PARENTS ANNOUNCE . . .

In some situations, the bride's parents cannot make the announcement—as when her family lives overseas or when she doesn't have family and prefers not to make her own announcement—and the groom's parents place the notice in their local newspaper. The wording will be similar to the following:

The engagement of Anna Livmann, daughter of Professor and Mrs. Ernst Livmann of Stockholm, Sweden, to Edward Dodd, son of Mr. and Mrs. Seymour Dodd, is announced.

ANNOUNCEMENTS FOR SAME-SEX COUPLES . . .

The *New York Times* made journalism history in 2002 when the newspaper began including commitment ceremonies among its traditional wedding write-ups. A number of large city newspapers have followed suit, and there are other outlets—notably gay and lesbian publications and some social news publications—that included same-sex announcements long before the venerable *Times*. If you'd like a published announcement, check with the editor of the Lifestyle, Social, or Weddings section of your newspaper. (Many papers do not have an established policy, and some may actually be looking for an opportunity to break new ground.) Be clear about the nature of your request, and remember that the person you speak with is not necessarily responsible when a paper's policy is not to cover same-sex unions.

The Engagement Party

An engagement is definitely something to celebrate, and a party may be the perfect way for family and friends to toast the future bride and groom. Today's engagement parties may be as formal or informal as you like—and are by no means mandatory.

The hosts. The bride-to-be's parents usually host the engagement party, but any family member or friend may do so. When families live in different parts of the country, the parents of the bride and groom might each host parties in their hometowns—an alternative to the more traditional post-honeymoon party given by the groom's family to honor their new daughter-in-law.

What kind of party? Cocktail parties and dinners are popular, but there is no standard party format. Sometimes, engagements are announced at surprise parties. From a casual brunch to a formal reception, there are many possibilities. Whatever suits the couple and the guests is just fine.

The guests. Generally the guest list is limited to the couple's relatives and good friends. It can be as short or as lengthy as you want and can comfortably accommodate. However, it's poor taste to invite anyone to an engagement party who will not be on the wedding guest list.

Invitations. Written or printed invitations are normally sent, but for an intimate gathering, phoned invitations are acceptable.

The announcement. Whether the news will be a surprise or is already known among the guests, the host, usually the bride's father, traditionally makes the "official" announcement and leads a toast to the couple. (When the engagement news is intended as a surprise for party guests, be sure to coordinate with any publication that will be running an announcement. The paper can delay, or "embargo," the announcement until after the party—but only if you inform them well in advance.) At a very large party with guests who already know about the engagement, the couple and their parents might compose an informal receiving line to welcome guests and make introductions.

Gifts for Engagement Parties?

Q: *I've attended a number of engagement parties, and I still can't figure out the etiquette of gifts. Some people bring presents; others don't. Do I need to bring a gift to an engagement party?*

A: It depends. In the past, engagement gifts were not obligatory or expected, and usually this is still the case. However, in many parts of the country, bringing a gift to an engagement party has become de rigueur. Gift instructions are not included on invitations, but couples who are very conscious of taxing their friends' budgets can tell guests (through the hosts) not to bring presents. If you really aren't sure what to do, call the host and ask. Or check with a local wedding planner to ask about the customs and trends in your area.

Ultimately, your decision whether to give an engagement gift depends on local custom, your relationship to the couple, and your budget. Often close friends and family members do give a gift.

An engagement gift is really a good-hearted gesture of affection, and it need not be expensive or elaborate. Something simple such as a cookbook or a good bottle of wine—intended to help the couple establish a collection—makes a great engagement gift. Or if you prefer, save your money for the wedding gift.

Gifts and thanks. If gifts are given by everyone, the couple might open them at the party, if there's time, and express their appreciation personally. Note, however, that written thank-yous are required even if the couple has thanked the givers directly. Handwritten thank-yous are also a must if a couple receives gifts later, such as after an announcement appears in the newspaper.

The Engagement Ring

A bride-to-be does *not* need a ring to make her engagement official. And if she does have a ring, it doesn't need to be the largest diamond the groom can find. Many couples prefer to put the money that would be spent on a ring toward the practicalities of building their life together. Some couples even postpone the purchase of an engagement ring until years after their wedding, when their finances enable them to buy the special ring they've envisioned. These days, the bride is often involved in selecting the engagement ring; in fact, only 30 percent of men do so alone. So it is wise for both bride and groom to bone up on the basics of engagement rings.

DIAMONDS: THE FOUR C'S AND MORE

The traditional gemstones for engagement rings, diamonds are the emblems of love and engagement. Knowing the four C's allows you to converse comfortably with jewelers when you are shopping for a diamond engagement ring.

Carat

Carat is the weight of a diamond. One carat is one-fifth of a gram (200 milligrams). There are 142 carats to an ounce. One carat also has 100 points. This system of measuring diamond weight began in India and was based on the weight of the seeds of the carob tree, which were used to balance scales.

Clarity

Diamonds are rated on the basis of blemishes that occur in nature, such as inner cracks, bubbles, and specks that are hard to detect with the naked eye. When a diamond is rated flawless (FL), it is given the highest clarity rating; a flawless diamond is rare. The size and placement of the blemishes determine a diamond's clarity rating, which ranges from flawless to varying degrees of small inclusions to the least-desirable rating: "imperfect."

Cut

The way a diamond is cut determines its brilliance. In fact, cut is generally considered the most important of the four C's of diamonds. When cut, a diamond is faceted in a series of flat, angled surfaces that reflect light off one another. This is what causes the stone to sparkle.

Color

Another criteria for determining the value of diamonds is color. If a diamond is clear and colorless, it is rated D, the highest color ranking. The lowest rating is Z, yellow. This indicates a stone that contains traces of earthy color. Some diamonds that naturally have some tint of color are placed in a special category called "fancies."

One More C

A fifth C for diamonds is certification. This is the written proof of a diamond's weight, grade, and identifying characteristics from the International Gemological Institute and should come with your ring.

Must She Wear the Family Heirloom?

Q: *I was presented with a family heirloom ring as an engagement ring. It was worn by both my future mother-in-law and her mother. My problem is, I really don't like it; it's too big and ostentatious and I had my heart set on a simpler one. Could I ask to have it reset by a jeweler? Or can I simply say, "Thank you, but I'm just not comfortable accepting the ring"?*

A: If you feel uncomfortable taking the ring, you needn't accept it. Decline graciously, and be sure to discuss your concern with your fiancé. A family has no right to demand that their future daughter-in-law wear an heirloom ring, passed along just because it exists, no matter how many generations it may have been in the family.

GEMSTONES

Instead of a diamond, many couples prefer a gemstone—a perfectly acceptable choice—for the engagement ring. Gemstones are classified as "precious" and "semiprecious," with "precious" stones being emeralds, rubies, and sapphires. Long prized as symbols of mystical powers, gemstones were also graced with symbolic meaning during Victorian times, when they became especially popular in engagement rings. Some couples select gemstones for engagement rings based on the birthstone of the bride or the groom or both. If you want your ring to symbolize something besides your engagement, you can choose the stone representing your birth month.

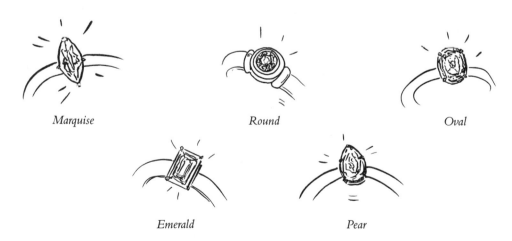

Marquise   Round   Oval

Emerald   Pear

If Parents Disapprove

It's hardly surprising that parents will feel somewhat anxious when their children become engaged, whether they express their concerns or not. Usually, the anxiety disappears as parents grow accustomed to the engagement and become involved in the wedding plans. But when a couple senses tension or a parent makes his or her objections clear, it's usually best to address the problem openly. First and foremost, stay calm and approach any discussion as adult-to-adult. Second, be willing to listen to parental concerns and to take them seriously. (For instance, parents may worry that marriage will adversely affect education or career plans, so explain your long-range goals.) Third, try to remember how important your happiness is to your parents and don't let minor disagreements get out of hand. Do you really want to draw lines in the sand over the choice of a florist or caterer?

When parents are on board, most other family members will follow. Yet it may be impossible to overcome parental objections, and you will have to proceed on your own. But don't sever family ties. Be sure that your parents—or any other family members who disapprove—know how much you want them at your wedding. When you act from goodwill, there's a very good chance that the doubting Thomases will put their misgivings aside and attend.

If Children Disapprove

If your children disapprove of the engagement, the dilemma is even greater, and family relationships can become quite strained. If time and communication cannot bridge the gap and basic civility and politeness have been abandoned, then professional counseling could be initiated to help the entire family understand one another's feelings.

When It Doesn't Work Out

One of the underlying purposes of a period of engagement is to give a couple time to test their commitment, and not every engagement ends in marriage. When an engagement is broken, it can be a time of great sadness, confusion, and, all too often, ill will. But whatever the feelings of the people involved, they shouldn't be embarrassed about taking a difficult step that prevents future and even greater unhappiness.

There are important do's and don'ts associated with a breakup—some are grounded in respect and consideration for all involved, while others concern practical matters, too.

Do tell close family as soon and as tactfully as possible. Your children and your parents should be the first to know. When children are involved, particularly if they have developed a good relationship with the person you were engaged to, they often feel an intense loss. Explain the breakup as best you can without demeaning the other person.

Don't expect family and friends to choose sides. A broken engagement should not be a declaration of war by either party. Some people will instantly rally around you, but many will not want to be drawn into your very personal decision, no matter how sympathetic they feel.

Do inform everyone involved in the wedding as soon as you can. A family member or friend may be able to help you out by getting in touch with people who have been contracted for services (caterers and the like), but you should personally speak with the officiant, attendants, and others who agreed to participate in the planned wedding. Remember to contact anyone who has planned a social event in your honor.

A QUESTION FOR PEGGY:

DIPLOMACY BETWEEN DIVORCED PARENTS?

Q: *My parents divorced when I was young and have had an antagonistic relationship since. I am close to both parents, and my engagement has brought a whole new set of problems. What can I do?*

A: Weddings often bring to light troublesome family dynamics. For example, the bride's mother may announce that she will not attend a single wedding party or the wedding itself if her ex-husband is going to be there. The groom's mother may insist that she will not participate if the groom's father's mother (her mother-in-law) is invited. Children in the custody of their other parent may refuse to attend the wedding out of fear that their custodial parent will be upset or angry with them. Ambassadorial-level diplomacy is called for in these situations. By addressing these concerns now, well before the wedding, you'll hopefully avoid any wedding-day dramas. Don't be afraid to discuss the matter directly with your parents individually. Assure them that you will do your best to avoid any situations that make them uncomfortable, but that you also expect them to behave appropriately. Try to keep feuding parties clear of each other as best you can through assigned seating and perhaps separate pre-wedding events.

SHOULD SHE RETURN THE RING?

Q: *My fiancé and I have just broken off our engagement. Our decision was mutual, so I hope we can be friends again someday. But what should I do with my engagement ring? He hasn't asked for it, and my friends say I should keep it.*

A: Most states consider an engagement ring to be like any gift—the property of the person who receives it—so you have no legal obligation to return it. But ethics trump law in this situation. Do you really want to keep a ring that was given to symbolize a pledge that you have both agreed not to honor? Since your decision was mutual, what is more important to you now, the ring or keeping some kind of positive relationship with your ex-fiancé? The decision is yours, and your conscience is a much better guide than the opinions of friends.

The unique circumstances of a broken engagement often determine what is done. When the man purchases the ring, he traditionally relinquishes it if he alone breaks the engagement, though the woman may choose to return it. If the woman cancels the engagement, it is correct for her to give back the ring—especially when it's an heirloom of the man's family—and any other jewelry she received from her ex-fiancé. But when a couple shared the cost, then the one who keeps the ring ought to refund the other person's money, regardless of who precipitated the breakup. Or they might sell the ring and divide the return based on the proportion each person originally contributed.

Do return all engagement, wedding, and shower gifts, including money gifts. This is generally the woman's responsibility, since gifts are traditionally sent to the bride-to-be. But there's no reason why the man cannot return gifts given to him and his former fiancée as a couple by his personal friends. Accompany returned gifts with a brief note such as the following:

Dear Claudia,

I am sorry to have to tell you that Roberto and I have broken our engagement. I'm returning the beautiful crystal bowl that you were so thoughtful to send.

Love,
Ashley

Do inform invited guests, but don't run a newspaper ad. Placing an ad was often done to announce a wedding cancellation in the days before telephones. But today when an engagement is broken after invitations have been mailed and there is sufficient time, you can send a printed card like the following:

Mr. and Mrs. Nathan Morris
announce that the marriage of
their daughter
Rebecca
to
Mr. Oliver Sandburg
will not take place.

If there isn't time for the printing and delivery of notices, call the people on the guest list. While it's preferable to talk personally with guests, you can leave a message and resort to e-mail if that's the most efficient way to reach someone.

BEHIND THE TRADITION:

What Is a Trousseau?

Your great-grandmother would know this one. A trousseau traditionally included the personal possessions—clothing and household goods—that a bride brought to her marriage. The word *trousseau* was derived from a French term meaning "bundle." The trousseau was originally part of a dowry (the financial arrangement between the families of a betrothed couple) and is associated with a time when marriages were arranged and the bride ceded all her possessions to her husband. For obvious reasons, the concept is high on the endangered list in contemporary American culture.

Beyond her wedding dress, party clothes, and honeymoon outfits, today's bride-to-be is unlikely to acquire a vast new wardrobe before her wedding. Items including linens, tableware, silver, and basic kitchen equipment, which comprised the household trousseau, are now purchased by the couple, acquired as gifts, or assembled when the couple merges their households.

One tradition that has survived is the hope chest—a good-sized wooden, often cedar, chest for storing linens and blankets. Although few mothers begin sewing and embroidering linens when their daughters are born, as they once did, and placing them in a hope chest in anticipation of a distant wedding day, hope chests remain a popular gift from parents to their engaged daughters and, like handmade wedding quilts, are often passed from one generation to the next.

IF ONE OF A COUPLE DIES

When one of an engaged couple dies, the survivor is unlikely to be able to handle many obligations. Family and friends should take over certain painful but necessary tasks, including notifying members of the wedding party, the officiant, the wedding location, anyone hired for services, and the people on the guest list if wedding invitations have been sent.

The bereaved bride-to-be can certainly keep her engagement ring, though she may later want to return it to the groom's family if it is a family heirloom. Returning gifts is a personal decision. If the survivor chooses to return some or all gifts, there is really no time limit. Only the most insensitive people would complain if gifts were not sent back or were returned after weeks or months. A note should be included with a returned gift, and family members can handle this task if the bereaved partner is not up to it.

CHAPTER 2

The Big Decisions: Turning Dreams into Reality

THE ENGAGEMENT IS ON! You and your loved ones are thrilled; the future is bright with hope and possibility. A beautiful bride, a beaming groom, elegant attendants, and a happy complement of family and friends . . . to make the dream come true requires time, effort, and major doses of the "three C's" of wedding planning—*consideration, communication,* and *compromise.*

Marriage is a legal and, for many couples, religious commitment. A wedding and its associated activities are the celebration of that commitment in the presence of family and friends. The success of the marriage, of course, depends on the two of you. But the success of the wedding often depends on how willing you are to adjust to outside circumstances, to include other people in the planning, and to consider their needs as well as your own.

This chapter focuses on the major decisions and also the initial steps of planning. While there will be many more decisions to come, some of the first ones you'll need to make will concern:

- The guest list

- The budget

- A wedding consultant

- The date, season, and time of day

- The style and formality

- The officiant

- The ceremony and reception locations

- Choosing the rings

- The honeymoon location

- A theme or destination wedding

Don't forget to relish this stage of planning. It's your opportunity to explore your wedding fantasies—and those your loved ones may share for you. Enjoy!

What Are Your Wedding Dreams?

Now is the time for the two of you to sit down and have a serious discussion about the kind of wedding you both envision. If you've always dreamed of floating up the aisle in a long white gown and your groom-to-be thinks a casual ceremony on the beach would suffice, don't despair. Keep talking. There are many ways to personalize your wedding and to bring in elements that you both think are important. Being part of a twosome means communicating clearly and honestly with the common goal of being contented and happy with each other—and with your wedding day. It takes some work, but that doesn't mean you have to shelve your dreams as you start the wedding-planning process.

In earlier eras, brides-to-be (and their mothers) generally took charge of wedding planning and preparation, but today, the decisions and tasks are far more likely to be shared. Grooms now tend to be closely involved and their wishes given equal weight. Blending your ideas could take some patience and honest discussion. Many brides have dreamed of their weddings since they were little girls; they think they know what they want. Often, grooms-to-be haven't thought about "the wedding" until they start the planning process. Brides: Give your grooms some time and some help! It's not that they don't care about the decisions that have to be made (fortunately, most do), it's just that they're beginning to focus on more than "buying the ring, lining up ushers, wearing a tux, and showing up." Couples who patiently consider the feelings of their partners, communicate honestly about matters large and small, and are willing to make compromises with each other usually find that the normal stresses of planning (and conflicts with others) can be kept to a minimum.

Think of the two of you as a team. Today's couples often feel pressured by family and friends telling them what they have to do, or should do, for their weddings. But the truth is, they want *their* weddings to be special—not just like everyone else's. They're looking for inspiration to incorporate different ideas into their plans, as well as permission to break from tradition to make their weddings unique. Most are simply seeking the confidence to merge tradition with their dreams to create their own wedding, one unlike any other.

So, begin with your ideas. Before you start debating the merits of large-versus-small or formal-versus-informal, take time to dream. What is your initial *vision* for your nuptials? Make a list of the qualities you have each admired about weddings you've attended or you see as important to your own wedding. Use descriptive words, such as:

intimate	contemporary	simple
grand	spiritual	family-oriented
elegant	secular	Hollywood-like

casual	tropical	friendly
luxurious	musical	overseas
ethnic	dramatic	friendly
traditional	huge	romantic

Next, pare down your list as you merge your wedding day dreams into one. What kind of celebration do these words describe? A gathering of close family and friends in your parents' backyard? An evening gala in a ballroom, with everyone decked out in formal garb? Let the qualities you have chosen as most important guide your decisions. You can adapt your dreams and personal touches to your circumstances, to have a wedding that is uniquely your own.

The Primary Decisions

Now is also the time for a reality check. Two of the biggest factors influencing the major decisions of your wedding plans are money and convenience.

"First things first" is a useful truism here. With your dreams fresh in your heads, begin by making the key decisions and then work your way toward the finishing touches. Taking things in logical order will help the two of you to gauge what you can accomplish in the time you have, what you can do on your own, how much help you will need from others, and what extras you may want to simplify or eliminate entirely.

Whether you have a long or a short time to plan your wedding, start by separating your primary decisions from those that can wait awhile. Once you've made the big decisions first, secondary decisions often fall into place. Think of the primary decisions as the foundation for every other choice you make.

Your initial decisions will be based on the following:

- The *Guest List*

- The *Budget*

- The feasibility of working with a *Professional Wedding Consultant*

- The *Date:* time of year, day of the week, and time of day

- The *Style* of your wedding (formal vs. informal, religious vs. civil)

- The availability of your wedding *Officiant*

- The *Locations* for both the ceremony and the reception

THE GUEST LIST

While your available budget is certainly the determining factor for your wedding, your guest list has everything to do with how the money is spent. Quite simply, any decisions about the type of wedding you will have cannot be made until you have some idea of the size of the guest list. If neither of you can imagine celebrating your nuptials without your mutually large families in attendance, the guest list will by necessity be a big one. If your guest list is large and your budget small, you may have to forgo a big, formal sit-down dinner reception. Otherwise, paring your guest list down may allow it. *The easiest way to cut costs? By shortening your guest list.* (See also Chapter 6, pages 91–92: "Trimming an Overambitious Guest List.")

THE BUDGET

The days when the bride's parents were automatically expected to bear all the expenses of the wedding and reception are over. It's now more common for engaged couples, especially established wage earners, to pay all or most of the costs or at least to share some of the expense with their parents. The groom's family may also make a substantial contribution.

As soon as possible, everyone—you, your parents, as applicable—needs to determine how much they can afford and to discuss finances. In the early days of planning, people have a tendency to over estimate their financial capabilities (and under estimate actual costs), so the first rule of budgeting is to be realistic. The second is to be considerate. A parent may be willing to take a second mortgage or deplete retirement savings in order to finance an elaborate wedding, but is this the kind of sacrifice you want? If you're paying for the wedding, you may have to borrow some funds. How much debt are you both comfortable taking on?

Be realistic about your expenses, and be appreciative of whatever your parents can contribute. If your parents have given you a figure that is the most they can spend, it is up to you to be appreciative and to work with that amount, combining your resources with theirs. Then tally the projected costs for your wedding, and compare it against your resources. Don't be concerned that you will have to cut quality to save costs. There are many smart ways of cutting corners without sacrificing quality.

If you are paying for your own wedding, take an honest look at your finances. If your budget is limited, you will have to decide what takes priority: a big, glamorous wedding with a shorter guest list, or a larger guest list and a more toned-down reception. This is the time to make compromises, by shortening the guest list, by choosing a time of year or time of day when costs are less, by choosing an affordable reception site, by forgoing a big wedding party. The variations are endless.

HOW A WEDDING CONSULTANT CAN HELP YOU

For busy people with hectic schedules, hiring a professional wedding consultant is a smart alternative to trying to do it all. Wedding consultants can be of great service: They can scout sites and oversee the budget, the caterer, the band, the florist, and any number of service providers. They can obtain discounts and bargains from vendors. In short, they can lift the load from your shoulders when you are feeling burdened, simply because they have encountered and solved in hundreds of ways the same problems you may be facing. Their purpose is not to take over your wedding but to help make your dreams come true and your plans a reality. Plus: Wedding consultants can save you money in the long run.

Think about what kind of help you need before making a decision. There are many different levels of service and types of consultants. A full-fledged wedding consultant can do anything and everything for you. A wedding day coordinator springs into action on the day of the wedding, making sure everything goes according to schedule. A wedding day director might be provided by the ceremony site to supervise all the details of the ceremony and make sure that the rules of the house of worship are followed. There are consultants and coordinators who handle varying responsibilities in between. Here is a general guide on wedding consultants:

- **What, exactly, does a wedding consultant do?** In general, a wedding consultant can provide the following services:

  - Listen carefully from the very beginning to learn your wedding vision, and then be your advocate for realizing your dream in the best way possible.

  - Help you set up a budget, and commit to helping you stick to it.

  - Help you locate and reserve ceremony and reception sites.

  - Help you select and hire reputable suppliers and vendors, such as the florist, the caterer, musicians, the photographer, and the videographer; advise you on vendor contracts and handle any negotiations.

  - Advise you on selection and wording of invitations, as needed.

  - Coordinate communication between vendors, suppliers, and sites, so that, for example, the florist knows when and how to obtain access to the ceremony site to decorate.

  - Draw up a time line to keep everyone on schedule, both pre-wedding and on the wedding day.

- Serve as a referee, friend, budget adviser and watcher, etiquette expert, shopper, detail manager and organizer.

- Coordinate your rehearsal with the officiant.

- Supervise all the last-minute details of your wedding day.

- **What are the qualities of a good wedding consultant?** Wedding consultants are known for saving time and money for their clients. Some qualities to look for:

  - **Experience.** A good track record is usually the best guide, so check references and talk frankly with some of the consultant's previous clients.

  - **Professionalism.** The consultant should understand the *business* of weddings. Certification and/or membership in a consultants association may be indicative of professional commitment.

  - **Congeniality.** A congenial consultant works *with* you; he or she isn't dictatorial and won't pressure you into decisions you aren't comfortable making.

  - **Good chemistry—with you.** It's important that you feel comfortable with the consultant that you'll work with. Is this someone who you'll want to spend time with? Confide in? Many couples refer to their consultant as "their new best friend."

  - **Excellent listening skills.** Your consultant is going to plan *your* wedding. Is he or she a good listener?

  - **Courtesy.** A consultant's manners may indicate how well he or she will work with you and others. This person will be your wedding etiquette expert and will also serve as your intermediary with officiants, site managers, suppliers, vendors, and even members of the wedding party. You want to be represented positively.

- **What is the typical cost of a wedding consultant?** You don't have to be among the wealthy to hire a wedding consultant, planner, or coordinator. Costs for a consultant's services depend on what the person does for you. In general, a consultant who provides full service will charge either a flat hourly rate or a flat fee. A good rule of thumb is to allow for 10 to 15 percent of your overall budget to be spent on the services of a wedding consultant who does everything for you. The many couples who have used the services of these professionals will tell you that the money was well worth it. You might need only planning advice and referrals. If so, you'll find that planners usually charge an hourly

Wedding Consultants Describe Their Skills

In speaking with several wedding consultants over the years, I've asked them to list the most important parts of their jobs and the personality traits of successful professionals. Here are some of their answers:

"First and foremost, the wedding consultant should be dedicated to the couple, always finding a way to accomplish their dream in the most appropriate way possible." "Being a good listener." "A master problem solver." "A dream/vision producer: the person who can pull all of the pieces together for the wedding that the couple wants." "Allowing couples to express their ideas and then bringing those ideas into reality." "A great illusionist: ability to keep a couple focused on what's most important to them, while also guiding them to stay within their budget. Make small budgets look like millions." "Being detail-oriented, well prepared, and able to be ready for any and every contingency." "The consultant must be honest." "A calm, professional demeanor is a tremendous help; a sense of humor helps, too." "Keys are being a diplomat, an etiquette adviser, and an intermediary among family factions." "Having the ability to make decisions on the spot, and with confidence." "Adaptable." "Highly regarded among suppliers and vendors." "Trustworthy." "Enthusiasm for each and every wedding."

rate for consultations. Or you might hire a consultant at a daily rate for help with specific events. All options are worth investigating.

Once you have an initial budget in mind, calculate what the cost of a consultant will be and weigh that against the value of your time. Keep in mind that a successful consultant will be able to pass along enough savings to defray much of his or her cost—and that time can be just as important a commodity to you as money.

To avoid unscrupulous consultants who attempt to increase their fees by adding extras or who have under-the-table agreements with suppliers and vendors, it's best to look for someone who provides wedding packages at fixed rates, or charges a flat fee based on the services you request.

THE DATE

Time of Year

The time of year for your wedding is a key consideration, for several reasons. First, *the most popular months for weddings* (starting with the busiest) *in most places are June, September, August, May, October, and July.* Accordingly, the most popular wedding locations will be at a premium during those months, in terms of both availability and cost. If cost is a factor, you will do better to select a month when rates and fees are lower. *In general, the best budget months of the year are January, February, and March.* Of course, if you plan a destination wedding or a honeymoon in February at a popular wintertime retreat like Florida, Hawaii, or the Caribbean, expect to pay peak prices. Time of year is also a factor for a wedding at a hot year-round destination such as Las Vegas or Disney World. In these cases, you might want to look at those seasons when the strip has a slow season or the park slows somewhat, such as the months when kids are in school.

Second, if your shared vision of your wedding *involves the outdoors,* you will be limited to warm-weather months, unless you are planning a reception at a ski resort. Even then, bear in mind that a winter ski resort may also be fully booked well in advance.

Third, *some religions have restrictions on weddings that take place during high holy days,* such as those of Lent or Passover. If you are hoping for an early-spring wedding, check the calendar—and then check with your priest, minister, or rabbi.

Fourth, consider *the effect your choice of timing will have on family and close friends.* Think about any hardships your wedding may cause guests. Thanksgiving, Christmas, and the Fourth of July are prime family vacation times, when people have longtime traditions and obligations they may find hard to forgo. When school is in session, it may be difficult for families to carve out a three-day wedding weekend. Consider as well any difficulties guests who live far away will have in making their travel plans.

On the other hand, having your wedding on a secondary holiday weekend, such as Memorial Day or Labor Day, may be a smart choice: Guests who have to travel will have an automatic three-day weekend and won't have to take an extra day off from work.

Day of the Week

Most weddings are held on weekends, and for good reason: Weekend days are the customary days off from work. Within the weekends, Christians don't usually wed on a Sunday, their Sabbath, and Jews don't usually wed on a Saturday, because it is their Sabbath day of prayer and rest. Historically, weddings were almost always held on Sundays because the workweek extended from Monday through Saturday, and who could afford to miss a day of work?

A weekday wedding can reap the benefits of lower prices and certain availability of ceremony and reception sites and vendor and supplier access. A weekday wedding, particularly in the late afternoon or evening on a Thursday, is also a logical consideration for a destination wedding. It provides an entire weekend for guests to fit in a mini vacation along with the festivities.

THE RIGHT TIME TO MARRY

There is an old folk saying that goes, "Choose not alone a proper mate, but a proper time to marry." If you don't need to contemplate practical considerations as part of choosing the month you will marry, there is folklore, myth, and tradition to guide you!

The Victorians loved attributing meaning to everything and many paid close attention to wedding rhymes that suggested certain results from certain wedding dates.

January	Marry when the year is new, he'll be loving, kind, and true.
February	When February birds do mate, you wed nor dread your fate.
March	If you wed when March winds blow, joy and sorrow both you'll know.
April	Marry in April if you can, joy for maiden and for man.
May	Marry in the month of May, you will surely rue the day.
June	Marry when June roses grow and over land and sea you'll go.
July	Those who in July do wed must labor for their daily bread.
August	Whoever wed in August be, many a change is sure to see.
September	Marry in September's shine so that your life is rich and fine.
October	If in October you do marry, love will come but riches tarry.
November	If you wed in bleak November, only joys will come, remember!
December	When December's snows fall fast, marry, and your love will last.

In actuality, these rhymes had a foundation that went beyond the fanciful. For example, the dire predictions for May weddings came from the custom of observing the Feast of the Dead during this month, when everyone worked hard to appease the souls of the departed. Queen Victoria took this so seriously that she permitted no royal weddings in the month of May. What made January a sure thing for a marriage to the ancient Greeks? This month was dedicated to Hera, defender of women and wife of Zeus. Anyone marrying in January received an extra blessing under Hera's power. In addition, this was the time for fertility rites, the results of which just might be passed on to the bride marrying then! September was recommended for fertility, too, because of the benefits of the full harvest moon. If love mattered most, then April was the month to marry, for it was the favored month of Venus, the Roman goddess of love.

Still undecided about when to be married? There is always the Victorian assurance that the luckiest time of all to be married is on the same day of the week that the groom was born, regardless of fertility rites, harvest moons, or when the goddess of love might be looking on. It is better yet to marry on his birthday.

Time of Day

The busiest booking times are, in order of popularity, *Saturday afternoon, Saturday morning, Friday evening, and Sunday afternoon*. The time of day your wedding takes place can also make a big difference in your budget. A late-afternoon or early-evening wedding is generally more expensive than a morning or early- to mid-afternoon wedding. Reception costs are affected as well—if you plan a reception in the middle of the day or anytime from four P.M. to eight P.M., your guests will expect to be served a meal or at least some substantial food. If cost is a factor, and you are planning to be married during the wedding high season when most sites may already be booked, consider switching your celebrations to a less frequently booked time of day. (The later the wedding, the more formal it is likely to be.) The time of day and the wedding's formality aren't necessarily indications of how elegant a wedding will be, however. Just because you are being married in the morning doesn't mean that your semiformal or informal wedding will be any less elegant than one held at night.

THE STYLE OF YOUR WEDDING

Now is the time to start thinking about *the color scheme of the wedding*. Your wedding color choices are often influenced by the time of year, seasonal flowers, the bridesmaids' dresses, the locale, and personal preferences.

Ultimately, however, the most important choice you have to make in deciding the style of your wedding is how formal or informal you wish it to be. There are three categories of weddings—*formal, semiformal,* and *informal*. The formality is related to the locations of the ceremony and reception, the size of the wedding party, the number of guests, and the time of day. While the style of a wedding in a church or synogogue may be formal or informal, a home wedding generally lends itself to informality, unless, of course, the home happens to be a mansion. In that case, drag out the white gloves and candelabra! The variations on each style are endless, but there are a few basic differences in the three categories:

The Formal Wedding

- **Where is the ceremony held?** The formal wedding ceremony usually takes place in a house of worship or in a large home or garden.

- **How many attendants should there be?** The bride and groom each usually have from four to ten attendants.

- **What is the typical attire?** The bride and her attendants wear long gowns in formal fabrics, and the groom and his attendants wear cutaways or tailcoats. Women guests wear street-length dressy clothing for a daytime wedding and usually floor-length gowns or cocktail dresses for an evening wedding. Men guests wear dark suits and ties for a daytime wedding and tuxedos for an evening wedding. An evening formal wedding that requires white tie is the most formal of all.

- **What type of reception is held?** The formal reception is usually a sit-down or semi-buffet meal. Invitations are engraved, decorations can be elaborate, transportation for the wedding party is usually provided by limousines, and music, if the reception includes dancing, is often provided by an orchestra or full band.

The Semiformal Wedding

- **Where is the ceremony held?** The ceremony can take place in a house of worship, a chapel, a hotel, a club, a home, or a garden.

- **How many attendants should there be?** The bride and groom each usually have from two to six attendants.

- **What is the typical attire?** For a semiformal wedding, the bride and her attendants may wear long, ballerina, or tea-length gowns, usually made of simpler fabrics than those for a formal wedding. The groom and his attendants wear gray or black strollers with striped trousers or a formal suit for a daytime semiformal wedding, and a dinner jacket with black trousers or a formal suit for an evening wedding. Women guests wear street-length tailored or semi-dressy dresses for a daytime wedding and cocktail dresses for an evening wedding. Men guests wear dark suits for both.

- **What type of reception is held?** The reception is generally a buffet or a cocktail buffet later in the afternoon with a small band or orchestra or a DJ.

The Informal Wedding

- **Where is the ceremony held?** The ceremony can take place in a house of worship, a chapel, or a rectory, or in a home or garden presided over by a justice of the peace.

- **How many attendants should there be?** The bride and groom each usually have from one to three attendants.

- **What is the typical attire?** At an informal wedding, the bride and her attendants wear simple white or pastel floor-length gowns or ballerina, tea-length, or street-length dresses. The groom and his attendants wear suits or sport jackets and slacks. Women guests wear what is appropriate to the location, usually street-length dresses. Men guests wear sport jackets and slacks.

- **What type of reception is held?** The reception can take place in a restaurant or at a home with a caterer and/or friends providing refreshments, usually a breakfast, brunch, or lunch in the morning or early afternoon and an informal buffet or simple hors d'oeuvres and wedding cake for an afternoon reception. Music may come from a single musician or background CDs or tapes.

THE AVAILABILITY OF YOUR OFFICIANT

If you place great importance on who performs your ceremony and wouldn't consider getting married without having him or her officiate, check on that individual's availability before making *any* other decisions about the date of your wedding.

THE LOCATIONS

Ceremony Location

You will need to decide *whether to marry in a house of worship or at a secular location.* If you plan to marry in a house of worship, try to briefly reserve a few dates pending your final decision to be sure the church or synagogue will be available when you confirm your reception location.

Otherwise you will want to consider alternative possibilities, whether indoors or outdoors, in a hotel or a wedding hall, at home or at city hall. Do you want a private ceremony with only a few close friends and family members attending? (See also Chapter 11, "Planning the Ceremony.")

Reception Location

Your choice of reception site will affect the type of food and beverages you serve, service, formality level, entertainment, and reception hours. Once you have drawn up your guest list and determined a date and time for your wedding, you can focus on the kind of reception you want and your location preferences. Begin checking out sites immediately, in terms of approximate cost and availability. In some parts of the country, reception sites are booked at least a year in advance. (See also Chapter 15, "Planning the Reception.")

The Second-Level Decisions

Once you have settled the who, when, and where of your wedding, it is time to start shopping, interviewing, and booking vendors, suppliers, and services. Because each of these next steps generally requires a good amount of lead time, there is no time like the present to:

- Shop for and make decisions about clothing and accessories—for the bride, groom, and attendants (see also Chapter 14, "Wedding Attire").

- Visit stores and list gifts you wish to receive with bridal registries (see also Chapter 8, "Gifts of Love").

- Begin reviewing reception menus (see also Chapter 15, "Planning the Reception").

- Interview and listen to bands or DJs, or start listing songs you would consider putting on tape for the reception (see also Chapter 17, "Let There Be Music!").

- Interview and talk to florists (see also Chapter 16, "Flowers for Your Wedding").

- Interview photographers and videographers and look at their portfolios (see also Chapter 18, "Photography and Videography").

- Order invitations, enclosures, announcements, and other printed material (see also Chapter 7, "Invitation Etiquette").

The Third-Level Decisions

With all your outside resources in order, you now can turn your attention to the details that will make your wedding day personal and unique. You might do the following:

- Listen to and choose music for your ceremony.

- Select readings for your ceremony.

- Make lists of music choices for your reception.

- Plan special events you want to include, such as your first dance at the reception, a bouquet toss, and a party for your attendants.

- Select gifts for your attendants, perhaps for your parents, and for each other.

- Begin to chart seating arrangements for your reception.

- Incorporate family and cultural traditions into your wedding.

Choosing Wedding Rings

Wedding rings may be selected at the same time as the engagement ring, but often they are not. Many times they are selected and ordered during the engagement period, when the bride and groom can take the time to find what will be a meaningful, serious purchase. Even if the groom has selected the engagement ring as a surprise for his intended, both should participate in the selection of the wedding ring or rings.

The bridegroom may or may not choose to wear a wedding ring. If he does, decide whether you want matching rings. If so, his will generally be a little wider and heavier than the bride's wedding ring. In the United States, the man's wedding ring, like the woman's, is traditionally worn on the fourth finger of the left hand.

- **Types of wedding bands.** Wedding bands are designed in platinum or yellow or white gold and come in a variety of finishes. If the bride is going to wear her engagement ring with her wedding band, the two should preferably be of the same metal and work well together.

- **Narrow or wide?** As with engagement rings, bands should be chosen with an eye to the shape of the bride's hand. If her hands are small, a narrow band looks best. Larger hands with longer fingers can wear wider and more elaborate rings. Still, for both the bride and the groom, comfort is of the utmost importance. A ring that is too wide or heavy or that gets in the way is not the right ring.

- **Engravings.** Wedding bands may be engraved with designs on the outside or they may be plain. The inside is usually engraved with words, initials, or simply the date. The engraved words may be a message that is a sentiment known only to the bride and groom. Before finalizing your purchase, ask the jeweler how many letters may be engraved on the inside of your wedding bands so that you can write out the inscription to be fit inside the rings.

Planning the Honeymoon

Many couples consider making honeymoon plans a top-priority decision, particularly if they plan to marry and vacation during a peak season or to travel to a popular honeymoon or travel site. In many instances, couples will make their other top-level decisions around their honeymoon plans. At the very least, the newly betrothed should make some preliminary choices regarding the honeymoon date, location, transportation, accommodations, and length-of-stay.

Honeymoons need to be planned up front not only to ensure a place to stay and transportation reservations, but for budget considerations as well. In the frenzy of planning the wedding and reception, couples often forget to compute into their total expenses the cost of a honeymoon. The expenses of a honeymoon trip are greater than just those of transportation and lodging—the honeymoon budget must include meals, transfers, souvenirs, sightseeing and sports-related costs, tips, taxes, and the little luxuries, like a massage or poolside charges for lounge chairs and towels. Always ask whether a gratuity is included in the final bill.

Commitment Ceremonies

If you are planning a same-sex ceremony, there are various resources available to help you with your decision making and planning. These resources include:

Vendors and suppliers. The wedding industry is considerably more open to same-sex celebrations than it was a decade ago, and suppliers are offering products such as invitations, rings, and cake toppers that are customized for gay and lesbian couples. Particularly in larger cities, you may find wedding consultants with considerable experience in staging commitment ceremonies and receptions. Even in less cosmopolitan areas, there may be consultants who will happily help you plan your event.

"Gay-friendly" vendors and suppliers—those that welcome gay customers—may identify themselves as such or be recommended via the grapevine. If a couple wishes to use gay-owned businesses, they can contact local gay and lesbian organizations and also consult on-line directories of retailers and service providers.

Whether or how extensively you explain your relationship depends on what you are seeking. Use common sense: The company that rents tents or folding chairs probably doesn't care what kind of party you're having. But wedding consultants, caterers, and travel planners need to know if they are to fulfill your dreams for the perfect ceremony, reception, and honeymoon trip.

Locations. Even though couples may not have a house of worship in their area that permits same-sex ceremonies, location options are many and varied. Your own home or that of a family member or friend; a hotel, club, or restaurant; a civic or historic site; a park or beach setting; a fabulous resort destination—the choice comes down to what you want and can afford. If you plan to rent a space, inform the management about the nature of the event. An increasing number of commercial sites have experience with same-sex ceremonies, but if you sense discomfort or antagonism in your initial contact, it's probably best to find another spot. If a clergyperson will officiate, you'll need to coordinate with him or her.

Theme Weddings

Theme weddings are becoming more and more popular. Perhaps you are thinking about having a wedding with a special theme. The theme may be carried into every aspect of the celebration: from the attire to the food to the decorations. (See also Chapter 11, pages 199–200: "Marrying to a Theme.")

Destination Weddings

Exchanging vows as the sun sets over the ocean. Marrying against the backdrop of a majestic mountain lodge or an ancient European castle. A romantic destination wedding can be realized with thoughtful planning. Destination weddings are increasingly popular. Choosing a dream location to marry, celebrate, and even spend your honeymoon is ideal for the couple who wants to get away with a few close friends and family for a combined celebration and vacation. It also is a smart solution for the couple who wants both a wonderful honeymoon and a lavish wedding but has to choose one over the other.

Unless you have the wherewithal to charter a plane for a slew of guests and rent rooms for all of them (customarily, these expenses are the guests' responsibility), you can't expect all of your invited guests to be able to afford such an expense. Begin with an assessment of your guests' ability to finance what is usually a three- or four-day vacation—especially if you won't be helping out by covering accommodations, something you need to communicate up front. There are often extra expenses for guests such as acquiring the correct attire for the location as well as the wedding. Understand that because of the costs and scheduling, some people you want at your wedding probably won't be able to attend.

The style of a destination wedding can be as formal or as casual as you like; there is no set guideline. The guest list will often be shorter than that of a wedding set in a traditional location, simply due to the logistics and expenses of a destination wedding; again, there is no absolute rule.

Unless you can commute back and forth to the location, you'll need someone on-site to manage the preparations, and you might work with a wedding consultant in your area who can coordinate with a planner in the wedding location. Hotels in popular travel sites may have a wedding planner on staff. There are also travel agents who specialize in destination weddings and can advise on the best times to travel as well as bargain rates for fares and lodging. With expert help, couples can sometimes achieve savings over a traditional at-home wedding—for themselves and their guests.

It's very important to inform guests of your plans as far in advance as possible—well before the traditional mailing of wedding invitations. Also, have a Plan B up your sleeve in case anything happens to prevent that planned wedding. If the site is struck by a hurricane or snowed in, for example, do you want to reschedule at another time or go ahead with your wedding in another location?

If your destination is outside the country, you and your guests will probably need passports and perhaps special visas. There may be recommended medical precautions and inoculations. Consult with both the U.S. State Department and the embassy of the country, and provide all necessary information to your guests. Also check on any legal requirements, such as a period of residency or a published announcement of intent to marry.

Remember, too, that the perfect destination may be closer than you think. There may be locations in your own state or region that meet all your requirements for romance, adventure, and convenience.

CHAPTER 3

EXPENSES AND OTHER PRACTICALITIES

WHATEVER THE SIZE OR STYLE of your wedding, the end result will depend not on how much money you spend, but on how you spend it. A wedding is an important milestone and should be a time of special indulgences. But that doesn't mean mortgaging the farm to do so. There are many ways to save without scrimping.

A large, elaborate wedding can cost tens of thousands of dollars. In fact, the average wedding in the United States today costs $22,000—although there are major regional variations. Excess does not necessarily equal success. A simpler, less elaborate wedding can be equally elegant and memorable. Remember: Your relationship is what is important, not the extravagance of your celebration.

The chart on pages 40–41 is intended only to explain the traditional division of expenses and to give you a structure for planning. Any of the items may be omitted entirely without making your wedding any less beautiful or meaningful. Use the chart as a guide—and make your own adjustments.

There are many variations not only in ways to save but also in how costs are divided. Traditionally the bride's family foots the bill for almost every expense, but today more often than not, the groom's family and the newlyweds pitch in, too. Forty percent of today's couples pay their own wedding costs, particularly if the wedding is a second one. Traditions evolve, but manners still lead the way. It is still not correct for the bride's family to ask the groom's family to pay any of the wedding costs. If, however, his family offers to pay a share, it is quite appropriate for the bride's parents to accept.

Who Pays?

WHO PAYS, TRADITIONALLY

As mentioned, traditionally the bride's family assumes the burden of most wedding costs, a custom most likely translated from the ancient practice of providing a large dowry to attract a good husband. This custom was eventually replaced in Victorian times by the provision of a settlement from the bride's family to the groom's family, along with a substantial trousseau, usually a year's worth of clothing and household items. Nowadays, however, just 27 percent of weddings are paid for solely by the bride's parents.

Who Pays? Variations by Culture

In Mexico and some Latin American countries, for example, the bride and groom might find as many as fifteen couples to be their sponsors, called *padrinos* and *madrinas*. These couples are responsible for a variety of the financial components of the wedding. They may pay for the bride's bouquet or for the music at the reception. In fact, there is a *padrino* and *madrina* for almost all wedding categories so that the costs are divided among the couples. The groom pays for the wedding dress; the sponsors pay for almost everything else. This custom is sometimes practiced in the United States by families of Mexican and Latin American ancestry, particularly in the southwestern states that border Mexico. In Egypt, the groom pays a bridal price to the bride and her family, but part of that price is used to pay for the costs of the wedding. Additionally, the groom and his family customarily pay for the couple's apartment, appliances, kitchen furniture, and lighting, and the bride's dress.

WHO PAYS, NONTRADITIONALLY

These days, up to 70 percent of weddings are paid for either by the couple or by some combination of the bride's and groom's parents. It's quite common for both the bride's and the groom's families to share the costs of the celebration, or for the bride and the groom to pay for all or part of the expenses themselves. Modern couples are older and generally employed and independent by the time they get married, enabling them to plan and pay for their own weddings.

When families are willing to share the costs, the bride and groom should consider the range of possibilities ahead of time and be certain that they are in agreement with each other before sitting down with their parents to discuss the budget. If they want financial help, they must be willing to compromise on some of their wishes for the wedding. Any conversation about money should be both dignified and candid.

Traditional Division of Costs

If age-old tradition is ruling the financial structure of your wedding, the following lists of traditional expense responsibilities should be of assistance:

TRADITIONAL EXPENSES OF THE BRIDE AND HER FAMILY

Services of a bridal consultant

Invitations, enclosures, and announcements

Bride's wedding gown and accessories

Floral decorations for ceremony and reception, bridesmaids' flowers, bride's bouquet

Formal wedding photographs and candid pictures

Videotape recording of wedding

Music for church and reception

Transportation of bridal party to and from ceremony

All reception expenses

Bride's gifts to her attendants

Bride's gift to groom

Groom's wedding ring

Rental of awning for ceremony entrance and carpet for aisle

Fee for services performed by sexton

Cost of soloists

A traffic officer if necessary

Transportation of bridal party to reception

Transportation and lodging expenses for officiant if from another town and if invited to officiate by bride's family

Accommodations for bride's attendants

Bridesmaids' luncheon

TRADITIONAL EXPENSES OF THE GROOM AND HIS FAMILY

Bride's engagement and wedding rings

Groom's gift to his bride

Gifts for groom's attendants

Ties and gloves for groom's attendants if not part of their clothing rental package

Bride's bouquet (only in those regions where it is local custom for the groom to pay for it)

Bride's going-away corsage

Boutonnieres for groom's attendants

Corsages for immediate members of both families (unless bride has included them in her florist's order)

Officiant's fee or donation

Transportation and lodging expenses for officiant if from another town and if invited to officiate by the groom's family

Marriage license

Transportation for groom and best man to ceremony

Expenses of honeymoon

All costs of rehearsal dinner

Accommodations for groom's attendants

Bachelor dinner if groom wishes to give one

Transportation and lodging expenses for groom's immediate family

Purchase of apparel and all accessories

Transportation to and from city where wedding takes place

A contribution to a gift from bridesmaids to bride

An individual gift to the couple (if being in the wedding is not the gift)

Optionally, a shower or luncheon for bride

USHERS'/BEST MAN'S EXPENSES

Rental of wedding attire

Transportation to and from city where wedding takes place

A contribution to a gift from groom's attendants to groom

An individual gift to the couple (if being in the wedding is not the gift)

A bachelor dinner if given by groom's attendants

OUT-OF-TOWN GUESTS' EXPENSES

Transportation to and from wedding

Lodging expenses

Wedding gift

Determining a Budget

A carefully prepared budget can spare you the nightmare of falling prey to impractical plans or of running up unnecessary debts. Whether you plan an elaborate wedding with 300 guests or a simple ceremony with 30 friends in your own home, a realistic budget will help make your preparations less stressful. If money becomes a source of tension, simply cut the guest list and adjust your plans accordingly.

Simply put: Base your budget strictly on what you or your parents can afford. A budget for a large wedding should include allotments for each of the expenses listed below. The budget for a simple wedding should include the items that you cannot provide yourself and intend to purchase, as well as the things you plan to do on your own or with the help of friends and family.

With imagination and good planning, a beautiful wedding can be held within any limits. Whatever you plan, stick to your budget, or the worry and insecurity will carry over to your relationship and you will start your marriage in a state of anxiety and stress.

- **Start with a figure.** Before you sign a single contract or make a firm commitment with any vendor, establish a dollar amount of what you believe you can spend on your wedding. If you have $5,000 to spend on your wedding, and the reception site you are hoping for will cost $3,500, you are probably not leaving enough money to cover other costs—accommodations for your attendants, fees, a band or DJ, wedding attire, and so on—unless some of those items will be paid for by someone else or given as wedding gifts. If this is the case, and you will indeed be paying all the expenses, adjust your sights and find a reception location that is not as costly. Choose a public garden or a friend's beautiful backyard. Have a morning wedding followed by a brunch, or an afternoon cocktail reception instead of a seated dinner. The variations are endless.

- **Economy versus value.** Value is really knowing precisely what you want and what you are willing to pay for so that you can satisfy your expectations for quality and service. If you pay for extras you don't want, you're not getting good value. For example, a band that charges for a master of ceremonies when you don't want a master of ceremonies is no value to you, just as a reception package that includes printed napkins and matchbooks has less value if you don't care about these incidentals. You can achieve economy if you plan well and give yourself the time to shop around and compare costs.

- **Tips on budgeting.** Almost every component of your wedding will have a wide range of choices and costs. Decide which components you consider important enough to splurge on; then find ways to economize with style and flair in the other areas.

    The best ways to economize on big-ticket items? Cut your guest list, find a smaller but no less elegant reception site, and choose a time of the year, a day of the week, and time of the day when prices are not at a premium. For fairly formal weddings, 50 to 60 percent of the costs generally go toward the per-person reception fees. Some caterers suggest making a budget for the reception and then cutting it back by 25 percent to cover any future overruns.

BUDGET CATEGORIES

The following chart includes traditional costs associated with a wedding. Some are mandatory, such as marriage license fees, and some are optional, such as limousines and a videographer. Whether an optional category is mandatory to you is your decision. For example, if it is really important to you to arrive at the ceremony in a white stretch limousine, then this will become a fixed cost in your budget. A fixed cost, yes, but adjustable—if you must have a stretch limo, call more than one car service to get the best value.

Don't forget the little costs that add up quickly. Things like stockings and lingerie are considered "bride's accessories," not just shoes and jewelry. Be as thorough as you can to get the most realistic picture.

ITEM	MANDATORY	OPTIONAL	COST
Attendants			
Accommodations			
Bridesmaids' luncheon			
Ceremony fees			
Officiant's fee			
Church, synagogue, or other location fee			
Organist's fee			
Cantor/vocalist/instrumentalist fee(s)			
Flowers			
Ceremony			
Reception			
Bridal bouquet			
Bridal attendants' flowers			
Corsages			
Boutonnieres			
Gifts			
Bride's gifts for attendants			
Groom's gifts for attendants			
Bride's gift for groom			
Groom's gift for bride			
Honeymoon costs			
Invitations/enclosures			
Announcements			
Calligraphy			
Postage			
Ceremony program			
Legalities			
Marriage license			
Health/physical/blood test fees			
Music for reception			

ITEM	MANDATORY	OPTIONAL	COST
Photography			
Engagement photographs			
Photographer			
Videographer			
Reception			
Location			
Food/beverage expenses (per-person cost)			
Reception favors (per-person cost)			
Wedding cake			
Transportation/parking			
Limousines for bridal party			
Traffic officials at ceremony, reception			
Valet parking			
Travel costs for ceremony officiant if necessary			
Trips home during planning if you live away			
Wedding attire			
Bridal gown			
Bridal accessories			
Groom's outfit			
Bride's ring			
Groom's ring			
Beauty costs (hair, nails, makeup)			
Wedding consultant fees			
Miscellaneous			
Telephone bills related to planning			
Wardrobe costs for wedding-related events			
Tips (if not included in above costs)			
Taxes (if not included in above costs)			
TOTALS			

Tips on Tipping

Wedding professionals, from bridal consultants to photographers, are tipped only for extra-special service. If your florist arrived to decorate the ceremony site only to find a locked door, which caused him or her to wait an extra hour, a tip would be an extra thank-you for professionalism, patience, and diligence. While you might set aside an extra 15 percent as an unexpected tip fund, you needn't anticipate tips for the consultant, club manager or caterer, florist, photographer, or videographer. Often a caterer's gratuities are imbedded in the total costs; many hotels include a service charge for the waitstaff. Always ask whether gratuities are included before signing any contract.

You should plan a gratuity budget for the following:

- Valet parking

- Coat check

- Powder room attendants

- Delivery truck drivers

- Limousine drivers

- Waitstaff

- Bartenders

- Table captains

In addition:

- Tip parking lot, coat check, and powder room attendants ahead of time so that your guests don't have to. Ask a friend to make sure that there are no tip dishes or baskets sitting on the coat check counter or the powder room shelf that would make guests feel obligated to tip. A general guideline is to tip attendants a flat fee or $1 to $2 per guest.

THE BEST MAN ASKS: "HOW DO I DELIVER CEREMONY FEES?"

Q: *As the best man, it's my responsibility to deliver the ceremony fees. What is the proper way to make these payments?*

A: Fees for the officiant, the organist, the soloist, and use of a church or other house of worship are not tips but should be delivered as you would tips, in sealed envelopes, addressed to each person, with the couple's "thanks" included. The groom will supply you with the money to cover the fees. Some grooms prefer to make the payments directly themselves, but most rely on the best man to distribute the envelopes.

- In the case of limousine drivers and the catering staff, you can request that gratuities be included in the total bill. (Make sure there are no tip receptacles on the bar making a guest wonder if he or she should leave a tip.) Sometimes a reception site requests that all tips be paid in cash in advance. Check your contract and take care of this detail before-hand so that no one has to settle a bill during or after the event. If gratuities are to be given after the wedding or are not included in the final bill, they still should be counted out and put in sealed envelopes beforehand so that they can be distributed easily at the end of the reception.

- When a tip is spontaneous and is given to a vendor who has done an extraordinary service, it can be given at the end of the reception or the next day, with a note of thanks included.

All About Contracts

You should expect to sign a contract with every supplier, from the stationer to the florist to the limousine service to the wedding consultant. *Every single* detail should be covered in writing in the contract, including taxes, gratuities, dates, delivery schedules, payment plans, cancellation fees, and refund policies. Take the time to read everything thoroughly; if you don't understand something, ask questions until you do. Never sign a contract under pressure. If you're still unclear about some aspect of the contract, take a copy of it to a friend who has experience in contractual agreements. Be sure you are clear on how and when bills are to be paid. And make sure there are clauses in the contract that ensure proper restitution in the event of a snafu that is clearly the vendor's responsibility.

CHECK FOR HIDDEN COSTS

Even deciphering the fine print on a contract can leave you with unanswered questions. Know exactly what you need up front so that you can ferret out hidden, unanticipated costs. You are entitled to know exactly what is included—and what is not—before agreeing to the service. If the service provider or contractor is unwilling to give you a detailed listing or breakdown of costs, consider looking elsewhere. For example, make sure that alterations to your gown are included in the service and price in the contract with a bridal salon. If they are not, ask what the general costs are. Does the salon charge extra to press your gown after alterations? Would it be less expensive for you to take the gown to a reputable and experienced dry cleaner for pressing?

Don't forget taxes and gratuities, which can add a significant amount to the total bill—especially in states that have a high sales tax. It's a good idea to make sure that taxes and tips are included in the total price. And inquire about such hidden costs as "plate charges."

Marriage Legalities

Along with the romance, fun, and excitement of a wedding come the absolutes—the legally required paperwork and to-do's without which a marriage cannot take place. In order to be married in the eyes of the law, a couple must live up to the letter of the law—and the law can vary, not just from country to country, but from state to state and even city to city as well. For example, you might find that Michigan requires a blood test, counseling, and witnesses for a marriage to take place (or a sixty-day waiting period for couples who ignore the counseling requirement), none of which Ohio requires. You certainly don't need to go so far as to hire an attorney to get married, but it is a good idea to check, in advance, what is required—whether you are getting married in your hometown or on an exotic island on another continent.

Where do you start? Write or call the county clerk's office or the Office of the Registrar in the town or county you are to be married. They may simply mail or fax you a list of legal requirements for acquiring a marriage license. Some states require that you register in the same state and even county where the ceremony will be performed, and some ask that you do so in person. The most important point is to start your research well in advance of the ceremony so that, come your wedding day, all will be legal and aboveboard.

The Who, What, When, and Where of Getting Married

LEGAL FACTORS

Age. In most states, the age one may be married is much younger than the age one may legally drive, drink, vote, or apply for a credit card. Age restrictions vary widely from state to state, so be sure to determine the requirements for your state. No one may legally take your word for it that you are indeed the age you say you are. You may be required to submit documentary proof of age. Generally, one or more of the following documents showing proof of age are required and acceptable:

- Birth certificate

- Baptismal record

- Passport

- Driver's license

- Life insurance policy

- Employment certificate

- School record

- Immigration record

- Naturalization record

- Court record

Familial restrictions. A marriage may not take place in the United States between those of the following relationships, regardless of whether they are legitimate or illegitimate offspring:

- Ancestor and descendant (parent, grandparent, great-grandparent, child, grandchild, great-grandchild)

- Brother and sister (full- or half-blood)

- Uncle and niece

- Aunt and nephew

In most but not all states, marriage between family members closer than first cousins is prohibited. If this is an issue, it is important to check with the town or city clerk or the marriage license bureau in the town where the marriage will take place.

Capacity to consent. It is the law that marriage requires two consenting people. If either person cannot or does not understand what it means to be married because of mental illness, drugs, alcohol, or other factors affecting judgment, then that person does not have the capacity to consent and the marriage is not valid. If fraud or coercion is involved, the marriage may also be invalidated.

Gender. Generally, couples must be of the opposite sex to form a valid marriage (see "A Question for Peggy: What's the Legality of Domestic Partnership?" page 52).

Remarriage. Applicants for a marriage license who were married before must provide information regarding previous marriages, including a copy of the Decree of Divorce or a Certificate of Dissolution of Marriage or a death certificate. Clerks and marriage licensing officials say the biggest problem that occurs for those who have been married before is that they neglect to bring the original document or a certified copy. The information the applicant needs to provide includes, but may not be restricted to:

- The month, day, and year of the final divorce decree

- The county and state where the divorce was granted

- The grounds for divorce

- Whether the former spouse or spouses are living

Similar documentation may be required for an annulment, and of a widow or widower. The preciseness of the legalities makes it necessary to check and double-check, because even one missing document can delay the wedding; this can be a disaster for the bride and groom who have contracted the services of countless others and who have to have their wedding postponed.

THE MARRIAGE LICENSE

A marriage license authorizes you to get married; a marriage certificate is the document that proves that you are married and is issued by the county office where you were married, usually within a few weeks after the ceremony. In general, a marriage license may be used only in the place it is obtained, and then within a certain period of time, usually between twenty-four hours and sixty days, depending on the state; otherwise the license expires. Some states require a three-day waiting period from the time applicants apply for a license to the time the license is issued. Those states with the strictest requirements strongly advise the bride and groom to obtain their marriage license two to three weeks before their wedding day.

HEALTH CERTIFICATES

The purpose of premarital health requirements and examinations is not to keep a person with an illness from marrying, but to ensure that the future spouse knows of the condition. Some states have no requirements for premarital examinations or blood tests in order to obtain a marriage license. In other states, the law says you need to be examined and found free of communicable syphilis. Even in states where no blood test or physical exam is required, failing to tell your prospective spouse that you have a venereal disease or a physical impairment (such as impotence or infertility) before you marry may make the marriage invalid.

Find out the requirements in your state by calling or writing the county clerk's office or the Office of the Registrar as soon as you decide to marry. States that require health certificates often add further restrictions of time, so factor those restrictions into your planning along with the confirmation dates you can obtain for ceremony and reception sites.

Who Can Perform a Marriage Ceremony?

Q: *We're considering being married on a cruise ship and want to know whether or not a ship captain can perform the ceremony—and if not, who can?*

A: Contrary to popular belief, ship captains often will not perform or are not universally authorized to perform marriage ceremonies. Increasingly, however, cruise lines are working out ways for legally recognized marriages to be performed aboard ship by ship captains. A list of persons specified by law as authorized to perform a marriage ceremony is available in each state's domestic relations law. The following are lists of those who *can* perform a marriage ceremony:

Religious Ceremonies

■ A member of the clergy (e.g., priest, rabbi, minister, or *imam*) who has been officially ordained and granted authority to perform marriage ceremonies from a governing religious body in accordance with the rules and regulations of the religious body

■ A member of the clergy who is not authorized by a governing religious body, but who has been chosen by a spiritual group to preside over their spiritual affairs

■ A tribal chief (for Native American weddings)

Nonreligious Ceremonies (also called civil ceremonies)

■ The mayor of a city or village

■ The city clerk or one of the deputy city clerks of a city with over 1 million inhabitants

■ A marriage officer appointed by the town or village board or by the city common council

■ A justice or judge in most courts

■ A village, town, or county justice

■ A court clerk who has legal authority to perform marriages

■ A person given temporary authority by a judge or court clerk to conduct a marriage ceremony

RELIGIOUS FACTORS

Mastering government legalities is just one step toward ensuring the legality of your marriage. Some religions also have rules and regulations that must be adhered to—points that are best checked, immediately, with the priest, rabbi, minister, or *imam* who will officiate.

In some religions, if one or both members of the couple have been divorced, the divorce is not recognized and they may not be married in the church. Then there is the matter of membership. For a wedding to take place at a Quaker meetinghouse, for example, at least one-half of the couple should be a Quaker. Otherwise, written support for the marriage must be obtained from two adult members of the Society.

The bottom line: Even if you are a lifelong Roman Catholic, Lutheran, or Presbyterian or a convert to Judaism or the Hindu faith who has seriously studied the tenets of the religion, inquire in advance whether the institution has any special requirements. If it is important to you to be married by a priest, rabbi, or minister or in a church, temple, or synagogue, you will need to know the requirements to make that happen.

ODDS AND ENDS

- *Marriage by an American to a foreign national* requires its own set of documents and qualifications, including certified English translation of any required documentation. You can get information on obtaining a visa for a foreign spouse from any office of the U.S. Citizenship and Immigration Services; U.S. embassies and consulates abroad; or the U.S. Department of State Visa Office.

- *If you are using an officiant from out of state,* know that some states require that he or she have a Certificate of Authorization from the state in which the wedding will take place.

- *Witnesses are required by some states,* in addition to an authorized member of the clergy or public official, to be present during the wedding ceremony. In some of these states, there is no minimum age for a witness, but it is suggested that he or she be deemed competent enough to testify in a court proceeding regarding what was witnessed. In other states, no witness is required other than the officiant.

WHAT'S THE LEGALITY OF DOMESTIC PARTNERSHIP?

Q: *I am a lesbian, and my partner and I have been in a long-term relationship. We would like to legalize our relationship. What are our options?*

A: Generally, couples must be of the opposite sex to form a valid marriage. Religions have their own gender regulations, but there is a growing trend among clergy to bless same-sex unions. Most states do not allow same-sex marriages, but in several states, arguments are being made in the courts that a marriage license cannot be denied based on the sex of the applicants. A few have passed legislation giving legal status to the union of same-sex couples, ensuring they receive the same benefits as those received by married couples. On the other hand, some states have passed laws designed to thwart same-sex marriages. Indeed, in 1996 the Defense of Marriage Act was signed into law, barring the federal government from recognizing same-sex marriages and permitting states to ignore same-sex marriages performed in other states.

Even though most states do not recognize same-sex marriages, many agencies and companies are adopting "domestic partnership" policies that accept same-sex relationships. Policies range from fair-housing regulations to the granting of traditional marital benefits, such as insurance coverage, family leave, and bereavement leave.

Premarital Counseling

Premarital counseling, whether mandated or merely recommended, is a short-term way to identify and work through important issues, to avoid conflict over the long haul. The purpose is to raise issues that you might not have considered, to discuss potential sensitive areas, and to give words to some of the things a couple may be thinking but may not know how to express. (Note: When premarital counseling is completed, it's thoughtful of the bride and groom to write a thank-you note or a letter to their clergyperson to express their appreciation for the guidance they received.) The couple who treats one another with respect and consideration has a much greater chance of making it over the long haul, and this counseling can help establish patterns of positive communication that will stand them in good stead for a lifetime.

THE LEGALITIES OF MARRYING IN ANOTHER COUNTRY

Many brides and grooms dream of being married outside the United States in a romantic spot like Tahiti or Paris or St. Thomas. But before you call that little French bakery for the perfect wedding cake or put down a deposit on a Caribbean island resort, you should first check the wedding legalities of the country you wish to be married in. Each country has a different set of requirements. Some ask for residency requirements of a certain duration. Others require a specific number of witnesses. And if you're marrying in another country, don't forget to look into your legal and religious requirements at home as well. Check your passport, medical requirements, and the documentation you need to bring back home to ensure your marriage's validity in the United States.

There are plenty of resources available to help you. One surefire way to get answers is to *telephone the country's consulate or tourist office located in the United States.* The office will provide specific instructions over the phone, by mail, or by fax. In some countries, such as Mexico, the requirements vary slightly from town to town, so once you've gotten the basic information from the tourist office, you will need to call the registrar's office in the town where you are getting married. And get all information in writing so you have all the facts.

Wedding consultants who specialize in destination weddings and travel agents who do wedding planning can also provide information on the documentation required and any restrictions.

Name Changes

There is no law, rule, religious dictate, or mandate that says the bride must take the groom's last name. A bride may take her husband's last name, retain her own surname, or hyphenate both her own surname and her husband's surname. When Linda Graham marries Mark Richards, she may be Linda Richards, Linda Graham, or Linda Graham-Richards. In spite of the range of acceptable choices, 90 percent of today's U.S. brides make the traditional choice of adopting their husband's names.

A bride who wishes to take her husband's last name may retain her given middle name or, more commonly, use her own surname as a middle name. Linda Beth Graham may become Linda Graham Richards or Linda Beth Richards. The only law governing the name chosen by the bride (or by the groom, who has the option of changing his name as well) is that the name be used consistently and without intent to defraud. Any name change occurs simply by entering the new name in the appropriate space provided on the marriage license, as long as the new name consists of one of the following:

- The surname of the bride (or the groom)

- Any former surname he or she has had

- A name combining into a single surname all or a segment of the premarriage surname or any former surname of each spouse

- A combination name separated by a hyphen, provided that each part of such combination surname is the premarriage surname, or any former surname, of each of the spouses

WHY CHANGE YOUR NAME?

The matter of changing names is traditionally more of a consideration for the bride than it is for the groom, for it is still rare for a man to change his name upon marriage. If a woman is being married for a second time, she probably has already changed her name once. She may have kept her ex-husband's surname, or she may have reverted to her maiden name. Another marriage can bring about more change. If the bride has kept her married name from her first marriage, it is likely that she will take her new husband's surname—if for no other reason than to avoid confusion for all concerned, but also out of consideration and love for her new husband (who will undoubtedly be pleased that she will be known by his name and not by another man's name).

Professional considerations. One way to deal with a name change professionally is for the bride to continue to use the name she has been using in work or professional situations and to use her new name in social situations. Therefore, she is known as Ms. Jane Johnson at work, while socially she is Mrs. Franklin Pierce (or Jane Johnson Pierce if she retains her maiden name as her middle name).

Children and names. If the bride has children from a previous marriage, their last name will very likely be that of their father, while their mother may be using her maiden name or taking the name of her new husband. How this is sorted out is up to each bride and groom, but it is important to let relevant persons and organizations know who is who and how each person is to be addressed. You may want to type up a note stating the proper names, phone numbers, and addresses in case of any calls or correspondence. Give copies to your child's school, to your pediatrician and dentist, and to any religious and sports groups.

NAME CHANGE: OFFICIAL NOTIFICATIONS

When a bride changes her name, she must notify a vast number of people, companies, agencies, and organizations. Use your wedding organizer to list them. Some organizations require proof of the name change and will require a copy of the marriage certificate, which is issued after the marriage. When an address change is occurring as well, it is a good idea to make both changes at the same time.

NAME CHANGE: ADVISING OTHERS ON NONTRADITIONAL CHOICES

Confusion often prevails when the bride decides to retain her maiden name or use some hyphenated form of both her and her husband's name. If you decide to go the nontraditional route, you will need to graciously advise those who assume you will be taking your husband's name as your own. If you need to correct someone, do so kindly. Some commonsense ways to notify friends and relatives: on stationery or in the return address on thank-you-note envelopes, in newspaper wedding announcements, or on "at home" cards enclosed in wedding announcements.

NAME CHANGE: WHAT TO CALL YOUR COMMITMENT CEREMONY AND YOUR SAME-SEX PARTNER

Although *commitment ceremony* has quickly become the most frequently used designation for same-sex ceremonies, it's not engraved in stone. Some couples prefer *wedding,* which is acceptable so long as the nature of the relationship is obvious. But describing the ceremony as a wedding might be confusing when the couple's names are not clearly gender-specific. Couples might choose a term that signifies the permanence of their relationship (*lifetime commitment, life partnership*) or the spiritual nature of the service (*rite of blessing, blessing of the union, vows of love, partnership covenant*). Other ideas include *affirmation ceremony, joining ceremony,* and *union ceremony.*

What do you call each other during the engagement? The traditional "fiancé" or "fiancée" is suitable. After the ceremony, many couples introduce each other as "spouse" or "life partner."

Regardless of how couples name their ceremony and refer to their relationship, the etiquette point is to choose language that will be readily understood by others.

NAME CHANGE: CHANGING YOUR MIND

If, at the time of the marriage, a bride (or groom) does not change her name and later changes her mind, she can file a petition for change of name with the court. However, the marriage license and certificate cannot be changed to record the surname she decides to use after she is already married and registered with a different name.

Pre- and Postnuptial Contracts

The matter of formalizing financial and legal matters through a prenuptial contract or premarital agreement is a sensitive one for brides and grooms, many of whom consider doing so a crass form of hedging bets on the longevity of the marriage. It is certainly an issue that needs to be discussed early in the relationship—and not something you spring on your partner-to-be right before the ceremony. Otherwise, serious doubts, hurt feelings, and even strong anger can result.

- **What is a premarital agreement?** Basically, a premarital agreement is a contract between two people that defines the rights and benefits that will exist during the marriage and after, in the event of divorce or death. It can expand or limit a person's right to property, life insurance benefits, or support payments. Usually, it addresses the rights to property that each brings to the marriage, retirement plan assets, and how money accumulated before the marriage will be distributed in the event of divorce or death. Without a premarital agreement, state laws define the rights and benefits of marriage. If the couple does not want to rely on state laws to determine their legal and fiscal fate, the premarital agreement allows them to make their own rules.

- **When is a prenuptial agreement used?** Although anyone can have a premarital agreement, it is most often used when the bride or the groom or both bring assets to the marriage that they want to protect in the event of divorce or death. This is particularly true for people marrying for the second or third time who want to make sure that certain assets are passed on to their children from a previous marriage.

- **What is not covered in a prenup?** What a prenuptial contract does not cover is child custody and support. The courts will disregard the contract on this point and make a decision that is considered in the best interest of the child. The courts will also disregard a premarital agreement that, in essence, leaves one person destitute.

- **What is a postnuptial contract?** A postnuptial contract is one made after a couple is married and can include the same categories of consideration, usually having to do with property and money, as in a prenuptial contract. This contract is usually drawn if the couple realizes that children from a previous marriage or other family members would be unprotected in the case of divorce or death.

- **What is meant by disclosure?** Because one person is usually giving something up by agreeing to a prenuptial contract, both the bride and the groom must fully disclose their finances to each other in advance. Most states require that the premarital agreement include separate asset listings that describe and show the values of each person's assets. If the couple doesn't do this, each is preventing the other from knowing what he or she is losing by signing the contract—and this may constitute fraud, which makes the agreement unenforceable. Because of this, and to ensure that the agreement is written correctly and legally, it is a good idea for both the bride and the groom to seek the advice of their respective lawyers before entering into the agreement.

- **What is the form of the agreement?** A prenuptial contract or premarital agreement must be in writing to be legally binding. It provides evidence of the terms of the agreement and demonstrates that both people understand and agree to the terms. It is generally legally binding as long as it is entered into voluntarily and without fraud and as long as it is reasonable and fair. It is not binding if a person is unfairly induced to sign the agreement or is coerced under excessive emotional pressure.

Wills and Finances

When there is no pre- or postnuptial contract, the bride and groom would be smart to put their wills and finances in order so that the disposition of their money and property is clear to each other or, should both die, to their families.

- **Changing beneficiaries.** Finances include such things as insurance policies and beneficiaries on retirement plan payouts. Assuming the bride and groom want to make each other the beneficiary on any existing policies they own, the couple should call an insurance broker and talk to their payroll coordinators at work to see what documentation is required to make this change.

- **Decisions about bank accounts.** How the couple will manage their finances is totally personal, but they should discuss their thoughts. They may decide to maintain separate accounts and open a new joint account or pool all their finances into a joint account. If the bride is maintaining a separate account but changing her name, she needs to take care of this paperwork when she changes other legal documents. If she is changing her name and has direct electronic deposit into her account, she needs to coordinate the account change at the same time as she changes her name at work.

Wedding Insurance

Weddings have taken place for centuries without wedding insurance, but no chapter on the legalities of getting married would be complete without including it as a topic of consideration. In many instances, the cost of a wedding is so astronomical that the additional cost of insurance is worth every penny if it protects such a large investment.

- **Why buy wedding insurance?** Wedding insurance, offered exclusively by the Fireman's Fund insurance company, may be taken out by a bride and groom to cover wedding catastrophes that are beyond anyone's control. Wedding insurance can also cover any retaking of photographs, wedding-attire or wedding-gift replacements, and public liability.

- **When is it beneficial?** Wedding insurance is beneficial in certain situations: when, for example, a reception site suddenly cannot accommodate the party for reasons including fire damage, a crime, or a health department quarantine occurring at the site. Insurance will cover the cost of rebooking elsewhere.

Consider every contingency when assessing the value and extent of the insurance you want. For example, if the reception site is suddenly not available and the wedding must be canceled because no other site is available on such short notice, other costs may be lost, such as formal-wear rental, car hire, hotel charges for the wedding party, and flower arrangements.

CHAPTER 4

WHAT'S A GROOM TO DO?

THERE'S AN OLD SAYING in wedding lore: "A man never knows how unimportant he is until he goes to his own wedding." Indeed, it wasn't so long ago that the groom's role was largely relegated to popping the question, selecting his groomsmen, planning the honeymoon, and making sure to show up on the scheduled day. Even the boutonniere he wore was someone else's choice.

Well, say good-bye to that shadow groom of old. These days, grooms are as likely as brides to be active participants in decision making and the carrying out of wedding duties, from setting a budget to hiring caterers to writing thank-you notes. More and more, the marriage partnership actually *begins* in the joint planning of the celebration that will cement a couple's future lives together.

The statistics confirm this trend: According to the Condé Nast Bridal Infobank, more than 40 percent of couples now plan their weddings together, and three out of four grooms help select items for their wedding-gift registries. This heightened involvement has a lot to do with the fact that some 75 percent of engaged couples are paying for some or all of their own weddings. As a result, grooms are more invested in what they're paying for, and they want more input. Another factor is the prevalence of second (or third) marriages. Nearly half of all weddings these days are encore marriages, and studies show that men are more involved in planning encore weddings—especially if children will be part of the celebration.

In addition, because people are getting married later in life (nearly twenty-nine for men and twenty-seven for women), many couples both have full-time jobs when they become engaged. Partnering to plan the wedding relieves the bride of the need to shoulder the bulk of the burden, when in her day-to-day worklife she may be just as busy as the groom. Sharing the duties is the loving, considerate thing to do—and it's also an excellent indicator of how the couple will work together on important issues in the years to come.

Even if they aren't involved financially, many modern men are clamoring to actively participate in what they increasingly see as "their" shared experience—a day not only for the bride to shine, but for both bride and groom to bask together in the radiant promise of love and happiness.

A Win-Win Collaboration

How is this new arrangement working out? Actually, quite well! Harried brides (and their harried mothers) are welcoming grooms' increased input, and their help is being deemed as eminently acceptable. In particular, more and more grooms are taking responsibility for choosing bands, transportation, liquor, and photography. And because many guys are committed foodies these days, they are jumping at the chance to help design the perfect wedding feast. Grooms are also readily embracing the trend toward more personalized weddings—ones that make a statement about who the couple is—as opposed to potentially having a cookie-cutter affair. Many like planning their ceremonies with their brides, as they personalize vows, choose music that has special meaning, and mix and match traditional roles—all of which serve to make the day even more memorable for everyone involved.

Finally, grooms are discovering that helping to plan one of life's major milestones can be sheer fun, and seeing it all played out a joy to behold. I recently heard of one groom, a former caterer, who took it upon himself to cook all of the food for his wedding reception. For the wedding party and sixty guests, he prepared a feast of roast beef, baked turkey, poached salmon, shrimp, and sides. Because of the personal stamp the groom put on the celebration—and all the love, time, and commitment it represented—the occasion was that much more meaningful. The bride, for her part, cried with joy.

Planning Together, from the Top

You're engaged, your families are thrilled, and you're about to get busy with plans. Now it comes down to the nitty-gritty of planning your wedding together. Here's where you both make your dreams and priorities known, and you'll also need to develop a budget accordingly.

A good place to start to bring your upcoming nuptials into focus is for the two of you to share your visions of a "perfect" wedding. For example, you may have always dreamed about being married outside in a garden, with lots of children about, a band playing foot-tapping music, and everyone you love present and giddy with excitement. This is where your mutual enthusiasm can take off, as you begin to realize what a celebration you can create together!

You may want to start by each compiling a list of your top priorities. Place all the major aspects of the ceremony and reception—location, number of guests, wedding party, attire, invitations, music, flowers, food, drink, photography, videography, cake, transportation, vows—in order of their importance to you. For example, the groom may have music at the top of his list, while the bride's top priority may be finding a wedding gown. Making these lists and discussing them can help you decide who takes the lead on planning in each of the categories.

A LAID-BACK GROOM—IDEAL PLANNING PARTNER OR ANNOYINGLY OUT OF IT?

Q: *Most of my friends' husbands had a big hand in planning their weddings and loved sharing in the success of their big days. But my fiancé just doesn't seem all that interested in the details of planning—such as choosing the food or selecting music. He works hard and is paying for everything, and he says he's happy to help out whenever I need him—which I don't, really, because I'm not working at this time. Still, I'd like for him to offer to help and I feel he may be sorry one day that he wasn't more active in the planning. Should I push him to get more involved?*

A: No matter what the current trends or fashions are, some grooms-to-be simply aren't interested in planning the details of the wedding. Your fiancé has expressed himself clearly, and you shouldn't force him to do something he's just not that into. Share your decisions with him as you make them, however, and do a little probing: You may discover one aspect of the wedding planning he's truly interested in. Plus, your enthusiasm is bound to be contagious; given enough time and space, your fiancé may find himself as excited about the details as you are.

Your first decisions will probably be to determine your ceremony and reception sites and to set the date for your big day.

This is also the time to talk about any aspects of a wedding neither of you want. "No baby's breath in the floral arrangements!" she might say. "No tacky emcee!" he might say. "No cash bars!" they both agree. By and large, if you've gotten this far together in life, you're likely to share many of the same aversions.

Deciding where to place your financial resources is often a trickier issue. Whether funding their entire wedding themselves or getting help from others, most engaged couples have to work within a budget. Thus, it's imperative to come to an agreement regarding your financial parameters at the outset: Which aspects of your wedding mean the most to you, in terms of cost, effort, and consideration for guests? (For example, you may be interested in having a destination wedding but know that doing so would be a hardship for a number of elderly or incapacitated relatives, or a financial burden for those you want to invite—and therefore out of the question.) You might want to start with a total figure and divide your resources from there. Whatever your approach, the ultimate goal is to find a level of expense you are both comfortable with. (For complete information on budgeting your wedding, figuring in fixed and variable costs, and learning about ways to cut costs, see Chapter 3, "Expenses and Other Practicalities.")

Deciding Who Does What

Once you've combined and fine-tuned your respective visions, it's time to divvy up the wedding duties. Here's where you refer to your priorities list. Many couples make the big decisions together: choosing the locations for both the ceremony and reception and the wedding date; coming to agreement on a budget; selecting their attendants; determining the size of the guest list; agreeing with each other about the style of the wedding (formal vs. informal, religious vs. civil); deciding on the wedding officiant. It's in the second tier of decisions that one person or the other typically takes the lead—things like researching and choosing the invitations, florist, photographer, videographer, music, food, transportation, and gift registries (although the latter is increasingly a mutually shared duty).

In splitting up these responsibilities, it's important to keep your partner informed about the vendors you're considering, and to avoid signing off on any final decisions until coming to agreement on your choices together.

One area where grooms often take the lead is in utilizing the resources of on-line wedding-planning sites, such as WeddingChannel (www.weddingchannel.com) and The Knot (www.theknot.com). Many grooms also enjoy creating and maintaining wedding blogs—personal wedding Web sites that may contain on-line planning updates, gift registry links, photos, helpful details for guests and other friends and family, and even personal advice and essays. (For more information on wedding Web sites, see Chapter 9, "The New Wedding Helper: Technology.")

Finally, the groom has another important role: that of including his parents—especially his mother—in the planning. Without the traditional responsibilities of a mother of the bride, a groom's mother (as well as his stepmother if he has one) may feel left out of the loop. The groom can avoid such omissions by being a good communicator, keeping his mother apprised of the latest details in the planning, and making sure she knows that her input and advice are not only welcome but highly valued.

GOING ALONG FOR THE RIDE

A groom doesn't have to be involved in a specific decision to be an active, supportive part of the planning process. Often, he can be helpful simply by joining his future bride on her errands, whether she is choosing caterers or making the rounds to find choices for bridesmaid's outfits. One man spent an enjoyable afternoon accompanying his food-loving fiancée and their wedding consultant to a food tasting at the reception site. The final menu was not his top priority, but the afternoon was a special bonding experience for everyone—including the restaurant staff—and he got to sample some terrific food in the process.

But What If He's Taking Over?

Q: *I'm a groom who's very excited about helping to plan our wedding. But lately, my fiancée accuses me of "taking over"! She says I'm making too many decisions without taking her interests into consideration. She even says I've become a "control freak." I thought I was doing the considerate thing. What gives?*

A: Remember: It's all a balancing act. Planning a wedding together is about sharing responsibilities, not steamrolling over everyone (especially your fiancée!) like some power-mad dictator. It's essential to know from the beginning which aspects of the wedding you hold most dear—so you can each pick your battles, so to speak. For example, your fiancée may have firm ideas about the type of flowers she wants, while working with florists is low on your list of priorities—making it an issue you can certainly be flexible on. Above all, do not commit to anything without getting the okay from your fiancée. In other words: Compromise, compromise, compromise. Also, be sure to include the other C's: Communicate and be considerate.

A Groom's Traditional Duties

Actually, the groom has always had a customary set of responsibilities to carry out before, during, and after the wedding. These traditional duties typically include:

- Selecting the engagement ring (though just as grooms have become more active in the wedding planning, so have brides become more involved in choosing an engagement ring)

- Choosing the groom's wedding party: best man, groomsmen, and ushers

- Choosing the attire for the groom's wedding party

- Selecting thank-you gifts for the groom's wedding party

- Arranging (and paying for) lodging for the groom's wedding party

- Selecting a gift for the bride

- Compiling the groom's part of the guest list and making sure that his parents make their guest list

- Planning the honeymoon (again, more and more a joint venture, with many brides-to-be now full partners in plotting a honeymoon trip)

- Choosing wedding bands together

- Making arrangements for transportation from the ceremony site to the reception site if necessary.

- Giving the officiant the fee for conducting the ceremony if applicable (or arranging for the best man to present such fees)

- Buying the marriage license

- Planning the bachelor party or event if applicable

- Standing in the receiving line (if there is one) or being sure—with the bride—to greet all guests during the reception

- Making toasts and responding to toasts at the rehearsal dinner and the reception (see "The Groom's Toast," pages 69–70).

- Cutting the cake with the bride

- Dancing the first dance with the bride, and dancing with the couple's mothers and the maid/matron of honor

Wedding Day Responsibilities of the Groom

On the wedding day, the groom has a number of traditional duties. He should make sure that the best man has the wedding ring and the necessary papers, and that he has the fee for the officiant. If the couple will be leaving directly from the reception for their honeymoon, the groom should also double-check on the transportation from the reception site and make sure the bags are packed and in place to be transported.

In preparing for the ceremony, the groom needs to be dressed and ready to go ideally an hour before the ceremony. He should arrive at the ceremony site at least fifteen minutes before the hour of the service. He generally spends his time waiting for the start of the ceremony with his best man in a private room, such as the vestry or the officiant's study. Here, the best man helps the groom pin on his boutonniere, assures the groom that he has the wedding rings in hand, helps to allay the groom's nerves—and generally shares in the excitement of the moment.

Coordinating Wedding Weekend Extras for Guests

In addition to their traditional duties, many grooms take it upon themselves to come up with creative ways for guests to spend their free time, especially when they've come a long distance to celebrate the wedding. One groom, whose afternoon wedding was held on a historic college campus, arranged for a morning walking tour of the university, complete with expert guide, for interested guests—and guests, as it turned out, were very interested! Another groom, whose destination wedding was held in San Francisco, treated out-of-town guests to their own sightseeing trolley tour of the city. Still another reserved tennis courts for his tennis-loving guests, while another made arrangements for foursomes to play golf at a nearby course. A groom whose tropical-destination guest list included a number of children set up a beach-party lunch. The activities don't need to be paid for by the groom, so be sure to communicate clearly with your guests if you're offering costly choices. If you decide to select an activity, consider your guests' interests, budgets, and allotted free time—and make sure they know that these extra activities are entirely optional.

Gifts from the Groom

It's traditional for the groom to present his best man and ushers with a gift, as a token of his appreciation for their participation in the wedding. A gift is also a powerful expression of how much it means to have good friends and loved ones there for you on your special day.

The ideal time to present your groomsmen with a gift is at the bachelor party, if you're having one. If you're not having a bachelor party, you can present the gifts at the rehearsal dinner or after the rehearsal.

The groom also shares in the giving of gifts to other members of the wedding party (except for the bridesmaids' gifts, which the bride is responsible for), including the flower girl, the ring bearer, and other people who have been of special help—for whom a simple nosegay or corsage (for women) and boutonniere (for men) make fine gifts. For the ring bearer, you might present a favorite classic book from your childhood or a silver piggy bank or other keepsake.

It's also a wonderful gesture to present both sets of parents with joint gifts from you and your bride. Wedding albums are a great idea, but even a simple rose, given to each of your mothers after the wedding processional—along with a kiss—can be a special touch.

Groom's Gifts to His Attendants: Some Ideas

Your groomsmen's gifts certainly don't have to be elaborate or expensive, but it's always nice to pick something that conveys a heartfelt personal appreciation. In that sense, anything monogrammed with each person's initials—cuff links, a pen, a pocket watch, a silver pocketknife set, or even a treasured book—are lasting mementos.

Other traditional gift ideas for the ushers include:

- Silver card-carrying cases
- Monogrammed silver key chains
- Silver money clips
- Etched beer mugs
- Leather address books
- Cocktail shakers

Less traditional gift ideas may include:

- Massage or other spa treatment
- Tickets to a sporting event or the theater
- Greens fees for a day
- Gift certificates to a sporting goods store, music store, or bookstore
- CDs of favorite music
- A hot-air balloon ride (if nearby)
- White-water rafting (if nearby)

The Groom's Toast

One tradition that has remained largely in the groom's domain is the toast—although more and more brides are also weighing in with toasts of their own.

The toasts usually occur during the reception or at the rehearsal dinner. At the reception, the best man traditionally leads off the toasting. The groom's toast can come anytime after the best man has made his toast. Most likely, however, the parents of the bride and groom will make toasts before the groom does. If you're making toasts at the rehearsal dinner, the host of the party (traditionally the father of the groom) makes the first toast. After that, the floor is open and the groom can stand to make his toast if he wishes.

If you're one of those people for whom public speaking is a nerve-wracking experience, join the crowd! Talking to a room full of people can be a daunting task. Add to that the adrenaline rush of your wedding day, an unfamiliar microphone, and perhaps a few glasses of champagne, and you have a formula for superbutterflies—or at least a toast that is difficult to give. Here are some tips on how to make your toast a smashing success:

Prepare ahead of time. Unless you're a stand-up comedian or a politician, don't try to wing it. In the days or weeks leading up to the wedding, take some time to jot down a few notes about what you want to say. Memorize your words. Practice them. When it's time for your toast, it's fine to take out your notes and refer to them. Stand up and take the microphone, if there is one. If you and your bride are making a toast together, don't speak in unison, but rather stand together as you take turns speaking.

Toasting basics. As for those words you've so carefully jotted down, here are some do's and don'ts:

- Do *keep it short*. Long is deadly, particularly after a long, emotional day of celebrating.

- Do *be sincere;* let your true feelings come through.

- Do *be sure to thank everyone for coming;* be sure to thank your parents (including the bride's) for their love and support.

- Do *tell brief personal stories* of moving experiences shared with your bride, but . . .

- Don't *make your guests suffer* through a year-by-year litany of youthful indiscretions or drunken high jinks—you may end up simply embarrassing someone, including yourself.

- Finally, do *turn to your bride and look her in the eye.* Tell her how proud you are to be her husband, how happy you are on this special day, and how much you love her.

After the Wedding

As with the pre-wedding planning, many modern grooms are sharing after-wedding duties with their brides. These duties may include returning any rental clothing, recording all gifts as they come in, helping return any broken gifts, and writing thank-you notes. This note writing, so long the sole domain of the bride, has now evolved into a clearly shared responsibility. In many cases, the bride writes to those people on her guest list, and the groom writes to those on his; however, you may certainly write to each other's relatives and friends—a great step toward building new relationships

Once the couple gets their wedding photographs back, it is customary to give some photos to members of the wedding party. Usually, the groomsmen receive portraits of the groom and his wedding party, while the bridesmaids get portraits of the bride and her wedding party; both ushers and bridesmaids might also each receive a portrait of the entire wedding party together. In addition, many couples give photo albums and/or copies of the wedding video to their parents. Couples who have a wedding Web site may also choose to post wedding and honeymoon photos. Some wedding blogs even present accounts of the big day itself—often written by the grooms.

So you've participated in the many aspects of the wedding planning with your bride. Congratulations on many fronts! One of the best outcomes of all is that your input and diligence are likely to translate into extra excitement, shared by your new wife and you, as you both savor the memories of the wedding day that the two of you created together.

CHAPTER 5

ATTENDANTS

ATTENDANTS ADD MUCH JOY and significance to the nuptial celebration. Including friends and loved ones in this happy milestone is one of our most cherished customs. Wedding attendants, whether bridesmaids or ushers, are chosen as witnesses to a couple's matrimonial union in a gesture of love, friendship, and support.

Choosing Your Attendants

For many couples, the choice of attendants is easy—sisters, brothers, and dearest friends. But if you have a large family or a wide circle of good friends, the decision can be quite hard. You aren't required to ask siblings, though it certainly promotes family unity. You can choose one best friend over another to be maid of honor or best man, but you may risk causing a break that is difficult to mend.

Fortunately, etiquette has kept up with the times, and today's couples have many options for organizing their wedding parties and choosing their attendants.

NEW RULES FOR WEDDING ATTENDANTS

- **There is no required number of attendants.** The average is four to six bridesmaids and at least as many groomsmen and ushers, but you can include as many or as few as you like. Some couples have a large number of attendants, but even a formal wedding with just one or two attendants on each side is perfectly acceptable. Since ushers have the practical responsibility of seating guests at the ceremony, the general rule is one usher for every fifty guests. But you can have more.

- **It's not necessary to have an equal number of bridesmaids and groomsmen/ushers.** Don't worry about pairing up. You can have more bridesmaids than groomsmen or vice versa. Don't alienate a good friend or family member for the sake of symmetry. One groomsman can easily escort two bridesmaids in the recessional, or bridesmaids can walk alone or in pairs.

- **You can have two maids of honor, a maid and a matron of honor, or two best men.** If you don't want to choose between siblings or very close friends, have two principal attendants. The attendants can share duties—for example, one maid of honor holds the groom's ring, while the other takes the bridal bouquet. This arrangement has practical benefits, too. If your matron of honor lives 300 miles away and has two young children, she may be your sounding board; your sister who lives locally can go with you to shop for bridesmaid dresses.

- **Toss a coin or draw straws to decide who will be maid of honor or best man.** When good friends are amenable to luck-of-the-draw decisions, leaving the choice up to fate eliminates any hint of preference or favoritism.

- **You can have pregnant bridesmaids.** Unless there's a religious restriction, brides can certainly invite a friend who is expecting, to be a bridesmaid. Just be considerate of her needs and capabilities. You may want to have a chair placed near the altar area so that the mother-to-be can sit during a lengthy service; to excuse her from a formal receiving line; and to make sure that she doesn't go too long without eating or drinking.

- **Brides and grooms can have attendants of the opposite sex.** *Honor attendant* is another, more modern term for an attendant of the opposite sex. Today many brides and grooms seek to pay tribute to their closest friends or brothers and sisters by including them in the bridal party in this unique way. Honor attendants perform the same duties as the maid of honor, best man, bridesmaid, or groomsman position that they represent, although some responsibilities are altered as necessary—for example, a male honor attendant wouldn't help the bride get dressed. Adaptations and personal touches are fine, as long as they are applied thoughtfully. The honor attendant should be completely comfortable with his or her role; otherwise, the special recognition their status is meant to convey is lost.

  While rules don't dictate the selection and number of attendants, there are some practicalities to consider.

- **Size and formality.** The size and formality of your wedding help determine the size of your wedding party. If you plan a small, intimate gathering, you won't want attendants outnumbering guests. If the ceremony site is small, you may have room for only one or two attendants. If you're planning a large, extravagant celebration, you may want an equally large wedding party.

SELECTING ATTENDANTS—HOW NOT TO HURT FEELINGS?

Q: I have several close friends and family members, but we have decided on a small wedding and can only select a few attendants. That means we're leaving someone out. How do you suggest we tactfully explain our choices to these dear friends?

A: It is perfectly fine to be direct in explaining to relatives or friends why you have chosen others to be in your wedding party. Choosing siblings over friends needs no explanation; a choice between friends might. If you have known the person you chose longer than the other friend, for example, say so. Be forthcoming, but convey anything you say in a kind and loving manner. Explain your desire for a smaller wedding. Some couples decide to flip a coin with friends and family in attendance to avoid any appearance of favoritism. There are other honors you can bestow upon these friends, such as reading a passage at the ceremony, serving as guestbook attendant, or working with the photographer to organize candid pictures and formal portraits.

- **Budget.** The more attendants you have, the more of a burden it puts on your expenses. The bride and groom are responsible for all bouquets, boutonnieres, wedding-party gifts, and attendants' accommodations. Also, the more attendants you have, the larger your rehearsal dinner and reception guest lists, because you are responsible for feeding and entertaining not only your attendants but your attendants' partners as well.

- **Religious restrictions.** Some religions have strict rules regarding official witnesses. Your honor attendants, at least, may be required to be members of your faith or may even have to attend pre-ceremony instruction classes before they can participate.

WHOM TO ASK

Participating in someone else's wedding is both a pleasure and a responsibility. When you consider which of your close relatives and friends to include, think about your expectations and how much you are likely to depend on your attendants—not just at the wedding but throughout the planning and preparation. Consider these fundamental traits:

Reliability. An attendant should be a person you can count on to stay in touch in the weeks and months preceding the wedding, to listen to instructions, to follow up on requests without being reminded, and to show up on time and ready for all events.

Consideration. Considerate attendants may offer suggestions but will understand that they aren't in charge. They will look for opportunities to be helpful but won't add to the bridal couple's worries with special demands or needless criticism.

Courtesy. In a sense, attendants are ambassadors for the bridal couple and their families. At pre-wedding events and during the wedding reception, they will mix and mingle with guests, make introductions, look out for people with special needs, and behave appropriately at all times.

FINANCIAL OBLIGATIONS

Expenses for attendants can add up quickly, from travel to clothing to participation in parties and showers. The number of pre-wedding events requiring a financial contribution or gift seems to be on the rise—such as engagement parties, showers, and bachelor and bachelorette festivities—and is often a source of economic strain for attendants.

Attendants coming from far away are expected to pay their own transportation costs. The bride and groom should cover the cost of accommodations or make arrangements for friends and family to put up members of the wedding party.

A QUESTION FOR PEGGY:

AN UNCOMFORTABLE HONOR?

Q: *I asked my best friend from college to be my matron of honor for my commitment ceremony. Although she said yes and has been supportive, I can tell that she's not really comfortable with the idea of my same-sex ceremony. Should I let her off the hook by taking back my invitation?*

A: You need to talk openly with your friend. Let her know that you sense her discomfort, but don't say anything that implies prejudice on her part. Be tactful and listen carefully to what she says. She may have a problem you don't know about, such as difficulty with her family, financial constraints, or simply nerves at being in the ceremony. Whatever the issue, you can tell her that being your attendant is her choice and that you won't be hurt or offended if she opts out. If she decides not to serve as an attendant, you might talk about another way she could be involved in the ceremony. Maybe she would give a reading. Or perhaps she won't participate but will be comfortable attending as a guest. Whatever her decision, you'll keep a good friend by showing your concern for her feelings.

People in their twenties and thirties may find themselves invited to attend or participate in several weddings in the same year. This can cause serious financial stress. Keep all of this in mind when you ask a friend or relative to be in your wedding.

For those who would find it a financial strain, you might thoughtfully ask them instead to participate in a different, less expensive way (see "Other helpers," page 86). If cost is a factor for a good friend you can't imagine being married without, you can certainly offer to pay his or her bills. No one but you and your friend has to know of this special arrangement.

WHEN TO ASK

Once you've decided whom you want in your wedding, give them as much advance notice as possible. Three to six months before the wedding date is fairly standard. This gives attendants time to organize their calendars, purchase clothing and have necessary alterations made, arrange transportation, and plan and host any parties they may wish to hold in your honor. If your schedule is very tight, you can find ways to cut a few corners (off-the-rack bridesmaid dresses rather than custom-ordered, a bridesmaids' luncheon and bachelor party but no shower or vice versa) to relieve the strain on you and your wedding party.

It's always nice to ask in person, but don't delay contacting someone who lives at a distance. Call, write, or e-mail your invitation—whatever is the easiest way to get in touch. Sup-

---

THE BRIDESMAID ASKS: "DOES APPEARANCE COUNT?"

Q: *I have been asked by my good friend to be one of her bridesmaids. I am overweight, and my mother thinks that unless I decide to lose some weight, I should decline.*

A: It goes without saying that friends' looks are not the criteria for their selection for the wedding party. A good friend's large size should play no part in any decision to ask her to be an attendant. The same is true if a friend is pregnant, disabled, short, tall, or not a physical match with the rest of the wedding party. Unless you personally feel uncomfortable taking on the role, you may accept with love and happiness. Your friend has extended a warm welcome to you to be part of her celebration; that should do nothing but make you feel comfortable, confident, and honored to be sharing her special day.

For brides who have friends or relatives who decline because they aren't comfortable in the role of attendant, be sensitive and understanding. As long as they know that being overweight or pregnant or whatever doesn't make a difference to you, you must respect their decision not to accept.

ply the wedding date even if you aren't sure of the time, the location, if travel will be required, and some sense of the formality of the event. The person may accept immediately, but don't push for an instant reply. Even your closest friend may need a day or two to consider.

It's a great honor to be asked to be in a wedding, but people have other obligations and accepting may not be possible. Don't be offended or expect a detailed explanation if someone turns down your invitation. A refusal is often based on important family, job, or financial concerns, so be sensitive. Express your disappointment without any hint of disapproval. Rather than jeopardize a relationship, assume that the person has made a conscientious decision and is doing what he or she thinks is best for everyone.

A QUESTION FOR PEGGY:

WHAT ARE AN ATTENDANT'S FINANCIAL OBLIGATIONS?

Q: *I'm a bridesmaid. What do I need to pay for?*

A: You will pay for your clothing—including dress, shoes, hose, and any special jewelry or headpiece the bride asks you to wear. You are also responsible for any travel expenses incurred traveling to and from the location of the wedding (airfare, taxi, rental car). Also, you might be asked to contribute to a joint gift from all of the bride's attendants. Flowers are paid for by the bride and groom. Local accommodations for attendants are also the responsibility of the bride and groom.

ATTENDANTS' OBLIGATIONS IN A DESTINATION WEDDING

If you are planning a destination wedding, it is especially important that you make that clear to possible attendants in your initial invitation. For example, "We're getting married in Bermuda! If you can get yourself there, we'll pick up the tab for your accommodations. We've rented several villas where everyone will stay. We hope you can come on Wednesday and stay until Sunday so you can have a little vacation at the same time." While the bride and groom are financially responsible for the wedding-party accommodations—and some will foot the bill for travel costs as well—the other costs fall to the attendants themselves. That's why they need to know the basic costs ahead of time before they can make a decision.

Keeping Everyone Up to Speed

From the time your attendants accept your invitation, it's your responsibility to keep them informed. Communication is essential to a well-planned wedding, and all the members of your wedding party need updates—especially about any changes that will affect them. Don't overload family and friends with details, but do maintain regular contact and be particularly attentive to wedding-party members who live elsewhere. Write, phone, e-mail, or establish a wedding Web site (see also Chapter 9, "The New Wedding Helper: Technology"). Keeping your attendants informed helps everyone stay organized. It also allows members of the wedding party to become informally acquainted. Disseminate information such as:

- A list of names, addresses, and phone numbers of the wedding party

- The dates and times of parties and showers attendants will be invited to

- The rehearsal time and place

- Rehearsal dinner arrangements

- Where they will stay

- The dress code for different wedding events

- Reminders to bridesmaids and ushers to break in their shoes

- Any plans for breakfast, lunch, or tea before or after the wedding

- Where they will dress

- The time and place for any pre-wedding photos

- Transportation arrangements to the ceremony and reception

Attendants' Duties and Responsibilities

Although attendants' duties will vary based on the size and style of the event, there are tasks common to most weddings. The list below details the basic responsibilities of all adult attendants. It is followed by specifics for each type of attendant, including children.

- Pay for their wedding attire and accessories (excluding flowers)

- Arrange and pay for their own transportation, unless provided by the wedding couple

- Attend prenuptial events

- Give an individual gift to the couple or contribute to a group gift from the attendants

- Understand specific duties and follow instructions

- Arrive at specified times for all wedding-related events

- Assist the bride and groom

- Be attentive to other guests at the wedding and reception

Hosting or co-hosting a pre-wedding party or shower is nice but by no means mandatory.

Attendants have a special duty to see that the wedding and the reception run smoothly. They are expected to be gracious and visit with guests, to assist the elderly and anyone else who needs help, to be attentive to young children in the wedding party, to be available for picture taking, and to generally help out whenever needed. If there's a formal receiving line, all bridesmaids may be asked to participate or only the maid/matron of honor and perhaps the best man.

MAID OR MATRON OF HONOR

- Helps the bride select the bridesmaids' attire

- Helps address invitations and place cards

- Organizes the bridesmaids' gift to the bride and often organizes the bridesmaids' luncheon if there is one

- Holds the groom's wedding ring and the bride's bouquet during the ceremony

- Witnesses the signing of the marriage certificate

- Helps the bride during the reception (gathering guests for the cake cutting, dancing, the bouquet toss)

- Helps the bride change into her going-away clothes and takes care of the bride's wedding dress and accessories after the reception

BRIDESMAID

- Attends the rehearsal, rehearsal dinner, and bridesmaids' luncheon if there is one

- Supervises the children in the wedding party if asked

- Assists the bride at the reception as requested

- Participates in activities such as a receiving line and a bouquet toss

- Gives an individual gift to the couple or contributes to the bridesmaids' gift for the couple

JUNIOR BRIDESMAID

A junior bridesmaid is a girl between eight and twelve years of age who serves as a bridesmaid but has fewer responsibilities than adult attendants. The junior bridesmaid's parents pay for her dress and accessories (excluding flowers). Junior bridesmaids attend the rehearsal and, depending on the girl's age and maturity, the rehearsal dinner. They may be invited to the bridesmaids' luncheon. They don't give bridal showers, though they can attend pre-wedding social events when invited. Other than participating in the ceremony, junior bridesmaids have no further obligations, but if asked, they should be in the receiving line. A junior bridesmaid may give a separate gift to the couple or be included in her parents' gift.

BEST MAN

- Organizes the bachelor party for the groom, if there is one

- Coordinates the groomsmen and ushers' gift to the bride and groom or gives an individual gift to the couple

- Makes sure that the groom's wedding-related payments are prepared; delivers prearranged payments to officiants, assistants, and musicians and singers at the ceremony

- Sees that the groomsmen and ushers arrive on time and are properly attired

- Instructs the ushers in the correct seating of guests (if there is no head usher)

- Keeps the bride's wedding ring during the ceremony

- Witnesses the signing of the marriage certificate

- Drives the bride and groom to the reception if there's no hired driver; has the car ready for the couple to leave after the reception and may drive them to their next destination

- Offers the first toast to the bride and groom at the reception; dances with the bride, the mothers, the maid of honor, and other single female guests

- Gathers and takes care of the groom's wedding clothes (returning rental items on the next business day)

GROOMSMEN AND USHERS

Groomsmen stand with the bridegroom during the ceremony. Ushers help prepare the wedding site for the ceremony and escort guests to their seats before the ceremony. Groomsmen may also serve as ushers, and this is fairly common at small to medium-sized weddings. When the guest list is large or when the bridegroom has only a best man and perhaps one other attendant, additional ushers are often needed. An older friend or family member might be asked to serve as *head usher;* his duties include supervising the ushers, seeing that all pre- and post-ceremony tasks are completed, and managing late arrivals. The head usher or best man will instruct the ushers in seating guests and the correct order for seating family members before the processional.

The duties of groomsmen/ushers include:

- Attending the rehearsal, rehearsal dinner, and bachelor party if there is one

- Contributing to the ushers' gift to the bride and groom or giving an individual gift to the couple

- Knowing the seating order; reviewing special seating arrangements prior to the ceremony

- Greeting guests and escorting them to their seats

- Handing each guest a program, if programs are provided

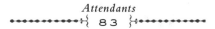

- Laying the aisle runner, if one is used, before the processional

- After the ceremony, removing pew ribbons, closing windows, retrieving any programs or articles left behind

- Helping guests who need directions to the reception site

- Coordinating the return of rental clothing with the head usher or best man

CHILDREN AS ATTENDANTS

Whether to include children in the wedding party is a personal decision for the couple. There are good arguments on both sides. When well behaved, children add a special charm, and being included in the wedding can be very meaningful for youngsters whose parent is marrying for a second time. But young children are unpredictable, and their charms can wear thin if they cry, whine, chatter, or freeze up during the service. No matter how often they've rehearsed, children under age nine or so need constant monitoring. You'll have to arrange for a parent, babysitter, or one of your attendants to supervise each child at all times before, during, and after the ceremony.

If you're prepared to manage potential situations, then by all means invite a child or children to participate. But you have no obligation to do so. Don't yield to pressure if you want to limit your attendants to adults.

In general, couples who want young attendants are advised to include as few as possible and to aim at the older end of the age range. Children of school age are better able to follow instructions than preschoolers. Young attendants aren't normally invited to prenuptial events unless their parents are included and other children attend.

Flower girl. Flower girls are usually between the ages of three and seven. Flower girls are often young relatives of the bride or groom. There may be more than one flower girl, and this is a nice way to include girls too young to be junior bridesmaids.

Their role is to precede the bride down the aisle, carrying flowers or flower baskets. The flower girl can scatter petals from a basket she holds, although this may be too overwhelming a responsibility for a young child to manage in front of a large group of people. It's usually easier for her to carry either a small basket of flowers or a tiny nosegay of flowers similar to those carried by the bridesmaids.

The flower girl stands with the bridesmaids during the service, though young children may sit with their parents or the bride's family. A flower girl's parents pay for her dress and accessories (excluding flowers). She attends the rehearsal but usually not the rehearsal dinner. In the recessional, the flower girl walks with the ring bearer (if there is one), directly behind the couple.

A parent, bridesmaid, or hired babysitter should be assigned to look after the flower girl: to make sure she's comfortable and well behaved and knows what to do; to check her appearance; to make sure she is present for formal pictures; to help her manage her food at the reception; and to escort her to the ladies' room.

Ring bearer. The ring bearer is a three- to seven-year-old boy who walks down the aisle and carries the wedding rings (or a reasonable facsimile) on a small cushion. He stands with the groomsmen or may sit with his parents or the groom's family during the service. His outfit is provided by his family. He is expected to attend the rehearsal but generally not the rehearsal dinner.

During the ceremony, the ring bearer traditionally enters after the maid or matron of honor. He is followed by the flower girl. But a very young boy and girl may enter together. The children exit together immediately after the bride and groom, but if a child has fallen asleep, has wandered back to his parents, or is in any way disagreeable, the recessional walk can be dispensed with.

Train bearers and pages. These are young attendants who hold and carry the bride's train and may assist with arranging the train when the bride reaches the altar. They are rarely included except in the most elaborate formal or state weddings.

Other helpers. In some parts of the country, it's customary for family members and friends who have a special relationship with the couple to assist at the wedding and the reception. Though not strictly members of the wedding party, these gracious helpers are usually presented with corsages and boutonnieres in the wedding colors. They are included in some wedding photographs, and their names and responsibilities are often listed in lengthier newspaper accounts of the wedding.

At a home or church reception, their duties, or "honor roles," might include serving cake, pouring tea and coffee, and greeting guests. They can hand out ceremony programs, be in charge of the guest book, or participate in the wedding service as readers, soloists, cantors, or altar assistants. It is appropriate to thank helpers with gifts, such as framed wedding photos, and notes of appreciation.

CHAPTER 6

FAMILY, FRIENDS, AND A CAREFULLY PLANNED GUEST LIST

It HAPPENS TO ALMOST EVERY BRIDE and groom: The guest list, carefully counted and coordinated within the budget, slowly but surely inflates. Don't think it can't happen to you. As cousins you've never heard of come out of the woodwork and your mothers' work friends inquire about the date, guest lists can grow at an alarming rate.

Most brides and grooms must work around financial considerations—and the biggest cost factor is the guest list, because the reception costs generally are the most expensive part of the wedding.

Guest list grousing can turn the most compatible of families into feuding factions and leave brides and grooms feeling that elopement is a reasonable resolution. Insisting that all involved whittle down their lists often makes the person who is paying feel guilty and petty. The bride and groom become anxious, parents complain, and tensions rise.

Tact and diplomacy, two of the cornerstones of etiquette, can save the day. Make sure you never lose sight of your first shared vision of your wedding—and give yourselves a budget reality check.

Guest List Survival Guide

1. **Realize that you have choices to make.** Do you want to plan your guest list and reception around a budget or make a guest list first and plan the reception around that? Either way, you will likely find that your list will require some fine-tuning.

2. **Remember: It's *your* wedding.** Don't automatically agree that cousins you've never met or Mom's office colleagues take precedence over your own good friends. Think and talk it through—calmly. You might end up inviting the cousins, but you'll be more understanding and less resentful if you agree it's the way to go.

3. **Don't opt for the easy solution.** Inviting a large number of guests to the ceremony but only a small number to the reception is no solution at all. It would be insulting to send a formal ceremony invitation to many and a reception invitation to a favored few. Two exceptions: You may invite children, or your entire congregation, to the ceremony

only. (For example, an open invitation to the ceremony issued to congregation members by the officiant, with your permission, carries no gift obligation for those who attend—nor any obligation to the bride and groom to invite them to the reception.) The reverse—inviting a small number of guests to an intimate or private ceremony and a larger number to the reception—is perfectly acceptable, too. The key: Carefully think through any variables in numbers of ceremony and reception guests.

Nuts and Bolts: The Guest List

- **What constitutes a guest list?** A guest list consists of a magical number of family and friends that (1) suits the size of your ceremony and reception sites, (2) corresponds with the level of intimacy desired for the wedding, and (3) can be accommodated within your wedding budget—an important reality.

- **How many guests can each family invite?** Traditionally each family is allotted half of the desired total guest count, a figure largely determined by the person hosting the wedding. A way of starting the process is to combine four lists, which when combined become the master list. Start with lists from the bride, the groom, the bride's parents, and the groom's parents. It is necessary that everyone make up their lists realistically. As acceptances and regrets become known, the "weights" of the lists may vary.

- Don't forget these guests:

Must Be Invited

  - The spouse, fiancé, or live-in partner of each invited guest—even if you've never met

  - The person who performs the ceremony, and his or her spouse

  - The parents of ring bearers and flower girls

Nice to Include

  - The parents of the bridesmaids. It's a nice gesture when feasible, especially when the bride knows them well.

Not Necessary, but Meaningful, to Include

  - Counselors, advisers, or mentors to the bride or groom who are not close friends but who have been an important part of their lives

- **Should children and guests of guests be invited?** It's a personal decision. Your budget and the size of your reception site play a role. Neither inclusion is necessary, but both necessitate "proper etiquette," meaning consideration and sensitivity. (See "All About Children," pages 94–95.)

- **Who should be invited to a destination wedding?** It's more difficult for people to attend a destination wedding, so your guest list will likely be limited to immediate family and closest friends. Even then, some may not be able to attend. (See also "Tips on Inviting Guests to a Destination Wedding," page 91.)

- **Should fewer guests be invited to an encore wedding?** It's up to you. Some encore couples prefer to limit the guest list at the ceremony and reception to close family and friends and to enjoy a later, larger get-together. Keeping the guest list short is considerate of guests who may have attended (and purchased a gift for) your first wedding. Other couples plan the large and elaborate celebration they've always dreamed of. As a general guideline, invite those you couldn't imagine getting married without.

- **What if a good number of guests send their regrets?** Be prepared. Wedding industry experts predict that 15 to 20 percent of invited guests send regrets. That means if you are planning to have 150 guests, invite 170 to 180 people. (Some people are more comfortable estimating a 10 percent margin for regrets.) Prior commitments, illness, and unseen circumstances will likely prevent more people from attending than you expect. Talk to your reception site manager to ensure that a few additional guests can be accommodated if more than 150 attend. This approach is far better than creating A and B lists of guests, the B list guests being sent invitations only after those on the A list send regrets. The potential for people discovering this and feeling hurt is too great. (See also "A Question for Peggy: What's the Etiquette of a Standby Guest List?," page 93.)

- **Is there any way to categorize the guest list?** Yes. It's a good idea to do this, so that if (or when) the guest list must be trimmed, clear distinctions can be made. Ask each family to identify their lists in the following way:

  - *First tier:* immediate family (parents, siblings, grandparents, the couple's own children)

  - *Second tier:* extended family members (aunts, uncles, cousins, nieces, nephews)

  - *Third tier:* family friends (parents' close friends, longtime friends and neighbors, childhood friends and their parents if close to you)

- *Fourth tier:* bride and groom's friends, in further tiers of closeness to you (childhood friends, high school and college friends, work friends, new friends)

- *Fifth tier:* parents' colleagues (associates, employers, employees)

Of course, these guidelines should be based upon what makes sense in your case. Any planning must be adapted to your situation. If you and your fiancé are established professionally, perhaps marrying for a second or third time, you will probably be paying for all or most of the wedding yourselves. Perhaps your wedding will take place far from your hometown or where your parents live. Under any of these circumstances, it could make sense to switch the third and fourth tiers.

Trimming an Overambitious Guest List

Your invitation guest list can be pared down in a number of thoughtful ways, including the following:

- **Make across-the-board, clear-cut distinctions.** To avoid hurt feelings when a guest list is limited, subdivide the groupings across the board. For example, if numbers are limited, you could invite all aunts and uncles and forgo cousins. Then, stick to categories equilaterally, treating each list as a whole.

- **Leave out work associates—all or some.** When space is absolutely at a premium, some couples delete work associates entirely. This can reduce the list considerably, while also keeping the wedding more personal, with only family and close, longtime friends attending. Or perhaps you invite only your boss and your respective assistants, or just your immediate department. Your other coworkers will clearly understand that you had to make a cutoff.

- **Beware parental paybacks.** This is not the time for parents to insist on reciprocity for all the gifts they've given and weddings they've attended in the past, nor does your wedding need to be the occasion for them to fulfill their own social obligations.

- **Remember: Shower guests are wedding guests.** Any guest who is invited to a shower must also be invited to the wedding, with a few exceptions, such as coworkers who give an office shower. Keep that in mind when drawing up your guest lists for wedding showers.

- **Talk to friends who live far away.** If you know that distance will prevent certain people from attending, call them to see if they think they can make the wedding. If not, factor this in.

- **Stick to your first-tier and second-tier guest lists.** Try to redraw your lines equilaterally, bumping entire groupings of people—second cousins, work associates with whom you've never socialized, or friends from the health club.

Organizing a Carefully Planned Master Guest List

A beautifully organized and orchestrated wedding, most brides will tell you, is the happy result of single-minded attention to lists. By incorporating your personal list, your parents' list, and your groom's parents' list into one alphabetical master list—and putting that list into your wedding planner and a computer file—you will have one of the most important documents of your wedding planning readily on hand. You will refer to this list endlessly as the weeks go by—to address invitations, delineate who needs maps and directions, check off acceptances and regrets, and record gifts received and thank-you notes written. You will also use this list to count heads. The master guest list is the *foundation of your wedding plans* and as such should be carefully thought out and maintained. A savvy guest list includes:

WHAT'S THE ETIQUETTE OF A STANDBY GUEST LIST?

Q: My future mother-in-law says it's appropriate to have a standby guest list ready when guests from the main list decline. Is this proper?

A: A standby guest list is a risky proposition. There is potential for feelings to be hurt and for guests to feel slighted. While I'm hesitant to encourage you to go this route, I understand that a standby list does provide a practical solution to controlling the numbers and budget. When possible, it's far better to invite your entire guest list. When the guest list is carefully planned, and when you consider the likelihood that typically 10 to 20 percent of invited guests send regrets—this approach is more straightforward and less deceptive than employing a standby list.

   If you and your fiancé decide to take the standby list approach, be very discreet. Guests must not have even the slightest idea that you have a standby list. Plan for enough time for responses from the master-list guests to be received—no less than four weeks—to invite guests who are on the standby list. Make this choice early in your planning process so that you will be ready to send the second group of invitations. Incorporate the names into the master list in your organizer or *Emily Post's Wedding Planner.*

- **Contact information.** Each guest's full name, address, telephone number, and relationship to bride or groom. Capture e-mail addresses, too. For many guests, e-mail may be the quickest way to update them on plans.

- **RSVPs.** A space to indicate (with a check mark or an X) whether or not a guest has RSVP'd, and how many members of the family or party will attend. Writing down the name of a single guest's date or fiancé will help you remember his or her name, as well as enabling you to extend your welcome with a personalized place at the reception.

- **Gifts.** A description of any gift received, and the date a thank-you note was sent.

- **Out-of-towners.** If you have the room, you might want a space to indicate if the guest is coming from out of town, so that you can mail him or her information on lodging and directions and any parties being thrown for out-of-town guests.

All About Children

One of the most hotly debated issues in planning a wedding is whether or not to invite children. Some people feel that having children at a wedding can be an intrusion or a distraction for guests intent on participating in and honoring a very grown-up ritual. Others can't imagine a wedding celebration without children. One undeniable factor is the additional financial burden inviting a number of kids can incur. If you are determined to include children on your guest list but your budget is tight, there are compromises you can make (see below). Here are some general guidelines on inviting children to wedding celebrations:

HOW TO LET GUESTS KNOW THAT CHILDREN ARE NOT INVITED

Simple. If children are not invited, the proper way to communicate this is to write only the parents' names on the outer and inner envelopes on your invitations. It is *inappropriate* to write "No Children" on the invitations.

HOW TO SET LIMITS WHEN INVITING CHILDREN

One of the most common problems is that of restricting the number of children attending the reception. In large families with dozens of cousins, nieces, and nephews, the costs of inviting them all may be prohibitive. Yet some relatives feel so strongly that their children be included that they will consider refusing the invitation altogether if the children are left out. One option is to draw the line by setting an age limit—inviting children ten and older, for example, to the wedding. Other ideas include inviting only the children of close family members and/or children of the wedding party, but this can get complicated. Either way, once you've made your decision, make no exceptions, since doing so will cause more hurt feelings than standing firm.

HOW TO EXPLAIN "ADULTS ONLY"

Launch a proactive campaign to get the word out that your wedding will be an adult affair. Discuss the situation with friends and relatives. Ask them to help spread the word. You may even want to enclose a note to those friends and relatives who may be the most upset by your decision, explaining that costs, space, and/or the formality of the setting prevent you from including children. Unfortunately, some guests choose to ignore (or truly misunderstand) the polite omission of their children's names on the wedding invitation and write or call to tell you that they are bringing their children. You'll have to have a direct conversation with the parents. "I'm sorry, Jan, but we aren't having any children at the wedding. We won't be able to accommodate Susan and Kurt." If this results in an angry "Then I'm not coming either," so be it. The breach of etiquette is theirs, not yours.

If you decide to include children in the wedding, you'll want to make the occasion special for them, too. Finding ways to keep them occupied can be great fun.

You could have your floral designer create a piñata, filled with inexpensive toys. Or you could set up a designated children's table with coloring books and favors. If children are seated with parents, you could still provide each with a coloring book and a small box of crayons. Make sure, too, that your menu includes some kid-friendly foods, like chicken fingers, little raviolis, or mini pizzas. Some reception sites even provide a separate room where children can be entertained. Fill the room with toys, games, coloring supplies, a television and DVD player, and snacks. Hire qualified babysitters to entertain the children. Aim for a reasonable adult-to-child ratio so that parents will feel comfortable with the arrangements. Companies now exist that you can hire to come to the wedding reception location. They will set up a fully staffed and organized kids' room. While adults are dining and dancing, children engage in age-appropriate activities and crafts.

One final option: Get the names and numbers of a few area babysitters. You provide the information to out-of-town guests who may wish to hire a babysitter during the hours of the wedding celebration to watch their children—either at a relative's home or at the hotel where the family is staying.

Out-of-Town Guests

It is not the bride and groom's obligation to plan constant entertainment for out-of-town guests who are not part of the wedding party. But you can offer information regarding activities and gatherings, and other forms of hospitality to those who have come from far away to celebrate your nuptials.

LODGING FOR OUT-OF-TOWN GUESTS

In general, out-of-town guests are expected to pay for their own lodging. It is a courtesy—and not obligatory—for the bride and groom to take responsibility for finding or recommending lodging for out-of-town guests. If your wedding is large and you expect many people to travel, pre-reserve a block of rooms at an area hotel. Many hotels will offer discount room rates if a minimum number of rooms are booked in a block. Some friends and family may offer to put up out-of-town guests at their homes. If so, it is up to you to make the best personality matches

Help! What Do I Do About . . .

Including Partners

Partners of invited guests must be included in wedding invitations. This includes couples who are married, engaged, or living together—whether you or anyone in the wedding party knows them or not. Allowing single guests who aren't attached to significant others to bring dates is a thoughtful gesture, but one that is certainly *not required* and often not realistic.

A single invitation addressed to both members of a married couple, or a couple who live together, is sent to their shared address, while invitations to an engaged or long-standing couple who don't live together are sent separately, to each address. An envelope addressed to a single friend that includes "and Guest" indicates that he or she may bring an escort or a friend. If it is possible to obtain the name of the guest, the name would be included on the invitation to the friend, or a second invitation may even be sent directly to the date at his or her home address instead.

Occasionally, a single guest will become engaged or will reunite with a separated spouse after the invitations have been mailed. In that case, the bride or groom can extend a verbal invitation to the guest's fiancé/fiancée or spouse.

Guests Who Ask to Bring Guests

The answer is straightforward: It is impolite of a guest to ask if he or she can bring a date—but it is not impolite of you to refuse. You may certainly answer no. Say, "I'm sorry, Stan, but we have very limited seating at the reception and we just can't accommodate any additional guests." However, if you discover that they are engaged or living together, invite your friend's partner, either verbally or by invitation.

Sending Invitations to Out-of-Town Guests Who Can't Possibly Attend

Apply careful thought. In most cases, invitations are not sent to those friends and acquaintances who cannot possibly attend the celebration. Since an invitation to a wedding carries an obligation to send a gift, inviting someone who can't possibly attend makes it look as if you are inviting those friends in order to receive a gift. Also, people with whom your only communication for the past several years has been holiday cards are generally not included on the invitation list either. Any of the above could receive a wedding announcement instead, which carries no gift obligation whatsoever.

There is a flip side to this dilemma. Some good friends who live far away might actually be hurt if you do not send invitations, even if your intent was to spare them from feeling obliged to send a gift for a wedding so far away. These friends, upon hearing news of your engagement, may actually have been making plans to travel to your wedding. In general, *always invite truly good friends*—even if they live far away.

so that all involved are comfortable with the arrangements. Either you or the hosts should send the out-of-town guests the names, address, and telephone number of their host and hostess. Also send along directions to their home, and let them know what to expect—whether their hosts have a pet, a swimming pool, children, and the like. The hosts need to be clear on the guests' arrival and departure dates and times, so encourage the guests to share this information promptly. Remember to give a thank-you note and gift to anyone who provides lodging.

EVENTS FOR OUT-OF-TOWNERS

Once your engagement is announced, you will likely be approached by friends and relatives offering to help out in some way. One ideal way for a group of friends and family to pitch in is to entertain out-of-town guests. Don't be afraid to tell someone who has asked to help how they can pitch in: "Aunt Lucy, it would be wonderful if you could host Allen's aunt and uncle for dinner on Friday night while we are all at the rehearsal."

> ## ACTIVITIES FOR OUT-OF-TOWN GUESTS
>
> If there is open time in the wedding-celebration schedule, or for guests who plan to make a vacation out of the trip, provide your out-of-town guests with a list of local activities, sports centers, museums, and other attractions, along with addresses and phone numbers. Here's where you can get creative: Your town may have a singular attraction that may be a must-see for any person new to the area. You might even provide tickets or passes. Don't make an activity mandatory, however; simply provide irresistible options. You might ask a friend to gather local information for you to arrange in an attractive "welcome pack" that will await guests at the hotel.

The costs and preparations can be shared by several people who join to host a gathering. It's your responsibility to provide the hosts of any gatherings or parties with a list of names and addresses of the out-of-towners so they can send invitations, if necessary, and plan accordingly.

If out-of-town guests are staying in private homes, their hosts should also be invited to any gathering, event, or party. And don't forget to send thank-you gifts or flowers to the party hosts, in addition to your words of appreciation.

There are several different opportunities to entertain out-of-town guests. Times when a get-together can occur include:

- **During the rehearsal dinner.** Friends and relatives may offer to host a cocktail party, barbecue, or other gathering for guests while the wedding party is at the rehearsal and rehearsal dinner. Note: Some couples, instead, include out-of-town guests at the rehearsal dinner. While this is not obligatory, if circumstances enable their inclusion in the rehearsal dinner, then it's a viable option.

- **The day before the wedding.** Many weddings are starting to feel like full weekend events. Events and gatherings are planned before and after the main event. A barbecue, miniature golf outing, or other casual outdoor adventure is a nice way for folks to get acquainted in a less formal setting before the wedding.

- **On the day of an evening wedding.** Friends might host a brunch or luncheon for guests on the day of a late-afternoon or evening wedding.

- **At a post-wedding brunch.** Out-of-town guests at an evening wedding generally stay the night. For them, a breakfast or brunch makes for a nice send-off.

Guest Etiquette

Guests invited to participate in a wedding celebration have as much of an obligation to exhibit good manners and thoughtful behavior as their hosts have to make them feel welcome and comfortable. Here are some guidelines for proper guest etiquette:

- **RSVP: Respond to the invitation immediately.** The most important obligation a guest has upon receiving a wedding invitation is to respond immediately to the invitation, *particularly* if he or she can't attend. This allows the bride and groom to promptly send an invitation to a new guest, if desired. At the very least, the hosts have realistic numbers of guests to relay to the caterer and others—as long as guests RSVP.

- **Send a gift.** Invited guests have an obligation to send a gift, whether they are attending or not. There are very few exceptions: If you receive an invitation to the wedding of someone you have neither spoken to nor seen in several years, or if you receive an announcement, rather than an invitation, you have no obligation to send a gift.

- **Be on your best behavior.** Just as there are guidelines to help the bride and groom and their families organize the most wonderful wedding possible, so guests have the responsibility to behave with decorum. This responsibility extends to immediate family members as well, regardless of any differences or rancor. A wedding is not the place to wage war. Best behavior is the code, so guests should practice civility during any and all proceedings.

The Good Guest's Pledge

Some behavior may seem harmless and trivial in casual circumstances, but within the context of a special occasion it can be ill-mannered and unruly. The good guest is almost invisible, busy enjoying him- or herself, communing with fellow guests, and, most of all, basking in the generous hospitality of the hosts. The good guest is thoughtful and solicitous, paying respect to the hosts, the wedding party, and the other guests. The bad guest, on the other hand, sticks out like a sore thumb and can be counted on to behave poorly, forcing the hosts to graciously grin and bear it when possible. Ultimately, it's up to the guest to do the right thing. Here is the Good Guest's Pledge—a promise to behave at his or her most thoughtful and respectful best during the wedding celebrations:

DURING THE CEREMONY

- I will respect the sanctity of the occasion and not talk during the wedding ceremony or interrupt the service by taking pictures with a flash camera. This is also not the time to mingle or loudly greet friends and acquaintances. I will turn off the ringers on my cell phone and pager.

- I will participate in as much of the ceremony as my own religion and that of the ceremony permit. If a mass or communion is offered and I choose not to participate, I will remain quietly in my seat. Otherwise, I'll stand when others stand and sit when others sit. I am not required to kneel or to recite prayers that are contrary to my own beliefs.

- I will not show up at the ceremony and reception with a surprise guest, whether a date, children, or extras in general.

DURING THE RECEPTION

- I will not grab the microphone to croon a few favorite numbers, no matter how impressive my singing voice, or broadcast stories or jokes, no matter how humorous I can be. The bride and groom have taken great care to orchestrate a few hours of entertainment that do not include an amateur hour.

- I won't monopolize the bride and groom in the receiving line. Guests in the receiving line should introduce themselves to the first person in the line, and then keep their comments to the bare minimum: "What a lovely wedding!" "I'm so happy for you." Then they should move quickly on. The same brevity of comment is appreciated during the reception, for the bride and groom have many people with whom to speak.

- I will not alter place cards or switch tables at a wedding reception. Instead, it is my responsibility to be as cordial as I can be wherever the bride and groom have designated that I sit. I won't stand on ceremony and wait to be introduced to tablemates and others. I will introduce myself and add a little explanation: "I'm Lorrin's aunt from Hawaii" or "Jen and I were roommates in college."

- I will be gracious and offer assistance. It is kind for men at a table to ask single women to dance at some point during the reception, and for anyone at the table to offer to assist an older or infirm guest with a buffet meal.

AFTER THE RECEPTION

- I will not take the centerpiece upon departing, scoop up matchbooks, or request that any uneaten portion of my meal be put in a doggie bag to be taken home. The centerpieces should be left in place unless the bride and groom have actually encouraged guests to take them; and asking for leftover food is not in keeping with the elegance or dignity of the event. The bride and groom may have made arrangements to have the flowers delivered to shut-ins, to hospitals or nursing homes, or to guests unable to attend the festivities because of health or family issues. The flowers, in other words, belong to the bride and groom to dispose of as they wish.

A Few Tips for Guests Invited to Same-Sex Unions

If you're invited to a same-sex ceremony and have not previously attended one, it's natural to wonder what is expected of guests. The answer is simple: Guest etiquette is the same as for a traditional wedding celebration. The following points address some common concerns, but common sense is always the best guide.

- Reply to the invitation as soon as possible. If you must regret, there's no need for excuses. Invitees who are genuinely opposed to or upset by same-sex unions would be wise to decline graciously rather than risk dampening the happiness of the couple.

- Whether you can attend or not, the invitation obliges you to send a wedding gift. (See also Chapter 8, pages 152–155: "All About Wedding Gifts.")

- When choosing attire, be guided by the time of the ceremony and the nature of the invitation (formal, informal, or casual).

- Follow the order of the service in the ceremony program if one is provided. Otherwise, take your lead from the wedding party and other guests. Chances are, the ceremony and reception will be similar to other weddings you've attended.

- Go through the receiving line if there is one. All the traditional expressions of congratulations are appropriate, except references to "bride and groom" or "husband and wife." If there isn't a receiving line, be sure to extend best wishes to the couple and their families at some point during the party.

- Refrain from making comments and asking questions that might be perceived as negative. This won't be hard if guests bear in mind that the ceremony, while it may not be legally sanctioned, honors the lifetime commitment of two people in love.

CHAPTER 7

INVITATION ETIQUETTE

Your invitation is the first important indication to your guests of the style and tone of your wedding, as it reflects the degree of formality of the celebration. It is also a keepsake for the bride and groom to cherish forever, and as such your choices should be based on personal preferences. The couple who enjoys a long engagement has the luxury of having more time to consider choices available to them before making a final selection.

Even with a long engagement, choosing, printing, and mailing invitations must be planned well enough in advance to allow time for the invitations to be mailed and guests to respond. The rule of thumb is to allow at least six to eight weeks for printing formal invitations and their related enclosures. Try to plot out the time so that you will be addressing your invitations no later than two months before the wedding and mailing them out six to eight weeks before the wedding date.

Of course, customs have loosened as busy couples find themselves pressed for time. For the bride and groom who decide suddenly to marry, tradition is often thrown to the wind. A couple may telephone, fax, or overnight-mail their requests for the honor of the presence of their family and close friends.

Timing for Ordering and Mailing

Wedding invitations are usually mailed six to eight weeks before the wedding date. To place your invitation order in time, count backward from your mailing date. As a general rule, plan on at least three months for printing and delivery of formal invitations, enclosures, and envelopes. The wait may be less for nontraditional invitations, but get a reasonable time frame from your stationer or supplier. Should you decide to laser-print or handwrite your invitations, you'll still need time to select attractive papers and envelopes and to develop your design. In addition to preparation time, schedule at least an additional two weeks to address and assemble your invitations. If possible, add a few "just in case" days into your ordering and addressing schedule—just in case something unexpected delays your preparations.

Here are some good ideas that should make the invitation process proceed without stress and strain:

- Make sure that your supplier can deliver invitation envelopes to you as early as possible, so you can get a head start addressing them.

- Mistakes happen, so order at least a dozen extra invitations and envelopes or just the envelopes. Also order extras as keepsakes for yourself and your family.

- Since replies and gifts are normally sent to the return address on the envelope or with the RSVP, be sure that the person or people at that address—the bride, parents, the couple—can keep track of responses and gift deliveries. Establish your system for recording all replies and gifts.

- For addressing, you need the full names and titles for all guests; be certain that spellings are correct. Make note of relationships ("Bob's mom's best friend," "Linda's fiancé") as you assemble your list; these details can be helpful when you greet guests whom you don't know personally, arrange table seating for the reception, and write your thank-you notes.

Invitation Styles

These days, the range of invitations is infinite. You'll want to shop around before making a final decision. You can get catalogs from the many wedding-stationery companies that advertise in the pages of bridal magazines. Local stationers and printers also have a wealth of sample books and catalogs on hand.

The general categories can be broken down into *third-person formal invitations, semiformal invitations,* or, in the case of a small, intimate wedding, *handwritten notes* on beautiful stationery.

The elements to consider when choosing invitations are *paper shades, paper weight, typefaces, size, and wording.* Visit several vendors and check costs for these various components as well as for coordinating *inserts and envelopes.* Then compare prices and the length of time required for printing. While some stationers require several weeks for an order to be placed and returned to them, printers who do the work themselves can often guarantee a faster turnaround time. If the delivery time is considerable, ask if you can receive your envelopes early so that you can get a jump on the often time-consuming task of addressing them.

Don't forget to keep samples of what you order so that you can coordinate the design scheme of other printed accessories—whether inserts, place cards, or personalized napkins—with that of the invitation.

THE PERSONAL TOUCH:

Shop the Museums

If your wedding is not so formal that it requires traditional invitations, look in museum gift shops for beautiful fold-over cards that replicate antique lace patterns on cutout paper. If they're too delicate to go through a print process, you could print the invitation on pastel paper and cut it to fit within the fold.

- **Color.** The traditional paper shades for the most formal and traditional wedding invitation are ivory, soft cream, and white. Today's invitations might consist of colored paper—perfectly correct.

- **Paper.** The heaviest-weight paper in these shades may cost a bit more, but its appearance and feel are substantial and bespeak formality. You may want your paper flat or prefer a raised plate mark or margin. It is correct to use either a large double sheet, which is folded a second time, or a smaller single sheet.

- **Typeface.** After choosing paper shade and weight, you should select a typeface. For formal invitations, shaded and antique roman faces are traditional choices. Remember, simple styles are in better taste than ornate and flowery styles—and are easier to read as well. No other ornament should be added to a formal invitation, with the exception of a coat of arms (if the bride's father's family has one). A coat of arms or a crest may be used without color at the top center of the invitation.

- **Designs, borders, and bows.** The choices are endless. Just be sure to tie your invitation into the style of your wedding. Invitations may be printed on paper with a design or border, often in a color carrying out the color scheme of the wedding. If your wedding has a theme, you can start out by apply the theme to your invitations.

- **Nontraditional alternatives.** Printed invitations that do not follow the traditional third-person wording style can be quite beautiful. These invitations may be engraved or thermographed in as formal a style as traditional ones.

PRINTING OPTIONS

Formal and semiformal invitations may be printed in several ways. Of course, whatever you use is a matter of personal preference and budget, but in general the more formal the wedding, the more formal the printing style.

- **Engraving.** Engraved invitations are the most traditional printing style for formal invitations, if only because the engraving method has been around the longest time. Engraving results in raised print that is pressed through so that it can be felt on the back of the paper. It is also the most expensive form of printing.

- **Thermography.** Thermography results in raised print that is shinier than engraved print and does not press through the back of the paper. Thermography is less expensive than engraving.

- **Lithography.** Lithography imprints lettering with ink but results in neither raised nor pressed-through lettering. It is less costly than either engraving or thermography.

- **Laser.** Invitations can be produced on a laser printer, either at a professional print shop or at home. The result is similar to that produced by lithography. Blank invitation forms are available at better stationers. A word of caution: Great care must be taken to ensure that the forms are fed through the desktop printer straight and evenly. You should also choose a typeface that is formal, crisp, and easy to read, duplicating other professionally produced print. Laser printing is the most inexpensive form of printing, but when it is used for a formal wedding it can also look inexpensive. Make sure to print out a few practice invitations to get the look you want before it's too late to have invitations professionally printed.

- **Handwritten.** A personal invitation may be handwritten on lovely stationery when it is an invitation to a very small wedding or when the bride and groom want to personalize their invitations, no matter how formal the ceremony may be.

The most formal invitations have the name of the recipient written by hand on an otherwise printed card. You may want to employ the services of a *calligrapher* for this form of invitation, unless you or someone close to you has beautiful penmanship. It is also possible to use a desktop laser printer to "write" in the name of the recipient, but to ensure a handwritten result it is imperative that a type font that duplicates a calligraphy style is used. Make sure, too, that the invitation (which must be a single sheet, not a fold-over style) can be fed evenly through the printer.

Invitation Wording

Traditional wording. For the bride and groom who cherish long-standing traditions, conventional wording and spelling will govern their invitation choices. Some specific rules for *formal* wedding invitations are as follows:

1. The invitation to a wedding ceremony in a house of worship reads "Mr. and Mrs. Henry Stuart Evans request the honour" (using the traditional "u" spelling) "of your presence. . . ." "Favour," as in "the favour of a reply," also uses the traditional spelling.

2. The invitation to a reception reads "Mr. and Mrs. Henry Stuart Evans request the pleasure of your company. . . ."

3. When a Roman Catholic mass is part of the wedding ceremony, invitations may include "and your participation in the offering of the Nuptial Mass" beneath the groom's name.

4. No punctuation is used except after abbreviations such as "Mr." and "Mrs." or when phrases requiring separation occur in the same line, as in the date.

5. Numbers in the date are spelled out, as in "the twenty-seventh of August," but long numbers in the street address may be written in numerals: "1490 Kenwood Parkway."

6. Half hours are written as "half after four o'clock"—not as "half past four" or as "four-thirty."

Doctor and Mrs. Reid W. Coleman
request the honour of
Mr. and Mrs. Christopher Wicke's
presence at the marriage of their daughter
Laura Jeanne
to
Mr. Patrick Desmond Whelan
Saturday, the eighth of May
two thousand and seven
at half after eleven o'clock
St. John's Church
Rehoboth, Massachusetts

7. Although "Mr." is abbreviated and "Junior" may be, the title "Doctor" is more properly written in full on formal invitations but may be abbreviated if the name is an especially long one. When addressing envelopes to a guest who is a doctor, it is correct to abbreviate the title.

8. If the invitation includes the handwritten name of the recipient, the full name must be written out. The use of an initial—"Mr. and Mrs. Scott E. Jenkins"—is not correct.

9. The invitation to the wedding ceremony alone does not include an RSVP.

10. On the reception invitation, "RSVP," "R.S.V.P.," "R.s.v.p.," and "The favour of a reply is requested" are equally correct. If the address to which the reply is to be sent is different from the return address appearing on the envelope of the invitation, you may use "Kindly send reply to" followed by the correct address.

11. Traditionally, the date of the wedding on a formal invitation does not include the year, but today it is considered correct to include it, spelled out: "two thousand and five." The year is always included on a wedding announcement.

The most common traditional wording used today for a formal wedding given by the bride's parents reads:

Mr. and Mrs. Henry Stuart Evans
request the honour of your presence
at the marriage of their daughter
Katherine Leigh
to
Mr. Brian Charles Jamison
Saturday, the twelfth of June
two thousand and five
at half after four o'clock
Village Lutheran Church
Briarcliff Manor

Less formal wording. When less formality is desired, alternatives to traditional third-person wording can be used. These invitations may be engraved or printed by a stationer in just as formal a style as traditional invitations.

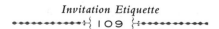

Our joy will be more complete
if you will share in the marriage of our daughter
Carole Renée
and
Mr. Domenick Masullo
on Saturday, the fifth of June
two thousand and seven
at half after four o'clock
7 Old Elm Avenue
Salem, Massachusetts
We invite you to worship with us
witness their vows and join us
for a reception following the ceremony
If you are unable to attend, we ask your
presence in thought and prayer
Mr. and Mrs. Earl Rinde
[or Lorraine and Earl Rinde]

RSVP

When the invitation is to come from both sets of parents, it might be worded:

Sharon and Elliot Karp
and
Hialri and Kenneth Cohen
would be honoured
to have you share in the joy
of the marriage of their children
Leah Rachel
and
Jonathan
This celebration of love will be held on
Sunday, the ninth of September
two thousand and eight
at five o'clock
Temple Shalom
Englewood, New Jersey

A reception will follow the ceremony
at the Palisades Lodge
Palisades Parkway

Kindly send reply to
Mr. and Mrs. Elliot Karp
[address]
[or]

RSVP

Less formally, the bride and groom may design and print or handwrite their own invitations on a simple card:

Elizabeth Upham and Michael Smithson
invite you to celebrate
their marriage
on
Saturday, June the 5th
two thousand and five
at four o'clock
2 Fox Run
Lander, Wyoming

Personal invitations to very small weddings are often issued in the form of a personal note. It is a most flattering invitation and typically would read:

Dear Aunt Ruth,
    Sean and I are to be married at Christ's Church on June tenth at four o'clock. We hope you and Uncle Don will come to the church and afterward to the reception at Greentree Country Club.

With much love from us both,
Laura Jeanne

Other personal forms of invitation for weddings that make no pretense of being traditional may be as original as the couple and/or the bride's parents wish, as long as the invitations are dignified and sincerely reflect the sentiments of the bride and groom and their families. Among the loveliest and most meaningful is the following example, written as a letter from the bride's parents:

Our daughter, Lisa, will be married to Frank Adams O'Gorman, on Saturday, the fifth of February, two thousand and six, at half after seven o'clock in the evening. Their vows will be spoken at St. John's Lutheran Church, Mamaroneck, New York.

We invite you to worship with us, witness their vows, and be our guest at the reception and buffet which follow at the Beach and Tennis Club, New Rochelle.

If you are unable to attend, we ask your presence in thought and prayer.

Helen and Davis Wilson

Wording for special cases. The wording in an invitation may undergo subtle changes for different circumstances. For example, if a formal invitation is to the ceremony only, the traditional wording should not include an RSVP. When a reception follows, a separate reception invitation or response card is inserted in the mailing envelope with the invitation to the ceremony. Circumstances dictate what kind of invitation is mailed, whether one to the ceremony only, one to both the reception and the ceremony, or one to the reception only.

Invitations to commitment ceremonies. Your invitations should reflect the nature of the ceremony—formal, semiformal, informal, or casual. You'll probably include an RSVP for the reception. Beyond the essentials of who, what, when, and where, the invitation style and wording is up to you. Some couples adapt traditional formats, as illustrated below; others opt for a blend of old and new styles. Or you may want to create an invitation that is uniquely yours. Although couples today are likely to issue their own invitations, certainly parents, grown children, or other family members can serve as hosts, and their names on the invitation are a loving way to demonstrate that they support the union.

A semi-traditional, first-person invitation issued by the couple:

Lucius Grisham

and

William Ryan Barker

invite you to share our joy

at the celebration of our Life Commitment

Saturday, the twenty-seventh of March

at half after eleven o'clock

756 Oriole Court

Westhaven

and afterward for brunch

RSVP

TO THE CEREMONY AND RECEPTION

When all the guests invited to the wedding are also invited to the reception, the invitation to both may be combined:

Mr. and Mrs. Kenneth McGuigan

request the honour of your presence

at the marriage of their daughter

Joanne Marie

to

Mr. Stephen Dempsey

Saturday, the ninth of April

two thousand and eight

at half after five o'clock

Church of the Resurrection

Evanston

and afterward at the reception

Lake Michigan Shore Club

The favour of a reply is requested

23 Soundview Avenue

River Forest, Illinois 60601

[or]

RSVP

When the wedding ceremony is private and a large reception follows, the invitation to the ceremony is extended orally or by personal note, and the wording of the reception invitation is:

Mr. and Mrs. Douglas Charles Campbell
request the pleasure of your company
at the wedding reception
for their daughter
Deirdre Mary
and
Mr. Jeffrey Keller
Saturday the twenty-fourth of June
two thousand and five
at seven o'clock
Horseshoe Harbour Yacht Club
Larchmont

RSVP

RECEPTION CARDS

A reception card, an invitation to the reception, is often sent when the ceremony and reception are held at different locations. The reception card is enclosed with the wedding invitation.

The reception card is also used when the guest list for the ceremony is larger than that for the reception. Here, the reception cards would be enclosed only with wedding invitations for those being invited to the wedding and reception. The most commonly used form is:

Reception
immediately following the ceremony
Knolls Country Club
Lake Forest

The favour of a reply is requested
Lakeside Drive, Lake Forest, Illinois 61300

INVITATIONS TO A BELATED RECEPTION

When a reception is not held at the time of the wedding, the couple or their parents may have one later, possibly when the newlyweds return from their honeymoon. Although the party is held to celebrate the wedding, the wording must be slightly changed:

Mr. and Mrs. Wayne Matteis
request the pleasure of your company
at a reception
in honor of
Mr. and Mrs. Scott Nelson
[etc.]

AT SOMEONE'S HOME

Even though the wedding and reception are to be held at a friend's house, the invitations should be written in the name of the bride's parents or sponsors or in the name of the bride and groom:

Linda Lanier-Keosaian and Gregory Keosaian
request the honour of your presence
at the marriage of her daughter
Peternelle Van Arsdale
to
Mr. Bryan Keith Oettl
Saturday, the twelfth of October
two thousand and ten
at half after three o'clock
at the residence of Mr. and Mrs. Robert Cozza
Kansas City, Missouri

RSVP

Sample Invitations

A growing number of wedding invitations issued today do not follow the traditional formal style illustrated in the previous sections but instead reflect the often complicated makeup of modern families. A bride may have two divorced and remarried sets of parents giving her away. A groom may have the blessing of one divorced parent but not the other. Birth mothers of adopted children may be involved. For brides and grooms in these situations, there is no need to panic. Etiquette accommodates almost any circumstance with elegance. These sample invitations are just a few that cover a variety of complex situations gracefully:

WHEN THE BRIDE HAS ONE LIVING PARENT . . .

When either the bride's mother or the bride's father is deceased, the invitation is issued only in the name of the living parent:

> *Mr. [Mrs.] Daniel Watson Driskill*
> *requests the honour of your presence*
> *at the marriage of his [her] daughter*
> *Susan Patricia*
> *to*
> *Mr. Drew Randolph Donney*
>
> *[etc.]*

However, there are circumstances when the bride very much wants to include the name of the deceased parent. This is acceptable, as long as the invitation does not appear to be issued by the deceased. In other words, don't word the invitation so that it reads ". . . the late William Tierney requests the honour of . . ."

> *Diane June Tierney*
> *daughter of Mary Ann Tierney and the late William Tierney*
> *and*
> *James Thomas Duffy*
> *son of Mr. and Mrs. Keon David Duffy*
> *request the honour of your presence*
> *at their marriage*
> *Saturday, the fifth of October*
>
> *[etc.]*

WHEN THE BRIDE'S MOTHER IS DIVORCED . . .

A divorcée giving her daughter's wedding by herself sends out her daughter's invitations using her first and last names:

Mrs. Ann Syverson
requests the honour of your presence
at the marriage of her daughter
[etc.]

WHEN DIVORCED PARENTS GIVE THE WEDDING TOGETHER . . .

In the event that relations between the bride's divorced parents (one or both of whom may have remarried) are so friendly that they share the wedding expenses and act as co-hosts, both sets of names should appear on the invitation. The bride's mother's name appears first:

Mr. and Mrs. Shelby Goldring
and
Mr. Michael Levy
request the honour of your presence
at the marriage of their daughter
Rachel Lynn Levy

[etc.]

If, however, the bride's parents are not sharing expenses, yet the bride wishes both parents' names to appear, a different situation exists. If the bride's mother is not contributing to the cost of the wedding, the bride's father's name appears first on the invitation and he and his wife host the reception. The bride's mother is then included only as an honored guest at the reception.

WHEN THE BRIDE HAS A STEPFATHER . . .

When the bride's mother has been widowed or is divorced and remarried and she and her husband are hosting the wedding, the invitations are worded:

Mr. and Mrs. Kevin Michael O'Callaghan
request the honour of your presence
at the marriage of her daughter [or, Mrs. O'Callaghan's daughter]
Kelly Elizabeth Quimby

to

[etc.]

If the bride's own father has no part in her life and her stepfather has brought her up (legally adopted or not) the invitation reads:

Mr. and Mrs. Kevin Michael O'Callaghan
request the honour of your presence
at the marriage of their daughter
Kelly Elizabeth Quimby

to

[etc.]

WHEN THE BRIDE IS AN ORPHAN . . .

"Miss," Ms," or "Mrs." is rarely used before the bride's name. The following case is an exception:

Mr. and Mrs. Paul John Carey
request the honour of your presence
at the marriage of
their niece
Miss Rosemary Gelbach
to
Mr. Karl Andrew Rauch

[etc.]

A bride and groom who send out their own invitations would also use a title ("Miss," "Ms.," "Mrs."):

The honour of your presence
is requested
at the marriage of
Miss Andrea Mignone
to
Mr. Robert White

[etc.]

OR

Miss Andrea Mignone
and
Mr. Robert White
request the honour of your presence
at their marriage

[etc.]

Or, less formally:

Beth Holland and Christopher Saladino
invite you to attend
their marriage
on
Saturday, October the twenty-ninth
two thousand and ten
at three o'clock
The Hopewell School
Richmond, Virginia
A reception on the grounds will follow the ceremony
RSVP
Ms. Beth Holland
87 Grace Street
Richmond, Virginia 23223

Mature couples or couples who have been living together may prefer to send out wedding invitations in their own names and not use social titles:

Mary Ann Schmidt
and
George James MacLellan
invite you to share with them
the joy of their marriage
Saturday, the tenth of July
two thousand and twelve
at half after four o'clock
First Congregational Church
Baton Rouge, Louisiana

WHEN OTHER RELATIVES ISSUE INVITATIONS . . .

If the bride has siblings or other relatives who are giving the wedding, then the invitations should be sent in their names:

Mr. Robert Mazzone
requests the honour of your presence
at the marriage of his sister
Elizabeth Ann

[etc.]

When a bride and groom's grown children are giving their wedding, the invitation may be issued in their names, with the bride's children listed before the groom's. When several children are involved, their names are given in the order of their age, from the oldest to the youngest in each family. When the bride's married son and the single daughter and married son of the groom are giving the wedding together, the invitation should read:

Mr. and Mrs. Brendan Shine
Miss Christine Barrett
Mr. and Mrs. William Barrett, Junior
request the honour of your presence
at the marriage of their parents
Madolyn Whitefield Shine
and
William Wyndham Barrett
Sunday, the tenth of September
two thousand and eight
at half after three o'clock
at the Belle Haven Club
Greenwich, Connecticut
RSVP

WHEN THE BRIDE IS A YOUNG WIDOW OR DIVORCÉE . . .

Invitations to a young widow's second wedding may be sent by her parents using the same wording used in the invitations to her first marriage. The only difference is that if she continues to use her married name, it should be included:

Doctor and Mrs. Daniel Thomas McCann
request the honour of your presence
at the marriage of their daughter
Sheliah O'Neill

[etc.]

A divorcée's second wedding invitation may read the same way. The bride's name would be the one she is using—either her first name, maiden name, and ex-husband's last name or if she has dropped her ex-husband's name, her own middle and maiden name.

A more mature woman whose parents are deceased or a divorcée who has been independent since her divorce would, along with her groom, generally send out her own invitations.

A widow's or divorcée's invitation would read:

The honour of your presence
is requested
at the marriage of
Mrs. Susan Green Millman
and
Mr. Elliot Franklin Aiken

[etc.]

If the bride prefers, she may drop the title and have her name simply read "Susan Green Millman."

WHEN THE BRIDEGROOM'S FAMILY GIVES THE WEDDING . . .

When the bride's family lives far away and she is alone, the groom's parents may give the wedding and issue the invitations. This is also true if the bride's family disapproves of the wedding and refuses to take part in it.

Mr. and Mrs. Wendell William Orr
request the honour of your presence
at the marriage of
Miss Latoya Kienisha Anderson
to
their son
Joshua Allen Orr

[etc.]

If any announcements of the marriage are sent to friends and colleagues who weren't invited to the wedding day celebrations, they should be sent by the bride's family. If that is not possible, then the groom's family should include the names of the bride's parents.

INCLUDING THE GROOM'S FAMILY IN THE INVITATION . . .

Increasingly, there are occasions when the groom's family shares in or pays the major part of the wedding expenses. In such a case, it is only fair that their names appear on the invitations. The bride's parents' names would be first, and the wording would be:

Mr. an Mrs. David Zimmerli
and
Captain and Mrs. John Gonzalez
request the honour of your presence
at the marriage of
Cynthia Ann Zimmerli
and
John Howard Gonzalez, Junior

[etc.]

When both the bride's and the groom's parents have been divorced and have remarried, and all are participating in giving the wedding and hosting the reception, it is not unusual for all their names to appear on the invitation. In this instance, the bride's mother and her husband would appear first, the bride's father and his wife second, the groom's mother and her husband third, and the groom's father and his wife fourth:

Mr. and Mrs. Michael Hannigan
Mr. and Mrs. Lawrence Anvik
Doctor and Mrs. Russell Healy
Mr. and Mrs. Jeffrey Jacobs
request the honour of your presence
at the marriage of
Lindsay Catherine Anvik
to
Andrew Lloyd Jacobs

[etc.]

A form followed in some foreign countries provides for a double invitation with the bride's family's invitation on the left and the groom's family's invitation on the right:

Mr. and Mrs. Arturo Mendel	*Mr. and Mrs. Roberto Perez*
request the honour of your presence	*request the honour of your presence*
at the marriage of their daughter	*at the marriage of their son*
Angelina Ruth	*Eduardo Robert*
to	*to*
Mr. Eduardo Perez	*Miss Angelina Mendel*
[etc.]	*[etc.]*

WHEN THE BRIDE HAS A PROFESSIONAL NAME . . .

If the bride is well known by a professional name and has many professional friends to whom she wishes to send invitations or announcements, she may include on the invitations her professional name in parentheses engraved or printed below her real name:

Margaret Marie
(Meg Drake)
to
Mr. Carl Louis Valentine

[etc.]

WHEN MILITARY TITLES ARE USED . . .

When the groom is a member of the armed services or is on active duty in the reserve forces, he uses his military title.

For officers whose rank is captain in the Army or lieutenant, senior grade or higher, in the Navy, the title should appear on the same line as the name:

Colonel Graham O'Gorman
United States Army

Those with lower ranks should have their names and titles engraved in this form:

John McMahon
Ensign, United States Navy

In the case of reserve officers on active duty, the second line would read "Army of the United States" or "United States Naval Reserve."

First and second lieutenants in the Army both use "Lieutenant" without the numeral.

A noncommissioned officer or enlisted man may, if he wishes, include his rank and his branch of the service below his name.

Henry Delucia
Corporal, Signal Corps, United States Army

OR

Marc Josephson
Seaman Apprentice, United States Naval Reserve

High-ranking officers of the regular armed forces should continue to use their titles, followed by their branch of service, even after retirement, with "Retired" following the branch of service:

General George Harmon
United States Army, Retired

When the father of the bride is a member of the armed forces, either on active duty, as a high-ranking retired officer, or as one who retired after many years of service, he uses his title in the regular way:

Colonel and Mrs. James Booth
request the honour of your presence

[etc.]

When the bride is on active duty, both her rank and the branch of the military are included in the invitation. The name of the bride appears on one line with her rank and the branch of the military on a separate line:

marriage of their daughter
Joanne
Lieutenant, United States Navy

WHEN OTHER TITLES ARE USED . . .

Medical doctors, dentists, veterinarians, clergymen, judges, and all others customarily called by their titles should have those titles included on their own wedding invitations and on the invitations to their daughters' or sons' weddings.

Holders of academic degrees do not use "Doctor" unless they are always referred to in that way.

Women use their titles only when the invitations are issued by themselves and their grooms:

The honour of your presence
is requested
at the marriage of
Doctor Laurie Neu
and
Mr. Norbert Rudell

[etc.]

Otherwise, she is, "their daughter, Laurie."

The bride's mother uses the title "Doctor" on her daughter's invitation if she feels strongly about it: "Doctor Lynn Josephson and Mr. Marc Josephson request . . ." Otherwise, the invitation would read, "Mr. and Mrs. Marc Josephson request . . ."

SAME-SEX UNIONS

A formal invitation to a gay or lesbian commitment ceremony may be issued by the couple themselves or by one or both sets of parents:

*The honour of your presence
is requested
at the marriage of
Susan Beth Gibson
and
Georgia Lee O'Dell*

[etc.]

OR

*Mr. and Mrs. Franklin Johnson
Mr. and Mrs. Jason Bolivia
request the honour of your presence
at the marriage of their sons
Victor Kenneth Johnson
and
Marc William Bolivia*

[etc.]

A gay or lesbian couple formally joining together may decide to use a different phrase than "marriage" on their invitation, depending on their feelings and the type of ceremony in which they are participating. Choices include *commitment ceremony, affirmation ceremony, celebration of commitment, rite of blessing, relationship covenant,* and *union ceremony.* (See also Chapter 3, page 55: "Name Change: What to Call Your Commitment Ceremony and Your Same-Sex Partner.")

DOUBLE WEDDINGS

Double weddings almost always involve the marriage of two sisters, and the form, with the elder sister's name first, is:

Mr. and Mrs. Roderick Thorn
request the honour of your presence
at the marriage of their daughters
Jessica Ann
to
Mr. Bradley Peterson
and
Amanda Lynn
to
Mr. Richard Suarino
Saturday, the twenty-second of October
at four o'clock

Good Shepherd Church

In the event that two close friends decide to have a double wedding, the invitation reads:

Mr. and Mrs. Richard McMillan
and
Mrs. Karen Clark
request the honour of your presence
at the marriage of their daughters
Kerry Ann McMillan
to
Mr. Stephen Bonner
and
Amanda Louise Clark
to
Mr. Kenneth Kienzle
[etc.]

Wedding Announcements

Sharing the happy news after the wedding in the form of a printed or handwritten announcement is never obligatory, but it is a nice idea. The year is always included as part of the date on an announcement.

- **Who receives wedding announcements?** Printed or handwritten wedding announcements sent through the mail can serve a useful purpose. These are generally sent to those friends and family who were left off the guest list because the celebration was too small to accommodate them or to acquaintances or business associates who, while not particularly close to the family, might still wish to hear news of the marriage.

- **Are recipients obligated to send a gift?** Announcements carry no obligation for the recipient to send a gift to the bride and groom, so many families send them rather than invitations to friends who are not expected to attend or to send a present. They are never sent to anyone who has received an invitation to the ceremony or reception.

- **When are announcements mailed out?** Ideally, announcements are mailed the day after the wedding but may be mailed up to several months later.

- **What is the traditional wording for announcements?** Announcements are traditionally sent in the name of the bride's parents, with wording as follows (still perfectly correct):

Mr. and Mrs. James Welch
have the honour of
announcing the marriage of their daughter
Amy Sue
to
Mr. Jonathan Scott Jamison
Saturday, the twelfth of June
two thousand and nine
Mansfield, Pennsylvania

VARIATIONS

Several other variations are equally correct. You may use "have the honour to announce," or merely "announce." Although traditionally the bride's parents send the announcement, today, however, when the attitude toward marriage is that it is a "joining" rather than a "giving" of a woman to a man, there is no reason that it should not go out in both families' names. The parents of the groom are also presumably proud and happy to share the announcement. The wording is as follows:

Mr. and Mrs. James Welch
and
Mr. and Mrs. Dewey Jamison
announce the marriage of
Amy Sue Welch
and
Jonathan Scott Jamison

[etc.]

The variations in circumstances, names, and titles follow the rules under wedding invitations. In general, the wording used for the wedding invitation is the basis for the wording of the wedding announcement.

All About Envelopes

ONE OR TWO ENVELOPES?

When formal third-person invitations are written, they are traditionally inserted into two envelopes, an *inner envelope* and an *outer envelope*. The outer envelope is the one that is addressed and stamped, while the inner envelope bears only the names of the people to whom the mailing envelope is addressed. For example, a married couple's inner envelope is addressed to "Mr. and Mrs. Anderson" with neither first names nor address.

This convention serves a useful purpose—it permits the bride and groom to be very specific as to who is invited. If, for example, a close friend is invited and the bride and groom want her to bring a guest (whose name they don't know), the outer envelope is addressed to the friend and the inner envelope reads "Miss Smith and Guest." Not only would it be awkward to address the outer envelope this way, but there is no other way, short of a personal note or telephone call, to let Miss Smith know that a guest is welcome. An inner envelope that reads only "Miss Smith" clearly indicates that Miss Smith is not supposed to bring a guest.

Of course, this kind of communication may be unnecessary for the type of guest list you have, and you may want to dispense with the custom of the inner envelope altogether; it is correct to do so.

If you do plan to use inner envelopes, you may write the names of intimate relatives and lifelong friends in informal and familial terms. For example, it is perfectly fine to write, "Aunt Deirdre and Uncle Tom" or "Grandmother."

USING ABBREVIATIONS

Just as abbreviations are not used in the wording of the invitation, so are they not used in addressing the envelopes. A person's middle name may or may not be used. If it is, it must be written out in full, as should "Street" and "Avenue." The name of the state is traditionally not abbreviated, but because the post office prefers the use of two-letter state abbreviations and no comma between the city and the state, it is fine to do so.

- **Including children.** Children over thirteen years of age should, if possible, receive separate invitations. Young sisters and brothers may be sent a joint invitation addressed to "The Misses Smith" or "The Messrs. Jones" on the outer envelope, with "Andy, Doug, and Brian," for instance, written on the inner envelope to make perfectly clear that all are invited. If there are both boys and girls, the outer envelope address may read:

The Messrs. Jones

The Misses Jones

If children are not receiving a separate invitation, their names may be written on a line below their parents' names on the inner envelope and do not have to be listed on the outer envelope at all. However, if no inner envelope is used, their names must be written on the outer envelope, or their parents won't know that they are included in the invitation. When possible, be specific and list names. Still, it is often difficult to know all of the names and relationships within a family. If, for example, relationships are so complicated or children so numerous that it seems simpler to address the envelope "Mr. and Mrs. Vito Sessa and Family," you may do so—but *only* in the following circumstances:

1. *When it is clear that you are inviting just the people living under that roof, not the aunt and uncle next door,*

2. *When the children are young (adult relatives who reside in the household should receive their own invitation), and*

3. *When every person living under the same roof is intended to be included in the invitation.*

How Can Bullying the Bride Be Stopped?

Q: I am getting married in a few weeks, and I am steamed about something. Friends of mine returned their invitation with their children's names written in as attending. I am not having children at my wedding, which was made perfectly clear on the invitation. What do I do?

A: There are those parents who go right ahead and write their children's names on the response card, even though the kids clearly weren't asked to attend. Some do this intentionally, believing they can bully the bride into having them; others truly believe it is understood that the children are included. Whoever is hosting the wedding may call immediately and explain in kind terms that the children are indeed not invited. If this results in an angry "then I'm not coming either," so be it. The breach of etiquette is theirs, not yours.

ADDRESSING ENVELOPES

- **To a married couple.** Wedding invitations are always addressed to both members of a married couple, even though the bride may know only one or knows that only one will attend.

- **To an unmarried couple living together.** Invitations to an unmarried couple who reside at the same address should be addressed to "Ms. Nancy Fellows" and "Mr. Scott Dunn," with each name appearing on a separate line. The same format is used for a same-sex couple living together; each of their names is written on a separate line.

- **To a married woman doctor/two married doctors.** If the woman uses her husband's name socially, the address is "Dr. Barbara and Mr. James Werner." If she uses her maiden name both professionally and socially, it is "Dr. Barbara Hanson and Mr. James Werner." If her husband is also a doctor, the address is either "The Drs. Werner" or "Drs. Barbara and Robert Werner." The same format would be followed if the woman were a reverend, or if both she and her husband were reverends.

- **Return address.** The U.S. Postal Service requests that all first-class mail bear a return address.

    This information also lets invited guests know where to send replies and gifts if an RSVP address does not appear on the invitation. The postal service prefers that the return address be printed or handwritten on the upper left-hand corner of the envelope. It is nonetheless acceptable to clearly emboss the return address by stamping it on the envelope's flap (although sometimes the embossing is difficult to read).

Insertions

In addition to the invitation, several enclosures may be placed in the inner envelope (or in the outer envelope if you omit an inner one).

ADMISSION CARDS

Admission cards are necessary only when a wedding is held in a popular cathedral or church that attracts sightseers. To ensure privacy in these circumstances, each guest is asked to present his or her card at the entrance. It is generally engraved or printed in the same style as the invitation and reads:

Please present this card
at
St. Patrick's Cathedral
Saturday, the twelfth of June

PEW CARDS

Small cards with "Pew Number _____" engraved on them may be enclosed with the invitations going to those family members and close friends who are to be seated in reserved pews. Recipients simply take the pew cards to the ceremony and show them to ushers, who escort them to their seats.

Similar cards are sometimes engraved "Within the Ribbon." This indicates that reserved pews or seats with white ribbons across the ends have been set aside for special guests. When ushers escort recipients of these cards to their seats, the ribbon is lifted and then replaced after the guests are seated. Guests receiving pew cards can sit anywhere within these seats.

Pew cards are sometimes sent separately after acceptances or regrets are received, when the bride knows how many reserved pews are needed.

AT-HOME CARDS

If the bride and groom wish to let friends know what their new address will be, they may insert an "at home" card with the invitation or wedding announcement. These cards traditionally read:

At home [or *Will be at home*]
after July second
3842 Grand Avenue
Houston, Texas 77001
(898) 555-4321

The problem with the example above is that many people receiving these cards often put them away, intending to enter them in an address book or file at some point in the future. When they come across the card weeks, even months, later, they may find they can't recall just who will be at home at 3842 Grand Avenue "after July second." Therefore, even though you are not married at the time the invitation is sent, it is perfectly all right to have an at-home card printed with the couple's names:

Mr. and Mrs. Bruce Moore
will be at home

[etc.]

An at-home card also gives the woman who plans to keep her own name the opportunity to let friends know. In this case, the at-home card would read:

Peternelle Van Arsdale and Bryan Oettl
will be at home

[etc.]

RECEPTION CARDS

When a separate reception card is used, it is placed in front of the invitation to the wedding ceremony (see also "Reception Cards," page 114).

RESPONSE CARDS

It used to be that the only correct response to a formal invitation was an equally formal reply, handwritten by the invited guest. This reply is still correct, but because fewer and fewer people these days will take the time to pen a formal reply, in the last decade or so response cards have replaced the handwritten reply in popularity. The response card is inserted with the invitation and is engraved or printed in the same style as the invitation on card stock, in the following form:

$$M\underline{\hspace{3cm}}$$

accepts ____

regrets ____

The favour of your reply is requested by July 26

The "M" precedes the space where the guest writes his or her title and name, as in "Miss Phyllis Reynolds" or "Mr. and Mrs. Joseph DeRuvo."

A *printed, stamped envelope* is included so that all the guest has to do is write in his, her, or their names—"*Mr.* and Mrs. Stephen Nelmes"—check "accepts" or "regrets," place the card in the envelope, and mail it. When one guest is able to accept and the other is not, it is necessary to make this clear on the response card.

Generally, a response card should not include the phrase "number of persons." The names on the outer and inner envelopes are those of the only persons invited, which means that other members of the family whose names do not appear on the envelopes are not invited. When "number of persons" is printed, recipients may confuse this to mean that other members of the family are indeed invited to attend, resulting in a wedding that overflows with too many guests.

When one invitation is received by a couple whose children are included, *every name* must be written in on the response card.

If one invitation is sent to a friend with "and Guest" written on the envelope, the friend should write in the name of the guest so that his or her name can be written on a place card. If the friend is not bringing a guest, then only the friend's name should be written on the response card.

HANDWRITTEN FORMAL REPLY

When a formal invitation does not include a response card insert, a guest should send a formal handwritten reply. The formal reply should be written on plain or bordered letter paper or notepaper in blue or black ink. The lines should be evenly and symmetrically spaced on one page. The formal reply, which mentions the hosts (by surname) and the date on the invitation, should read if accepting:

Mr. and Mrs. Mark Ross
accept with pleasure
Mr. and Mrs. McCullough's
kind invitation for
Saturday, the twenty-second of May

OR

The longer version of the formal reply follows exactly the form of the invitation, and should read if accepting:

Mr. and Mrs. Mark Ross
accept with pleasure
the kind invitation of
Mr. and Mrs. Frank McCullough
to the marriage of their daughter
Kristin Lynn
to
Mr. Brent Brown

Saturday, the twenty-second of May

Regrets are sent in the same manner:

Mr. and Mrs. Charles Coletti
regret that they are unable to accept
Mr. and Mrs. Aliberto's
kind invitation for

Sunday, the fourteenth of March

When one invited guest is able to attend and the other is not, the form reads:

Mrs. Lawrence Hires
accepts with pleasure
Mr. and Mrs. Benson's
kind invitation for
Saturday, the fifth of February
but regrets that
Mr. Hires
will be unable to attend

TISSUES

The delicate tissues that are sometimes included in a wedding invitation are optional today. Their prior usage had a real function: to keep the oils from the ink on engraved invitations from smudging as it slowly dried. Improved printing and engraving techniques have made tissues unnecessary for decades, but their use continues as a bow to tradition. While the tradition is fine, it is perfectly correct to exclude the tissues if a couple chooses to do so.

MAPS

You can provide maps and directions to the wedding sites in a number of ways. You may enclose them with the invitation or you may mail them after you have received an affirmative response to your invitation. Sometimes maps are supplied by the ceremony and/or reception sites. If they are not, you will have to order them or design them yourselves. Be sure your directions are clear and accurate, and that they are written in as concise and abbreviated a manner as possible, to avoid adding extra bulk to the invitation.

THE PERSONAL TOUCH

TRAVEL INFORMATION FOR GUESTS

If you have the time and the inclination, gather as much travel and lodging information as you can for your out-of-town invited guests. This information can be sent by e-mail after you receive a response or can be included with the invitation, perhaps laser-printed on a card or a single sheet of small stationery. Helpful information to include: the names of airlines that fly into nearby airports; hotels, motels, inns, and bed-and-breakfast lodging; ground transportation services; and car rental rates. If events are planned for out-of-town guests, this information should be sent as soon as a response is received, along with travel directions. That way your guests can best plan their arrival and departure times. Along with the travel information, the schedule of events can be e-mailed or printed right from your own desktop computer, and coordinated in color and paper, if possible, with the other printed pieces.

RAIN CARD

When a ceremony and/or reception are planned for outdoors, you must have an indoor contingency plan of action in the event of inclement weather. A rain card is a small card that gives the alternate location for the wedding and/or the reception. It might read, "In case of rain, the ceremony and reception will take place at 33 Elm Street, Traverse City."

Stuffing the Envelopes

1. When two envelopes are used, the invitation (folded edge first for a folded invitation, left edge for a single card) and all enclosures are put in the inner envelope, facing the back.

2. The inner envelope is then placed, unsealed, in the outer envelope, with the flap away from the person inserting it.

3. When there are insertions, they are placed in front of the invitation, so that they face the flap (and the person inserting them).

4. In the case of a folded invitation, insertions are placed in the same direction but within the fold.

A Change in Plans

Even the best-laid plans can go awry. Here are some of the more typical situations that warrant some sort of communication that plans have changed:

WHEN THE WEDDING IS CANCELED AFTER INVITATIONS ARE MAILED . . .

If the decision to cancel the wedding is a last-minute one, guests must be notified by telephone. If there is time, printed cards may be sent:

Mr. and Mrs. Oliver Grant
announce that the marriage of
their daughter
Debra
to
Mr. Christopher Bronner
will not take place

WHEN THE WEDDING DATE IS CHANGED . . .

When it is necessary to change the date of the wedding and the new date is decided upon after the invitations have been printed but before they are mailed, it is not necessary for the bride to order new invitations. Instead, she may enclose a printed card, if there is time to print one, saying, "The date of the wedding has been changed from March sixth to April twelfth." If there is not time for the card, she may neatly cross out the old date on the invitation and insert the new one by pen.

If the invitations have already been mailed, she may mail a card or a personal note or, if the guest list is small, telephone the information.

When the wedding is postponed, not canceled, and there is time to have an announcement printed, it would read:

Mr. and Mrs. Roy Westgate
regret that
the invitations to
their daughter's wedding
on Saturday, December fourth
must be recalled

OR

Mr. and Mrs. Scott Pierce
announce that
the marriage of their daughter
Janet Ann
to
Mr. Peter Norton
has been postponed

If the new date is known, it is added: "has been postponed to February third." If there is no time to have a card printed, the information must be communicated by telephone, fax, e-mail, mail, or personal note.

Invitation Do's

Here are some invitation issues that warrant particularly careful attention:

- **Order extras.** Even the most carefully held pen can experience a slipup, so it is the wise bride who orders at least a dozen extra invitations and envelopes. At the very least, order extra envelopes. It is far less costly to print extras that you may not need than to go back to the printer to order more. Remember to order an extra for yourselves, to include as a keepsake in your album or organizer, as well as extras for your family and in-laws, who may want to do the same.

- **Think about where you want responses sent.** Do think about where you want responses sent. Usually, gifts are sent to the return address on the envelope or to the address printed by the RSVP. If the bride lives in New York City but her wedding will be held where her parents live in Chicago, it is far handier to have gifts sent to her New York City home than to her parents, who will have to pack them up and ship them to New York. Then there is the question of who is keeping track of responses. If it is the bride, then by all means her address should be used. If it is her mother, then the question of which is easier to ship back and forth—responses or gifts—is the determining factor.

- **Allow plenty of time.** This is both an invitation do and an invitation don't. Don't run out of time. Do allow plenty of time to carefully address, assemble, and mail your invitations, especially if you are using a calligrapher to do the writing. If other obligations leave you pressed for time, ask to have envelopes sent to you well in advance of the invitations so that you can start addressing early.

- **Get organized.** Develop a system of organization that makes the process of addressing and mailing your invitations pleasurable, not painful. Prepare in advance by writing in your wedding organizer the names and addresses of everyone on your guest list. Perhaps family and future in-laws could be persuaded to send you their complete lists with full names and addresses (including names of any children or unmarried partners to be invited). Other brides find a computer database or file cards helpful. Otherwise, you'll spend all your time looking up addresses in the phone book and other sources.

Use proven time-management systems and handle each piece only once if possible. Arrange each element that goes into an invitation in a stack, in the order it will be picked up, assembled, and inserted.

As replies are received, make helpful notes to yourself, such as "friend of Andy's parents" or "Susie's date" so that you'll know who's who when finalizing your table arrangements and greeting guests in the receiving line.

- **Check postage.** It would be extremely annoying (and time-consuming!) to mail all your invitations, only to have them returned because of insufficient postage. Before you buy stamps and apply them, take an assembled invitation to the post office and have it weighed. It's likely that the inserts, or even an unusually shaped envelope, will necessitate extra postage. Remember that maps and other directional inserts sent to out-of-town-guests will make heavier invitations than those sent to local guests and may require a postage adjustment. In that case, be sure to assemble two sets, have both weighed—and pay close attention when affixing postage so that the appropriate stamps go on the right envelopes.

- **Double-check spelling and site names.** Ask for the business cards of the contacts at your ceremony and reception sites before you order your invitations. You'll want to get the spelling and names of the sites absolutely correct. Guests directed to "St. John's Church" could easily miss the wedding ceremony at "The Evangelical Lutheran Church of St. John."

- **Use correct names and titles of guests.** It is most flattering when invitations are addressed correctly. This means using correct titles, as well as spelling names right. Some professional titles that are also used socially and that would be used when addressing an invitation include: *The Honorable* (judge, governor, mayor, United States senator, member of Congress, cabinet members, ambassadors) and *The Reverend, The Most Reverend,* or *The Right Reverend.* When in doubt, ask before addressing.

- **Use the names of guests of invited guests when possible.** It is so much warmer and more welcoming to use the correct names of those who will be guests of your friends on invitations and place cards. Whether you also send these guests their own invitations or include their names on your friends' invitations is up to you, but the guest feels personally invited when his or her name is actually written on the envelope. This also enables you to write a place card using the person's name instead of "and guest" on your friend's place card or a card that reads "Miss Johnston's Guest."

Invitation Don'ts

Certain information should never be included on or placed inside a wedding invitation:

- **Registry or gift information.** Although a wedding invitation demands a gift in return, it is in extremely poor taste to insert a "helpful" list of places where the bride and groom are registered or a checklist of the things they want or don't want. This information should be shared with parents and attendants who can be resources for guests who want to know.

- **The inclusion of "No Gifts."** Often a second-time bride or groom or an older couple feels that they have everything they need and prefer that their guests not give them gifts. Regardless, the joy and happiness a wedding represents include the giving of gifts to celebrate that happiness, and the printing of "No Gifts, Please" on the invitation is not acceptable. Again, family members and attendants can share this information with guests or can provide the name of a favorite charity to which guests may contribute in lieu of giving a nuptial gift.

- **The inclusion of "No Children."** Never print "No Children" or "Adults Only" on an invitation. The way an invitation is addressed, whether on the outer or inner envelope, indicates exactly who is—and by omission who is not—invited to the wedding.

- **Bulletin board invitations.** It is not a good idea to post an invitation on a bulletin board at work. It implies that anyone reading it is welcome to attend, and each person may feel he or she is also welcome to bring a spouse, a date, or children—which would surely skew the count for the reception. Instead, it is better for each person to receive his or her own invitation at home, not at work, particularly if some colleagues are invited and others are not.

- **Dictating dress.** It is incorrect to put "Black Tie" or "White Tie" on the invitation to the ceremony. If it seems essential to include this directive, it can be added only to the invitation to the reception and is placed in the lower-right-hand corner. Avoid writing "Black tie invited" or "Black tie preferred," as these phrases can be confusing.

- **Labels.** Do not use labels to address wedding invitation envelopes, even when inviting hundreds of guests. Instead, plan ahead and take the time to handwrite (or hire a calligrapher to do so) every envelope, so that it is in keeping with the personal tone of the wedding.

- **Choice of entrée.** It is preferable not to put entrée choices on the response card or the envelope. If you are offering menu choices, work out arrangements with the club, restaurant, or caterer to provide French service—where each waitstaff member carries a tray with both or all entrées already plated and offers each guest his or her choice—or have the waitstaff ask each guest his or her preference at the table before serving. The waitstaff could also offer a little of each entrée to each guest. Note: Some reception sites simply do not allow guests to make menu choices on the day of the wedding. If this is the case for you, you may correctly include the entrée choices on the response card for attending guests to check their selection.

- **Alcohol information.** It is unnecessary to put "Alcohol-Free" or "Wine and Beer Only" on the invitation. Surely this information will not be the deciding factor as to whether or not guests attend. You are inviting them to a wedding, not a cocktail party.

- **Don't underestimate your time.** Count on the printing of your invitations and their related inserts to take six to eight weeks. Keep in mind that in the case of a large, formal wedding, invitations should be mailed six to eight weeks in advance. Factor in the fact that it can take an extraordinarily long time to address, assemble, and mail invitations. Don't underestimate the time this takes. Allow several extra weeks in your schedule to prepare your invitations for mailing.

- **Don't mix typefaces.** Once you have selected a typeface for your invitation, stick with it for all related printed insertions and other printed material. The typeface you choose is part of your overall theme, and even though you may love both a shaded roman and a flowery script, you should avoid mixing them.

- **Don't offend your guests.** Inviting people at the last minute makes it obvious that they are last-minute invitees—a notion that will make them feel more unwelcome than if you had not invited them at all.

Miscellaneous Stationery Items

SAVE-THE-DATE CARDS

Save-the-date cards, giving advance notice of an upcoming wedding, can be very helpful to guests who must make travel plans or when the wedding will be held at a time when there may be conflicts with other activities, such as on major holiday weekends. They are especially helpful for alerting guests about a destination wedding. Save-the-date cards are also increasingly sent for other social events such as formal parties and charity balls.

Save-the-date cards are usually mailed from three to four months prior to the wedding or event, but may be sent earlier for a destination wedding at a distant location. Cards can be sent to all guests or only to those who need more time to plan. Be sure that everyone who receives a save-the-date card also receives an invitation.

Printed on single standard-invitation-size or postcardlike cards, save-the-date cards can be informal or formal to match the style of the upcoming wedding or event. The more informal ones might be colorful. The usual wording is as follows:

Please save the date of
Saturday, June 5, 2009
[or for a formal card: *Saturday, the fifth of June/two thousand and five*]
for the wedding of
Angie Henrickson
and
Jim Marrero
[or full names for a formal card]
Invitations to follow [this line optional]
Mr. and Mrs. Byron Henrickson [the hosts]

CEREMONY PROGRAMS

Programs can be smart additions to your ceremony and are especially helpful to guests of other religions who may not be familiar with your service. This is particularly true when the wedding is a mix of religions and cultures and not all guests necessarily understand the liturgy or ritual. Programs are not Broadway playbills, however, nor are they a forum for lengthy biographies of the bride, the groom, their attendants, or their families. (*Very* brief bios are okay.) Under no circumstances should programs be advertisements for wedding service providers, such as florists or consultants. They may, however, be embellished with art, poetry, or fine calligraphy or may simply list the order of the service in a fold-over bulletin. (These bulletins can often be ordered from the diocese, synod, or home center of the church, synagogue, or other house of worship or they can be printed on a desktop publishing system.) Ushers hand programs to guests as they seat them, or children can hand them out as guests arrive. Programs can also be placed in pews or on chairs or in baskets by the door. Flower girls can offer them to arriving guests if the girls are at the ceremony site early and are not arriving with the rest of the bridal party.

Program elements can include:

- The processional

- The service music

- Translations

- The order of the service

- An explanation of the symbolic meaning of service components

- The text for group prayers or readings

- A poem or thought of thanks and love

- The names of soloists (particularly if they are contributing their talents as a gift to the couple), the officiant(s), and the attendants, altar assistants, organist, and readers.

PLACE CARDS

While the use and placement of place cards and table cards is discussed in Chapter 15, "Planning the Reception," page 285: "Place Cards," they are mentioned here because they are a stationery item that is often ordered with the other paper and printed items. Place cards and table cards should be written or calligraphied in one hand. Because they will all be presented together on one table, they should have a uniform look. Place cards may be decorated, have a gold or colored border, or be simple white or colored fold-over card stock. Place card forms are available at better stationers. Place cards created and printed by computer (using 8½″ × 11″ sheets to run through a laser printer) are acceptable as long as the typeface chosen looks handwritten and as long as the individual place cards are separated carefully with no rough edges left to indicate that they were from a computer-designed tear-off form.

PRINTED ACCESSORIES AND FAVORS

Some couples like to have personalized cocktail napkins, matchbooks, or other memorabilia at their receptions. If this is your choice, it is a good idea to see if they can be done by the printer who is printing your invitations, announcements, and other inserts. Sometimes you can get a better price when ordering everything from one source.

PERSONAL STATIONERY

Don't forget to order stationery for your thank-you notes. Fold-over note cards are perfect for this purpose and can be printed with your monogram or name on the front. Remember: The groom can also write thank-you notes. You might want to order "his" and "her" stationery to use before you are married and at the same time order stationery with your married name, monogram, or initials to use after you are married. "Mr. and Mrs." stationery or a monogram of just the initial of your last name can be used by both of you.

Newspaper Wedding Notice

Most newspapers request wedding information at least three weeks before the big day. The wedding announcement generally appears the day following the ceremony. Since newspapers often receive more wedding announcements than they can print, the sooner yours is sent and the clearer and more concise the information, the better your chance of having it published. Each paper generally uses as much of the information as it wishes and rewrites it to match the paper's style. It is a good idea to call the paper ahead of time and request a form, but in general you should provide the following:

> *Bride's full name and town of residence*
>
> *Bride's parents' names and town of residence*
>
> *Bride's parents' occupations*

Bride's maternal and paternal grandparents

Bride's school and college

Bride's occupation

Groom's full name and town of residence

Groom's parents' names and town of residence

Groom's parents' occupations

Groom's maternal and paternal grandparents

Groom's school and college

Groom's occupation

Date of wedding

Location of wedding and reception

Names of bride's attendants and relationship to bride or groom, if any

Names of groom's attendants and relationship to bride or groom, if any

Description of bridal gown and bouquet (optional)

Description of attendants' gowns (optional)

Name of minister, priest, rabbi, or other officiant

Name of soloist, if any

Where couple will honeymoon

Where couple will reside (town) after wedding

Photograph of bride or couple

If a photograph of the bride is to be included, the photo needs to be taken in time to be provided with the announcement information. If a photograph of the bride and groom together is to be included, the announcement is usually printed a week or two after the wedding so that a portrait can be taken on the day of the wedding.

CHAPTER 8

GIFTS OF LOVE

WEDDING GIFTS HAVE A LONG HISTORY. In ancient cultures, whole communities celebrated weddings as times of renewal and hope for the future. Each union was greeted as the beginning of a new family, and families ensured the survival of the community. Wedding couples were showered with symbols of fidelity, fertility, and prosperity. In many cultures, household items were given to help newlyweds establish their home and prepare for children.

The showering of gifts on the newly betrothed is a tradition that seems to become only more deeply ingrained with time. And no wonder: Wedding-gift giving has become big business. Still, the idea behind wedding gifts is a fine one. Gifts are a tangible representation of love and support, a generous offering to help young marrieds get a head start in their lives together. Wedding gifts may be practical or fanciful, inexpensive or extravagant, but each one represents the giver's happiness for the bride and groom.

In this chapter, you'll learn the do's and dont's of gift registries and the guidelines for the newest registries such as honeymoon- and charitable-gift registries. You'll learn how to keep track of the gifts you receive, how to politely communicate your gift suggestions to your guests, and tips on the most gracious and timely ways to express your thanks.

For guests, gift giving for weddings can flummox even the most sophisticated. From the engagement to the shower to the main event, this chapter covers gift giving for all types of wedding celebrations—the what, when, how, and how much.

Gift Registries

Throughout most of the twentieth century, brides typically registered with only one or two stores, listing their patterns for traditional household gifts, including fine and everyday china, crystal, silverware, and linens. Wedding guests could select a place setting or serving piece within a couple's pattern, and experienced salespeople kept track of what was purchased. This kind of registry still prevails, but there have been some major changes to how gift registries work these days.

While the tradition of registering at department and gift stores continues to be popular, more and more couples are selecting other types of gifts—particularly in second- and third-time marriages, where multiple sets of china and crystal have already been amassed. The practice of registering items at different types of specialty stores is now very much in vogue, with creative retailers offering registries for nontraditional wedding gifts. Couples can register with stores specializing in items including hardware, garden supplies, and sporting goods. Computers enable national chains and catalogers to track gift purchases at all their outlets. (See also Chapter 9, pages 172–173: "On-Line Gift Registries.")

In addition, more and more grooms are involved in setting up the couple's wish lists. Major home and appliance centers, for example, tend to have items well suited to grooms' interests and tastes. The use of computerized scanning "guns" has caught on, with many a groom seen walking through stores "zapping" items for their registry lists.

Today's gift registries remain a convenience for guests, especially those who don't know a couple's tastes, have little time for shopping, or live at a distance and can't shop at local stores. But many guests enjoy shopping for gifts and take pleasure in selecting "just the right thing," and no one is obligated to select an item from the couple's gift registry.

WHEN, WHAT, AND HOW TO REGISTER

If you plan to register, do it as soon as you can, and complete the process before your wedding invitations are sent. Registering simply means completing a list of things you would like to have, in the quantity you would like to have them. You can register even if you're marrying on a short schedule, so guests can shop after the wedding. Encore couples should also register.

Stores will do their best to see that you receive the gifts you want, and many retailers can assist you by determining whether your registry includes the right number of gifts based on the number of invited guests. The following suggestions should help you select registry items wisely and with consideration for your guests:

Do think about what you need. A registry is a "wish list," based on your real needs and lifestyle. If your style is casual, you may not be interested in fine china and silver. On the other hand, you may look forward to the time when your life is more formal and want to register for more traditional gifts. Whatever you select, be sure that you and your spouse-to-be agree on the choices.

Do leave the choice of gifts to your guests. Always remember: No dictating to guests what they "must" select for you. It's a guest's prerogative to choose. Sometimes, a gift is not selected from a couple's registry at all; in fact, surprises are often the best gifts of all.

Do register items in a variety of price ranges. Just as guests have varying budgets, so your list should contain items in different price ranges. It's the courteous thing to do. Also, your registries may include choices for more moderately priced shower gifts.

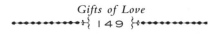

Do register with national chains and/or catalog services when possible. This makes gift selection easier, especially for out-of-town guests. They can order through the stores' Internet sites, major planning sites such as www.weddingchannel.com, catalogs, toll-free numbers, or local branch stores. There's no limit on the number of stores where you may register, but be sensible.

Don't register for the same items at different stores. Since retailers do not coordinate information with other retailers, you might receive many more of an item than you want.

Do politely inform guests of your registries. It's best done the "old-fashioned" way, via word of mouth. Wait until someone asks either you or one of your relatives or friends. Then, it's okay to say where you are registered. If asked directly, a courteous response not only includes retailer names but also your kind comment: "*Whatever* you choose would be special. Thanks for thinking of us!"

Don't include any lists of registries in your wedding invitation. Although at first glance it might seem practical, including registry information offends others. Guests report being turned off by receiving wedding invitations that include "what-to-buy-us" lists. Why? The emphasis on gifts seems more important than the invitation to join a couple on their special day. Also don't include registry lists in engagement party invitations or wedding announcements. However, it's okay for shower hosts to include your registry information in invitations, because gift giving is the highlight of a shower.

Do monitor your registry. Most guests select gifts in the week or two just before the wedding day. As your day approaches, check your registries to make sure that items remain on the lists. Add choices in varying price ranges, as necessary, so that your guests who shop at the last minute have something to choose from.

GETTING THE WORD OUT

The tried-and-true method of telling people about your gift registry is word of mouth. Once you've registered, provide your parents, your attendants, and anyone else who is close to you with a list of your registry sources, their addresses, and how to contact them via phone and Internet. Most people know to ask a couple's close family and friends—or the bride or groom directly—about registries.

It's worth stating again: *Do not include registry lists or information of any kind about gifts in your wedding invitation,* even though store personnel may tell you that this is okay. There are stories of some couples mailing registry lists with their invitations, only to offend their guests with the emphasis on gifts seeming more important than joining them on their wedding day.

REGISTRY ALTERNATIVES

Not every couple is comfortable registering, and not everyone needs or wants tangible items. Alternatives, like the following, can fulfill your wishes, can help your guests with gift selection, and may even spread your happiness in unexpected directions.

No registry. Couples do not have to register for gifts. If you plan an intimate wedding or your guests are all family and friends who know your tastes and needs, there may be no reason to register. Or you might register at only one or two locations for a limited number of items.

Charitable gifts. Couples who don't want gifts might steer guests to special charities and nonprofit services. Give close family and friends a list of the causes and contact information you consider worthwhile and ask them to inform other guests. Established charities will notify you of donations made in your name. It's advisable to avoid political or highly controversial causes. Some people may not hear about your desire or may prefer to give more traditional gifts, so be gracious if you receive traditional items.

Financial registries. Check with your bank or investment house about financial gifts; some now have registries for savings accounts, stocks, bonds, and other investment vehicles. There are even registries for couples who are saving for down payments on houses or automobiles. One caveat: If you want monetary gifts, let your family and friends tell others. Don't initiate discussion about your desire for funds or imply that money matters most to you.

Cash and checks. Cash gifts are perfectly acceptable *if* the guest feels comfortable with the idea. (Although cash gifts are traditional in some areas and ethnic groups, some people just don't like to give money, and that's their prerogative.) If asked, a couple might say, "We're saving for dining room furniture, so if you like the idea of giving a check as a gift, that's how we will use it. Whatever you decide would be terrific!"

Honeymoon registries. Now available through many travel companies and agents, these registries allow guests to contribute to a couple's honeymoon-trip fund. Just be sure you work with a reputable company and that they have a system for advising you of each person's gift.

All About Wedding Gifts

A gift is, by definition, voluntary. Although gifts are customarily expected for some occasions, including weddings, this is a matter of social convention, and no one should regard a gift as an entitlement. Local and cultural traditions may influence gift choices and methods of delivery or presentation, but as every child knows, receiving gifts is a thrill; and that childhood pleasure will bubble up again when your wedding gifts begin to arrive. Knowing the following fundamentals of wedding-gift etiquette should increase the fun of every unwrapping and enhance your appreciation of the gift, the giver, and your own responsibilities as the recipients.

When should wedding gifts be opened? It's especially delightful when couples open their gifts together, but circumstances don't always cooperate, as when the future bride and groom live some distance apart. Don't put off opening gifts, however; delays will hold up your thank-you notes and may cause red faces when you run into a friend whose unopened package you've squirreled away for a week or two.

Is a wedding gift expected? Yes. Following long-established tradition, everyone who receives a wedding invitation should send a gift—whether they attend the wedding or not. There are a few exceptions: If you send invitations to casual acquaintances, business associates you don't know well, or people you haven't seen in years and they do not attend the festivities, then gifts are not expected.

Married couples and nuclear families generally send one gift, as do couples who live together. When you invite someone "and Guest," the person you invite is responsible for a gift, but the guest or date isn't. Group giving, when guests pool their resources to purchase a more elaborate gift, is fine.

What about wedding gifts for encore couples? Wedding gifts for encore couples (either the bride, the groom, or both have been married before) are optional. Guests who have attended a prior wedding of the bride or groom and given a gift then are under no obligation to give another. Still, there are some close friends and relatives of couples who know this but want to give a present anyway, to share in the couple's happiness. They certainly may, if they wish. New friends who had not attended a first wedding for either member of the couple may also want to give something, and usually do, unless the word has been spread that the couple requests no gifts. (See also Chapter 13, pages 243–244: "Gifts, the Second Time Around.")

How much should guests spend on gifts? A wedding gift is a social obligation, but the choice of the gift is based on the giver's affection for and relationship to the couple and their families, and on the gift giver's financial capabilities. People have tried to come up with formulas and average dollar amounts. One, for example, is a pure myth that each guest should spend an amount on their gift that is equal to the per-person amount spent on a guest at the reception. Expecting this kind of tit-for-tat exchange is impractical and thoughtless.

When are gifts sent? Traditionally, gifts may be sent as soon as the wedding invitation arrives, and some may come earlier if people know for certain that they'll be invited. Most guests send gifts before the wedding, but gifts may arrive afterward, particularly when the wedding is held on short notice.

Gifts should be delivered as close to the wedding date as possible, but circumstances such as an invitee's illness may cause a delay, and couples shouldn't question a late arrival. Some guests think they have up to a year after a wedding to send gifts; not the case (although "it's never too late," one year is neither correct nor the norm).

When you receive a gift that has been mailed or shipped and you're unable to write a thank-you note immediately, it's thoughtful to tell the giver (in person, in a phone call, or via e-mail) that the item has arrived. Regardless of whether you thank the person verbally, *every wedding gift must be acknowledged with a written thank-you note.* (See also "The Importance of 'Thank You,'" pages 162–166).

In some localities and certain ethnic and religious groups, it's customary for guests to take their gifts to the wedding ceremony or reception. In some cases, gifts in the form of checks are handed to the bride or groom in the receiving line or at another time during the reception. If gifts are brought to the celebration, they should be placed on a table set up for them and in a safe place. Newlyweds are not expected to open the gifts during the reception, but they should arrange to have someone oversee the packages and transport them to a secure place afterward.

How are gifts delivered? Gifts are usually sent by mail or delivery service. Traditionally, gifts are addressed to the bride and delivered to her or her parents' home before the wedding, or addressed to the couple and sent to their home after the wedding. Today, gifts may be addressed to both the bride- and groom-to-be, and sent to both of them if they are already living together. Gifts may also be sent to the groom or his family if that's most convenient. When gifts are being delivered to different people and different addresses, communication among the couple and their families is important, and you must keep an accurate record of what has been received and when gifts arrive.

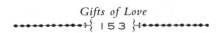

Is record-keeping really necessary? Yes, absolutely. Gift cards can easily be lost or mixed up, and it's hard to remember who gave what. Keeping a record helps you associate specific gifts with the givers, so you can say something nice when you next see your guests and personalize your thank-you note. A detailed list also serves as a record for insurance purposes.

Most couples keep a written or computer-based log, recording information as soon as gifts arrive. This information should include:

- **The date the gift is received.** Also note how it was shipped in case there is damage or breakage.

- **A clear description of the item or items.** Writing "platter" won't help much if you receive three or four. Be specific: "18-inch pottery platter, sunflower design." Include the quantities of multiple items ("4 monogrammed pillowcases, pale blue").

- **The source of the gift.** Store, catalog service, etc., if known.

- **The name and address of the giver or givers.** Save gift cards to double-check spellings.

- **A notation of when your thank-you note is sent.**

It's also a good idea to number the gifts in your log and attach the corresponding number to each gift. If gifts are going to several addresses, be sure that everyone who might take delivery knows to jot down the date, the delivery service, and other pertinent information and to attach the note securely to the package. If children might accept deliveries, instruct them clearly on how to handle and where to store packages. Another tip: Open deliveries as soon as you can. You may be expecting something from a store, but don't assume that the store's label on a shipping package means that it contains the item you bought. It could be a gift.

What happens to the gifts if the wedding is canceled? The gifts must be returned. This means that all wedding, shower, and any engagement gifts are sent back to the gift givers. All monetary gifts are to be returned, too. Possible exceptions to returning gifts: monogrammed items, gifts you've already used, or items that the givers insist you keep. In these latter cases, it's your judgment call as to how to "return." You might want to do something nice (a treat such as a gift, a dinner out) for the gift giver.

If it is too difficult to return gifts in person, they may be sent by mail with an accompanying note. (See also Chapter 1, page 16, for a sample note). This is generally the woman's responsibility, since gifts are traditionally sent to the bride-to-be, but the man may also do the returning.

In the event that one of the couple passes away before the wedding takes place, gifts may be kept. However, the bride or groom who is left without a mate might prefer to return gifts that are painful reminders of the loss.

Wedding-Celebration Gifts

ENGAGEMENT-PARTY GIFTS

Except when part of a couple's culture, no engagement gifts are expected, regardless of whether there is an engagement party. Engagement gifts, if given, are generally tokens of affection (for example, picture frames, guest books or photo albums, bottles of good wine, sets of guest towels) and not too expensive. (See also Chapter 1, page 11: "A Question for Peggy: Gifts for Engagement Parties?")

SHOWER GIFTS

Unless culture and custom rule that shower gifts should be the equivalent of wedding presents, gifts given to the bride or engaged couple at a shower should not be elaborate. Years ago, shower gifts were handmade for the occasion, and while such gifts are still treasured, most shower guests buy the gifts these days. Shower gifts should be appropriate to the shower if the shower has a theme, such as a kitchen, lingerie, or bar shower. Sometimes, guests contribute to a joint gift for the bride or the couple, but no one should be told they must participate, and no other shower gift is expected from people who do contribute.

- **If a guest can't attend, must she send a gift?** If an invited guest can't attend the shower, it is not obligatory that she send a gift. Sometimes, close friends or relatives wish to, however, which is fine. If a nonattending invitee does send a gift, she should send it directly to the shower hostess, and not from the store directly to the bride. The gift should be accompanied by a card to let the guest of honor know the name of the donor.

- **When are shower gifts opened?** Shower gifts are opened at the party, and each guest is thanked personally then and there.

- **Are thank-you notes required for shower gifts?** Yes. Even though the bride (or couple, if given a couple's shower) might have thanked guests in person, she should still send written thank-you notes. Why? Most people *expect* a note for their shower gifts. Also, with showers having grown more elaborate with more guests than in previous times, it's difficult for each guest to fully be thanked in person.

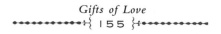

ANOTHER SHOWER, ANOTHER GIFT?

Q: *I am my best friend's maid of honor and as such am invited to two showers. I know I'm not required to give a gift at these showers, but I would like to present a token of my affection for the bride—maybe even something she could really use on her wedding day. Any thoughts?*

A: The maid of honor is not expected to take a gift to each shower and party she is invited to, but she can bring a small token. A great gift idea, especially coming from the maid of honor, who is supposed to be the bride's most important helper, is a little emergency kit for the day of the wedding. In it she could place an extra pair of panty hose, a mirror, hair spray, hairpins, a small comb, a nail file and nail polish, all sizes of safety pins, a small sewing kit, white masking tape, a package of tissues, bottled water, breath mints, scissors, super-adhesive glue, and packages of hand wipes.

- **Is it appropriate to have a gift shower for an encore bride?** It is perfectly acceptable to have a shower for a second marriage or for an older couple who have been independent for a number of years. For couples who may already have all of the basic necessities, food showers, garden showers, and ticket (to some entertainment) showers may be more appropriate than traditional kitchen or linen showers. In general, the guest list is made up of new friends of the bride or couple, or very close friends and relatives. Other than the closest of friends, it is better not to invite guests who attended a shower for the first marriage.

- **How to keep a shower simple.** Conscious of the financial burden that shower gifts, plus wedding gifts, can place on friends, considerate couples and shower hosts often choose a clever low-cost themed event such as a recipe shower or a best-wishes shower. For more ideas, see also Chapter 10, page 178: "Showers on a Shoestring."

GIFTS FOR THE WEDDING PARTY

Gifts are often exchanged among members of the wedding party, and gifts from the bride and groom to their attendants are considered especially important.

Bride and groom's gifts. It's traditional for the bride and groom to give a special gift of appreciation to each attendant. Usually the bride chooses the gift for her bridesmaids and the groom for his groomsmen and/or ushers, but a couple might give the same gift to everyone. (Glassware, picture frames, engagement books, and decorative boxes are typical of gifts that cross gender lines.) Gifts need not be expensive but should be a meaningful commemoration of the occasion. This is not the place for joke presents.

If you have children in your wedding, personal and age-appropriate gifts will be a special treat for each youngster.

Gifts to attendants are usually presented at the rehearsal dinner, at the rehearsal if there is no dinner, or at bridesmaids' and groomsmen's parties. Sometimes gifts are presented at the wedding, but there's always the risk they could be mislaid or stolen.

Attendants' gifts. Wedding attendants often present gifts to the bride and groom, though this isn't an absolute. The expense of being in a wedding can put a serious strain on an attendant's budget, so couples need to be sensitive. If attendants host a prenuptial party or give shower presents in addition to their individual wedding gift, a considerate couple will be clear that no other gifts are expected. (You might tell your honor attendants of your wishes, and ask them to speak to the other attendants.) Although costly gifts shouldn't be expected in any case, a group gift—bridesmaids to the bride, groomsmen/ushers to the groom, or all attendants to the couple—can be the ideal way to express love and best wishes at the least expense for each attendant.

Attendants' gifts are usually presented at bridesmaids' and groomsmen's parties, at the rehearsal or rehearsal dinner, or possibly at the reception, when other gifts are taken to the wedding.

Gifts to each other. Though not essential, couples often give each other personal engagement and wedding gifts, in addition to their rings. Gifts can range from jewelry engraved with the wedding date or a special sentiment to fun items to share in your new life together.

Gifts for family. Though not expected, gifts for parents, stepparents, and grandparents are a lovely tribute to the people who have cherished and supported you both through thick and thin. Expense isn't the issue: A family gift can be as simple as a rose and a loving note placed on their seats at the ceremony or a small book of verse or meditations with a special personal inscription. Gifts are very important for the young and teenage children of either or both of the couple (see also Chapter 13, pages 237–239: "When Children Are Involved)."

Wedding announcements. Sent soon after the marriage to inform people who were not invited to the wedding, announcements are a courtesy and carry no obligation for a gift. Some people may send gifts, but you shouldn't expect them.

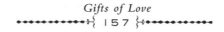

Monogramming Gifts

Traditional monograms for married people consist of three initials (the bride's) or the last-name initial only (the husband's). But today, with couples using both last names and some wives keeping their maiden names, monograms can be a bit more complicated.

Initials in a couple's monogram generally include first names. However, a middle-name initial can be substituted if that is the name a person uses. The initial of a nickname is not normally included in a monogram.

The following chart should help couples and gift givers choose the type of monogram that best suits items. The order of initials depends on whether the letters are of the same size or the last name is centered. The monograms illustrated below are for a couple named Judith Alice Brown and Thomas Roland Neuberger.

	When Initials Are the Same Size	When Center Initial Is Larger	Single Initial
Single woman (used for personal items and stationery before marriage)	First, Middle, Last JAB	First, Last, Middle JBA	Last B
Single man (used for personal items and stationery before and after marriage)	First, Middle, Last TRN	First, Last, Middle TNR	Last N
Married couple		Initials of Wife's First Name, Couple's Last Name (Husband's), Husband's First Name JNT	Married/Last Name N
* Married woman (for (for personal items andstationery)	First, Maiden Name, Married/Last Name JBN	First, Married/Last Name, Maiden Name JNB	Married/Last Name N
Married couple with hyphenated last name		Wife's First Name, Hyphenated Married Name, Husband's First JB-NT	Hyphenated Last Name B-N

Married woman with hyphenated married/ last name (married men use the same form)	First, Middle, Hyphenated Last name JAB-N (or) First, Hyphenated Last Name: JB-N	First, Hyphenated Last Name, Middle JB-NA	Hyphenated Last Name B-N
Married couple when wife keeps her maiden name	Wife's Maiden-Name and Husband's Last-Name Initials Separated by a Dot, Diamond Shape, or Other Design: B ● N		

*Women who remarry do not use initials from previous marriages in monograms. Follow the forms above, using your maiden name and new married-name initials.

When having a wedding gift monogrammed, givers should be guided by the way a couple plans to write their name(s). If you aren't sure of the correct monogram, you might check with the couple's parents, one of their attendants, or the couple directly.

Some tips for the monogramming of specific items include:

Monogramming linens. Many people today prefer the single last-name initial or hyphenated initials. The other monogram choices are also appropriate. Towels are marked at the center of one end. Rectangular tablecloths are monogrammed at the center of each long side, and square cloths at one corner. Dinner napkins are marked diagonally at one corner or centered. Top sheets are monogrammed so that when the sheet is folded down, the letters can be read by someone standing at the foot of the bed. Pillowcase monograms are centered approximately two inches above the hem.

Monogramming flatware. If silver flatware is monogrammed, a triangle of block letters—last-name initial below and the first-name initials of the bride and groom above—works well on modern patterns. If a single initial is used, it is the last-name initial of the groom.

Monograms on flat silver are usually placed so that the top of the letter is toward the end of the handle. In other words, when the piece is on the table, the monogram is upside down as seen by the diner at that place. If you prefer, you can have initials engraved the other way, so that they can be read by the diner.

Displaying Wedding Gifts

Whether to display gifts is your decision. Gift displays are for the home. Because of transportation and security problems, gifts are rarely put on view in hotels, clubs, restaurants, and reception halls. Security is always an issue; thieves search the newspapers for wedding days and times. If you're uneasy, you can hire a guard to watch the house when everyone is away. Also check with your insurer about additional coverage for gifts.

How to display. Gifts can be displayed during a home reception or for guests who are invited to stop by in the days before or after the wedding. Sometimes couples or their parents host a tea or cocktail event at which the gifts are on display—usually in a separate room from the party area. Normally, gifts are placed on a table or tables covered with cloths or sheets; the covering can drape to the floor so that boxes can be hidden underneath. Shower and engagement presents are not usually included in displays.

Tactful displays. Organize the table so that there's no visual comparison between the items. For instance, don't place a single piece of silverplate next to an elaborate sterling service. Sometimes, gifts are arranged by purpose: utilitarian items such as kitchen equipment or hardware on tables or areas separate from china and silver. With tableware, a single place setting (two if you have formal and everyday settings) is displayed rather than all the plates, utensils, and glasses you've received. If you receive multiples of any item, display only one.

Display cards. There's no rule about displaying gift cards. Some couples think that who gave what is a private matter. But showing cards can be a nice acknowledgment and save you from endless "Who sent that?" questions. You can place the cards with each gift or arrange them in a separate spot, overlapping cards so that the givers' names show. If you show one giver's name, however, you should show every name. People who do not see their names on your display may worry that their gifts never arrived or, worse, that you don't value their gifts.

Cards are advantageous when you receive large items that are difficult to display. On a folded card (small note size), write the item and the name of the giver or givers ("Gas Outdoor Grill" on the first line, followed by the names in the order they appeared on the gift card); then prop the card among the gifts on the display table.

Displaying checks. The custom of displaying gift checks is waning, largely because financial gifts come in so many forms—certificates, cash, contributions to bank and investment accounts. Should you receive financial gifts of different sorts, listing the givers, but not the amounts, in your gift-record book may be the best approach (see also "Is record-keeping really necessary?" page 154). When checks are displayed, the amounts are never revealed. Checks are overlapped so that only the signatures are visible. Place plain paper over the top check to cover the bank name and the amount. Secure the checks to the table, so they can't be lifted or moved; a sheet of clear glass or acrylic over the checks should keep them safe and sound. Be sure to deposit checks fairly promptly, and keep a private record of the amount of each one.

Exchanging and Returning Gifts

What can be done with duplicate presents? You may discreetly exchange duplicate presents. If friends who have given a gift realize that you have more than one, they should encourage you to exchange theirs for something else.

Can unwanted gifts be exchanged? If a gift is not a duplicate but rather is something you neither like nor need, you may exchange it—unless it is from a close friend who would be hurt if he or she found out. If the gift was from someone you rarely see, simply write a thank-you note for the gift, even though you've exchanged it. You should not, however, exchange the presents chosen for you by your own families unless you are specifically told to do so. Nor should you discard a gift that was made especially for you.

Do I have to let the giver know I exchanged his or her gift? When you write a thank-you note for a duplicate gift that you have exchanged, simply thank the giver for the present with enthusiasm. You don't have to explain that you exchanged the gift for something else.

What do I do if a gift arrives broken? If a gift that was sent directly from the donor arrives broken, immediately check the wrapping to see if it was insured. If so, notify the person who sent it at once so that he or she can collect the insurance and replace it. If it was not insured, you may not want to mention that it arrived broken; otherwise the person who gave it may feel obligated to replace it. When a broken gift arrives directly from a store, simply take it back without mentioning a thing to the donor. Any reputable store will replace merchandise that arrives damaged.

Is it proper to return a gift to the donor? The only time that gifts are returned is when a marriage is either canceled or immediately annulled. When wedding plans are canceled, gifts that have already been received must be returned. If there is simply an indefinite postponement, but the couple still intends to be married, the gifts that have arrived are put

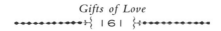

away carefully until such time as the ceremony takes place. If after a period of six weeks to two months, it becomes doubtful that the wedding will take place at all, the couple must send the gifts back to donors to return.

The Importance of "Thank You"

There are two fundamentals of expressing gratitude. First, every gift—whether a tangible item, money, a social event in your honor, or a gift of time or talent—should be acknowledged in writing. And second, your acknowledgment should be prompt.

Personal, handwritten thank-yous remain the gold standard of courtesy in this age of cell phones, pocket computers, and instant messaging. Written notes demonstrate that the writer cares enough about the giver to compose an individualized message and put the words on paper.

HOW TO THANK

Respond in a timely fashion. Ideally, you'll write on the day you receive a wedding gift. If you put off all note writing until after the wedding, it can truly become a chore. In fact, it is both wise and correct to write thank-you notes for any gifts received before the wedding. For couples stymied by the large number of notes to be written, a good suggestion is to set a daily goal. Completing three or four notes each day doesn't seem nearly so impossible as writing a hundred notes within a month. The accepted standard: Your thank-you notes should be written and sent *within three months* of receipt of each gift.

Share the responsibility. The days when thank-yous were the sole duty of the bride are over. Today's brides and grooms share the responsibility, which greatly decreases the time involved, and each writes to the people he or she knows best. This makes it easier to tailor notes to the individual givers.

Include your fiancé/fiancée or new spouse in the thanks. Though you sign your notes with your own name, your message expresses gratitude from both of you. There may be exceptions (when someone does a favor or entertains specifically for you), but in general people are giving to you as a couple.

Don't take shortcuts. Simply signing store-bought cards shows very little consideration. Likewise, writing virtually the same message to everyone is mechanical, and people quickly recognize a "fill-in-the-blanks" note. If you have a Web page, you might put up a general thanks to everyone for sharing your special day, but this is not an acceptable substitute for personal notes. Stationery printed with "Thank You" or a short quotation or verse is fine, so long as you write your own note. But it's unacceptable to use a card with a pre-printed message.

WHOM TO THANK

As you write notes, remember that not all gifts come wrapped in pretty paper. The following categories include both gift givers and the people who make a wedding special through their efforts and goodwill:

Everyone who gives you a wedding present. This includes people who literally hand you a present, no matter how effusively you thank them in person. You should write to each person or couple who contributed to a group gift. The one exception is a group gift from more than four or five coworkers. (See "People who entertain for you," page 164.)

Note: Thank-you notes are expected for shower gifts even though you thanked the givers in person when presents were opened. Written notes must also be sent to anyone who couldn't attend the shower but sent a gift.

WHAT KIND OF STATIONERY?

There's no single stationery required for thank-you notes, though you'll probably use a standard one-sided or single-fold note card and matching envelope. The paper can be plain or bordered, white, ecru, ivory, or a pastel color. Use ink that's easy to read; black ink is always legible.

A bride signs with her maiden name (or pre-marriage name, if an encore bride) before the wedding, married name afterward. When using monogrammed stationery, the notes sent by the bride before the wedding have her maiden name initials; post-wedding notes have her married initials or the couple's last-name initial.

Grooms write thank-yous, too. When husbands and wives share monogrammed stationery, the last/married-name initial, hyphenated initial, or double last-name initials (when the wife retains her maiden name) are used.

Everyone who gives you money—cash, checks, contributions to savings and investment accounts, donations to designated charities. You can mention amounts if you want, and doing so assures givers that currency arrived intact and account deposits were correct. Always include some indication of how you plan to use a monetary gift.

Anyone who sends you a congratulatory telegram on your wedding day. Though an old custom, this is still done and deserves a note of thanks. E-mail responses are fine for e-mailed congratulations.

Your attendants. In addition to thank-you notes for wedding presents, be sure to attach to the gifts you give your attendants a card or note with a personal sentiment. ("Thanks for everything, baby brother. You really are the *best* best man I could ask for. Love, Mitch.")

People who entertain for you. When there is more than one host for a shower or party, write to each person or couple. These notes should go out no later than two days after the event. The one exception is when a large number of people in your office or workplace host a shower or party in your honor and give a group gift. While it's preferable to thank everyone with an individual note, it is acceptable to write to the organizer or organizers only. Be sure your note includes your appreciation for everyone's participation. The person who receives your note should forward it to coworkers or post it in a common area. But if individual presents are given, write individual notes.

People who house and/or entertain your guests. When family and friends invite out-of-town guests or attendants to stay in their homes, you should write notes to the hosts and send thank-you gifts. The gift, with your card or note attached, might be an item for the home such as a potted plant or a basket of soaps, or something special for the hosts, like tickets to a concert or a book by their favorite author. Friends who entertain your visitors—inviting them to dinner, taking them shopping, showing them the sights—deserve a note from you, though gifts aren't necessary.

People who do kindnesses for you. The neighbor who accepts delivery of your gifts when you're at work, the cousin who supervises guest parking at your reception—anyone who assists you during your preparations, the wedding itself, and after the big event should be graciously thanked. It's also nice to send notes to your officiant and anyone else (the organist or music director, for instance) who worked with you on the ceremony, even though you've paid them the customary fee.

Suppliers and vendors. You don't have to write everyone you hire for services, but anyone who exceeds your expectations will appreciate a courteous note of thanks.

WHAT'S IN A NOTE?

While there's no formula for the perfect thank-you note, the notes people remember are the ones that express real feeling. Think about the people you're thanking before you write anything. How would the conversation go if you were thanking them in person? Another hint: Look at the gift when you prepare to write; it may provide inspiration.

The first two examples below illustrate the difference between a note that gets the job done adequately and one that expressed thanks for a gift and real interest in the givers.

A simple note:

Dear Mr. and Mrs. Gresham,

How did you ever find the beautiful vase? It is perfect in our apartment, and Phil and I thank you for your special gift! We're so sorry you couldn't be with us on our wedding day, but we hope to be back in St. Paul during the holidays and we look forward to seeing you then.

Thanks again for thinking of us in such a nice way.

Love,
Courtney

A more personal note:

Dear Mr. and Mrs. Gresham,

I'm looking right now at the lovely vase you sent and imagining how pretty it will be on our Thanksgiving table next month. (We're hosting Phil's family for the first time!) It really is one of my favorite things, and Phil and I are so grateful to you.

We were both sorry that you couldn't come to the wedding, but I know your trip to New Zealand must have been amazing. If all goes according to plan, we will be in St. Paul for Christmas, and we'd love to see you and the girls and hear about your travels.

Again, thank you so much for the vase and for the beautiful thoughts in your note.

Love from both of us,
Courtney

There's no reason for a note to be stuffy and formal. Write from your heart and the words will come—as they did in this warm and humorous example:

Dear Uncle Jim,

Well, you really saved the day—the Big Day—when my car conked out. If it weren't for you, I'd probably still be standing in front of Bartlett's, hanging on to my tux bag and trying to hail a cab in that downpour. Meg considers you our personal guardian angel. First you get me to the church on time, and then we arrive in Antigua and discover that you've treated us to three days of our trip! I'm enclosing a photo so you can see the incredible view of the ocean from our hotel.

We can't thank you enough for everything you've done. And I promise never to leave home without my jumper cables again.

Much love from your grateful, if forgetful, nephew,

Peter

Ten Do's and Don'ts of Thank-You Notes

This checklist should help couples avoid common missteps when expressing their gratitude in writing:

Do personalize your notes, making reference to the person as well as the gift.

Do be enthusiastic, but you don't need to gush. Avoid saying that a gift is the most beautiful thing you've ever seen, unless you mean it.

Don't send form letters or cards with printed messages and just your signature; don't use e-mail or post generic thank-yous on your Web site in lieu of personal notes.

Don't mention that you plan to return or exchange a gift or indicate dissatisfaction in any way.

Don't tailor notes to the perceived value of gifts. No one should receive a dashed-off, perfunctory note.

Do refer to the use you will make of money gifts. Mentioning the amount is optional.

Don't include wedding photos or use photo cards if this will delay sending notes.

Do promptly acknowledge receipt of shipped gifts; either send your thank-you within a few days or call or e-mail the sender—following up with a written note soon.

Don't use lateness in writing as an excuse not to write. If you're still sending thank-you notes after your first anniversary, keep writing.

Do remember that a gift should be acknowledged with the same courtesy and generous spirit in which it was given.

CHAPTER 9

The New Wedding Helper: Technology

NEW ADVANCES IN TECHNOLOGY have entered the realm of wedding planning with a bang. In particular, the growing use of computers and the Internet has ushered in a sea change in the way wedding preparations are conducted: E-mail now allows you to communicate instantaneously with anybody and everybody involved in your wedding; numerous wedding-planning Web sites offer everything from advice on budgeting to personalized wedding Web pages; and on-line gift registries now give guests the option of shopping for wedding gifts from the world's great stores simply by logging on to the Internet.

As wonderfully convenient as they may be, these advances also bring their own unique etiquette challenges. Sending an inappropriate e-mail, sharing overly personal information on your Web page, or trumpeting your registry information too prominently can backfire and come across as crass, greedy, or disrespectful. To avoid such missteps, keep in mind that no matter how new an invention may be, the basic principles of etiquette always apply in its use. Ask yourself: How does this new technology enable me to treat others with consideration, respect, and honesty—and how might it have the opposite effect? Cell phones, for example, can be a great help in coordinating everyone's activities on your wedding day; but many a ceremony has also been jarred by a ringing cell phone that was left on by an inconsiderate owner. (See "A Question for Peggy: Noises Off: How Can We Stop the Cell Phones?," page 174.)

One thing is certain: Using the latest technologies to streamline the wedding-planning process is here to stay. Here are some tips on how to use these new technologies wisely and appropriately:

The Etiquette of E-Mail

The first thing to remember about e-mail is that just because you *can* send an e-mail doesn't mean you always *should*. The more formal the communication, the more appropriate it is to use postal mail rather than e-mail. A good test of whether it's acceptable to e-mail an invitation or other communication is to ask yourself if you'd feel comfortable extending the same invitation over the phone. If the answer is yes, then e-mail away.

E-mail is also not the place for highly personal or delicate communications, which are best handled in a real-time conversation. Remember, too, that e-mails are *not* private. You should never put anything into an e-mail that you aren't willing to have the whole world read.

When Not to Use E-Mail

For wedding invitations. E-mailing a wedding invitation, even to your closest friend or relative, generally is not appropriate. It's customary always to send each of your guests a printed wedding invitation mailed in an envelope. (See also Chapter 7, "Invitation Etiquette.") The only exception is in the case of highly unusual or rushed circumstances—if, for example, you and your fiancé are moving overseas and you've decided at the last minute to get married before you leave. Again, a good rule of thumb is that if the invitation is so hurried or informal that your alternative is to convey it over the telephone, then using e-mail is acceptable.

For thank-you notes. For each wedding gift you receive, you should always pen a separate handwritten note and send it through the mail. No exceptions, unless you're stuck on an unreachable island. (See also Chapter 8, pages 162–166: "The Importance of 'Thank You.'") If you've fallen behind on your note writing, however, you *can* send an e-mail as a stop-gap measure to let the gift giver know you've received his or her gift and will be sending a formal thank-you soon. ("Wonderful to see you at the wedding. We love the vase! Note to follow . . .") Just remember—this message does *not* replace the actual thank-you note.

When discussing personal or thorny issues. Not only is e-mail not private, but it's also a difficult medium for working out compromises or resolving emotional conflicts. If a tricky issue comes up, pick up the phone and call to talk it over, or arrange to meet face-to-face with the parties involved.

When the groundwork hasn't been properly laid. Similarly, while it's extremely convenient to be able to send out group messages about wedding-related plans via e-mail ("As mother of the groom, I'm pleased to invite you to a bridal shower for my future daughter-in-law . . ."), it's still important to check your plans personally with other key people before announcing them to the world. Otherwise, you run the risk of ruffling feathers ("Why, as mother of the bride, I thought we were going to host the shower together!") and possibly putting a serious damper on the whole event.

When E-Mail Is Appropriate

Aside from the specific instances cited previously, e-mail is generally an acceptable option for wedding-related communications—including the following:

"Save the Date" notices. Many couples, once they've pinned down their wedding day, choose to send out an early informal note alerting friends and family to put that date aside. It's perfectly fine to e-mail this note.

Wedding RSVPs. When sending out your wedding invitations, it is acceptable to give your guests the option of e-mailing their RSVPs to you. Just make sure that it's an option. Simply add a printed sentence at the bottom of your printed response card saying, "You may also reply by way of our e-mail address, which is happycouple@rsvp.com." This is especially appropriate in the case of a last-minute wedding, if you are planning a relatively informal wedding, or if you're already in regular e-mail contact with many of your invited guests.

Wedding announcements. These optional notes, sent out after the wedding itself, typically go to friends and family who were left off the guest list, as well as acquaintances and business associates you think might wish to hear the news. Traditionally, these are printed or handwritten announcements that are sent through the regular mail. (See Chapter 7, pages 128–129: "Wedding Announcements.") While most couples still prefer this more formal way of sharing their happy news, it is also acceptable to send wedding announcements out via e-mail—particularly if you and the recipient are on informal terms or if the wedding itself was an informal affair.

Invitations to informal or casual engagement parties, bridal showers, and other pre-wedding get-togethers. These are all extremely important occasions, and most couples and their families will want to honor this fact by sending out printed invitations. E-mailed invitations can be an acceptable alternative, however, particularly if you are planning an informal affair or the people on your guest list are especially computer-friendly. This is *not* the time for a group e-mail, though—each e-mail should begin with an individual salutation to the intended recipient.

Information on lodging, etc. When sending out your formal wedding invitations, it's also fine to include in each a sheet containing a map and directions for out-of-town guests. To avoid overloading the mailing, however, any other material—including information on hotels, restaurants, and points of local interest—should be sent out in a separate mailing. For those of your guests who are Web-connected, a group e-mail is ideal for this purpose. Simply begin with a general salutation—"Dear All"—and sign off on the e-mail as you would on an individual message.

Wedding updates. Many couples enjoy keeping their family and friends updated on the month-to-month progress of their wedding plans through regular mailed updates. Group e-mails are perfect for this sort of informal communication—and can even make such mailings more feasible, since a single key stroke now replaces the hours needed to assemble, address, and mail ordinary envelopes. Again, though, this convenience factor makes it all the more important to use common sense and consideration whenever e-mailing: Don't flood the in-boxes of your entire guest list with daily news flashes; don't share overly personal details that are best saved for your closest friends; and if you do decide to send out a regular e-mail "wedding newsletter," be sure that you also send a printed copy to any friends and family who are not set up to receive e-mail.

"Wed"-Surfing on the Job

With honeymoon locales to research, Web pages to update, e-mails to answer, and gift purchases to peruse, the temptation to spend hours on-line tending to your wedding plans will be strong—especially when you're at work, with your computer staring you in the face. So what's an ethical employee to do? First, find out what your company's policy is regarding the use of office Internet connections for personal purposes. Some businesses accept it as inevitable; others don't, and may even employ software to block access to non-work-related Web sites. Second, resist the urge to jump on-line when you should be working. Instead, do all wedding-related Web-surfing on your personal time— during coffee breaks or lunch breaks, or before or after office hours.

Assembling Your E-Mailing List

E-mail should be used to augment your communications—and never to limit them. If you plan on sending out any additional mailings to your guest list, be sure to let each guest indicate whether he or she would like to receive these mailings by regular mail or by e-mail. Some guests may not use e-mail at all, while others may check their e-mail accounts only sporadically. The best time to assemble your e-mailing list is immediately after you've drawn up your list of invited guests. It can even be done at the same time you send out your "Save the Date" alert. Phone or drop a note to any invitees you're not in regular e-mail contact with, asking if it would be all right for you to contact them via e-mail about wedding details and, if so, what address you should use. Meanwhile, send out individual e-mails to the people you are already in e-mail contact with, asking them which e-mail address they'd like you to use when sending wedding-related communications. (Some people prefer getting such messages at home rather than at work, for example.)

The most important thing is to avoid leaving anyone out of the loop. Whenever you send out a group e-mail to people on your wedding guest list, *always* mail printed copies of your message to any invited guests you aren't in e-mail contact with.

On-Line Gift Registries

Most major American retailers now have Web sites offering access to the gift registry lists of any couples who are registered with them. It's no understatement to say that this advance—together with the invention of the "zapper," a computerized light gun that lets a couple roam a store, adding gifts to their registry by simply pointing and firing—has revolutionized the experience of giving and receiving gifts. Guests can simply log on to a store's Web site from their home computer, click on the "Gift Registry" link (typically posted on the Web site's home page), and type in the name of the couple, and they'll have instant access to every item on the couple's list that is still available. Meanwhile, you—the couple—can log in anytime you wish to check on which items have been purchased.

As accessible as these on-line registries are, word of their existence should still be spread discreetly, as with any gift registry. You and your close friends and relatives can pass along the Web site addresses once someone asks for them—but not before. Also, don't let convenience beckon you to excess: Registering at two or three stores is plenty, and four is pushing the upper limits. Be careful, too, not to select the same item at two different stores—otherwise, since the stores' lists aren't cross-referenced, you run the risk of getting duplicate gifts. (See also Chapter 8, pages 148–151: "Gift Registries.")

Creating Your Own Wedding Web Site

One of the most popular new trends is for couples to create their own personalized wedding Web pages (sometimes referred to as "wed sites"), which can include photos, information on travel and lodging, wedding-planning updates, an option to RSVP electronically, and even links to department-store gift registries. This is all easier to do than you might think: Wedding-planning Web sites such as Wedding Channel (www.weddingchannel.com) and The Knot (www.theknot.com), besides offering all manner of wedding advice, also provide step-by-step instructions for designing your own free Web page, reachable through their Web addresses. Other Web sites will show you how to create a Web site at your own Web address for a fee. Whichever way you go, keep these guidelines in mind when designing your Internet site:

- **First and foremost, your Web page should be representative of who you are** as a couple. Take the time to develop a design and content that you are both comfortable with—one that reflects your personal aesthetic and style.

- **If you plan to offer people the option of leaving an RSVP on your Web site,** simply *add a printed sentence at the bottom of the reply card* sent out with the invitation, saying, "You may also reply by way of our wedding Web site, www.happycouple.com."

- **As tempting as it may be, don't list your Web site on your actual invitation.** There are plenty of other ways to let people know about the site, such as including the Web address on other items enclosed in the invitation packet (for example, the response card or the directional map).

- **Don't overwhelm your visitors with content.** A few well-designed pages will speak volumes.

- **Don't include overly personal information.** Some pre-designed Web templates prompt you to type in personal details such as when you shared your first kiss, what you did on your first date, and so on. This may be good fodder for a bachelor(ette) party, but there's no need to share such intimate moments with your entire guest list (and whoever else may be peering over their shoulders). Keep your postings tasteful and inclusive—remember, this is a space where you want every visitor to feel comfortable and welcome.

- **Don't overemphasize your gift registry links.** It is perfectly acceptable to post links to your various on-line gift registries on your home page—in fact, these one-stop shopping links are now expected, if only because of their sheer convenience. Still, it's important to strike a balance between discretion and your desire to make things easy for your guests, by placing such links to the side of the page, in modestly sized type.

- **Don't overlook your unwired guests.** Remember, not everyone has ready access to the Internet. If you know that a certain invited guest is not connected to the Web, be sure to send him or her hard copies of any pertinent information posted on your Web page.

- **You can make good use of your Web page after the wedding** as well, by posting pictures from the wedding and honeymoon along with any anecdotes you care to share and, most important, a heartfelt thank-you to everyone involved.

A QUESTION FOR PEGGY:

Noises Off: How Can We Stop the Cell Phones?

Q: I recently attended a wedding. The ceremony was very beautiful, except for one thing: It was interrupted several times by the ringing of different people's cell phones. Is there some tactful way to tell wedding guests to turn off their cell phones and other noise-making devices before things get under way, so these unpleasant intrusions can be avoided?

A: Your best bet is to stop the cell phone use before it even starts. You can do so in one of several ways: Print a tasteful little notice in your ceremony program if you decide to give programs to guests. You could write something like: "We wish to remind you to please turn off your cell phone ringer and to refrain from using your phone during our wedding ceremony. Thank you!" Or you could notify everyone as they sign a guest book just before they enter your ceremony site. You could have someone ask all guests to sign a guest book before taking their seats; while they're writing, they would see an attractive little sign (perhaps in a picture frame) positioned next to the book. The sign would have the same message mentioned above, "reminding" guests about turning off their cell phones. There's one other option if you don't have either a ceremony program or a guest book: Have someone make an announcement just before the start of the ceremony processional, asking everyone to "please turn off your cell phones, as the ceremony is about to begin!" While this last choice is acceptable, it is not as good as the other two less invasive ones. A verbal announcement could deflate some of the upbeat anticipation of your impending ceremony by taking away from the positive joy of the moment that is about to begin.

CHAPTER 10

Wedding Celebrations

A WELL-PLANNED WEDDING PARTY or pre-wedding event can be as fun, joyous, and celebratory as the wedding itself. While no events other than the wedding itself are necessary for the marriage to be celebrated, those that occur should be festive occasions that heighten the excitement of the impending big day.

As soon as your engagement is announced, friends and family may begin asking how they can entertain for you. Even events like the rehearsal dinner, held very close to your wedding day, require advance planning. The occasions discussed in this chapter are considered customary, though none is obligatory. Nor is it essential to have showers and other parties that include gift giving. It is perfectly acceptable for the bride and groom to suggest a "non-gift" occasion when others ask about entertaining in their honor.

Wedding Showers

A shower is an intimate gathering of friends to extend good wishes to the bride, the couple, or, occasionally, only the groom and to present the honoree(s) with gifts. A shower may have a theme that indicates the type of gifts expected. Opening the presents is usually the high point of the party, but the real purpose is to bring good friends together to celebrate the upcoming marriage. Gifts are great but secondary to conversation, conviviality, and gracious manners.

- **What form must a shower take?** A shower can be held in any form the hostess or host chooses—a brunch or supper, a traditional afternoon tea, an evening get-together—and is more often casual than formal these days. Unless the shower is a surprise, the honoree is consulted about the date, time, theme, and guest list, but party planning is up to the hostess or host. These days, some showers are for both the bride and groom. In fact, couple's showers have become quite popular.

- **When is a shower held?** The ideal timing is from two months to two weeks before the wedding—after the couple has firm wedding plans. Showers held fairly soon after the wedding day are also acceptable, especially when the wedding was arranged on short notice. A shower that takes place too close to the wedding date may be more of an inconvenience than a party for the bride, who is likely to be inundated with chores in the last busy days. A shower held too early may occur before the bride knows what she needs and before her wedding plans are finalized. A shower may be held on any day of the week that is convenient for the guest of honor, the hostess, and the majority of guests.

- **Who hosts the shower?** The traditional hosts are friends of the bride, the couple, or their parents. Workplace showers hosted by coworkers are popular, as are showers for the couple hosted by mutual friends and attended by men as well as women. Showers for the groom (only) are a recent phenomenon. A couple never hosts a shower for themselves. Contrary to some misconceptions, bridesmaids are *not required* to host a shower. One of an attendant's duties is to "host a shower"—*if* she chooses to do so.

A QUESTION FOR PEGGY:

ARE SHOWER GUESTS WEDDING GUESTS?

Q: Must everyone invited to a wedding shower be invited to the wedding?

A: Yes, normally, anyone invited to a shower should be invited to the wedding. One exception: when coworkers wish to throw an office shower for the bride, even though all are not being invited to the wedding. The shower in this case is their way of wishing the couple well.

- **Can a family member host the party?** It has long been considered a breach of etiquette for family members to host showers, because doing so gives the appearance of being self-serving. But it's becoming increasingly correct for family to host in certain situations, as when the bride is visiting her future in-laws and the groom's mother or sister invites hometown friends to meet her. Also, more mothers or sisters of the bride are giving showers. Today, people should be guided by individual circumstances when deciding if family members will host.

- **Who is invited?** A shower guest list is generally made up of close friends, attendants, and family members. Anyone invited to a shower should be invited to the wedding. The one exception is a workplace shower to which a large number of coworkers contribute. (If an office shower involves only a few coworkers, thoughtful couples will probably include these colleagues in the wedding guest list.) Showers are *intimate* gatherings for people you know very well—not excuses to haul in more gifts. The days of the strictly all-female wedding shower are fading fast. More and more, grooms-to-be and their male friends are included on the shower guest list.

- **How many showers can be given?** One of the basic principles of good manners is consideration for others. Inviting the same people to the wedding and multiple showers and expecting them to bring gifts every time puts a serious strain on guests' budgets and is inconsiderate. As a general rule, *two showers is the limit,* with different guests invited to each. Parents, close family members, and wedding attendants can be invited to multiple showers, but they are not expected to bring presents. Some choose to bring small or homemade gifts, such as a collection of favorite recipes.

- **How many people can be invited?** Since the hostess is the person footing the bill and providing the space, she decides the number of guests. If the shower is not a surprise, she most likely gets input from the bride on the guest list. A huge shower that includes almost everyone invited to the wedding is in poor taste. The idea of an intimate party is lost, and the shower becomes little more than a demand for gifts, which can often be more of an imposition on those invited than a reason to celebrate.

SHOWERS ON A SHOESTRING

Conscious of the financial burden that shower gifts plus wedding gifts can place on friends, considerate couples and shower hosts today are coming up with clever, low-cost ideas like the following:

- **Book and CD showers.** Reading and music make great themes for showers for couples. A VHS/DVD shower might be perfect for movie lovers.

- **Recipe showers.** In this revival of an old custom, the presents are favorite recipes, usually written on standard recipe cards and collected in recipe boxes or files.

- **Pantry showers.** For couples who already have well-equipped kitchens, guests bring useful and often exotic pantry supplies—spices, condiments, coffees and teas, paper products, bamboo skewers, and the like.

- **Stock-the-bar showers.** Guests needn't buy expensive vintages to help a couple acquire the basic bar components, including non-potables like measuring utensils, bottle openers, swizzle sticks, cocktail napkins, bottled garnishes, and tins of fancy nuts.

- **Best wishes showers.** Instead of things, guests bring sentiments—original writings, favorite quotations, humorous sayings. These expressions can be written on pages supplied by the hostess before the party, read aloud at the party, and then collected in an attractive notebook for the couple.

THEME SHOWERS

A shower needs no theme other than to celebrate the upcoming marriage of a couple. Sometimes, however, a hostess narrows or custom-designs the focus of a shower to a certain theme (often after discussions with the bride regarding the wedding couple's needs). Guests are then expected to bring gifts related to that theme, and the hostess may even provide theme-related food and decorations. Ideas for themes are limitless. Choices include:

KITCHEN SHOWER
Suggested gifts: Glasses, knives, linens, utensils.

SPA SHOWER
Suggested gifts: Massage certificates, aromatherapy oils, candles, robes.

HONEYMOON SHOWER
Suggested gifts: Travel clock, sewing kit, first-aid kit, travel book.

GOURMET COOK SHOWER
Suggested gifts: Gourmet foods and wines, utensils, cookbooks.

THE GREAT OUTDOORS SHOWER
Suggested gifts: Badminton net, flower seeds and gardening tools, picnic basket, Japanese lanterns, croquet set.

HAPPY HOLIDAYS SHOWER
Suggested gifts: Decorations for every holiday of the year.

LABOR OF LOVE SHOWER
Suggested gifts: Promises, not gifts, are brought to this shower, where friends pledge to paint, wallpaper, garden, or donate their talents in any number of ways.

- **How are invitations issued?** Usually, the hostess sends pre-printed invitations with the party details filled in or handwritten notes. Invitations may also be issued in person or by phone—a convenient method for workplace or surprise showers. Invitations should include the theme of the shower and any pertinent information, such as the couple's color preferences in the case of kitchen, bath, and linen showers. It's fine for the hostess to include gift registry information in the envelope with the invitation.

- **Can an encore bride have a wedding shower?** If the bride has been married before, she may be given a shower, but it's better to cut back on inviting friends and relatives who were invited to a shower for her first wedding. If the bride is marrying for the first time but her groom has been married before, she certainly may have a shower.

- **Showers for same-sex couples.** The choice of whether to register for gifts or have a shower is up to the couple. If you register, be aware that today's electronic and on-line registries may not include spaces for same-sex couples on their registry forms. You may need to register one name as "bride" and the other as "groom," enabling guests to search under either name. You might also consult with your favorite local stores. Even a retailer who has little or no experience with same-sex registries may welcome new business and be happy to assist you.

THE ETIQUETTE OF SHOWER GIFTS

Showers are the one pre-wedding event where gifts are expected. In fact, giving gifts is largely the purpose of showers. In general, shower gifts should be relatively inexpensive. People who can't attend are not obliged to send a shower gift, though sometimes close friends and relatives do. Here are some guidelines for hosts and guests alike on sharing information about and selecting shower gifts:

- A group gift, often organized by the hostess, is a popular way to give a more elaborate present. No one should be forced to participate, and no other present is expected from people who do contribute.

- Any shower theme (kitchen, bath, books and CDs) should be noted on the invitation.

- For kitchen or bathroom showers, note the couple's color preferences on an insert that can be included in the envelope with the invitation.

- Don't include registry information on the invitation itself. It's fine to enclose a list of where the couple is registered on a separate sheet inserted into the invitation envelope. The hostess can also compile a list of specific gifts that the couple needs and make recommendations to people who ask for gift suggestions.

- For a lingerie shower, it is helpful to include the bride's sizes.

- Gifts are generally opened after refreshments have been served. The guests gather around while the bride (or the bride and groom together if it is a joint shower) opens the packages one by one and thanks each giver.

- Someone—often one of the bridesmaids—is designated official "note taker." The note taker sits beside the bride and makes a list of the gifts and who gave them, making sure the gift cards are kept with their respective gifts.

- Often gifts are passed around the room so that everyone can see them—and so that the giver can be showered with praise for her good taste and thoughtfulness.

Saying Thank You

- The bride (and groom, too, if honored at a shower) is required to send a thank-you note for each shower gift. Don't forget to send thank-you notes to those who were unable to attend the shower but sent gifts. (See also Chapter 8, pages 162–166: "The Importance of 'Thank You.' ") *Do not* ask guests to fill out envelopes with their addresses at the shower. This is occasionally done as a convenience for the bride when she writes thank-you notes, but it implies laziness and an assembly-line approach to what should be a personal communication in response to a guest's personal gesture.

- When the shower is a surprise, it's a delightful idea for the bride to send flowers to her hostess with a personal note of thanks after the shower. She should also call the hostess the day after the shower to say thank you.

- When the shower is not a surprise, the bride should give the hostess a thank-you gift, as a way of showing her appreciation. She can give her a personal gift or send flowers beforehand so that they can be used by the hostess as a shower decoration. The bride then follows up with a thank-you telephone call and a note of appreciation.

A QUESTION FOR PEGGY:

WHICH STATIONERY TO SAY THANK YOU?

Q: *I have note cards with my married initials on them. Should I use these to write thank-you notes for my shower gifts or should I wait until I'm married and use something else in the meantime?*

A: Wait until you're married before you break out the stationery monogrammed with your married initials. Fold-over note cards are fine to use for shower thank-yous. You can use your monogrammed maiden-name stationery, too.

The Groom's Mother Asks:
"Can I Host a Shower for an Absentee Bride?"

Q: *My son is marrying a wonderful woman who lives a long away from here. Her work prevents her from coming to town for a shower before the wedding. We have lots of friends and relatives who can't make the wedding but who would love to honor the couple. Can I give the bride and groom a wedding shower without their being present?*

A: Certainly you can! Throw the bride and groom a proxy shower, the name for a shower for a bride who cannot attend or who lives far away. Although a proxy shower is an acceptable way of celebrating, it can pose problems for the hostess, who is responsible for sending the gifts to the bride. One solution is to have the hostess ask guests to bring their gifts unwrapped so that everyone can see them. She then provides a variety of wrapping paper and ribbons for the guests to wrap their gifts, so that she can pack them into large cartons and mail them to the bride. At most proxy showers, a telephone call is made to the bride or the couple so that they can thank their friends.

Bridal Shower Do's and Don'ts

Don't coerce anyone—especially bridesmaids—to host a shower. It's a financial burden that many aren't able to take on.

Do send thank-you notes to all shower guests—even if you thanked them in person at the shower.

Don't invite anyone to a shower who won't be invited to the wedding. The only exceptions would be coworkers who throw you a shower who already know they won't be invited to the wedding.

Don't ask guests to address their own thank-you notes.

Do send a thank-you note and a gift to anyone who hosts a shower for you.

Do include registry information in the envelope with your shower invitation—but not on the invitation itself.

Don't invite guests to more than one shower.

Bridesmaids' Luncheon

In many communities, it's traditional for the bride, her mother, and the bridesmaids to get together for a "farewell" luncheon or maybe a tea or dinner for the bride, either in addition to a shower or instead of a shower.

- **When does the luncheon take place?** This luncheon usually takes place very close to the wedding date, particularly if bridesmaids live in different communities and will be arriving only for the wedding celebrations.

- **Can someone else host?** Often, the bride and her mother host a luncheon for the bridesmaids as a respite in the midst of a busy time—and as a thank-you to the attendants for their presence and support.

- **What type of celebration does it involve?** A bridesmaids' luncheon is a little different from any other lunch party. The table may be more elaborately decorated and the linens are often white or the bride's chosen wedding colors. The bridesmaids' luncheon is the perfect time for the bride to give her bridesmaids their individual gifts, personally thanking them for being a part of her wedding. For the bride and attendants who work during the day, a more convenient get-together may be after work, at a small cocktail party or intimate dinner. Another venue could be a day spa, where they all could share a pre-wedding pampering.

Bachelor and Bachelorette Parties

The bachelor party of legend is a sodden farewell to bachelor days, an event where the groom and his ushers traditionally share an evening of debauchery before the wedding. These days bachelor parties and dinners are much more low-key affairs than they used to be.

- **What kind of celebration?** It may be a simple gathering of good friends over beer and barbecue; a night at a restaurant or an intimate dinner party; a day on a boat, at the beach, or on the golf course; or an afternoon of baseball or football, followed by a picnic. A dinner may be held, in the private dining room of a restaurant or in a club. Aside from toasting the bride and reminiscing over he-man steaks, wine, and cigars, the bridegroom's farewell dinner is like any other dinner among friends.

- **Who hosts?** The bachelor party is usually arranged by the best man. Often the groomsmen help with the planning, too.

- **Who pays?** Many bachelor parties are Dutch treat, with the best man and groomsmen pitching in to cover the groom's expenses. But any combination that is communicated in advance and is financially feasible for all involved is acceptable.

- **Who's invited?** In addition to the best man, the groomsmen, and the groom's closest friends, sometimes the father of the groom and the father of the bride are included in part or all of the celebration. Generally, anyone invited to the bachelor party is also invited to the wedding.

- **Can a second-time groom have a bachelor party?** A bachelor party is certainly not off-limits for a second-time groom. His status as a bachelor alone fits the bill.

A bachelorette party is very similar to the bachelor party and is given by a bride's female friends. It is different from the bridesmaids' luncheon in that it is often held at night and may include toasts and a dinner, similar to the bachelor party. The guest list may also include other friends in addition to the attendants.

The basic idea for these events is to treat the groom or bride to one last night out as a single person. The guests are good friends, the atmosphere is relaxed, and there's no reason not to have a great time—so long as everyone is willing to exercise self-control. If alcohol will be served, a designated driver should be appointed or arrangements should be made for taxi or limo service. Whatever entertainment is planned, it should not embarrass, humiliate, or endanger the honoree or any of the guests. It's wise to hold a bachelor or bachelorette party a week or more before the wedding, so everyone can rest after what will probably be a late night. If gifts are given, they're usually inexpensive and often humorous, and guests should be able to find items that are both funny and in reasonably good taste.

Bachelor and bachelorette celebrations are by no means necessary. No one should be "guilted" or bullied into organizing or hosting such a gathering. Some brides and grooms prefer to skip it altogether, and good friends should honor the couples' wishes.

And the Party Never Ends . . .

If the traditional wedding parties are not enough celebrating for you, here are some ideas for filler events, whether held to thank a group of people, to honor out-of-town guests, or simply to keep the party going through the wedding weekend.

The Appreciation Party: Instead of trying to schedule a series of luncheons and bachelor and bachelorette parties, a couple might host one big appreciation party instead. Invited are attendants and anyone else who has given generously of their time and ideas to help make the wedding wonderful. The appreciation party is often a casual affair, a barbecue or picnic, especially if the rehearsal dinner is to be formal. It is usually held just before the wedding, when everyone has gathered, and is another opportunity for the bride and groom to give their attendants gifts of appreciation. An appreciation party can also be held after the couple returns from their honeymoon if their attendants and special friends live close enough to attend.

The Pre-Wedding Luncheon: For a late-afternoon wedding, a small luncheon for the bridal party may be given by friends or neighbors. This takes the burden off the busy mother of the bride to host yet another entertainment on her daughter's wedding day. It may be as simple or as elaborate as the host and hostess wish, but laid-back and relaxing may be just the ticket to put an excited and nervous bridal party at ease. The bride and groom are absolutely not required to attend, however; it depends on their schedules and energy levels.

Parties for Out-of-Town Guests: A lovely gift for the couple from relatives or friends is a party for out-of-town guests and early-arriving wedding attendants. This, too, relieves the bride's parents of extra work before the wedding and gives guests a chance to spend time together in an informal atmosphere. Invitations should be sent well in advance so that guests can plan their travel itinerary accordingly. Often the party is given by multiple hosts, who share the expenses and work. These parties may be held at home or in a club or restaurant. Guests may include the attendants, the couple's families, their close friends, and friends of their parents. Outings, too, can be arranged rather than parties—bowling, miniature golf, hiking, visits to local tourist attractions. It's a great way for visitors to relax and explore the area before the wedding.

The Wedding Rehearsal

Although the traditional marriage service is a familiar one to most, it is easy to forget the sheer volume of details that go into its planning. Add to that the excitement and nervousness all involved may be feeling on the big day. It is essential, therefore, that the wedding-party participants be fully involved in the wedding rehearsal. It is even more important for those involved to pay close attention when a service is unfamiliar or nontraditional. Here are some guidelines to consider for the traditional wedding rehearsal:

- **Who attends?** Other than the bride, the only other people required to attend the rehearsal are the groom, the attendants, and the bride's parents. Since typically the groom's parents have no active part in the ceremony, they don't need to be present—but usually enjoy being there.

The officiant and the organist or musician must also be present. The wedding consultant, if one has been hired, should be on hand to help instruct the ushers, line the wedding party up correctly, and help with the spacing and pace of each person as he or she practices walking down the aisle. If there are young children participating in the ceremony, their presence is required only if the rehearsal is not held too late at night. If they come, their parents generally accompany them.

- **When is the rehearsal held?** The rehearsal is scheduled with the officiant at a time when all attendants can be present. For a Saturday wedding, it is usually held on Friday afternoon or early evening. The closer to the wedding the rehearsal takes place, the better the chances that all will go smoothly.

- **What should participants wear?** People taking part in a church-wedding rehearsal or attending as observers should remember that they are in a house of worship and should dress accordingly. This means no shorts or jeans and in some houses of worship no bare arms or legs. When the wedding is taking place at a secular location, clothing might be more informal, unless the rehearsal is to be followed immediately by a dinner requiring dressier attire.

- **What happens during the rehearsal?** At the rehearsal, the officiant reviews the order of the service with the couple. The couple does not say their responses or vows at the rehearsal. The officiant might ask the bride and groom to recite one verse, so they can find the right tone and volume.

  If there will be an aisle runner, its use and the timing and signals of placing the runner are determined and discussed with the ushers so that the officiant knows when the bride's mother has been seated, that the bride has arrived, and when the service should begin.

  The organist is also present at the rehearsal and plays the processional so that pace and spacing can be practiced.

  The order of the procession is established, and the attendants walk up the aisle two or three times until all goes smoothly.

  Everyone lines up at the chancel to make sure that all fit comfortably and that the order looks symmetrical. The maid of honor learns when to take the bride's bouquet and how to rearrange the bride's train without fussing or attracting attention to herself.

  The best man and the maid of honor learn when to give the rings to the officiant and how to remove the rings if they are affixed to a pillow carried by the ring bearer.

The officiant will explain when a veil, if worn, should be turned back, and a decision is made on who will do so.

The ushers are given instruction by the officiant or the wedding consultant on their roles in escorting guests. The ushers are the first people guests see, and they should be confident about what they are doing and look as though they have done it for years. They should be shown how to offer an arm and how to remove pew ribbons, noting which pews have been set aside for special seating. The ushers will learn how to escort guests in and out of the ceremony site in an orderly fashion.

How attendants will leave the chancel is arranged at the rehearsal, whether in pairs or singly. They should all practice the recessional at least once, to ensure that the attendants know how they will exit. The pace of the recessional is set by the bride and groom on the day of the wedding, and the others should follow at a natural, non-stilted walk.

The Rehearsal Dinner

The rehearsal dinner has become a popular tradition of the wedding-party weekend—and is nearly as festive as the wedding reception. It's a time to celebrate and savor the upcoming nuptials in a relaxed atmosphere, without the pomp and ceremony reserved for the wedding day.

- **When is the rehearsal dinner held?** The rehearsal dinner generally takes place the night before the wedding, regardless of when the rehearsal is held.

- **Who hosts?** It has become customary, but not obligatory, for the groom's family to host the rehearsal party. If they do so, they may elicit the help of the bride or her mother in selecting a location—especially if they are from another town and unfamiliar with what is available. In this case, preliminary plans are made by telephone or confirmation letter, and the final arrangements are made when the groom's family arrives for the wedding celebrations.

  If the groom's family does not or cannot give the rehearsal dinner, one may be arranged by the bride's family. It may take the form of a picnic, a simple buffet, or a formal dinner. The only guide: The rehearsal party should never be more formal than the wedding reception, particularly if the party is given by the groom's parents.

- **Who is invited?** The guest list at a rehearsal dinner should include the members of the wedding party, the officiant, parents and grandparents of the bride and groom, and any siblings of the bride and groom who are not in the wedding party. If the bride and/or groom have stepparents, they are invited with their spouses but should not be seated next to their former spouses. The wedding party's husbands, wives, fiancées, fiancés, and live-in companions should be invited, but dates are not included. Any children of the bride and groom from a previous marriage also attend, unless they are too young. The flower girl and ring bearer may be included, unless the hour or formality makes it difficult for them to attend.

- **What type of invitation should be extended?** Invitations are generally written on informals or fill-in cards or may simply be handwritten or telephoned. If a good number of out-of-town guests are being invited, the written invitation is the best way to go; it serves as a tangible reminder of the date, time, and address of the party. Send out invitations three to six weeks in advance.

- **What happens during the dinner?** The rehearsal dinner is the perfect occasion for the presentation of attendants' gifts, whether from the couple to the bridesmaids and ushers or from the attendants to the bride and groom. Often the latter gifts are presented by the maid of honor and the best man and may be accompanied by a short speech or toast.

Toasts can be made during dinner, preferably not after; otherwise, the night can drag on interminably. The host—often the groom's father—should make the first toast, welcoming the guests and expressing his feelings about the forthcoming marriage. He is generally followed with a return toast by the bride's father or stepfather and then with toasts from ushers, bridesmaids, and anyone else who wishes to say something.

The attendants' toasts, while sentimental to some extent, are often filled with anecdotes, jokes, and poems regaling guests with tales from the bride and groom's past. Sometimes the bride and groom stand and speak; even if they don't, they generally end the toasting by proposing a toast first to their respective parents and then to all their friends and relatives in attendance. (See also Chapter 21, pages 367–370: "Toasts.")

A QUESTION FOR PEGGY:

WHO'S INVITED TO THE REHEARSAL DINNER?

Q: *My fiancé says we are required to invite all out-of-town guests to the rehearsal dinner. I say we're not. Who is right?*

A: The guest list for a rehearsal dinner traditionally consists of the bride and groom, all attendants and their spouses or partners, the couple's immediate families, and the clergyperson and spouse. It's a nice gesture to include out-of-towners if your budget allows, but it's by no means a must. Sit down with your fiancé and discuss the situation. Perhaps the guests who are coming from a far distance can meet up informally at an easy-to-get-to restaurant.

Wedding-Night Afterglow

When out-of-town guests are staying overnight on the day of the wedding, the bride's family might spontaneously invite them home for a late snack or even for dinner after an afternoon reception. This is not necessary or expected. In fact, the last thing the parents of the bride may want to do is entertain, but often the afterglow of all the events leading up to that moment carries them on to an impromptu gathering with friends. Any post-wedding entertainment, which can also be hosted by a close friend or relative, can be as simple as take-out pizza offered to guests who have changed into comfortable clothes or as elaborate as a next-day brunch.

The fun of the gathering is in hearing and sharing post-wedding stories and impressions. Often the parents are so busy and swept up in the emotion of the occasion that they miss some of the details.

Morning-After Gathering

If the reception ends late and guests prefer to turn in for the evening, sometimes there is an after-wedding party that takes the form of a breakfast or brunch the next day. In this case, the gathering is probably planned, and it is generally the bride's parents, the groom's parents, or a friend who offers to host the occasion. Notes or informal invitations are often extended to out-of-town guests ahead of time so that they can plan their departures around the party.

Another Wedding Celebration: A Belated Reception

When a small, private, or destination wedding has taken place, some couples decide to give a party in the weeks following the ceremony to share their happiness with friends and family.

The couple may host their own wedding party, or the bride or groom's family can host a wedding reception for the couple. This is frequently done when the couple has married privately or away from home or did not have a reception at all. Following are some guidelines for a post-wedding party:

- **Who hosts?** The couple, the bride's parents or the groom's, or other family members or good friends may host.

- **What kind of reception?** If no wedding reception was held or if only a small reception was held, this celebration may include all the components of any wedding reception. It can be as formal or as informal as the couple wants. If the bride wore a wedding gown for the ceremony, she may wear it again at the reception party if she wishes. They can even have a wedding cake ready to be cut and served to guests.

- **What kind of invitation?** Fill-in cards or printed invitations can be used and should be sent four to six weeks in advance. Invitations for a reception hosted by the bride's parents would read:

> Mr. and Mrs. William DeRosa
> request the pleasure of your company
> at a reception
> in honor of
> Mr. and Mrs. John Nelson
> [etc.]

- **What about gifts?** No gifts are expected. However, some guests choose to bring gifts. The couple should open any gifts after the party and send prompt thank-you notes.

- **A party to welcome the bride to the groom's family.** If the bride and groom were married in her hometown or elsewhere, and the friends of the groom and his family live too far away to attend, his mother and father might give a reception for them the first time they come to visit after the honeymoon. They may even host a celebration if the couple visits them a short time before the wedding takes place.

  Invitations to such a reception are generally fill-in cards or informals, with "In honor of Priscilla and James" or "To meet Priscilla Holmes" written at the top. They should be mailed two to four weeks before the party.

  This party *does not* parallel the couple's wedding reception, because a reception has already been held. There is no wedding cake, and the couple and any attendants who live near enough to be there do not wear their wedding clothes. However, when the party is held after the wedding and the groom's mother would like guests to see the wedding gown—and the bride would like to wear it—she may certainly receive in it and then change after everyone has arrived. Or some of the wedding pictures (or the proofs) might be on display for guests to peruse.

  This party is usually in the form of a tea or cocktail buffet. The host and hostess stand at the door with the newlyweds and introduce them to everyone who has not met them. The bride's parents are invited as well, but they certainly don't have to attend. Gifts are optional—close friends and family members usually give gifts.

CHAPTER 11

PLANNING THE CEREMONY

First Things First

Planning the type of ceremony you want will likely be a collaborative affair. The ceremony, more so than the reception, is often influenced by family and cultural traditions—such as your parents' religious preferences, your church or other affiliation, and the customs of your community. Many couples follow traditional ceremonial customs as a way to honor their family and their cultural heritage. It provides a spiritual connection to the generations that have gone before and infuses the ceremony with meaning.

Whether you choose to follow a traditional service, tinker with certain aspects of the ceremony to personalize it, or forgo a traditional ceremony altogether, you will need to make a few big decisions as soon as you become engaged. Following is a list of decisions to make when developing the plans for your wedding ceremony:

1. Choose the Site of Your Ceremony: Traditional venues include a church, side chapel, synagogue, wedding facility, or home. (See also Chapter 2, page 31: "Ceremony Location.")

2. Decide on the Date and Time of Your Ceremony.

3. Choose an Officiant: If the officiant is affiliated with the church or house of worship where the ceremony is being held, you will likely be discussing the date and time of the ceremony with him or her from the start. Note: Never show up to see an officiant without making an appointment first!

4. Discuss the Following Issues with Your Officiant:

- Reconfirm *the date and time* of your ceremony.

- Discuss any *issues or concerns* you may have, as well as any ways you might like to *personalize the ceremony,* such as tinkering with the vows or including a reading or a musical interlude.

- Discuss the *length of the ceremony.* If yours is a Christian ceremony, for example, discuss whether communion will be a part of the ceremony.

- Discuss the *number of guests* the site will comfortably hold.

- If your chosen officiant is a priest, rabbi, or minister, before doing anything, you will need to let him or her know if yours is an *interfaith marriage* or if neither of you is a practicing member of that particular faith. Each religion has different standards, rules, and restrictions. You will need to discuss whether you plan to marry in a house of worship or at a secular site. Clergy often have restrictions on whom they can marry and where they can marry them. Catholic priests, for example, can marry couples only in a Catholic church.

- If you haven't already done so, be sure to make a *reservation for the wedding rehearsal* at this meeting. You should do so as soon as possible—the site schedule that is heavily booked on your wedding day is likely to be equally tight on the day before, the traditional time to hold the rehearsal. Ask if there are restrictions or rules for the rehearsal, such as clothing regulations, or guidelines on who may attend. Find out how long the rehearsal will run so that a rehearsal dinner can be planned. Note: Make sure to include a few extra minutes in the schedule in case the rehearsal runs over.

- If you and your partner plan to participate in *premarital counseling* from the officiant (and some religions require that you do so), this is also the time to set the dates for appointments.

- Finally, provide the officiant with the *names* you'll use in the ceremony. Also mention whether or not you will be taking the groom's last name.

Nuts and Bolts: Questions to Ask at the Ceremony Site

Before you begin formalizing your plans, you must check with your officiant or the ceremony-site manager to determine what is permitted and what isn't, and to ensure access for your vendors. For example, it is imperative to get clearance to install your floral decorations at the ceremony site. It would be a colossal disappointment to finalize your floral plans, only to find out that your selections weren't allowed at the site in the first place. Indeed, the answers your officiant or ceremony-site manager provides about the wedding ceremony will likely inform many other decisions. For example, if photography or videotaping is allowed only during certain times in the ceremony, you will need to discuss this with the photographer or videographer. Important questions to ask your officiant or ceremony-site manager are:

How Is Visiting Clergy
Asked to Perform the Ceremony?

Q: I would desperately love for my hometown minister to marry us in the church we now belong to, but I'm not sure of the protocol and I certainly don't want to hurt the feelings of our current officiant. Any advice?

A: If you want a clergyperson from out of town to officiate at your wedding, and you plan to marry in a church or synagogue he or she is not affiliated with, talk to the local clergy immediately. Explain that your hometown minister is an old friend whom you've always wanted to be involved in your wedding. In some cases, it is required that the local officiant be present and participate in the service. In others, there is no such requirement, and the church or synagogue is literally turned over to the visiting officiant. Sometimes, a payment to the local clergyperson is customary for his or her help in making arrangements.

Your obligations?

- Check what the regulations are before asking the out-of-town officiant to perform all or part of the ceremony.

- Get permission to use the church or synagogue.

- Coordinate the communication between the out-of-town officiant and his or her contact person at the church or synagogue. Details may include borrowing a key to the building to have access to a robing room or to set up for Holy Communion.

- If the out-of-town clergy is to be the sole officiant, you should get a list from him or her of any ceremony needs ahead of time.

- Finally, it is your responsibility to pay the travel, lodging, and meal expenses of any clergyperson you invite from out of town.

SITE SPECIFICS

- What is the site contact name and number? Write these down in your planner, to give to any vendors or wedding consultants.

- Are any other weddings or ceremonies planned on the same day as your wedding? Does that give you a time restriction? (On the other hand, you may be able to share flowers with another bridal party—and floral costs.)

- Is there a room for dressing prior to the service?

- Is there a way to ensure that space is left vacant for the cars that will carry the bride and her attendants to the front of the building? Is there enough space that traffic congestion won't occur when the wedding takes place? If not, are the services of a traffic officer or an off-duty police officer to direct traffic advisable?

- If the site is outdoors, is there some sort of podium for the officiant?

- Is the throwing of rose petals permitted outside the building?

- What fees are required for the use of the facility; for the organist; for the cantor; for additional musicians; for the sexton; for the minister or rabbi? If there will be other service participants such as altar boys or acolytes, is it the officiant's duty to arrange for them to be there? Should they be paid and if so, how much? And should they attend the rehearsal?

- May a receiving line be formed at the ceremony site, if desired? In some instances, there may be another ceremony following yours or there may not be enough room for a receiving line.

PLANNING A CEREMONY AT ANOTHER SITE

Even if you plan to marry at a site separate from the officiant's house of worship, many of the same questions for the officiant still apply. In addition, you will need to ask:

- Are there any restrictions on the kind of ceremony you can have if it is not conducted in a house of worship? If so, what? If not, is there perhaps more room to deviate from the standard wedding service?

- What are the travel needs of the officiant? Would he or she prefer to come in a hired car? If your officiant chooses to drive, can you reimburse him or her for time, gas, and mileage?

- Will you need to provide an altar? A kneeling bench or cushions? An altar cloth? Candles? Any other liturgical items? If the answer is yes to any of these questions, ask for the names of resources that provide these articles. Ask whether makeshift arrangements will do, such as a table that can be used as an altar or a table runner that doubles as an altar cloth. If the ceremony site is a frequent wedding location, you may find that these items are already available.

FLOWERS AND DECOR

- Are there any decorating restrictions or rules? What kinds of floral arrangements/decorations are permitted?

- At what time may decorations be delivered and how will access be arranged? How do you arrange access for a florist to decorate?

- What is the site policy on the disposition of flowers after the ceremony? Is there a policy on removing the flowers after the ceremony? Couples often wish to use flowers as reception decorations; to deliver them to shut-ins, area hospitals, or nursing homes; or to give them to friends.

- Are candles permitted as decorations other than within the sanctuary?

- Does the ceremony site provide an aisle runner, should you want to use one, or do you need to order one from the florist?

- For a Jewish ceremony: Who will provide the *chuppah* and may it be decorated with flowers?

ATTIRE

- Are there restrictions concerning dress? Bare shoulders or arms? Head coverings? What about restrictions on attire for guests?

PHOTOGRAPHY

- Are photography and videography allowed? If so, when may photographs and/or a video be taken? Before, during, and/or after the ceremony?

- What are site rules on lighting, whether flash or videocassette lighting?

MUSIC

If you're being married in a church or other house of worship, keep in mind that some sites stipulate that any musician performing in a wedding ceremony must be engaged through the in-house music department. In that case, the house of worship may have its own music director or organist. Other religious sites might forbid secular music.

- Does the site have any restrictions on the type of music, the type of instruments, or whether or not music is played with a microphone or not? Does it have any restrictions on recorded music?

- Are secular, classical, or popular selections allowed? Must the prelude, processional, ceremony, and recessional music, for example, all be sacred music?

- Are there certain hymns that can or can't be sung at the ceremony?

- Can additional music be inserted in the ceremony—such as a solo by a flutist, a trumpeter, a guitar player, or a vocalist—and if so, where?

- Does the site have modernized sound-recording equipment and can it provide audiocassettes or CDs as mementos?

Personalizing the Ceremony

Often couples like to include personal readings, musical interludes, or self-penned vows in the wedding ceremony. These are great ideas, but keep in mind that any additions will lengthen the total time of the ceremony and affect the timing of your reception.

- What latitude may you have in writing some or all of the ceremony by yourselves or including additional readings? If you are being married in a house of worship, ask your officiant for a copy of the liturgy for the wedding ceremony and to mark those places where you may add a reading. Find out whether the readings must be scriptural or can include secular pieces. Your officiant may even be able to provide a list of reading choices. Finally, find out whether the officiant needs to review your selections.

- Can you use a second officiant at the wedding? If you want a co-officiant at your wedding—a relative, perhaps, or a retired minister you are particularly close to—ask your officiant if this is permissible. If so, provide his or her name, telephone number, and address and send the reciprocal information to the visiting clergy. That way, they can communicate directly if they wish and plan the order of officiating. If the visiting clergy is from another faith, your officiant may be unable or unwilling to include him or her. If your officiant agrees to include a co-officiant from another faith, discuss ways the service may be structured.

Discuss the inclusion of religious rituals, readings from other religious texts, or cultural traditions with your officiant. Some faiths do not allow deviation from their standard services, but it may be possible to include other rituals either before or after the ceremony or at the reception.

For more information on religious rituals and cultural traditions to personalize your ceremony, see Chapter 12, "Multicultural Weddings." Your options are limitless—unity candles, religious customs, secular readings, musical mixes, jumping the broom, handfasting, and the shared cup are just a few elements that can be added to your ceremony to make it personal and unique.

Including children from a previous marriage. Children of divorced or widowed parents should be included in the wedding party if they wish to be. Including them in the ceremony, whether as attendants or in some other role, will help them adjust to the new family situation much more readily. They will feel they are part of the formation of that family.

One meaningful way to include children from a previous marriage in the wedding ceremony is by placing family medallions around their necks after vows have been exchanged. The medallion, sometimes a circle with three intersecting circles inside, represents a promise of family love and inclusion. It is first blessed by the officiant, who then shares with those gathered the meaning of the medallion and gives it to the parent to give to the children. The children may then stand alongside the attendants or return to their seats for the conclusion of the service. (See also Chapter 13, pages 237–240: "When Children are Involved.")

Honoring the Deceased. Increasingly, some couples are finding ways to honor deceased family members, either privately or publicly, in their ceremonies. This is a way to remember loved ones, especially parents and grandparents, and to give tribute to the importance of family and tradition. If you decide to include a tribute in your ceremony, be sure that it is neither morbid nor lengthy. A simple declaration of love, a moment of silence, or the lighting of a candle may be the most eloquent commemoration. Often, couples find it too difficult to publicly honor the deceased, so they make their memorials private. They may do so by offering a silent prayer, wearing something of the person who has died, or laying a bouquet of flowers on the front pew or by the altar.

Themed weddings can carry personalization into nearly every aspect of planning, from the look of the invitations to the shape of the wedding cake. Themes should be meaningful to both of the couple—and not so far out that guests won't get the idea. A theme shouldn't be an imposition on guests, as acquiring period clothing would be. It's also important to consider budget; a themed wedding complete with costuming for the wedding party and reception staff, elaborate decorations, and complicated menus can be very costly.

But themes—whether carried through the entire occasion or just the reception—can be great fun and a satisfying outlet for creative thinking. The following categories and examples are provided as idea starters for themes that are both practical and memorable:

- **The season or the month of the wedding.** An October wedding might be the inspiration for autumn colors, country dances, even a hayride to the reception site.

- **A favorite place.** A couple who met in Paris, Nairobi, or Hong Kong might theme their reception around the foods and music typical of that city.

THE PERSONAL TOUCH:

TIPS FOR AN AT-HOME CEREMONY

- If you're having an evening wedding outdoors, line your walkway with white paper bags filled with sand and luminaria candles. Hang Japanese lanterns in the trees or on ropes from tree to tree.

- Borrow or rent chairs from a church, school, social club, or rental company for seating your guests.

- Hang a wedding banner on the front porch, or rent topiary or potted trees to place at the entrance.

- Recruit neighborhood children to usher, to take guests' coats, and even to give corsages and nosegays to special guests.

- Hire off-duty police or responsible teens as parking valets.

- Avoid having muddy footprints in the house—don't water the lawn the day of your ceremony!

- **A historical period or era.** The spectacle of ancient Egypt, the romance of medieval courts, the sleek style of 1930s Art Deco—history is a treasure trove of ideas.

- **A shared interest.** A mutual love of Shakespeare might suggest an Elizabethan theme with sonnets as guest favors. A couple devoted to water sports or camping could create a nautical or outdoors theme.

- **The wedding location.** A floral theme might be perfect for a wedding in a beautiful garden. A clambake, luau, or barbecue could just right for the reception for a beach or lakeside wedding.

- **The honeymoon.** A couple planning their dream trip might stage their reception as a bon voyage party with a travel theme.

Religious Ceremonies

Even with so many different religious rituals and cultural traditions being used in weddings today, there is generally one common thread. Most of the major religions share a mutual belief that marriage is a joyous occasion worthy of high celebration. Using happiness as the common denominator, today's brides and grooms from different religious and ethnic backgrounds are able to blend the cultural traditions of one with the rituals of the other, by weaving those aspects that matter most to them and their families into the events surrounding their marriage.

Deciding on a ceremony can be a challenge, especially when families and friends have a wide range of practices and beliefs, but there are ways you can foster understanding and help everyone be a part of your wedding. One solution is to provide a wedding program, with the help of your clergyperson, that explains the symbolic meaning of different parts of the ceremony so that guests can follow along. Programs can also provide translations if parts of the ceremony are in another language.

Whether yours will be a marriage of mixed faiths, one that integrates age-old traditions and rituals into a modern ceremony, or one that follows religious tradition to the letter, your officiant can best help you choose the right ceremony rites for you.

INTERFAITH MARRIAGES

If your faiths have strictures against interfaith marriage and offer no way for you to incorporate the two faiths in one ceremony, you should either be married in a civil ceremony or hold two separate ceremonies, one right after the other. If you do the latter, you'll need to decide whether to invite guests to both ceremonies or to invite all instead to a reception after the two private ceremonies.

ROMAN CATHOLIC CEREMONIES

One of the seven sacraments of the Catholic Church is marriage, and as such it is treated seriously.

Preparing for the Ceremony

Interfaith Marriages: Interfaith marriage is accepted as long as the partner of another faith complies with counseling requirements, and most priests will co-officiate with the clergy of the non-Catholic.

Marrying Divorced Individuals: Divorce is not recognized, so the bride or groom whose previous marriage did not end in annulment but rather in divorce is not permitted to be married in the Catholic Church if that partner is still living. It is likely, however, that someone not married in a Catholic ceremony but in a civil service and later divorced will be allowed to remarry in the Catholic Church, which does not recognize civil marriages in the first place.

Premarital Counseling: The Catholic Church requires a prescribed series of religious and personal counseling sessions for both the bride and the groom, even if one of them is not Catholic.

The Ceremony

- Inclusion of a nuptial mass is common, although not required. If it is conducted, it lengthens the approximately twenty-minute ceremony to about an hour. (It used to be that a nuptial mass could be conducted only if both the bride and groom were Catholic, but today this is not a requirement.)

- Only Roman Catholic guests are permitted to receive Holy Communion.

- Throughout the ceremony, personalization and the participation of lay readers may take place, as well as the singing or playing of religious music.

The Service

1. At the beginning of the service, the groom stands by the priest at the altar as the bride proceeds down the aisle, preceded by her attendants.

2. The bride is met by the groom, and the two remain in front of the altar either kneeling, sitting, or standing throughout the ceremony. Their attendants either flank them or move to front pews in the church.

3. The priest then often welcomes those present and gives a homily about marriage.

4. After the homily, he asks if the couple has come freely to marry. They respond and join hands to exchange marriage vows.

5. The priest blesses the rings, the groom puts the bride's ring on her finger, and she puts his ring on his finger, and then the nuptial blessing is given, followed by the mass if one is included.

EPISCOPAL CEREMONIES

Like the Catholic Church, the Episcopal Church considers marriage a sacrament and requires that at least one partner must be baptized in the name of the Holy Trinity.

Preparing for the Ceremony

Interfaith Marriages: Interfaith marriage is accepted, and Episcopal priests are usually willing to co-officiate with other clergy if the couple wishes.

Marrying Divorced Individuals: If either the bride or the groom has been divorced, she or he must receive a dispensation to marry again from the area bishop. If this is not done, the marriage may not take place in the church.

Premarital Counseling: Premarital counseling with the priest who will marry you is customary.

The Ceremony

- Personalization is permitted in the form of any number of readings and the inclusion of religious music—usually solos but sometimes hymns sung by the guests.

- The ceremony, with the celebration of Holy Eucharist, takes about forty-five minutes. Without communion, the service is about twenty minutes long.

- The celebration of Holy Eucharist may follow the wedding ceremony if the bride and groom wish. All baptized Christians are welcome to receive communion.

- The attendants stand on both sides of the bride and the groom throughout.

The Service

The Episcopal ceremony is taken from *The Book of Common Prayer* and has four parts, which follow the processional of the bride and her attendants:

1. The priest begins with the call to worship: "Dearly Beloved, we have come together in the presence of God to witness and bless the joining together of this man and this woman in Holy Matrimony."

2. It is followed by the declaration of consent.

3. The ministry of the Word follows, using one or more scriptural passages.

4. This is followed by the exchange of vows and the blessing of the rings, and then the blessing of the marriage.

MAINSTREAM PROTESTANT CEREMONIES

The wedding ceremonies of Baptist, Lutheran, and Presbyterian churches are familiar to many; they are the ceremonies most frequently portrayed in movies and television shows. Mainstream Protestant ceremonies, in general, are quite similar. Marriage is not a sacrament, but it is considered holy.

Preparing for the Ceremony

Interfaith Marriages: Interfaith marriages are permitted and co-officiants welcomed, although the more conservative synods or branches may not permit a co-officiated Christian or non-Christian marriage.

Premarital Counseling: Premarital counseling is customary, usually conducted in a series of three or more private meetings with the minister who will conduct the ceremony.

The Ceremony

- Holy Communion may be part of the ceremony if the bride and groom wish. The bride and groom may add readings and music to the ceremony and may write their own vows to replace the ones included in the church's worship book.

The Service

The service, without additional readings and music or communion, can take as little as fifteen minutes. When the minister enters, followed by the groom and his best man, who stand to the side, the bride and her attendants begin the processional.

The ceremony consists of three parts:

1. The welcome and introduction by the minister

2. The exchange of vows and rings

3. The final blessing

In the charge to the couple, the minister may say, "Will you have this man to be your wedded husband to live together in holy matrimony? Will you love him, comfort him, honor and keep him in sickness and in health, in sorrow and in joy, and forsaking all others, be faithful to him as long as you both shall live?" He then repeats this charge to the groom.

ROMAN CATHOLIC, EPISCOPAL, AND MAINSTREAM PROTESTANT TRADITIONAL ORDER OF SERVICE

While individual clergy members proscribe specific procedures and may require a certain processional, order of service, and recessional, most Christian wedding ceremonies follow this order:

1. Guests are ushered to pews.

2. Prelude music is played.

3. Grandparents and other honored guests are ushered to their seats.

4. The parents of the groom are ushered in.

5. The mother of the bride is ushered to her seat.

6. The aisle runner, if used, is rolled out by the ushers.

7. The music selected for the processional of the attendants begins.

8. The clergy member enters the sanctuary.

9. The groom and best man enter and move to the right side of the head of the aisle.

10. Attendants enter, ushers first, followed by bridesmaids, the maid of honor, and then the ring bearer and the flower girl.

11. If separate processional music accompanies the entrance of the bride, it begins.

12. The bride enters accompanied by her father, her father and mother, her mother, another escort, or by herself.

13. The ceremony is conducted.

14. The clergy member pronounces the couple husband and wife.

15. The bride and groom kiss.

16. The recessional music begins.

17. The bride and groom turn and walk up the aisle followed by their attendants.

18. The ushers return and escort the family members from the front pews.

19. The remaining guests exit beginning from the front.

EASTERN ORTHODOX CEREMONIES

Marriage is a sacrament in Eastern Orthodox congregations, which can be Greek, Russian, Serbian, Syrian, Polish, or Yugoslavian, among other backgrounds.

The Ceremony

- The ceremony is filled with symbolism, beginning outside the church doors with the betrothal, when the rings are blessed and exchanged. The couple is then led by the priest into the church to stand on a white cloth in front of a wedding platform. A wedding icon is carried in the processional, and the couple is given lighted candles, which they hold during the service.

The Service

1. Much of the symbolism of the service, which can last up to one hour, is represented by threes. During the betrothal, the priest beseeches God's blessings upon the rings and proceeds to bless the groom and the bride with the rings. He does this three times, in the name of the Father and of the Son and of the Holy Spirit. He then places the rings on the ring fingers of the right hands of the couple, and the rings are exchanged three times.

2. The ring blessing is followed by the sacrament of Holy Matrimony, which is followed by three prayers.

3. This service, along with the Byzantine Catholic Church service, then uses crowns, whether metal crowns or floral wreaths, as a solemn part of the service, called "the crowning." The crowns, often attached to each other with a ribbon as a symbol that the two are now one, are placed on the heads of the bride and the groom and exchanged between them. The crowns have several meanings, the two most important being the conformation to biblical teachings that say God bestows his blessing upon his children in the form of crowns; and the identification of the bride and the groom as the beginning of a new kingdom.

4. The service continues with readings, with the presentation of the common cup to the bride and groom to symbolize that from that moment on they will share the same cup of life, and that whatever life has in store for them they will share equally and with the expression of joy.

5. The priest takes the arm of the bridegroom and leads him and the bride around the table three times, as an expression of joy.

READINGS FOR YOUR CEREMONY

Many couples include in their ceremonies scriptural passages, poems, and prose pieces, often read by special friends and relatives. Within some religions, readings may be selected from secular as well as scriptural sources. Within others, readings must be confined to the scriptural. Talk to your clergyperson about the requirements of your faith.

Readings are generally taken from three categories: those that are scriptural and are about marriage, love, and the nature of joy; those that are classical poetry or prose and similar in theme to the scriptural readings; and those that are original poetry or prose.

Following are a few selections that are popular with brides and grooms:

SCRIPTURAL

Love is patient and kind; love is not jealous or boastful; it is not arrogant or rude. Love does not insist on its own way; it is not irritable or resentful; it does not rejoice at wrong, but rejoices in the right. Love bears all things, believes all things, hopes all things, endures all things.

Love never ends; . . . So faith, hope, love abide, these three, but the greatest of these is love.

—I Corinthians 13:4–8, 13

Two are better than one, because they have a good return for their toil. For if they fall, one will lift up his fellow; but woe to him who is alone when he falls and has not another to lift him up. Again, if two lie together, they are warm; but how can one be warm alone? And though a man might prevail against one who is alone, two will withstand him.

—Ecclesiastes 4:9–12

SECULAR

Love is something you and I must have. We must have it because our spirit feeds upon it. We must have it because without it we become weak and faint. Without love our self-esteem weakens. Without it our courage fails. Without love we can no longer look out confidently at the world. We turn inward and begin to feed upon our own personalities, and little by little we destroy ourselves. With it we are creative. With it we march tirelessly. With it, and with it alone, we are able to sacrifice for others.

—Chief Dan George

You have become mine forever.
Yes, we have become partners.
I have become yours.
Hereafter, I cannot live without you.
Do not live without me.
Let us share the joys.
We are word and meaning, unite.
You are thought and I am sound.

May the nights be honey-sweet for us.
May the mornings be honey-sweet for us.
May the plants be honey-sweet for us.
May the earth be honey-sweet for us.

—Hindu marriage poem

Now you will feel no rain, for each of you will be shelter to each other.
Now you will feel no cold, for each of you will be warmth to the other.
Now there is no more loneliness, for each of you will be companion to the other.
Now you are two bodies, but there is only one life before you.
You will now go to your dwelling place to enter unto the days of your togetherness.
And may your days be good and long upon the earth.

—Apache wedding poem

How do I love thee? Let me count the ways.
I love thee to the depth and breadth and height
My soul can reach, when feeling out of sight
For the ends of Being and ideal Grace.
I love thee to the level of every day's
Most quiet need, by sun and candlelight.
I love thee freely, as men strive for Right;
I love thee purely, as they turn from Praise.
I love thee with a passion put to use
In my old griefs, and with my childhood's faith.
I love thee with a love I seemed to lose
With my lost saints,—I love thee with the breath,
Smiles, tears, of all my life!—and, if God choose,
I shall but love thee better after death.

—Elizabeth Barrett Browning

Jewish weddings may be held anywhere that a canopy, or *chuppah,* can be erected and are most often held where the reception will follow. The *chuppah* symbolizes both the tents of ancient ancestors and the formation of the new home of the family being created beneath it. The *chuppah* can be decorated with flowers and may be constructed in a fixed position or held by special attendants.

Preparing for the Ceremony

Interfaith Marriages: Interfaith marriage is not encouraged but nonetheless occurs, usually with a Reform rabbi presiding. Some Reform rabbis will also permit a co-officiant of another faith, but Orthodox and Conservative rabbis, as a rule, will not.

Marrying Divorced Individuals: Usually, even in a Reform congregation, a divorced woman cannot be remarried without a *get,* an official rabbinical document of divorce.

The Ceremony

- The ceremony lasts about twenty minutes.

The Service

1. The bride and groom are escorted by their parents in the procession and gather, with the attendants, under the *chuppah.*

2. To begin the service, which is usually conducted in a combination of Hebrew and English, the bride and groom take a sip of ceremonial wine and are blessed by the rabbi.

3. The bride is given a plain gold wedding ring by the groom, and the marriage contract, or *ketubah,* is read aloud and presented to the couple.

4. A member of the family or a special guest then reads the Seven Blessings, after which the bride and groom again take a sip of wine, this time symbolizing the commitment of the marriage.

5. The ceremony ends with the groom stomping a glass wrapped carefully in a cloth to prevent shards flying, while guests cry, "*Mazel tov!*" meaning good luck and congratulations. The breaking of the glass represents the destruction of the Temple in Jerusalem and is a reminder that even on such a joyous occasion it is important to remember that others may not be so fortunate.

6. The service ends with the recessional, led by the bride and groom and followed by the bride's parents, the groom's parents, the attendants, the rabbi, and the cantor, if one is participating.

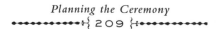

7. Following the recessional, the bride and groom retire to a private room for several minutes before they join the reception. This lovely tradition is known as *yichud,* or "seclusion." These few minutes give the couple a brief time to be alone before the excitement of the rest of the day. It symbolizes the couple's right to privacy. Tradition also says that the couple is to share their first meal together, so they are often brought a small plate of favorite foods.

8. The reception is often begun with a blessing of the challah, a loaf of braided bread that here symbolizes the sharing of families and friends. The meal often concludes with grace and seven special benedictions, sung in Hebrew.

THE PERSONAL TOUCH:

Writing Your Own Vows

Your wedding vows are the expression of your personal commitment to each other. Most clergy are willing to allow certain adaptations of traditional vows, as long as the basic tenets of those vows are expressed in one form or another. These tenets, in most religions, are promises to be true to each other in good times and in bad and in sickness and in health; and to love and honor each other "until death do you part." They may also include pledges to cherish and respect each other. If you decide to write your own vows, keep in mind the following tips:

- Make sure your vows express who you are, reflecting your beliefs and sensibilities.

- If you decide to personalize your vows, avoid sweeping generalizations—make your words personally meaningful.

- Keep it brief. Simplicity and brevity can be far more eloquent than overblown metaphors.

- Even if you plan to memorize your vows, make sure you or the officiant has a written copy in case you go blank and forget what comes next.

- If you come from two different cultures or two different faiths, vows that commit to building bridges of understanding and honoring each other's traditions are particularly meaningful.

MORMON CEREMONIES

Members of the Church of Jesus Christ of Latter-day Saints (Mormons) may be married in one of two ways: in a *marriage ceremony* or a *civil ceremony*. The marriage ceremony, the "sealing ordinance," is for couples of great faith. This sacred ceremony is always held in one of the church's dedicated temples. Members of the Mormon faith believe that when they are married (sealed) in a temple by proper priesthood authority, their union may continue forever; they believe that marriage and family relationships can extend beyond the grave. Mormons proclaim that the family is ordained of God, and that marriage between man and woman is essential to his eternal plan. Only faithful members may be participants in—and guests at—a temple wedding.

If Mormons choose to be married civilly, the ceremonies are simple, sacred ceremonies usually held in a church or a home. They may be attended by anyone. Bishops from the church are authorized to perform civil ceremonies, but receive no pay for conducting such services.

It is typical after both types of ceremonies that a reception is held (often later in the evening) for any number of guests. Gifts for the couple are usually taken at this time.

ISLAMIC (MUSLIM) CEREMONIES

Marriage is a holy and desirable union under Islamic law. Although marriage is not a sacrament, it is a sacred covenant or contract.

Preparing for the Ceremony

Interfaith Marriages: There is no objection to interfaith union, but there may be objection to intercultural marriage, another issue entirely.

Civil Preliminaries: Prior to the religious ceremony, the bride and groom are required to undertake civil preliminaries and may be required to go through a civil ceremony in addition to their religious ceremony.

The Ceremony

- A Muslim marriage ceremony usually takes place in a mosque, at the bride's home, or in an office. The main wedding reception should not take place until after the religious ceremony and also after the civil ceremony, if there is one.

1. When the groom, who is attended by a *serbala* (the youngest boy in his family, usually the son of a sister), arrives at the ceremony, he and his *serbala* are given floral garlands, in welcome.

2. The ceremony is conducted by an *imam,* who reads from the Koran.

3. The bride, who is heavily veiled, and groom are seated apart during their wedding, often on opposite sides of the room.

4. The bride's father and two witnesses ask the bride if she has agreed to the marriage, and the *imam* asks the groom if he has agreed. Assuming they have both agreed, the *imam* completes the marriage certificate.

5. A meal is served after this ceremony, but the bride and groom are still separated, each sitting with their own families.

6. After the meal, the bride leaves, puts on all the jewelry she has been given for her wedding, and returns to sit next to the groom. Her veil is lifted.

HINDU CEREMONIES

Marriage is one of a series of holy sacraments in the Hindu faith, just as it is in the Roman Catholic Church. It is believed that marriage has a purifying quality.

Preparing for The Ceremony

Interfaith Marriages: Interfaith marriages are accepted.

Civil Ceremony: It is important for the couple to be aware of the possibility that a civil ceremony may be required by law. Since the requirements for civil and religious ceremonies are separate, the civil ceremony may take place first, but the couple is not deemed married by the community until they have had a religious ceremony.

The Ceremony

- In India, the Hindu wedding ceremony, which is conducted by a priest, can last all day. In the United States, the Hindu ceremony has been shortened to about ninety minutes, although cultural traditions surrounding the wedding can last several days. It does not have to be performed in a temple and is often conducted in the bride's home.

- Throughout the ceremony, whether of a duration of ninety minutes or an entire day, the couple is instructed in lessons for married life. There is frequent chanting of mantras, or prayers in Sanskrit, which ask for blessings on the union. A traditional Hindu mantra is "I am the word and you are the melody. I am the melody and you are the word."

- The bride usually wears a sari made of a single piece of red fabric embroidered in gold. She is also adorned with 24-karat-gold jewelry, presented to her by the groom's family. The groom wears white trousers, a tunic, and a ceremonial hat.

The Service

1. At the beginning of the ceremony, the bride and groom, usually seated under a decorated canopy called a *mandaps,* may exchange garlands of flowers.

2. After emphasizing the importance of marriage, the priest ties the couple's right hands together with cord and sprinkles holy water over them.

3. The bride's father then gives his daughter to the groom.

4. A sacred flame is lit, and the bride and groom make an offering of rice to symbolize their hope of fertility.

5. The most important part of the ceremony is the Seven Steps, and until this rite is completed, the couple is not married. The Seven Steps symbolize food, strength, wealth, fortune, children, happy seasons, and friendships. Together the bride and groom either take seven steps around the sacred flame or walk around it seven times.

6. Now married, the bride and groom feed each other five times with little bits of sweet food, and the ceremony ends with prayers and readings.

SIKH CEREMONIES

The Sikh wedding ceremony is called *Arnand Karaj,* which means "the Ceremony of Bliss." It solemnizes the union of the couple's souls and seals their religious, moral, and legal obligations.

Preparing for the Ceremony

Civil Ceremony: A civil ceremony may be required to legalize the union.

The Ceremony

- The ceremony may be performed in a *gurdwara,* the Sikh place of worship, or not. It most often takes place in the bride's home.

- It almost always takes place before noon, because according to Sikh belief, the morning is the happiest time of day.

- The bride wears either red trousers and a tunic or a red sari made from a single piece of cloth, and a red head scarf. She also wears all the jewelry the groom's family has given her. The groom wears a white brocade suit, a scarf, and a turban, or he may wear Western dress.

- Wherever the ceremony is performed, a central platform is used, upon which the Holy Book is displayed by the priest who conducts the ceremony. (It is not necessary for a priest to be present; actually any Sikh may be in charge of the ceremony as long as both families agree.)

- Guests sit on the floor around the platform, with men to the right of the Holy Book and women to the left.

The Service

1. Flower garlands play a role, as they do in Muslim and Hindu weddings, beginning when the parents of the bride welcome the groom and his parents by placing garlands around their necks. The bride is brought to greet the groom, and they exchange garlands.

2. The couple stands before the priest and the Holy Book, and the bride's father hands one end of a sash to the groom and the other end to the bride. This symbolizes giving her away.

3. The wedding ceremony comprises four verses from the Holy Book that explain the obligations of married life. Each verse is read and then it is sung. During the singing of each verse, the groom leads the bride around the Holy Book one time, sometimes with the help of guests to symbolize their support. After they have walked around four times, they are married.

4. A prayer and a short hymn follow, and the sharing of a sweet food by all the guests is symbolic of God's blessing on the marriage. Guests place garlands around the necks of the couple or throw flowers petals, a symbol of happiness.

UNITARIAN-UNIVERSALIST CEREMONIES

The roots of this society are Judeo-Christian, making it a pluralistic religion. It is not a church with ecclesiastical rules or rituals, so wedding ceremonies may be personalized and individualized, and couples are encouraged to design their own service from a combination of religious, spiritual, or other traditions that are meaningful to them.

A Quaker wedding is the simplest of all Christian marriages, for it has no music or set order of service. Couples who wish to marry in a Quaker meetinghouse must apply for permission in advance, often two to three months; several levels of approval are required for the marriage to take place. The bride and groom pledge their lifelong love and loyalty to each other but do not exchange rings during the ceremony, for it is believed that the words of the pledge are sufficient. A ring may be given to the bride at the end of the ceremony, however.

Commitment Ceremonies

Sharing the News: Ceremonies celebrating the partnerships of gay and lesbian couples are planned much the same way as heterosexual weddings. The current, nearly universal lack of legal status affects some aspects of the engagement and ceremony—notably the absence of a marriage license, mandated health testing, and a marriage certificate signed by a licensed officiant and witnesses—but in no way limits the joy of the couple and those who share their happiness.

There isn't any one-size-fits-all formula for telling family and friends about an engagement and impending union ceremony. Each situation is personal, and couples have to be guided by their knowledge of the people involved. Reactions can range from unfettered delight, to concern about the public nature of a ceremony (even when families approve of the relationship), to rejection and outright hostility. But patience is a virtue to be cultivated; a negative initial reaction may be transformed when family and friends have time to consider their true feelings. There may be people who never accept the union, but couples should try to give their loved ones the opportunity to come around.

The first people most couples should inform are their parents, but if either partner has children from a previous marriage, his or her children should be told even before the couple's parents. This is particularly important for young children and teenagers whose lives will directly be affected by the union. However, before speaking to parents or children, some gay and lesbian couples may prefer to tell supportive friends. This is often the case when family members are not likely to accept the union or may be uncomfortable with the idea of a same-sex wedding. By telling friends first, couples can enjoy the "lift" of sharing their news with people whose approval is certain—a morale-builder prior to family discussions that are likely to be difficult—and get advice from friends who have had their own commitment ceremonies.

It's wise not to attribute every negative response to prejudice. People who love you may be worried about issues including your choice of partner (is he or she the right person for you?) and lifestyle changes that the union may bring about. (How will career or education goals be affected? Will you be moving far away?) Listen carefully to any objections before assuming motives that may be not be real.

Planning Commitment Ceremonies: Gay and lesbian couples today are creating their own traditions but also following some of the steps of traditional wedding planning. A couple's first major decisions involve the guest list, the budget, the date and time for their ceremony, and the style of the celebration. While most of this book applies directly or can easily be adapted for commitment ceremonies, there are some specific guidelines that can help same-sex couples plan their big events.

Same-sex ceremonies can be religious or secular, and couples are free to plan the kind of occasion that is meaningful to them. They might consult friends who have celebrated their own unions. Gay and lesbian organizations can often provide information about ceremonies, officiants, and local vendors and suppliers. Internet searches might provide links to resources in the immediate area of the ceremony.

While there are many religions that refuse to be associated with commitment ceremonies for gay and lesbian couples, there are others that are willing to affirm same-gender unions in one way or another. Still, which services they will perform varies greatly. For example, within the Universal Fellowship of Metropolitan Community Churches, a couple may participate in a Rite of Blessing (a simple prayer that acknowledges the relationship and offers it to God) or a Holy Union (a covenant or contract between two people), but not a Rite of Holy Matrimony. The Unitarian-Universalist religion performs a Service of Union; some Episcopalian priests will perform a Commitment Ceremony; and some Presbyterians, a Holy Union. Many other clergy, within the structure of their religion or outside it, will perform a ceremony that acknowledges the commitment of the couple.

Because many churches do not sanction a gay or lesbian union through wedding liturgy, gay couples actually have more latitude in planning the ceremony. Most write their own vows in some form or another, using both religious and secular sources, as they wish. In thinking about how to structure a ceremony of commitment, couples generally follow the standard guidelines of Jewish or Christian ceremonies.

The Actual Ceremony: Although there is no set structure for a commitment ceremony, it often includes the following:

> *The introduction.* Any activity before the actual service begins, including the processional, a gathering together and welcome, and an invocation. Some couples want a statement made about being gay, believing that their sexuality is so integral to their being and their relationship that they wouldn't think of not addressing it. Others choose not to address their sexuality, preferring a ceremony that focuses on love and commitment.

The service. Consists of prayers, songs, readings, a homily, and an address by the officiant. If readings are included, some gay couples like to read from the Book of Samuel, chapter 18, verses 1–5, and chapter 20, verses 16–17. Lesbian couples often select readings from the Book of Ruth, chapter 1, verses 16–17. Unless the ceremony is taking place in a house of worship that prohibits the use of secular readings and music, the couple also has a wide range of sources from which to choose.

The vows. The expressions of the couple's intent. The couple may borrow vows from any service book ("I, Jane, take you, Beth"), write their own vows to be read by an officiant, or declare to each other with no prompting.

The exchange of rings. May be preceded by the rings being blessed.

The pronouncement. The public proclamation by the officiant that the couple is recognized as married. This part of the ceremony can be worded several ways, such as "Since you have consented to join together in the bond of matrimony, and have pledged yourselves to each other in the presence of this company, I now pronounce you married" or "In the presence of this company, by the power of your love, because you have pledged to one another your vows of commitment, we recognize you as married."

The closing. The kiss, the blessing of the union, the recessional.

Military Weddings

Any enlisted man or woman on active duty or any officer or cadet at a military academy may have a military ceremony. The military wedding is different from other weddings in the following ways:

- Military weddings are formal in attire. Those who are entitled to do so wear full dress uniform, including the bride, if she, as a member of the military, so chooses.

- Other attendants wear civilian formal attire.

- Men in uniform do not wear boutonnieres.

- The American flag and the standard of the groom's and/or bride's unit is displayed.

- During the recessional, the bride and groom—if the groom is a commissioned officer—pass under an arch of drawn swords or sabers that is formed outside the church or chapel.

- At the reception, the cake is cut with the groom's sword or saber.

Otherwise, the rest of the ceremony is conducted according to the religion and traditions of the bride and the groom.

Civil Ceremonies

In general, you will need to make few arrangements for a civil ceremony to be held at the office of a justice of the peace or at town hall.

- **What do you need for a civil ceremony?** The ceremony itself is simple and brief. The only things you'll need to do are to fulfill the legal requirements and, often, to provide two witnesses.

- **What arrangements are needed for a civil ceremony at another site?** If a civil ceremony is to be conducted at another site, such as the bride's home, a garden, or a rented facility, the same arrangements need to be made as those for a religious ceremony outside of a house of worship; the exception being the need for liturgical items, which aren't required for a civil ceremony.

- **Can the service be personalized?** Of course. If the bride and groom wish to personalize the order of a civil ceremony, they should arrange to meet with the justice of the peace or whoever will officiate to discuss the length of the service, any requirements, and a list of elements they may add to the service.

BLESSING A CIVIL MARRIAGE

Couples who did not have a religious wedding originally can usually get approval from their church at a later date for a church or chapel ceremony for the blessing of the marriage. There is such a service in *The Book of Common Worship.* The widely used Protestant service book follows the traditional marriage service, except that the minister says, "Do you *acknowledge* [rather than *take*] this woman . . ." and makes other similar changes. No one gives the bride away, nor does the groom give the bride her ring again.

- **Who attends?** The service is generally attended only by family and close friends, and there are no attendants. This is, after all, a blessing and not a new celebration of the marriage.

- **What is the attire?** The bride wears a street-length dress or suit, and the groom a dark suit. She may carry a bouquet or wear a corsage.

- **What can be included in the ceremony?** There may be music, and the altar may be decorated with flowers.

Double Weddings

Double weddings may honor two sisters, two cousins, or two best friends. Each couple should have the same number of attendants. All ushers are dressed alike. The bridesmaids' dresses, while not necessarily all the same, should be complementary. One difficulty of a double wedding is the seating of multiple sets of parents. They may either share the first pew, or draw lots to determine who sits in the first row and who sits in the second.

THE CEREMONY AND SERVICE

- If the wedding involves two sisters, the ceremony begins with the two bridegrooms following the clergyperson to the altar. Each stands with his best man beside him. The groom of the older sister stands nearer the aisle.

- The ushers—half of them friends of the first, and the other half friends of the second bridegroom—go up the aisle together.

- Then come the bridesmaids of the older sister followed by her maid of honor, who walks alone.

- The older sister follows, holding her father's arm.

- Then come the bridesmaids of the younger sister, her maid of honor, and, last, the younger bride on the arm of a brother, uncle, or other male relative.

- The first couple ascends the chancel steps and takes their place at the left side of the altar rail, leaving room at the right side for the younger bride and her bridegroom. The father stands just below his older daughter.

- The younger daughter's escort takes his place in a pew with his wife or family.

- The service is read to both couples, with responses made twice.

- Generally, if the service includes a father "giving" two daughters away, he does so—first his older daughter and then the younger. Then he takes the place saved for him beside his wife in the first pew.

- At the end of the ceremony, the older sister and her husband turn and go down the aisle first. The younger couple follow. The bridesmaids and ushers of the first sister pair off and follow. The attendants of the second walk out last.

Reaffirmation of Vows

Traditionally, couples who reaffirm their vows do so on a big anniversary, such as the twenty-fifth or an even higher one. This practice is popular today as a way for some couples to celebrate earlier anniversaries. In addition to wanting to recommit to each other publicly, they may want to have the big celebration they missed out on the first time around. A big party will usually do the trick, as it sometimes will have to, since some clergy will not perform a duplicate of the first wedding ceremony. Most clergy, however, will conduct a simple reaffirmation of vows.

- **When is the ceremony held?** The ceremony can occur during a regular Sabbath service or at a separate time.

- **What type of service is performed?** The form of the service varies, depending on the wishes of the officiant and the tenets of the house of worship.

- **Who attends?** The couple is joined by any members of their original wedding party, plus their children.

- **Can a celebration be held after the ceremony?** Yes. Most reaffirmations of vows are followed by a party or reception, whether at the church, at home, at the home of friends, or at a reception site. Some couples make a reaffirmation of vows a destination affair, inviting family (and perhaps close friends) to a vacation location for both the ceremony and the party.

CHAPTER 12

MULTICULTURAL WEDDINGS

The Universality of Love and New Traditions

Love is a universal phenomenon, and the ceremonial commitment a couple makes to each other is an expression of a timeless trust. Each culture has its own special ways of celebrating and honoring the combining of two lives, many of them traditions that have been lovingly passed on for many generations.

The revival of these multicultural traditions among contemporary brides and grooms is proof of their lasting power and significance—and attests to the desire of modern couples to invest their ceremonies with meaning and a personal and historical context. It's a way to honor your heritage and personalize your ceremony. If the bride and groom come from different cultural backgrounds, incorporating different traditions into the wedding events can be a connective thread linking both families. Fusing traditions of old with 21st-century nuptials only serves to enhance and enrich an already remarkable milestone event.

Today's bride and groom wants their wedding day to be an intimate reflection of themselves, their heritage, and their love. In fact, personalization is one of the most visible trends in contemporary weddings. You have the freedom to fashion a wedding that is unique. You have the best of both worlds—new and novel ideas reflecting your personal interests and values, combined with timeless traditions.

TRADITIONS IN NEW CONTEXTS

Most guests will enjoy unconventional weddings, but their enjoyment will be greater if they know what to expect. When you include elements that are unique to your heritage, life experience, or religion, the result should be a pleasant surprise for guests—not a shock. The ceremony program is a good place to include explanations of customs and rituals that are likely to be unfamiliar. Or the officiant or members of the wedding party can explain specific rituals to the guests during the service.

Discuss the inclusion of any religious rituals and/or readings from other religious texts with your officiant. Some faiths do not allow deviation from their standard services, but it may be possible to include other rituals either before or after the ceremony or at the reception.

Today, weddings are truly a melting pot of old and new customs, drawn from cultures and traditions all over the globe. Below are some of the more common manifestations that couples employ to personalize their weddings. This is followed by examples from around the globe of cultural wedding traditions.

Unity candle. An eloquent and popular addition to many marriage services, the lighting of a single candle symbolizes a couple's unity. Usually, the bride and groom each hold a lighted candle and set a third candle alight together. The individual candles can then be extinguished, but some couples keep them lit throughout the service as a sign that they remain individuals within their union.

The unity candle ceremony is easily adapted. Family members may be included, and parents and stepparents can participate if everyone agrees. Sometimes, the bride's and groom's mothers light the candle. A unity candle lighting is also a good way for an encore couple to involve their children in the service. The ceremony can take place at any point in the service, but if more than the couple are involved, it's often staged after the exchange of vows.

Customs from other faiths and cultures. In religious and secular services, couples may adopt and adapt elements from faiths other than their own. One example is the Jewish tradition of having mothers and fathers in the processional. Some couples have adapted the Greek Orthodox crowning, or wreath, ceremony as a symbol of their unity. Another gracious addition to some American weddings is the Chinese tea ceremony, during which the couple offers cups of sweet tea to each other's families. Native American ceremonial sand painting has inspired sand-blending rituals to signify the mingling of two individuals and their families into a single family.

Secular readings. Including non-religious poetry and prose readings in marriage ceremonies enables couples to express their commitment in words that have special significance for them—and also allows personalization of the service by couples who do not compose their own vows. Couples may ask family members and friends to be readers. Religious and secular officiants might suggest sources for readings, and an Internet search will yield many ideas. Appropriateness and brevity are important, so discuss your options with the officiant early in the planning process.

Musical mixes. Maybe you'd like to open your ceremony with the ringing of a Tibetan gong. Or walk up the aisle to the sound of Scottish bagpipes. Or include Balinese dancing at your reception. Music provides innumerable ways to personalize (and internationalize) wedding celebrations. Ask your officiant about any restrictions on secular music. Musical selections are usually listed by title and composer in the ceremony program, and a brief explanation can also be included.

Jumping the broom. This custom, most often associated with African American weddings, is done to honor the slaves, who were not allowed to marry legally, but who did marry and form strong families. The ritual is said to symbolize the establishment of a new household and is usually performed just after the wedding service or at the reception. The broom (a regular house broom is fine) is decorated with ribbons, flowers, and perhaps special trinkets. The broom is laid on the floor, and guests gather round. On the count of three, the newlyweds, hand in hand, jump over the broom and into their new life as husband and wife. (In the pre–Civil War era, the broom was held above the floor, behind the couple, and they jumped it backward!)

Breaking the glass. In a traditional Jewish ceremony, the bride and groom stand beneath the *chuppah,* or wedding arch or canopy (often adorned with flowers). They sip wine during readings by various guests. Wine is poured into a new glass, and the bride and groom drink from it. The groom then places the glass, wrapped in cloth, on the ground and breaks the glass with his foot—an act symbolizing the destruction of the Temple in Jerusalem that is meant to underscore the fragility of love.

Handfasting. A custom most associated with pagan Celtic tradition, handfasting is now included in some religious as well as secular services. During the service, the couple's hands are ceremonially tied with rope or cords to symbolize their union. Though the Celtic handfasting ceremony probably originated as a contract between a couple to stay together for a year and a day (if the arrangement worked, the contract was renewed), handfasting today signifies the enduring nature of the marriage commitment. It may be the source of the phrase "tying the knot."

The shared cup. In many traditions, both religious and secular, the bride and groom share a cup of wine during the wedding ceremony—a custom unrelated to Christian communion services. In Chinese tradition, the couple drink wine and honey from goblets tied together with red string. In Japan, couples who wed in the Shinto tradition take nine sips of sake, as do their parents, to symbolize the new bonds of family.

Sharing a wedding cup is also a reception custom in many cultures. French couples drink wine from a *coupe de marriage,* or double-handled cup. Irish guests gather round the newlyweds, and toasts are made over cups of mead, a fermented drink made from honey, malt, and yeast.

CAN'T I SEE MY FIANCÉE
BEFORE THE WEDDING ON THE BIG DAY?

Q: My mother insists that I not see my bride-to-be on the day of the wedding until the ceremony. Is this customary in today's weddings?

A: Most couples today have disregarded the musty old superstition of the bridegroom not seeing his bride before the ceremony on the day of the wedding. The superstition stems from the days when marriages were arranged and the groom might never have seen the bride. There was the chance that he might take one look at her and bolt—so it was often safer for them to meet for the first time at the altar! This, of course, is a custom that these days certainly does not need to be followed, unless of course it's something you both feel strongly about.

More Traditions from Around the World

Included below are more ideas from around the globe, for making your wedding day a unique expression of your heritage. Add your personal touch—through music, food and drink, and even good luck charms.

INSPIRATION FROM WHERE?

Want to add some cultural touches but unsure where to look for ideas? Start at home by talking to your family members—parents, grandparents, aunts, and uncles. There may be traditions from their weddings that you can incorporate into your own. Check on-line for ideas as well. Try a search for "Latino wedding traditions." Or Russian, Italian, Greek—whatever your heritage or interest. A little research will likely yield interesting ideas. Explain cultural traditions you include in your ceremony in the program. At the reception, announce the meanings of any rituals that are performed, or put little cards on the tables that note the symbolism.

AFRICAN TRADITIONS

In addition to the broom jumping tradition described above, some couples use fabric and color to highlight their African American heritage. Kente cloth, a woven red, gold, and green design, is often used in African American weddings. This cloth reflects personal, societal, religious, and political culture. The traditional red, gold, and green repeated in the design are liberation colors recognized by people of African descent all over the world: red for the blood shed by millions in captivity, gold for Africa's mineral wealth (prosperity), and green for the vegetation of the land of Africa (home). Boxes arranged in an X in the fabric represent all ideas coming together at one point, symbolizing leadership, consensus, and the voice of the people. The stepped border motif symbolizes defense against assaults and obstacles encountered in the course of an African lifetime. The traditional color of African royalty is purple, accented with gold. These color and fabric accents can be used in many ways—in invitations, as accent colors worn by the bridal party, on place cards, and in decorations.

CHINESE TRADITIONS

Red is the Chinese color for joy and luck—and can be integrated in wedding invitations, flowers, the aisle runner, candles, favors, tablecloths, napkins, and even bridal clothing.

In the Chinese culture, great importance is placed on dates and numbers. Auspicious days for marrying are determined by fortune-tellers and feng shui experts, who examine the Chinese almanac along with the day and hour of the bride's and groom's birth.

Dowries for marriages are still honored in many families, whether in the form of a whole roasted pig, a live chicken, or some other representative swap. For the wedding banquet the bride often changes from her wedding dress into a long red cheongsam, which may be adorned with dragon and phoenix images, representing the union of man and woman.

The Chinese Historical and Cultural Project (www.chcp.org) is a great resource for couples wishing to learn about Chinese wedding customs. The wedding banquet revolves around a feast of elaborate courses, serving foods that have special symbolism for the Chinese, representing such attributes as prosperity, happiness, and long life. Eight courses are generally served—eight, of course, being considered a lucky number. Popular foods for wedding banquets include shark's fin soup, which represents prosperity; "red" foods, such as lobster (another good-luck symbol); and noodles, which symbolize longevity. Lotus seeds, in soup or steamed bread, represent fertility. The Chinese icon representing "double happiness" is often hung on the wall behind the bridal party table.

Chinese couples traditionally honor their relatives and new family members with a tea ceremony—the couple kneels before older relatives and family friends and offers each of them a cup of tea as a gesture of respect. Each honoree hands the couple an envelope of money or gold jewelry in return.

ENGLISH TRADITIONS

If a couple marries in a church, banns announcing the proposed wedding are read aloud in the church three Sundays before the wedding. It is unlucky for the bride and bridegroom to be present at the calling of the banns. The bride and groom and their wedding party often walk together to the church. Weddings are traditionally held at noon; afterward there is a seated luncheon, often called a "wedding breakfast." It is good luck for a chimney sweep to kiss the bride when she comes out of the church. Orange blossoms may be sprinkled on the ground in front of the bride, who might carry or wear a small horseshoe for good luck. When the bride and groom enter and leave the church, bells are rung to scare off evil spirits. The top layer of the wedding cake is called the "christening cake." It is saved and served at the baptism of the first child.

FRENCH TRADITIONS

The bride and groom and the wedding party walk to the church together. Children run to stand in front of the entrance with white ribbons that the bride cuts before entering the church. A silk wedding canopy is held over the couple to protect them from evil spirits during the ceremony. The bride and groom often drink a reception toast from a *coupe de marriage,* a two-handled silver cup that is shaped like a small bowl on a pedestal. The bride drinks first, then the groom, and in so doing they make their commitment to each other.

GERMAN TRADITIONS

In Germany, a couple's silver marriage cup is made in the shape of a young girl wearing a full skirt, holding the cup over her head. The bride and groom drink from it at the same time to symbolize their joining together. Start your own "marriage cup" tradition at your wedding—and save the cup for the next in the family to wed.

At the wedding eve party, called *Polterbend* (rumbling night), the couple is teased and dishes are broken as a method of dispelling evil spirits. Friends and family, and even the couple, purchase cheap china for the event. Only the couple has the privilege of tossing the china down the stairs the night before the ceremony. The festivities continue until the early hours of the morning and may be followed by a breakfast at the bride's parents' home.

Another playful exchange occurs at the end of the ceremony, when guests "rope" the couple in with a barricade of ribbons and garlands of flowers. To get out, the couple has to promise the guests a party.

GREEK TRADITIONS

In Ancient Greece, brides wore wedding veils of yellow or red, which represented fire. These brightly colored veils protected the bride from evil spirits and demons. A Greek bride may carry a lump of sugar on her wedding day to ensure she has a sweet life, or she might carry ivy, as a symbol of endless love.

At the ceremony, the bride and groom are "crowned" by the best man to show that the couple are the king and queen of their union as man and wife. The Greek tradition of the *kalamantiano,* the circle dance, is done at the reception. Candy-coated almonds are given to the guests as favors.

HISPANIC AMERICAN TRADITIONS

Brides and grooms of Mexican descent who are removed from their heritage by time and distance can reconnect by adding long-standing cultural traditions to their nuptials. In addition to the common customs of decorating the church with white roses and holding the mass at nine o'clock in the evening, they can ask those closest to them to be "godparents," giving a responsibility to each. One responsibility is to make three bouquets—one to place on the altar, one to keep as a memento, and one for the bride to toss at the reception. Another godparent holds a dish with thirteen gold coins (*arras*) and rings: The groom takes the coins from the dish and hands them to the bride as a sign of giving her all his possessions; he also promises he will use all he possesses for her support. Two more godparents carry a very long rosary rope (*lazo*), which they drape around the bride and groom as the couple kneels at the altar. Besides the appointing of godparents, musical tradition may also be included: At the reception, the band can play music for *la vibora,* a line dance that the single women perform. It is traditional for one of the attendants to carry flowers for the Virgin Mary. Traditional foods might include tapas, paella, and sangria. Wedding cookies known as *pastelitos de boda* can be served with dessert or given as favors.

INDIAN TRADITIONS

The Hindu bride usually wears a red and gold sari with lots of jewelry and a veil that covers her head. For the ceremony, an orange powder, made from the henna shrub, is put on the bride's forehead. Prior to an Indian wedding, the bride hennas her hands and feet, a practice known as *mehndi*. This ritual is also performed in Pakistan and many other Muslim countries. It originated as a way to mimic or augment the precious dynastic jewelry worn by rich Muslim brides. Typically, a hired henna professional visits the bride a week before the wedding to draw elaborate flowery scrolls on her hands and feet. The groom often rides to the wedding on horseback; his arrival can be heralded by the beating of drums.

How to Combine Traditions?

Q: *My husband is Jewish and I come from an Irish Catholic family. We would like to incorporate some traditional Jewish customs, like the* chuppah *and the breaking of the glass, into our ceremony. We'd like to make our reception more of an Irish celebration, with Irish music and pipers and traditional set dancing. We certainly don't want to make anyone uncomfortable, but we thought we'd combine what we consider to be the best of both culture's customs. Is it proper for us to do this?*

A: If yours is an interfaith marriage, you will need to first make sure that performing your ceremony is acceptable to the officiant and that the ceremony site allows interfaith marriages to be performed. If it is unacceptable to either, you might have to select a different site for your ceremony or find a different officiant. It is important for you and your fiancé to meet with officiants from both faiths to discuss your plans, especially if you intend to have children and want to teach them the ways of both your faiths. Second, it is correct for you to be concerned about guests feeling comfortable. Assess the mix of the majority of the guests—if they are traditionalists or Orthodox Jews, the events might make them uncomfortable. Finally, if your officiants and your site approve, by all means, go ahead and combine your cherished customs. Today, many couples enhance their weddings and receptions with such personalized touches.

IRISH TRADITIONS

The Irish bride sometimes carries a horseshoe for good luck—a decorative porcelain version is now used rather than the real horseshoes brides used to carry. According to legend, the chime of bells keeps away evil spirits and reminds the couple of their wedding vows. For this reason, giving a bell as a gift has become an Irish tradition. A popular toast is the Irish wedding blessing: "May the road rise to meet you. May the wind always be at your back. May the sun shine warm upon your face, The rains fall soft upon your fields."

The musical traditions of the Celtic world are naturally celebratory, perfectly suited to the joyous events surrounding a wedding. Irish *célilí* bands play toe-tapping music for social dancing. The Scots' equivalent are *céilidh* bands and dancing. Irish set dancing is an elaborate form of social dancing, traditionally practiced by four couples in a square. Many modern Irish weddings feature performances by set dancers; others opt for less frenzied accompaniment, such as soothing music from an Irish harp.

GOOD-LUCK CHARMS

Horseshoes. The Irish bride often wears a little porcelain horseshoe on her wrist for good luck.

Coins in shoes. The Swedish bride wears a gold coin from her mother in the right shoe, and a silver coin from her father in the left shoe, while the Irish bride traditionally puts an Irish penny in her bridal shoes for luck.

Jordan almonds are traditionally given to guests at weddings in the Mediterranean countries. They represent the bitter and the sweet sides of marriage.

The evil eye. A good-luck charm or pin in the shape of an eye is worn by attendants in Greece to protect against evil spirits.

Plates are broken in Germany on the doorstep of the bride to drive away evil, and the remaining shards are considered good luck.

The art of mehndi. *Mehndi*—the ancient art of painting beautiful designs on the hands and feet with henna—was practiced for centuries by friends of Pakistani, Moroccan, and Indian brides; it's still done in some villages. In these countries, friends gather before the wedding to color and paint with henna the hands, feet, and sometimes arms and face of the bride in intricate floral patterns as good luck and protection against unfriendly spirits.

Gifts for guests. Japanese brides and grooms sometimes give their wedding guests *kohaku manjyu,* round steamed buns with sweet bean paste in the middle. A pair of buns, one red, one white, is made and given to guests in a special box. Other gifts for guests include a pair of chopsticks imprinted with the date and names of the bride and groom, tied with a ribbon; a collection of origami cranes; and a bag of candied almonds. The reasoning behind this gift giving? The Japanese believe that guests bring so much luck with them that the bride and groom should thank them in return!

Orange blossoms. In a tradition that began in twelfth-century Spain, brides fashion fresh orange blossoms into wreaths to crown their heads or carry them in their bouquets. According to legend, the orange blossoms represent purity and chastity and symbolize everlasting love.

ITALIAN TRADITIONS

On the day of the wedding, the bride is not supposed to wear any gold until after her wedding ring is slipped on. Wearing gold during or before the wedding is thought to bring bad luck. Traditionally, the ceremony (*sposalizio*) itself has been officiated by the priest or civil authority. Old church traditions and folklore banned marriages during Lent and Advent. Religious custom held that weddings should not be scheduled in May and August. May was reserved for the veneration of the Virgin Mary, while August, according to folklore, was considered bad luck. Sunday marriages were believed to be luckiest for the wedding couple.

The best man greets everyone coming to the reception with a tray of liquor. Sweet liquors are served to the women and strong drinks served to the men before any food. The purpose of this is to give everyone an opportunity to toast the bride and groom. A common toast would be "*Per cent'anni,*" which means "For a hundred years." All the men at the reception kiss the bride for good luck—and to make the groom jealous. One Italian celebration, known as the *buste,* began years ago and is very much a part of most modern Italian weddings today. At a *buste,* the bride carries a satin bag (*la borsa*) into which guests deposit envelopes containing their gift checks. In the past, the money helped the bride's family to defray the cost of the wedding, which was their financial responsibility, exclusively. Today, the checks are the guests' wedding gifts to the couple.

Wedding knots, or *farfallette dolci,* made of twisted dough, are popular wedding treats in Italy. Sugared almonds, called *confetti,* are given as favors. The *tarantella,* a traditional circle dance, is danced at the reception.

JAPANESE TRADITIONS

In choosing a wedding date, a Japanese couple looks for an auspicious day of good fortune. The predominant religion in Japan is Shinto, which means "the way of the *Kami*" (God). The traditional Japanese religious wedding ceremony is held in a Shinto shrine. Shinto wedding ceremonies are very private with only family and close friends in attendance.

Today, only one-third of couples in Japan marry in the traditional Shinto wedding ceremony. As part of the ceremony, the bride and groom partake in the sake ritual. They are served sake in three cups. They each take three sips from each cup, repeating this process three times, to complete what is known as the three-times-three ceremony (*San-San Kudo*). Then their parents also take sips, cementing the bond between families. The bride will normally change her dress several times, a Japanese wedding tradition dating from the fourteenth century called *oiro-naoshi* that signifies that she is prepared to return to everyday life. Favors are always given to guests.

SAYING IT WITH BAGPIPES

Scottish wedding receptions often feature music for dancing jigs and reels, keeping up the high-energy custom of Scottish wedding days of old, when pipers played all day in the fields and fiddlers played all day in the house. Bagpipes continue to be a popular instrument at both Scottish wedding ceremonies and receptions, announcing the entrance of the bride and other important events.

SCOTTISH TRADITIONS

In Scotland, at the end of the wedding ceremony, the groom takes off his colorful tartan sash—often the tartan of his clan or family—and places it on his bride, whether gently over her head or on her shoulder, with the sash running diagonally across her gown. It symbolizes the welcoming of the bride into the family and the joining of two into one.

CHAPTER 13

ENCORE WEDDINGS

FEW TRENDS UNDERSCORE the durability of marriage in modern culture more convincingly than the popularity of encore weddings. In spite of increasingly complex family divisions and the prevalence of divorce, the faith in forging a spiritual lifelong union with another person remains strong and steadfast.

Indeed, it is estimated that more than 40 percent of all weddings are encore weddings. An encore wedding is defined as the marriage of two people in which the bride, the groom, or both have been married before—the new wedding is a second or third or fourth. More and more, questions are being asked about the proper etiquette surrounding encore weddings. Can a bride wear white again? Can the bride's father walk his daughter down the aisle again? Is it okay for the couple to register for gifts?

To these questions, the answer is *yes*. There is nothing wrong with an encore bride wearing white, and the wedding can be as festive as a first wedding—and often is. If the bride's father is able and willing, by all means he can walk his daughter down the aisle once more. Certainly, a couple marrying for a second or third or fourth time may register for gifts. An encore wedding may be celebrated with an engagement party, the bride may have the same maid of honor she had for the first wedding, and the ceremony may be as formal as the bride and groom want. The wedding might also be a personalized celebration, with the couple blending the traditions and characteristics that best represent them.

The nature of an encore wedding, however, often dictates a different sort of celebration. An encore couple has to consider how their wedding will affect other people. It is especially important for them to think carefully about the impact their marriage will have on the lives of those whom they love.

The differences between encore and first-time weddings arise chiefly from these two factors:

- When one or both of the couple have children, the marriage is the joining not only of two people but also of pre-existing nuclear family units. Other family members, former spouses, and former in-laws will also be affected.

SHOULDN'T THE EX-SPOUSE BE TOLD
ABOUT THE UPCOMING WEDDING?

Q: I am very hurt and perplexed. I heard about my ex-wife's remarriage the same way the general population did—in a newspaper announcement. While we didn't have children together, we divorced on good terms. Why couldn't my ex-wife have made a simple phone call to me in advance as a courtesy?

A: It certainly would have been thoughtful if she had advised you. Even if there are no children, it is a discourtesy to let an ex-spouse hear this news from anyone other than the former husband or wife. When there are children from the first marriage, it is particularly important to let an ex-spouse know about the impending nuptials. The ex should be told early on, at (or close to) the time the children are informed. This courtesy allows an ex to better deal with the news and help the children deal with it.

- Encore couples are usually older than first-time couples and often fairly or entirely independent (financially and emotionally) of their parents.

The couple may be wholly responsible for wedding planning and expenses, yet every decision they make is likely to have an enormous effect on other people. When there are children, the wedding will begin the formation of a new family and bring changes (not all of them welcome) in the children's established relationships and routines. For other family members and friends, the happiness of a remarriage may be tempered with memories of sad or difficult times.

Whether celebration of an encore marriage is low key or grand, it is usually a powerfully unique and personal experience. Weddings should be occasions of joy, and many remarriages are doubly so. They reaffirm faith in the power of love and commitment.

Ten Guidelines to a Joyous Encore Wedding

1. Keep it simple; don't let the details take over. Plan together. Today, both brides and grooms are actively involved in planning their weddings.

2. Find meaningful ways to include your children (if they concur) in the celebrations, and in your future lives. Tell them first—no matter what their ages.

3. Reassure family and longtime friends that they will continue to play an important part in your lives.

4. Build your celebrations around those traditions and themes that are most meaningful to you, and have confidence in your choices. Make sure, however, that in making these choices, you have given consideration to those involved, and that your choices will not alienate them or make them feel uncomfortable.

5. Be realistic about your budget—in all likelihood it's just the two of you footing the bill.

6. Make sure you have put closure on your first marriage, legally, financially, and emotionally. Put away engagement rings from past marriages; you can save them for the next generation or have stones reset into other jewelry.

7. Register for gifts if you want. Even if you don't expect gifts, many guests will want to give them. Registries are helpful to those trying to select something that a couple would like to have. Be sure to register in a range of prices.

8. Remember that thank-you notes never go out of style. A written note should be sent for every wedding gift you've received, within three months of the date of receipt of the gift. And remember: Grooms can write thank-you notes, too!

9. Whether verbally or with a small token of thanks, be sure to thank anyone who has done anything for you—vendors, service providers, clergy, or friends.

10. When the big day arrives, relax and enjoy your wedding!

A QUESTION FOR PEGGY:

"Must She Wear Her Old Engagement Ring?"

Q: *Both my wife and I were married before. We are very happy together, except for one thing: She insists on wearing the engagement ring given to her by her deceased first husband. Frankly, it bothers me to see her wearing the ring. Is it appropriate for her to do so?*

A: When a widow or divorcée becomes engaged to marry again, she should stop wearing her rings from her previous marriage, whether or not she receives a new engagement ring. She may want to consider keeping it for a son to use as an engagement ring for his future bride, or she might have the stone or stones reset in another piece of jewelry for herself or for her daughters.

A divorcée does not continue to wear the engagement ring from her previous marriage. She may, if she wishes, have the stone or stones from that ring reset in another piece of jewelry. She does not need to return the ring to her ex-husband when she becomes engaged again.

Essential Etiquette for Encore Weddings

WHEN CHILDREN ARE INVOLVED

- **Who tells the kids?** A good percentage of couples marrying again have children from a previous marriage. If you have children from another marriage, it is your responsibility and yours alone to tell your own children about the new wedding; the same applies if your fiancé has children from a previous marriage. You should talk to your children without your fiancé present, so they will feel comfortable about expressing any anxieties they may have. The two of you should then talk to them together, addressing their concerns and asking for their input in making plans. Remember, too, that your children should be the first people you tell about your engagement, even before you tell your parents, other relatives, and close friends.

- **Should children be included in the wedding ceremonies?** Even if your children or your fiancé's children don't live with you or you don't see them as much as you'd like, it's always a good idea to try to include them in the wedding in some way. Second weddings, whether for the bride, the groom, or both, are often about building a family. No matter how you feel about it, your fiancé's children will become part of the new life you create, even if he sees them only on alternating weekends. Talk to your future husband about his feelings on this. It's likely that he feels strongly that any children should be included in the wedding. Most important: Ask the children if they want to be included. This sometimes becomes complicated if an ex-spouse is angry over the remarriage and objects to the children's participation in the wedding. If the ex can be convinced that the children's inclusion in your wedding plans does not detract from their relationship, he or she may be willing to allow it. Still, it's in the best interests of everyone to make every effort to get to know your future stepchildren. Use the time before the wedding to spend time with them. That way, when the wedding day arrives, you both will be much more comfortable sharing this important moment together.

- **Can children serve as attendants in an encore wedding?** This is a great idea, especially if your children are happy about the marriage. You may ask them, your siblings, or your close friends—whomever you would like to have share these moments with you and serve as official witnesses to your marriage. Some encore brides have even asked their children—whether a son or daughter or both—to walk them down the aisle. Instead of "giving the bride away," the child is participating in forming a new family. (No more than one or two kids should escort you, however, as you don't want to crowd the aisle.) It's a wonderful personal touch to hear the officiant ask, "Who will support this new family?" and hear the music of children's voices happily answering, "We do."

- **Can grown-up children be involved?** Of course! For older couples with adult children from a previous marriage, including these children (and even grandchildren) in the celebrations only adds to the joy and community of the occasion. If you both have children who have never met one another, it's a nice idea to bring them all together to announce your engagement, particularly if you are planning a wedding where all will be present. Still, arranging a gathering for your children to meet is not absolutely necessary. You needn't assume that you have to set the stage for all your children to become friends. In other words, don't push them together; give them some time to get used to the idea that you are remarrying.

WHEN FUTURE STEPSIBLINGS MEET

If you both have children from previous marriages, you'll want to get them together before the wedding; but try to make first meetings as casual as possible. A ball game or a movie-and-burgers night makes for a lot less stress at a first meeting than a formal family dinner or an engagement party. It can be hard, but work at dividing your attention equally among all the children. Avoid remarks such as "I know you're going to be great friends" or "Isn't it wonderful that you're going to have a big brother now?" Kids are naturally curious about and wary of new stepsiblings, so let them take early meetings at their own pace. If their manners aren't the best, you can let minor missteps slide.

It's vital to discuss discipline issues with your future spouse before you get the children together. Anticipate problems or conflicts that might arise, so you can present a united front. If your child is deliberately rude or hostile, take him or her aside to correct the behavior. Chastising one child in front of the others can breed only resentment at this point.

Adult children also need some TLC. Give your grown children opportunities to meet, if possible, before the wedding, but don't try to force relationships. Adult stepsiblings may never become close, but they should always treat one another—and you—with respect and courtesy.

As you work with your children—and former spouses—to plan a family-oriented wedding, the following guidelines should help you maintain family harmony:

Do consult each child individually to determine if he or she would like to be in the wedding. Avoid simply expecting children to participate. Respect the wishes of a child or teen who doesn't want to take part, but also leave the door open for a change of heart.

Don't question your future spouse's children about their other parent. Your interest may be benign, but questioning children may be seen as prying and can undermine the children's trust in you.

Do answer children's questions about your previous marriage. You can be honest without being explicit.

Do speak respectfully about former spouses. If you demean an ex-spouse, your future stepchildren may conclude that you will talk the same way about their mom or dad after the wedding.

Do consult your former spouse to schedule events involving the children, especially if wedding activities may conflict with regular visits. Set the pattern now for cooperation with ex-spouses.

Don't use wedding-related activities as an excuse for missing your regular visits and special events with the children.

A Gift a Day

If you are leaving children at home—especially young children—while you and your new mate enjoy a honeymoon, here's a nice way to remember them and make them feel special. Before you leave, buy fun little toys or gifts, wrap them, and have the children's caretaker present one to each child every day that you're gone. The gifts don't have to be big or expensive; they are simply loving remembrances that let the child know that he or she is in your thoughts every day. You could even make a scavenger hunt out of it, providing the child with a written clue each day on the whereabouts of that day's gift.

CHILDREN AND THE HONEYMOON

If your children are young, sooner or later they are likely to ask, "What is a honeymoon?" followed by, "Can we go?" Whether they raise the subject or you do, be very sensitive to their feelings.

An encore wedding followed immediately by a honeymoon trip can be like a one-two punch for children. The disappearance of their parent and new stepparent right after the wedding may cause very young children to fear that their natural parent will not return. Older children may feel hurt or angry at being excluded, especially if they worry that your remarriage will relegate them to second place in your affections.

Young children tend to live in the present moment. They may not really grasp why you are going away after the wedding—no matter how well you explain. If children are genuinely troubled or upset, there are alternatives that couples might consider, including:

- Dividing the honeymoon into two parts—for example, several days devoted to the children followed by time on your own as a couple.

- Delaying the wedding trip. Give the children some time to settle into their new family life (and perhaps new home) and also to adjust to the idea that you and your new spouse will be going away on a trip by yourselves.

- Forgoing the honeymoon. This might be an option when both spouses have children who will live with them. Devote the weeks or months following the wedding to integrating the families and establishing stable routines. Once the children are secure in their new lifestyle, they'll probably have no problem with their parents taking off for some "alone time."

Invitations for Encore Weddings

Just as for first-time weddings, invitations to encore weddings reflect the nature of the occasion—formal, semiformal, informal, or casual. Invitations to small weddings are often made in phone calls or personal notes.

Parents may issue the invitation, especially if the bride is young. Or the invitation can be sent in the names of both sets of parents, with the bride's family listed first. These options are correct even though parents may not be paying for the wedding.

When the couple have been living independently, they often issue the invitation themselves. The following example is a traditional invitation from the couple. The use of social titles is optional. (See also Chapter 7, "Invitation Etiquette.")

The honour of your presence is requested
at the marriage of
Clara Miller O'Connor
and
Arnold Neumeyer
Friday, the twenty-seventh of August
two thousand and ten
at half after four o'clock
The City Club
San Antonio
And afterwards at the reception

RSVP

OR

Clara Miller O'Connor
and
Arnold Neumeyer
request the honour of your presence
at their marriage

[etc.]

When adult children host. It's particularly nice when grown children host their parents' wedding and/or reception. On the invitation, the children (and their respective spouses) are listed as hosts. Traditionally, the invitation lists the bride's children before the groom's children. Each set of children is listed by age, from eldest to youngest.

Mr. and Mrs. Patrick Howell
Mr. and Mrs. Keven Howell
Mr. and Mrs. John Restin
Miss Kristin Restin
request the honour of your presence
at the marriage of their parents
Margaret Diane Howell
and
Stanley Restin
Saturday, the twelfth of June
two thousand and eight
at half after four o'clock
Village Lutheran Church

WHOM TO INVITE

The guest list may play an especially significant role in the size and style of an encore wedding. The size of the guest list is up to you (and your budget). But whom to invite can be problematic if a previous marriage ended in discord and you retain mutual friends with your former spouse. If friends sense that attending the wedding means choosing sides between you and your ex-spouse, they may legitimately feel trapped between a rock and a hard place. In this instance, you might decide on an intimate wedding with only close family and friends in attendance. Another option might be a small ceremony and a larger, informal reception.

If you include guests who attended your first (or most recent) wedding, it's usually best to plan a ceremony and reception that will not invite comparisons. Instead of the formal evening church wedding you had last time, you might host an informal midday service and brunch reception at home.

Inviting your former spouse. It's not a good idea to invite an ex-spouse to an encore wedding. Friends can feel awkward celebrating a new marriage when the former husband or wife is there. Even if you and your ex are on good terms, there are other family members to consider, and there's no reason to open old wounds when it can be avoided.

Most important, consider your new spouse and any children you both bring to your marriage. It can be difficult and confusing for them to celebrate your new family if your former spouse is present. Even if you and your ex are friendly, it's best to leave him or her out of the festivities.

Inviting your former in-laws. Widowed and divorced people who remain close to their former in-laws may certainly invite them. But be conscious of their feelings; your new marriage may be bittersweet for your former spouse's parents. It's a good idea to talk with them personally and tell them how much you would like them to attend. But also let them know that you understand if they choose not to. It's also considerate to discuss your wishes to invite your former in-laws with your fiancé/fiancée beforehand.

Gifts, the Second Time Around

- *How do you let guests know that you don't want gifts?* Many encore wedding couples already own the wedding china, silverware, and other gifts traditionally given to first-time brides. They may even feel they want for nothing, desiring only to enjoy the company of family and friends in celebrating their happy event. Often, too, the issue of "no gifts" comes up when the guest list includes people who were at your first wedding, who you don't feel are obliged to give you a gift the second time around.

  First of all, you should make no mention of gifts on your invitations. Instead, rely on word of mouth, mentioning to close friends and relatives that you hope guests know your wish about "no gifts." You can ask them to pass this message along to anyone who asks them what you would like. Although it may seem odd that there is a prohibition against asking people not to bring you gifts when all you are doing is trying to be thoughtful, there is a reason. The moment you mention gifts, you put an *emphasis* on gifts, which is the opposite of your intent. And, indeed, friends and family who have attended a first wedding and given a gift are under no obligation to give another wedding gift to the same person, even if, as is usually the case, the marriage is to someone new. Still, there will be many who know this but who will want to give you a gift anyway, as a way to share in the celebration of your happiness.

- **Should you register for gifts?** Registering is actually a thoughtful thing to do. New friends who have never given you a wedding gift before will probably want to give you something. Even though many encore couples have little need for china, silver, and other traditional gifts, registering at one or two stores for items you'd like to receive can be helpful for guests. You could either register at a few stores for the things that you don't have or make a list for your parents and attendants to share if asked. Your ideas could be anything from a two-by-four for a new deck to a bunch of movie tickets for a nearby theater to a welcome mat for your front door. Think about your interests. Sporting goods, hardware, garden tools, books and CDs, videotapes and DVDs—you can register for items that are both useful and inexpensive. Remember, you can keep your ideas restricted to reasonably priced items that would be fun for your friends to find or create to commemorate your marriage.

- **What happens to the monogrammed linens and sterling silver flatware from a first marriage?** It's really up to you and your fiancé/fiancée to decide what's best and practical for the both of you. With regard to the linens, unfortunately their monogram may be a daily visible reminder of your previous marriage. Your new partner could face a lifetime of having to see your former spouse's initials everywhere he or she looks. Here's a suggestion: Why not pass them down to any children you have, or give them away?

The flatware is a different story, however. Sterling silver flatware is exorbitant to replace. Again, ask your partner how he or she feels about using the flatware. It is very likely that you are both bringing belongings to the marriage, and the flatware can be thought of as no different from furniture or other household items from your pasts that work well together in your new home with each other.

Encore Ceremony Ideas

The following are some ways that today's encore couples are reaching out to make their weddings into genuine family affairs:

Children as attendants. This is practical when there aren't too many children or children too young to take an active part. To avoid any appearance of favoritism, if one younger child or teen is included, all should be. Equal treatment is extremely important to youngsters and teens, so try to assign each child a role that is significant to him or her. For example, if the bride wants her teen daughter to be a bridesmaid, then it's advisable to ask the groom's teen daughter as well.

If the bride has more than two children, it's usually best not to have them all escort her down the aisle. Since girls as well as boys can be ushers, this can be a responsible role for older children. Children who are comfortable before an audience might present a reading. Just be sure that each child is happy with his or her role, whatever it is.

A family addition to the service. After the couple are pronounced husband and wife, the children can be asked to come forward to join them. The officiant then addresses a special message to the children. A family prayer is often included in religious ceremonies. This brief part of the service usually emphasizes the creation of a new family, and the children are mentioned by name.

A candle-lighting ceremony. After the ceremony, the children and perhaps the parents of the bride and groom come forward, or the couple could go to where the family members are seated. Candles are lit by everyone as an expression of the union of the families.

Special remembrance gifts. The couple might present each of the children with something unique to the occasion, such as an engraved medallion, picture frame, or photo album. Include the children in wedding photos. Be sure your photographer knows who they are and captures them in plenty of candids as well as in formal photos.

Flowers. Small tokens can mean a great deal. Whether they take part in the ceremony or not, be sure that each child has a boutonniere or flower. Corsages are fine for girls, but a particularly memorable idea is a small nosegay including the same flowers as the bride's bouquet.

Attire, the Second Time Around

- **Is an encore bride restricted in her choice of attire?** It used to be that second-time brides were advised to wear a pastel suit or, for a more formal wedding, a pastel or off-white gown. This custom dated back to earlier days when white symbolized purity or virginity—thus making it an inappropriate color for a person who already had been married. Today this is no longer the case—white is thought of as a color of joy and celebration. You may wear as beautiful a white bridal gown as you can find—but make sure that it is appropriate to your age and figure.

Although it is preferable for an encore bride to go the more low-keyed route, it is okay to wear a veil if you really want. These days, wearing a veil can be regarded as a fashion choice—and for some religions, it's required. Do, however, apply some common sense if you plan to wear a veil. You'd preferably choose a veil style that matches your gown, and one that isn't overly frilly or long.

ETIQUETTE FINE POINTS:

ENCORE BRIDES AND THE BLUSHER VEIL

With a nod toward the tradition that said only a first-time bride could wear a veil, you should forgo a blusher veil that covers your face. This style is still an option reserved for the very young or first-time bride.

The Wedding Party, the Second Time Around

- **Can the wedding party of an encore wedding include attendants from previous weddings?** Yes. While your upcoming wedding should not be a flashback or replica of your first wedding, it is absolutely fine to include people who remain near and dear to you in your encore wedding, whether they were attendants in a previous wedding or not. If, for example, your sister was your maid of honor for your first wedding and you remain the best of friends, it's perfectly acceptable for her to serve as your maid of honor again. All you need to do is make sure your sister is comfortable with the idea. Tell her you feel so fortunate to have her by your side, supporting you and welcoming her new brother-in-law. It's a fresh start for you, and who better to have with you than your best friend?

Showers, the Second Time Around

- **What is the etiquette of an encore wedding shower?** A second shower is okay only if it's carefully planned—other than a few close friends and relatives, the guest list should not include people who came to a first shower. Of course, if you've changed jobs or moved to a new town since the first get-together, another party could be in order. But if your friends plan to invite people who have already "showered" you, a small luncheon or afternoon tea—sans gifts—would be a better way to go. (See also Chapter 10, page 178: "Showers on a Shoestring"; and page 179: "Theme Showers.")

    As for the shower gifts for an encore wedding, often theme showers work well, because they allow the couple to be specific about the things they really need. So, for example, if the couple wants to replace monogrammed linens from a previous marriage, a linen shower would be a great way to accomplish this.

When Is a Prenuptial Agreement Advisable in an Encore Marriage?

Q: *My fiancé has asked me to sign a prenuptial agreement before our wedding, which is the second marriage for both of us. He suggests that doing so will benefit me as well. What exactly is a prenup, and when is signing one advisable?*

A: A prenuptial agreement is basically a contract between two people that defines the rights and benefits that will exist during the marriage and after, in the event of divorce or death. Although anyone can have a prenuptial agreement, it is most often used when the bride or groom or both bring assets to the marriage that they want to protect in the event of divorce or death. This is particularly true for people marrying for the second or third time who have children from a previous marriage and who want to ensure that certain assets will be legally passed on to their children. Prenuptial agreements can be sensitive matters for brides and grooms, but they actually protect a couple and allow them to make their own rules about the distribution of their finances, should they someday seek divorce or should they either or both die. (See also Chapter 3, pages 56–57: "Pre- and Postnuptial Contracts.")

CHAPTER 14

WEDDING ATTIRE

M ANY BRIDES-TO-BE BEGIN SHOPPING for their gowns as soon as they become engaged. But before you dash off to the stores, your first step is to determine how formal or informal your ceremony and reception will be, when and where they will take place, and how much money you're prepared to spend. (See also Chapter 3, pages 41–44: "Determining a Budget.") Religious and cultural considerations can affect your selections. So will the choice of attendants, since bridesmaid's dresses should be chosen with the women who will wear them in mind.

Most brides purchase new wedding gowns, and it's smart to begin shopping as soon as the critical planning decisions are made. Special dress orders can take months—sometimes as many as ten months to a year for designer creations. If you're having your dress made, you need plenty of time to work with your designer or seamstress. Even off-the-rack dresses usually require alterations, so fittings will be part of your and your attendants' busy pre-wedding schedule.

Men's clothing is easier to select, but don't wait until the last minute. Many grooms and their attendants rent formal, and sometimes informal, wedding clothes. Because formal-wear rental stores can run out of stock at certain times during the most popular wedding months, prom season, and holidays (June, September, May, and December), you should investigate rental sources and place orders well in advance.

The following discussions and the dress chart at the end of this chapter apply primarily to traditional American wedding attire, but the basic guidelines and etiquette of selecting clothing for the wedding party are applicable to virtually every culture.

The Wedding Gown

White is just one of a rainbow of colors that brides wear, and though it has been the main custom since the 1800s—boosted by the fashion for white gown and orange blossoms set by Queen Victoria at her 1840 wedding—it's not the only choice for today's women. In fact, until the late nineteenth century, most American brides wore their best dress, whatever the color, because the expense of a special gown was prohibitive except for well-to-do families. During the twentieth century, white came to signify joy rather than virginity and is now considered appropriate for all brides, including those marrying again.

Other colors—especially those drawn from non-European ethnic and cultural traditions—are equally acceptable. Although white, in all its many shades and pastel tints, is still the conventional choice for long formal and semiformal bridal gowns, the ultimate decision about color belongs to the bride. In fact, more and more brides are opting for some color, whether it's choosing an accent such as a large bow for the gown or a deep-champagne-colored fabric (more golden than ivory, often referred to as "champagne rum") from head to toe. These days, the choices are limitless.

FABRICS AND STYLES

As a general rule, the more formal the wedding, the more formal the fabric of the wedding dress. Fabrics are selected with the season in mind, as the general guidelines below indicate. But you have to take into account the weather in your area. In a cold climate, for example, velvet or brocade might be worn earlier in the fall and later in the spring than in temperate and hot zones.

Spring	*Lace and tissue taffeta*
Summer	*Organdy, marquisette, cotton, piqué, linen*
Fall/winter	*Satin, brocade, taffeta, velvet, moiré, crepe, peau de soie, wool (informal)*
Year-round	*Silk, jersey, blends*

Think about your comfort, and don't be guided by looks alone. Lace is beautiful but can be itchy over bare skin. Ball gowns of multi-layered or bead-encrusted fabrics can literally weigh a bride down after several hours of standing or dancing. Synthetic fabrics tend to be hotter than natural ones, so a blend might be the better choice. Since formal gowns may be boned and often require more structured undergarments than women today are used to, try on the dress with the correct undergarments to get a sense of its weight and ease of movement.

Your choice of style, or silhouette, is a matter of what is most flattering to you and most appropriate to the formality of the wedding. Floor-length gowns are usually worn for formal and semiformal weddings but are seen at less formal weddings, too. A long, summery, cotton or piqué dress might be just right for a casual garden or beach wedding. In addition to factors such as the setting and time of year, the style, length, and color may also be determined by the couple's cultural heritage. Many of today's brides, grooms, and their attendants wear full ethnic and national ensembles or adapt elements such as the Japanese marriage kimono, Turkish tunic, African *bubah* and symbolic patterned fabrics, and Chinese cheongsam.

CLASSIC WEDDING GOWN SILHOUETTES

Ball gown   *Floor-length "Cinderella" style with big, full skirt*

A-line   *In the shape of an A, slimmer at the bodice and widening from the bodice down*

Empire   *High-waisted with the bodice cropped just below the bust*

Basque   *U- or V-shaped waistline dropped several inches below the natural waist*

Sheath   *Narrow, following the body's contours; no defined waist*

Ball gown   A-line   Empire

Basque   Sheath

Neckline, sleeves, and back. Brides often ask how revealing their gowns may be. Your personal sense of decorum is generally paramount, but it's important to think about where and in what tradition the wedding will be held. For a religious ceremony, ask your officiant about any dress restrictions or expectations. (Are bare shoulders and arms acceptable? Is a face veil required? Do dress rules differ for religious services in a house of worship and at a secular location?) For an interfaith or inter-sect service, there may be several traditions to observe, so talk to each officiant.

There may be more freedom of choice for secular ceremonies, but issues of good taste and consideration for others still apply. If you will be married in a judge's chambers, for instance, respect both your officiant and the solemn civil office he or she holds, by dressing appropriately.

Think about your guests. What is acceptable to your contemporaries may make older guests uncomfortable. While it's tempting to say, "My wedding, my way," a gracious bride would never deliberately shock or discomfort the people invited to share her wedding day.

Train. A train adds visual interest to the back of a floor-length gown, but it is by no means necessary. The train may be sewn into the dress, and many sewn-in trains can be "bustled," or gathered up, at the back, so the bride need not carry her train after the ceremony. Detachable trains are easily removed for the reception.

Popular styles include:

The sweep or brush train	*Drapes from the waistline to 6 inches on the floor.*
The court train	*Extends 3 to 4 feet from the waistline.*
The chapel train	*Extends 5 feet from the waistline.*
The cathedral train	*Extends 2½ to 3 yards from the waistline; very formal.*
The Watteau train	*Drapes from the back yoke of the dress.*

RENTED AND BORROWED

The average cost of today's new wedding gown, plus headpiece and shoes, is between $1,000 and $1,800, with designer gowns running into the multiple thousands. Gowns tend to be purchased from department stores, wedding gown specialty shops and outlets, and designer studios (for the more expensive creations). But brides have less expensive options, including renting, borrowing, or buying secondhand gowns—even off the Internet. All routes are acceptable and sensible, especially if you want to save money and feel no real need to preserve the dress. Nor do you have to purchase your gown and accessories from bridal industry sources. You may find just the thing for an informal or casual wedding at your favorite department or clothing store.

The Bride's Accessories

You have many options, from regally elaborate to stately simplicity. Accessories are best selected to complement your gown and the formality of the wedding, but your comfort is basic.

Veil and headdress. Historically, the bridal veil probably relates to the face coverings worn by unmarried and married women in many cultures as a sign of modesty and female subservience. But today's bridal veil is directly descended from French and English practice beginning in the 1500s and is particularly related to the nineteenth-century fashion for veiled headgear in all social situations.

Veils and headdresses may be a matter of religious custom but otherwise are strictly personal choices. Many of today's brides prefer nothing more than flattering hairstyles, perhaps enhanced with flowers, hair combs, or elegant barrettes.

Veils can be worn over the face or trail from the top or back of the head and are usually attached to or draped under a headdress. Veils come in a variety of semi-transparent materials, including lace and tulle, and lengths. Among the most popular styles are:

ETIQUETTE FINE POINTS:

LIFTING THE VEIL

Some brides like to wear face veils for their wedding, and some religions even require that face veils be worn. If the bride chooses to wear a veil over her face coming up the aisle and during the ceremony, it should be short and about a yard square. It is either taken off by the maid of honor when she gives the bride's bouquet back to the bride at the end of the ceremony (if it is a separate piece attached to the headdress), or the bride or the groom may gently lift it back.

The blusher veil   *Short veil worn over the face; may fall just below the shoulders.*

The fingertip veil   *Falls to the tips of the fingers.*

The mantilla   *Scarflike veil that drapes over head and shoulders.*

The sweep veil   *Touches the ground.*

The chapel veil   *Trails 1 to 2 feet behind the gown.*

The cathedral veil   *Trails 1 to 3 yards behind the gown.*

A face veil, worn for the processional and during the ceremony, is usually about a yard square and may be detachable. At the end of the ceremony, the face veil is either removed (if it is a detachable part of the headdress) or lifted by the maid of honor when she returns the bride's bouquet, or lifted by the groom or the bride herself.

The blusher veil

The fingertip veil

The mantilla

The sweep veil

The chapel veil

The cathedral veil

Bows, headbands, tiaras, Juliet caps, and floral wreaths can be worn with a veil or without. Fashion hats and headbands, with or without short veils, make attractive accessories with informal attire such as a wedding suit.

wreath of flowers

Must She Wear Her Mother's Gown?

Q: *My mother has always hoped that I'd be married in her wedding gown. It's really beautiful and I'd love to wear it, but my mom is four inches shorter than I. She's petite, while I'm more full-figured. She's offering to have her dress altered for me, but I'd rather get something new that really fits. How can I get out of this without hurting my mom's feelings?*

A: Wearing an heirloom gown is a wonderful tradition, when it's practical. On the basis of the differences you describe, however, your mother's dress would probably need to be completely remade. When you talk with your mother, be sure she knows that you would really like to wear her dress if you could. (You aren't criticizing her taste.) Be respectful, but also be clear that you won't feel comfortable in a dress that doesn't suit you. You might also talk with a seamstress or tailor who can explain to your mom how extensive the changes would be. Then involve your mother in your dress selection; seeing you in a beautiful new gown is likely to cure her disappointment. If it's feasible, incorporate something from her wedding attire (a piece of her jewelry, some lace, or her veil) in your outfit—a loving way to show how much you appreciate your mom and to create a new family tradition.

Undergarments. Your dress shop or dressmaker should be able to recommend bras and other undergarments. You should wear these for your fittings and make sure they complement your gown. Since women today are not used to wired, boned, or strapless bras or waist-length and full-torso undergarments, "practice" by walking around, bending, moving your arms, dancing, and generally getting comfortable in all new undergarments.

Shoes. The bride's shoes are traditionally satin (with a satin gown) or *peau de soie,* dyed to match her gown. Though pumps were once the only choice for formal weddings, sandal styles have become popular, particularly for warm weather or for more casual weddings. Whatever the style, shop for comfort, avoiding stiletto-heeled shoes that can snag on a long gown, crinolines, or an aisle runner. Since comfort is so important, it's okay to wear flat or low-heeled shoes, which are now a fixed element of modern dress. Traditional retailers are offering fashionable ballet-type flats, especially enjoyed by brides who are conscious about being taller than their grooms. Low or flat shoes are mostly hidden under a long gown anyway, but if you have your heart set on higher heels, you can always change into attractive flat or low-heeled shoes for the reception and dancing.

Gloves. Wearing gloves can often enhance the look of a wedding dress but is optional except for very formal weddings. Fabrics range from cotton and soft kid to satin and lace and should be in keeping with the wedding gown. A short, loose glove can easily be removed by the bride and handed to the maid of honor when rings are exchanged. Tight or long gloves are trickier. When it's difficult to remove a glove, you can snip open the seam on the underside of the ring finger before the ceremony and then slip off only that finger of the glove when you receive your ring. Finger-less gloves are another way to solve the ring-finger problem.

Jewelry. Traditional bridal jewelry is classic in design and neutral in color, such as a pearl or diamond-and-pearl necklace and earrings or simple gold ornaments. But colored stones are fine, too. Sometimes a bride wears heirloom family jewelry, either the gift of the groom and his family or something from her own family. Very ornate jewelry used to be avoided if it would distract from the bride's overall look, but these days some fashionable brides are wearing chandelier earrings and jeweled chokers.

THE PERSONAL TOUCH:

VARIETY FOR YOUR BRIDESMAIDS

Countless tales have been told of unhappy bridesmaids who had to walk down the aisle in dresses they disliked or that were clearly unflattering. Some brides have hit on the clever idea of letting their bridesmaids choose their own dresses. It's practical, too: Why not let each attendant pick out a dress she actually likes and can use again? It is perfectly proper for your bridesmaids to wear different dresses. There is absolutely nothing wrong with variations on a theme. Bridesmaids' dresses may be identical in texture and style but not necessarily in color—or vice versa. The trend these days is away from costume-like sameness. It is, however, a good idea to give your attendants some general guidelines so that the wedding party doesn't clash visually. Have the attendants select dresses of similar lengths, styles, and colors, for example. You can have each bridesmaid wear a slightly different variation on one color—red, for example, with one attendant in rose, another in soft pink, and another in sunset red. One bride asked her attendants to pick floor-length dresses with short sleeves in various shades of purple. The result was a glorious blend of lavender, violet, and magenta—a living, breathing wedding bouquet!

Bridesmaids' Attire

Because attendants generally pay for their own dresses and accessories, the bride is obliged to carefully consider the cost of their outfits. It's also important to think about your bridesmaids' heights and figures and look for styles that will be as flattering as possible for everyone.

Though the maid or matron of honor traditionally assists in the selection of bridesmaids' attire, try to consult with all your attendants. Unless someone requests that you order her gown, it's best to respect your attendants' privacy and not to ask for sizes and measurements. Try to let your attendants do their own ordering. Alterations are usually handled by the store where the gowns are purchased, but inform your attendants if you have better sources.

APPROPRIATENESS

Bridesmaids' dresses should match the bride's dress in formality, though not necessarily in style or fabric. For example, if the bride wears satin, her attendants would wear a similar material, though not organdy or linen. As long as the dresses are complementary, the bride can wear a long gown, while the bridesmaids can wear a shorter length. At very formal weddings, however, both the bride and her attendants traditionally wear floor-length. Virtually all colors are acceptable today, including black and shades of white. If choosing white, be careful that attendants won't look like the bride.

A QUESTION FOR PEGGY:

THE BRIDESMAID ASKS:
"WHAT IF I'M ON A TIGHT BUDGET?"

Q: *I have been asked by a dear friend to be a bridesmaid in her upcoming wedding. The problem is, I am on a strict budget and I am sure she will select extravagant dresses for us to wear. Can I hint that I have a limited income to spend on a dress and shoes? Or should I simply turn her down and tell her why?*

A: Tell her truthfully that you cannot realistically afford an expensive dress, and that even though you would love to be a bridesmaid, it is simply out of the question economically. That way, you give her the choice of finding someone else or selecting a less expensive dress. If you are really close, the bride may decide that her wedding would not be complete without you and offer discreetly to buy the dress for you herself.

BRIDEZILLA ALERT!
WHAT TO DO WITH A DEMANDING BRIDE?

Q: *I'll be a bridesmaid in a couple of months, but the bride is making all her attendants crazy with her instructions. She sends us lists with the color and brand of lipstick, eye shadow, and nail polish we have to wear. We're all supposed to have our hair and nails done at one very expensive salon. Our shoes aren't open-toed, but she expects us to have pedicures. She's even asked one bridesmaid to have her ears pierced and another to get her hair highlighted. Is this normal? What can we do?*

A: It's understandable that brides want their wedding day to be perfect, but some get carried away and obsess about details. Your situation could be worse. There have been brides who have told attendants to lose weight, have teeth capped, hold off getting pregnant, or undergo skin treatments before the wedding.

You and the other attendants should meet with the bride now and talk about your issues. Be as kind as you can (she may not realize that her instructions are excessive), but let her know that you are united. Explain your objections clearly and rationally. Look for some compromises. You'll be glad to discuss makeup and hairstyles, but the final choice is up to each of you. You might bring up costs, but don't make it your main issue; if the bride says she'll pay, you will be back to square one.

For the discussion to go well, be prepared with positive as well as negative comments. A few well-deserved compliments can do wonders. If she reacts badly, give her time to calm down and think. If she still insists on having her way, you have two choices: Go along graciously or get out (though hopefully, it won't come to that point). Should you decide to "resign," avoid blaming or saying anything that could end your friendship. Good people can do very foolish things under stress, and your friend may someday regret her imperious behavior.

Whatever you decide, the goal is to create a look for the entire wedding party that is harmonious and suitable for the occasion. Before selecting attendants' outfits, however, be sure to check with your officiant about any dress requirements.

DIFFERENT SHAPES, DIFFERENT DRESSES

Attendants' dresses don't have to be exact matches, so brides may offer their bridesmaids a range of styles—dresses in the same fabric and color (or range of colors) but of different cuts. Another option is to ask attendants to select their own dresses within general guidelines for fabric, length, color, and degree of formality. Another twist: The maid or matron of honor's dresses and flowers may be of a different color and style than the other attendants'.

Attendants' shoes are usually the same type—pump or sandal—and color but need not be exactly the same shoe. Dyed fabric shoes are one choice. (If the bride herself will have all the shoes dyed, she should ask her bridesmaids to buy their shoes and deliver them to her in advance. The dying can then be done at one time to ensure that the colors are a perfect match.) Or you can ask your bridesmaids to wear dressy black or white shoes in the same basic style. When attendants are wearing street-length or midcalf-length dresses, you'll want to coordinate the color of panty hose.

Although the bride selects the headdress for her attendants, she should never dictate hairstyles. If you expect attendants to wear matching jewelry, you should provide it, perhaps as your bridesmaids' gifts. Otherwise, discuss jewelry with your attendants but leave the final choice to them.

Clothes for Young Attendants

When children are included in the wedding, their parents are expected to pay for their outfits. The bride and groom or their families provide all the necessary accoutrements, including flowers, baskets, and ring cushions.

Junior bridesmaids and junior ushers wear the same clothing as their adult counterparts. A young bridesmaid's dress, accessories, and flowers are the same color and style as the other bridesmaids', through dress style can be adapted so that it is suitable for her age and size. A ten-year-old, for instance, could wear a strapped version of the bridesmaids' strapless dresses. A junior usher dresses like his elders, usually in a tux or dark suit and tie.

Flower girls. A flower girl traditionally wears a white or pastel dress of midcalf length, white socks, and party shoes like Mary Janes. The dress may be similar to the bridesmaids' gowns but should be appropriate for a young child. Headdresses include wreaths of artificial flowers or ribbons or flowers braided in the child's hair. (If headwear makes a child uncomfortable, it can be dispensed with.) Flower girls carry a small bouquet or a basket of flowers, but as a rule, they no longer scatter petals before the bride.

Ring bearers, train bearers, and pages. Very young boys often wear white Eton-style jackets and short pants with white socks and shoes. Or they might wear boyish blazers and kid-appropriate good clothes. Older boys usually wear navy-blue suits with navy socks and black shoes and a boutonniere. It's best to forgo dressing boys in tuxedos; wait until they're high-school age.

The Groom and His Attendants

Though formal and semiformal attire for grooms, groomsmen, and ushers hasn't changed significantly (aside from updating of cuts for trousers and lapels) for a century, today's groom does have more fashion choices, especially for informal and casual weddings. Even the traditional black or midnight-blue tuxedo can be paired with modern shirt and tie styles, and the ubiquitous dark suit or blazer and trouser combination offers room for variation. Clothing from other cultural or religious traditions can be worn for any degree of formality.

| Tailcoat | Waistcoat | Cutaway | Tuxedo | Suit |

The point is to select outfits for yourself and your attendants that are appropriate to the style of the wedding and solemnity of the marriage service. The chart on pages 264–265 will give you the specifics of daytime and evening dress for traditional formal, semiformal, and informal weddings, but the general guidelines are as follows:

Formal evening. A tuxedo is often the choice. Traditionally, a tuxedo is not correctly worn until six o'clock or after. For the more formal evening wedding, attire includes black tailcoat and matching trousers, stiff white shirt, wing collar, white tie, and white waistcoat: this outfit is referred to as "white tie."

Formal daytime. Worn for any wedding before six o'clock. Black or Oxford gray cutaway coat and black or gray striped trousers, pearl-gray waistcoat, stiff white shirt, stiff fold-down collar, black-and-gray four-in-hand tie or dress ascot. Customs have loosened with regard to wearing a tuxedo before six o'clock. These days, it is correct to wear a tux *before* six—if the wedding or event starts in the mid- to late-afternoon and continues into the evening. In some parts of the United States, it has become customary for tuxedos to be worn earlier in the day, even in the morning. It is wise to check with either the officiant or a professional wedding consultant to determine local custom.

Semiformal evening. Black or midnight-blue tuxedo and matching trousers, piqué or pleated-front shirt with attached collar, black bow tie, black waistcoat or cummerbund. A white dinner jacket and black cummerbund can be substituted for hot-weather ceremonies.

Semiformal daytime. Suit-style dark gray or black sack (straight-backed) coat, matching trousers, soft shirt, and four-in-hand tie.

Informal day or evening. Lighter-weight suits or jackets and trousers, soft shirts with attached collars, and four-in-hand ties in a dark, small pattern. In warm weather, grooms and attendants might wear dark blue or gray jackets or blazers with white trousers, with either white or black dress socks and shoes. In hot climates, white suits can be worn.

Attendants' Attire. There are basically two ways to organize attendants' attire. The groom might tell his attendants what he will wear and ask them to rent or purchase the same. Or it may be more convenient for the groom or best man to ask for sizes and measurements and then order all the outfits and accessories from a single rental source. (Formal-wear rental stores may offer discounts for multiple orders and normally provide alteration service.) Dress shoes can also be rented, and this is a good way to ensure that everyone is shod in the same style.

Except for boutonnieres (supplied by the groom), attendants are responsible for their rental and/or purchase costs. It's normally the duty of the best man or head usher to see that everyone is dressed appropriately.

Don't forget comfort when selecting attire. Coats should lie smoothly across the back but give you freedom of movement. Coat sleeves should reveal a half inch of shirt cuff when your arms are straight at your sides. Trousers are hemmed even with the tops of the backs of the shoes and have a slight break in front, so the hem rests on the shoes.

Mothers and Fathers of the Wedding Couple

This will be your children's day, but you have the right to shine, too. Parents and stepparents should choose clothing in keeping with the style of the wedding. Comfort matters as well, since you're likely to be busy for the entire event, so select garments that feel and fit as good as they look.

MOTHERS

Fashionable mother-of-the-bride (and the groom) outfits—whatever the formality—are generally easier to find today than in the past, when even youthful mothers were expected to appear matronly. No one now expects mothers to look anything other than their age. Still, there are a few issues of dress etiquette to remember:

- Try not to wear colors that are the same as or very similar to the bride's and bridesmaids' dresses. If you want a light color, look for pastels and light or medium tones rather than white.

- It's preferable that the mothers wear different colors, so consult with the other mother and/or stepmothers about color. Hopefully, everyone is on good terms, and you can discuss your plans so that each mother will be both distinctive and comfortable with her choice of attire.

- The length of your gown or dress is your choice, even for formal weddings. Long dresses and skirts are fine for any wedding from noon on. Mothers of the bride and groom do not have to wear the same length, though many do, feeling that the same length creates a more harmonious look, especially in wedding photos.

- Gloves and hats or headpieces are normally worn for formal weddings but are optional otherwise, so be guided by the bride's preference and any religious requirements. Gloves are worn for receiving lines but can be removed afterward and are always taken off when eating.

FATHERS

When they participate in the ceremony, fathers and/or stepfathers almost always wear the same outfits as the groom's attendants. This is also the case for any man who escorts the bride down the aisle.

When the father of the groom doesn't have an active role, he can either match the formality of the male attendants or "dress down" a bit—choosing a tuxedo or dark suit instead of more formal attire. But if the groom's father is to be in a receiving line, his outfit will often conform to that of the bride's father or the groomsmen.

DRESS FOR THE WEDDING PARTY

This chart provides general dress guidelines for traditional American formal, semiformal, and informal weddings. Standards for dress are often different in other traditions, and religious practice may affect decisions about head coverings, veils, and other clothing choices.

	MOST FORMAL DAYTIME	MOST FORMAL EVENING
Bride	Long white dress, train, veil. Gloves optional.	Same as the most formal daytime.
Bride's attendants	Long dresses, matching shoes. Gloves at bride's option.	Same as the most formal daytime.
Groom, his attendants, bride's father or stepfather, and groom's father if in the service	Cutaway coat; striped trousers; pearl-gray waistcoat; white stiff shirt, turndown collar with gray-and-black striped four-in-hand tie or wing collar with ascot; gray gloves; black silk socks; black kid shoes.	White tie: Black tailcoat and trousers; white piqué waistcoat; starched-bosom shirt, wing collar, and white bow tie; white gloves; black silk socks; black patent-leather shoes or pumps or black kid smooth-toed shoes (or see Semiformal Evening).
★ Groom's father and/or stepfather if not participating in the ceremony	Dark suit, conservative shirt and tie.	Tuxedo if wife wears long dress; otherwise, dark suit.
Mothers and/or stepmothers of the couple	Long or short dresses. Hats or hair ornaments optional. Gloves optional.	Usually long evening or dinner dresses or dressy cocktail-length dresses. Head coverings or hair ornaments optional. Gloves optional.
	SEMIFORMAL DAYTIME	SEMIFORMAL EVENING
Bride	Long white dress. Short veil and gloves optional.	Same as the semiformal daytime.
Bride's attendants	Long or short dresses, matching shoes. Gloves at bride's option.	Dresses of same formality and length as bride's dress. Gloves at bride's option.
Groom, his attendants, bride's father or stepfather, and groom's father if in the service	Black or charcoal sack coat; dove-gray waistcoat; white pleated shirt, starched turndown collar, or soft white shirt with four-in-hand tie; gray gloves; black smooth-toed shoes.	Winter: black tuxedo. Summer: white jacket. Pleated or piqué soft shirt; black cummerbund and black bow tie; black patent-leather or kid shoes. No gloves.
★ Groom's father and/or stepfather if not participating in the ceremony	Dark suit, conservative shirt and tie.	Tuxedo if wife wears long dress, or dark suit.
Mothers and/or stepmothers of the couple	Long or street-length dresses. Gloves and head coverings optional.	Same as semiformal daytime.

	INFORMAL DAYTIME	INFORMAL EVENING
Bride	Short afternoon dress, cocktail dress, or suit.	Long dinner dress, short cocktail dress, or suit.
Bride's attendants	Same style as bride.	Same style as bride.
Groom, his attendants, bride's father or stepfather, and groom's father if in the service	Winter: dark suit. Summer: dark trousers with white linen jacket or white trousers with navy or charcoal jacket; soft shirt with conservative four-in-hand tie.	Tuxedo if bride wears dinner dress. Otherwise, dark suit in winter, lighter suit in summer.
★ *Groom's father and/or stepfather if not participating in the ceremony*	Hot climate: white suit. Winter: dark suit. Summer: light trousers and dark blazer.	Dark suit.
Mothers and/or stepmothers of the couple	Short afternoon or cocktail dresses.	Same length dresses as bride's.

★If the father or stepfather of the groom is not among the attendants but will be taking part in the receiving line or wishes to dress formally, he may wear the same outfit as the groom and groomsmen.

"BEST WOMAN" AND "MAN OF HONOR"

When the customary roles are reversed in the choice of attendants—a man as the bride's honor attendant or a woman serving as the groom's "best person"—the question of what to wear arises. The solution is surprisingly easy. A male honor attendant simply wears the same attire as the groom and groomsmen. A woman may wear a dress in the same color family as the bridesmaids', or she can choose a dress in black, gray, or whatever the primary color worn by the groomsmen. Her attire is in keeping with the formality of the wedding, but she wouldn't wear a tux or dress like the groomsmen. A man wears a boutonniere, and a woman usually wears a corsage featuring the same flowers as in the groomsmen's boutonnieres.

BEHIND THE TRADITION: THE TUXEDO'S TALE

It's not uncommon nowadays to see all formal male attire classed as tuxedos, but in fact, a tux is a semiformal dinner jacket, worn with matching trousers to make a tuxedo suit. The man who started the fashion was Pierre Lorillard IV, of the tobacco fortune. Inspired by the traditional scarlet English hunt coat (and perhaps by the Prince of Wales, who reportedly had the tails cut from his coats while on a visit to India), Lorillard asked his tailor to make several tail-less black jackets. The jackets were first worn by Griswold Lorillard, Pierre's son, and several young friends to a ball in Tuxedo Park, New York, in the fall of 1886—and a style was born. The tux got its name from the town, but "tuxedo" goes back to the Algonquin word for "wolf."

Griswold Lorillard and his friends wore scarlet vests under their daring new coats. But the cummerbund, most often worn with a tux today, owes its origin to an item of Hindu formal wear—the *kamarband,* or "loin band."

Attire for the Military Wedding

A military wedding can be anything from an informal service in a civilian setting to a full-blown, spit-and-polish affair complete with the American flag, unit standards, and the romantic Arch of Steel. The etiquette for military weddings varies somewhat from service to service, and members of the military should check their service manuals or consult with a protocol officer or base chaplain.

In general, brides and grooms in the service may wear either civilian clothes or their uniforms, as may their colleagues who serve as attendants. Depending on the formality of the occasion, everyday and dress uniforms are equally correct, since young and noncareer personnel often don't have dress uniforms. For commissioned officers, evening dress uniforms are the equivalent of civilian white tie, and dinner or mess dress is the same formality as a tuxedo. Noncommissioned officers can wear dress or everyday uniforms for formal and informal ceremonies.

Regulations vary by service branch, but as a rule, only commissioned officers in full uniform wear swords. Hats and caps are carried during an indoor ceremony, and gloves are always worn by saber or cutlass bearers. Flowers are never worn on uniforms, but brides in uniform may carry a bridal bouquet. Service members not in uniform and nonmilitary members of the wedding party dress as they would for any ceremony.

CHAPTER 15

PLANNING THE RECEPTION

THE WEDDING RECEPTION is not just a celebration party; it's your chance to share your good fortune with the family and friends who form the most important relationships in your life. Whether you plan a grand affair with elegant food and service or prefer a barefoot clambake under the stars, the reception should be a reflection of your personality. Combining personal and traditional touches is an homage of sorts to the people and influences who formed you—and an introduction to the person you have become.

Reception Decisions

There are many decisions to be made about the reception. Here's a review of the major decisions you'll need to make that are covered in this chapter:

- How will you work with your vendors?

- Where will you hold your reception?

- What type of food service will you have?

- Do you need to hire a caterer?

- What type of beverage service?

- How will you handle the seating arrangements?

- Transportation: How will you and the wedding party get from the ceremony to the reception?

Forming a Successful Partnership

The goal of a wedding reception is twofold: to create a celebratory atmosphere and to ensure the physical and emotional comfort of your guests. You and your vendors are in partnership to meet that goal.

The success of your reception depends on the choices you make and your success in conveying your vision and desires to the people you have hired to help you. Ultimately, the onus

HELPING THE CATERER HELP YOU

The caterer is an important member of your wedding team. It is the caterer's job to tailor his or her skills to meet your needs and wishes. You can make your caterer's job easier by viewing the relationship as a collaboration working toward a common goal: the success of the occasion. Here are suggestions and advice on ways to make working with a caterer a positive, joyful experience for all involved:

1. First decide what your vision is and see if the caterer can accommodate it. Think it through thoroughly, so that you can articulate your goals.

2. Stick to your vision. Don't give in to the instinct to just let the caterers do what they do. Speak up; gently insist on attention to detail. If you want a variation made or have a special request, say so. Don't let yourself get lost in an assembly-line wedding machine. A wedding consultant or an event planner can be invaluable in helping fight for your vision.

3. Recognize the strengths of your caterer. Ask what the company's signature and most popular dishes are.

4. Be up front with the caterer from the start on the amount of money you want to spend on catering—and stick to that figure. If you are firm about your budget, then it's the caterer's job to work within that figure. Have faith: Reliable caterers are not in the business of inflating budgets, certainly not at the expense of customer relations.

5. Just as it's helpful to say up front if there is something you really want on the menu, it's also invaluable to specify any food you don't want. This is especially important if you're aware of allergies of any of your guests, for example, or if there are certain religious restrictions regarding foods. No one wants to have to handle special food needs on the day of the wedding.

6. Even perfectionists need to know when to pull back. You may have articulated a vision, but you don't necessarily need to know exactly how your caterers will achieve it.

7. Remember that the kitchen and the front of the house—the waitstaff, manager, bartenders—are two parts of the same team. You'll want to make sure the communication between the two is there so that your plans are carried out.

8. Don't forget to check on any site restrictions before the caterer gets to work.

is on you to make sure that your vision is executed. But it is also to your benefit to place your trust and good faith in your vendors. Taking an antagonistic approach or assuming that the vendor is out to fleece you at every turn is a recipe for uninspired execution at best and ill will at worst. I can't tell you how many professionals have told me how much it means to be treated as a respected collaborator, not simply as hired help. Good manners and a personable approach go a long way toward making your wedding a positive experience for both you and your vendors. Establishing a partnership up front gives your vendors confidence to work to the best of their abilities.

Finding the Perfect Place

Finding a reception locale is a top-priority decision, a process that begins once you have determined the size of your guest list—and the size of your budget. Your choice will affect the style of wedding you have, the food you serve, and the entertainment you choose. Typically, the later in the day the wedding is, the more formal it is, and the more expensive the reception is likely to be. Be thorough in selecting just the right space. Most sites require hefty deposits the day you reserve them and have equally steep cancellation fees.

In addition to cost, there are a few other important considerations in selecting a reception site. These include:

1. **Size and comfort.** You may fall in love with a space the first time you see it, but until you determine its comfort capacity—not its standing-room-only capacity—refrain from booking it. No matter how lovely it may be, your guests will be uncomfortable if they have no room to move. Look for potential bottlenecks: The entrance and coat check, for example, should be spaced so that guests will not have to wait in line. Consider the flow of the space, making sure aisles and hallways are not cluttered and won't precipitate traffic jams.

   If the guest list for your reception is small, don't pick too spacious a space. Otherwise, tables could be miles apart, and the room will feel cavernous and empty. If you plan on hours of dancing, you will want a dance floor large enough to accommodate guests. If you plan to have food stations instead of a single buffet line, you don't want guest tables that are so close to the food stations (or a buffet line) that no one can move.

   Other comfort factors to scope out include sufficient restrooms and a place for coats. Make sure there are plenty of chairs, even if you are having an afternoon tea or a cocktail reception where guests will stand more than they sit. Check the acoustics so that your music is neither too low nor too deafening. And finally, make sure the space offers good air circulation. A church hall may be a perfect space to decorate, but if it has few windows, it may need extra fans to provide better air circulation.

2. **Time availability.** The lag time between the ceremony and the reception depends on several factors—including whether formal photographs of the wedding party will be taken after the ceremony; whether a receiving line will be held at the ceremony site; the distance from the ceremony site to the reception site; and the time availability of both spaces. The ideal lag time is thirty minutes. While that may not be possible, avoid keeping reception guests waiting and aim for as short a lag time as possible.

3. **The level of formality.** The degree of your celebration's desired formality is set by both the time of day of your wedding and the environment you choose for the reception. While a morning or afternoon reception can be as informal or formal as you like, an evening reception usually indicates a formal reception and therefore requires a more formal site. Certain spaces, by virtue of their casual ambience, are unlikely choices for formal weddings. No matter how you decorate, these casual spaces—such as a backyard garden or a hunting lodge—will never look like a country club or hotel and are more appropriate for a morning or afternoon wedding that is informal or semiformal.

4. **Accessibility.** When scouting sites, think about how your guests will get there. If access is difficult, consider hiring minivans or a bus to transport guests to and from the reception. (Be sure to clear with the ceremony site that cars may be left there). If the parking lot at the reception site is a distance from the entrance, arrange valet parking (the tab and tips are on you), so that guests don't have to walk far in high heels or in rain or heat. Also check for access for the disabled. No matter how enchanting, the tower room at the golf club isn't for you if any of your wedding guests are older or have disabilities and the room is up three flights of stairs (with no available elevator).

5. **The layout.** How easily can tables be set up? How big will the bridal table need to be and where will it be situated? Where will speakers be located for the music? Will you require a table where guests may pick up their seating assignments, a table for gifts in case guests bring them to the reception? Is so, is there room? Is there a place to do a receiving line? Is there a separate room or space for children to play?

CHECKING OUT THE SITE

Before you sign a contract and formalize your plans, meet with the reception site manager. Whatever site you select, have at least one guided tour before signing an agreement. Look at the place from a practical point of view. Check the lighting, electrical supply, and food preparation areas. Most sites have guidelines as well as restrictions that you and your vendors will need to follow. Have the details spelled out before signing a contract. You'll want to ensure that all your vendors will have access to the space to do their work. You'll need to communicate specific details to the site manager, such as the final guest count. Before the wedding, make arrangements for outside vendors to inspect the site. Later you may need to set up delivery times; make sure parking spaces are available for vendors (such as the band, the florist, and the photographer).

Here is a list of important questions to ask the site manager before signing a contract:

- What policies and restrictions does the site have for food, beverages, music, flowers, decor? Are there restrictions on the use of candles? Are there restrictions on photography or videography lighting?

- What are the laws in the state regarding the serving of alcohol? Does the site have a liquor license?

- How large a band or orchestra is recommended?

- Is there adequate wiring and are there sufficient outlets for a sound system or would the band or DJ have to bring extra cords and plugs?

- Ask about any restrictions on floral decorations. Some reception halls, for example, aren't keen on having flower garlands twined around statuary and staircases or have restrictions on moving furniture to make room for, say, potted plants or carpet runners. It would be a colossal disappointment and waste of time and money to finalize your floral plans, only to find out at the last minute that your selections weren't allowed at the site in the first place.

- At what time may decorations be delivered and what access will the florist be given for putting them in place?

- Who assumes liability if a guest becomes inebriated and has an accident?

- Is there a place for the wedding party to change clothes, if necessary?

- Does the site provide baby-sitting services? Is there a place where a children's room can be set up, with a television and DVD, if necessary?

A World of Receptions

There are three basic types of reception sites:

Hotels, private clubs, and reception halls. Food, beverages, and service are generally provided by the site. The location may offer complete wedding packages, leaving you with little to do but select the color table linens you prefer. Wedding packages may vary according to the time and style of your reception. Most facilities have a minimum number of guests for larger spaces or main ballrooms.

Sites that offer only space. The reception areas of most houses of worship; private meeting halls; civic sites; public parks; historic sites; galleries; museums; and private homes are examples of places that generally provide physical space only. You must take care of everything else and also arrange access for your suppliers and vendors. Some couples or their parents choose to hold a reception at home. This can be a great way to save money or it can be the elaborate setting for a very upscale reception. Pride in home and family is often the overriding reason to hold a reception at home.

Restaurants. A restaurant reception is a kind of hybrid. Some restaurants offer a full array of services, but most provide only the space, food and beverages, waitstaff, and cleanup. It may be possible to rent the entire restaurant or a private party room.

A restaurant reception is a smart choice for the busy couple who has little time to plan but prefers a more intimate setting than a hotel or club. It's all there in one place: food, service, ambience, and a built-in cleanup crew. A restaurant is often chosen for lunch or dinner after a civil ceremony or after a marriage attended only by family and close friends. Unless you are inviting guests to order off the restaurant menu, the food and choice of beverages are ordered ahead of time. Having a set menu—whether served by waiters at a sit-down meal or offered buffet-style—is most often the economical choice. It also eliminates any complications in paying the check. Many larger restaurants have party-menu choices and even reception consultants to help out.

THE MILITARY ADVANTAGE

When one or both of an engaged couple are on active duty, they may have access to base facilities, including chapels and officers' clubs, for their ceremony and/or reception. The principal advantages are price (often lower than comparable off-base locations), convenience for guests who are also in the service, and flexibility. Base clubs will generally accommodate scheduling changes when a groom or bride is re-posted—without charging extra.

Retired servicemen and -women and reservists also have access to military facilities, but children and other relatives of veterans do not.

OUTDOOR CEREMONIES AND RECEPTIONS

An outdoor service and/or reception might be held at home; at a club, restaurant, reception hall, or house of worship with outdoor facilities; at a favorite natural spot like a park or beach; or at a historic site that is available for entertaining.

Be weather-conscious. Whatever the general climate, the weather on your wedding day is the great unpredictable. But you can check with meteorological sources in your area about historical weather trends such as periods of high wind or frequent thunderstorms.

Have a Plan B. You might feel as if you're planning two weddings, but you must have a fall-back plan. This will include an alternate indoor site and a plan to notify guests. (You can prepare "just in case" phone lists and provide these to attendants and family members.) Be ready to make a quick decision as early as possible if the weather doesn't cooperate.

Check on fees and permits. For a public site, there may be fees and you may need special permits, so talk with the appropriate authorities. Ask about any restrictions, such as bans on alcohol or campfires.

Think about access to the site. That remote sandy cove or field of wildflowers may be beautifully romantic but nearly impossible to get to. Consider your suppliers and your guests. Caterers, florists, and other vendors will need access for their vehicles. Where will guests park? If walking to the site is difficult, you'll have to provide some form of transportation. Also plan ways for your guests, particularly the elderly or disabled, to get around easily. If the site has uneven walking surfaces, installing temporary level walkways may be necessary.

Provide directions. If the site is off the beaten track, include maps and detailed directions in your wedding invitations.

THE PERSONAL TOUCH:

All About Tents

If you are considering using an outdoor tent for your reception, there is a long list of options. Tents today run the gamut from simple to palatial. There are arched entryways, bridges and pathways, parquet floors, stained-glass panels, and chandeliers. You can get a colored tent that matches your wedding colors or a climatized tent, with generators for heating or cooling and ceiling fans to keep air circulating.

Because the choices vary so widely, it is a good idea to get a referral from a caterer or club manager, who may be able to recommend reputable suppliers. You will want recommendations; whom you rent the tent and supplies from is crucial to your budget. There is often a big discrepancy in costs from one tent supplier to another. Don't order a tent over the phone; go in person to see what you are paying for.

In general, you need at least one 60′ × 60′ or 40′ × 100′ tent per 200 people, for dinner and dancing. If you want restrooms or plan on having a cocktail hour, you'll need extra footage. You'll need to consider sound system hookups, a generator and a backup generator, ground cover, a dance floor, any permits required by local ordinance, and what supervisory and other personnel are required for tent installation and maintenance.

Planning the Wedding Feast

Once you have located a reception space, it is time to decide what the menu will be for your reception. Keep your guests in mind. You will want a menu to please most everyone, but you don't have to settle for bland or boring. You don't want to alienate your reception guests, presumably the people who mean the most to you, by forcing a quirky, trendy, or bizarrely alien menu on them. But you can find foods that will excite your guests, that perfectly fit the season and the setting—and that are a meaningful expression of your personality. Be creative in choosing your menu—but never at the expense of your guests.

Before you decide on the menu, consider logistics. There will be many different factors in determining the final menu—the size of your guest list, the type of food service (discussed below), the season, the time of day, the formality of the occasion, and your budget.

Serve It Up: Types of Reception Service

SIT-DOWN OR SEATED MEAL

At a traditional sit-down dinner or luncheon, guests are usually assigned places at dining tables and are served by waitstaff. Place cards can either be set on the tables or be laid out alphabetically (complete with instructions regarding assigned tables) on a separate table where guests pick them up early in the reception. At a large reception, tables are often numbered, and the individual place cards indicate which table a guest is to go to. (See also pages 283–285: "The Fine Art of Seating Arrangements: Who Sits Where?")

Generally, a seated wedding meal comprises three courses—soup, salad, or appetizer; entrée (or entrée choices) with vegetables; and dessert—but can be more lavish. Whether you offer a choice of entrées, the food items are predetermined, so it's easier to estimate quantities than for a buffet. Per-person cost may actually be less than for a buffet, but the primary deciding factors will be the food itself (lobster will be more expensive than chicken) and the number of waitstaff required.

There are several variations on the method of service, including:

Plated service. The food is already arranged on the plates when they are set before the guests at the table.

Russian service. Empty plates are on the tables, and the waitstaff serve each course from platters. There may be more than one waiter; one serves the meats, another the vegetables, and a third might serve salad.

French service. One waiter holds the serving platter while another serves the plates. French service can be very efficient when guests are offered a choice of entrées.

You can also mix these styles—perhaps having plated salad and dessert courses and Russian or French service for the main course.

BUFFET

Buffet service adapts to any wedding style and is particularly well suited for brunch and luncheon receptions. Whether a buffet is more or less expensive than a seated meal depends on the costs of the foods served, the number of service staff required, and the amount of food likely to be consumed. Though a buffet doesn't involve separate food courses, guests are welcome to return to the buffet for second helpings, so people tend to eat more. Guests serve themselves or are served by a staff standing behind the buffet table. The advantage of a buffet is that you can serve a varied menu from which most people will find things they like.

Guests select what they want from a single long service table or several food stations devoted to different types of food. Self-service is one option, but you may want waiters to serve at the buffet table, especially if the menu includes items such as large roasts that are carved on the spot or sauced dishes that can easily be spilled or dripped.

Guests sit at dining tables, which may or may not have assigned places. These tables can be large or small, though very large circular tables tend to impede cross-table conversation. Normally, places are set with tableware, glasses, and napkins, but guests might pick up their own utensils and napkins at a casual buffet. Drinks can be served from a separate service table(s) or at the dining tables by waitstaff.

When guests return to the buffet, they leave their used plates on their tables and receive a clean plate at the buffet table. (Waiters remove the used plate.) At a small or very casual reception (such as an outdoor barbecue or a clambake), guests usually take their plates back to the buffet for another helping.

> ### THE PERSONAL TOUCH:
>
> ## LITTLE BUFFET FOR LITTLE KIDS
>
> If you plan to have children attend your wedding, one lovely way to serve them at the reception is to set up a separate children's buffet table—of kid-friendly height. Locate a shorter table, decorate it with colorful linens or butcher paper with crayons, and include such kid-pleasing foods as stacks of peanut-butter-and-jelly tea sandwiches, fish sticks and chicken fingers, mini raviolis, and brownies and cookies.

Passed-tray service is ideal for afternoon and cocktail receptions when a full meal isn't provided. Waiters or helpers circulate among the guests and offer hors d'oeuvres from trays. Finger foods are the general rule, and cocktail napkins are provided. Sometimes the food trays are supplemented with crudités, cheeses, and fruit served from a buffet table or tables. If sauced or dipping foods are served, small plates, napkins, forks, skewers, and other utensils can be placed on these tables.

Determining costs for a passed-tray reception requires a reasonable estimate of quantities, and it's better to have too much than too little. Caterers and reception sites usually charge a per-person fee for hors d'oeuvres and can provide guidelines (say, six or seven servings per guest), but you may want to increase quantities if you expect a hungry crowd. Hiring servers or using a caterer's serving staff will add to the cost.

Passing hors d'oeuvres may precede a full buffet or seated dinner that includes a cocktail hour. In this case, fewer servings are probably needed.

Do You Need a Caterer?

If you are planning a small reception and have the help of family and friends, you probably don't need professional help in preparing and serving reception food and beverages. By preparing food in advance and by keeping the menu and the decorations as simple as possible, a small wedding reception can be both inexpensive and, within reason, easy to manage.

Planning a larger reception in your home or anywhere else that provides no services, however, can be a lot of work. Entertaining a large group of guests with any degree of pleasure and relaxation requires the aid of professional catering services. Caterers, in other words, let you be a guest at your own party.

In general, *hiring a caterer is recommended for a reception of more than thirty guests.* Depending on the size of the catering company, they can provide just the food or the works: food, beverages, the wedding cake, the serving staff, crystal and china, tables, chairs, and linens. Some even provide tents, dance floors, and party decorations—or can recommend reliable suppliers and vendors.

Before you enter an agreement, check the caterer's references. Friends are a good source for recommendations, but it's essential to talk with people who have actually hired the caterer you're considering. Also, be sure you understand all costs. Is breakage insurance included or extra? Are gratuities and taxes included in the caterer's estimate? How will you be charged for any overtime?

What Do Caterers Cost?

Q: *We are planning our wedding and would like a general idea of how much we will need to budget for catering. Can you give us a rough idea of what we'll be paying?*

A: Caterers generally set prices based on a per-person figure. That figure varies from region to region, state to state, urban area to rural area. Costs are dependent on other factors as well: the formality of the occasion, the time of day, the day of the week, the number of guests, what kind of food service you choose, how you choose to serve alcohol and other beverages, and the number of service people needed for the job.

Costs can run from $25 per person for an informal beach party to $600 per person for a grand sit-down dinner in a major city. Having an open bar can add more than $10 per person to the total cost. Don't forget to figure gratuities and taxes into your total costs; they can add up to 25 percent of the total bill.

Once you and your caterer have toured the reception site and agreed on arrangements, be absolutely sure that every service and item to be provided is listed in an itemized contract. Make sure that everything, down to the last canapé, is specified.

You may choose to use the on-site caterer at your reception location. Banquet facilities often offer wedding packages that include on-site catering. It's a convenient and cost-efficient alternative to renting a space and hiring independent vendors.

If you decide to go with an off-site caterer, set up a preliminary meeting. Be sure to set up a time to meet at your reception site before proceeding too far into your planning. A caterer's experience can be extremely valuable in assessing how well equipped the site is, deciding where to place tables, determining how many guests can be accommodated comfortably and how much staff will be required, and addressing any number of other details essential to the perfect reception.

Selecting the Caterer for You

Food and food service are among the most important elements of your wedding celebration. So if you've decided to use a caterer, finding the right person or company is one of the most important goals of your wedding planning. When you start to interview caterers, consider the following criteria:

Tips on Tastings

Most reliable caterers offer potential clients tastings of their foods, from hors d'oeuvres to main courses—and it's a smart idea to take them up on it. The tasting has become increasingly important; it's the only dress rehearsal for food you have. Here are some tips on things to watch for during your tasting:

- If you have hired a *wedding planner or consultant,* you should include him or her in the tasting; it's the wedding planner's job to be the clear-eyed troubleshooter, and to make sure you get the service you want.

- Looks for signs of *good-quality foods and ingredients.* If the ends of cheese slices appear dry and discolored, that could mean that the cheese was cut hours before—or even yesterday. Are the vegetables brightly colored and not soggy? Is the salad fresh and not wilting? Are baked breads soft and chewy and not stale and hard? Even little things, like butter having a refrigerator taste, can be a clue to a caterer's attention—or inattention—to detail.

- Notice the *attentiveness of the staff.* If you're attending a buffet tasting, note whether food is allowed to sit out for long periods without being replenished. The caterer should have sufficient staff to keep the presentation as fresh looking at 3 P.M. as it was at noon.

- Ask if it's possible to *meet the chef* at your tasting. Be sure to thank the chef and offer positive feedback. Once you empower a chef with your attention and confidence, the results can be amazing.

Portfolio. Some caterers keep albums containing photographs of previous receptions. Look for creative touches: fruits and vegetables skillfully cut into beautiful shapes or arranged in eye-catching ways; interesting and complementary color schemes; a variety of dishes; well-organized and attractive presentations if you're considering a buffet. In other words, the food should be pretty enough to stand on its own.

Creativity and variety. The catering menu reflects the chef's breadth of preparation know-how and awareness of food trends. If a menu seems fussy and complicated, the chef may be overreaching—especially problematic when you consider the challenges of efficiently serving large groups of people. On the other hand, if the menu appears uninspired, offering the same old standards prepared the same old ways, then that's exactly what you are likely to get.

Flexibility. Most caterers have set menus with several selections to choose from in each category. The best caterers are happy to accommodate special requests or tailor the menu to your needs. Any caterer who is adamant about not veering from his or her patented script is a caterer you probably don't want to work with.

Taste, presentation, and service. Most caterers are more than happy to set up a food-tasting session. Ask for a variety of dishes, from hors d'oeuvres to a main course to a dessert. Note *how* the food is served as well as how it looks and tastes. The success of your reception will depend on service as well as food. Ask how the caterer plans to time each presentation.

Details indicating quality and freshness. Tastings are a great way for you to evaluate the caterer's attention to fresh, quality ingredients.

NUTS AND BOLTS: QUESTIONS FOR THE CATERER

When you interview a caterer, take a list with you of the nuts-and-bolts questions you'll need answered. Consider the following:

- How will guests arriving at the reception be served? Will there be champagne or drinks ready for arriving guests? How soon will appetizers be introduced (ideally, twelve to fifteen minutes after the drinks are served)? How will switching from serving hors d'oeuvres to serving dinner be coordinated?

- What is the ratio of serving staff to guests? (Ideally, for high-end service, that ratio should be ten to one, or one and a half tables per waiter. For medium-end affairs, the ratio is more like twenty to one.)

- What does a sample place setting consist of?

- Is insurance against china and crystal breakage included in the costs? If not, what are additional insurance costs?

- What are the selections of table linen colors? Are there choices for china, silver, and crystal? Can tables and chairs be provided if necessary? What about tents, heaters, portable toilets, and other miscellaneous items?

- How are meals for the band, DJ, photographers, videographers, charged?

- Can the cake be provided and served? Does the caterer have a cake portfolio?

- What is the price difference between brand-name liquors and house brands?

- What is the price difference between an open bar just for the cocktail hour and an open bar throughout the reception? Between a consumption bar (where drinks are charged on a per-drink basis) versus an open bar?

- At what time do servers go on overtime pay? What would the overtime charges be?

- Are gratuities and taxes included in the total bill? What are delivery charges? Are the fees for setup and cleanup included in the total bill?

ADDITIONAL QUESTIONS TO ASK ON-SITE CATERERS

- Ask to see a book of on-site wedding cakes and whether you can sample a selection. Ask whether you can provide your own wedding cake at no extra cost. If not, what is the extra cost? Can arrangements be made for your baker to finish decorating the cake on premise?

- Will a manager be on-site during the reception to oversee the event?

A QUESTION FOR PEGGY:

ARE CASH BARS ACCEPTABLE AT THE RECEPTION?

Q: *My fiancé really wants to serve alcohol at our wedding reception, but it would really put a crimp on our budget. Someone suggested a cash bar, where guests would pay for their own drinks. What are your thoughts?*

A: You wouldn't think of asking someone to pay for a cocktail in your home, so don't have a cash bar at your reception. When you invite guests to your reception, they are just that—your guests. If a bar is not in your budget, serve soft drinks, wine, or champagne. Or perhaps you'll cut back on the size of your guest list and serve a full array of drinks. Just do not let the hotel or club or reception-site manager talk you into selling tickets for drinks or having guests pay their way!

The Wedding Drinks

WHAT TO DRINK?

You will provide beverages, but you don't have to serve alcohol if you don't want to or you have religious or moral reasons not to. Some couples and their families don't drink alcohol themselves but do provide alcoholic drinks for their guests. Others restrict alcohol to wine; wine and beer; or just champagne for toasting. Budget is always a consideration, but these days, people are also limiting or eliminating liquor for health and safety reasons.

If you serve liquor, carefully estimate the amount of alcoholic drinks likely to be served. If you plan a seated dinner, your needs will include drinks for the cocktail hour and also with the meal. The two basic ways a caterer or a reception site can charge are:

Open bar. The hosts pay a flat fee for drinks served during a specific time period—either during the cocktail hour or for the entire event.

Consumption bar. Drinks are charged at a per-drink rate, and a running tab is kept for the time the bar is open. The hosts are charged for what is actually served.

The word *bar* doesn't have to be taken literally. Whether you offer liquor or not, beverage service may mean that drinks are passed on trays or served at drink stations (tables set up at convenient locations in the room) or from the buffet table. At a seated dinner and often at a buffet, wine is poured at the dining tables. For a very casual outdoor reception, drinks might be kept in ice coolers so guests can serve themselves.

You have many non-alcoholic beverage options. Juice-based punches are traditional, but not everybody wants sugary drinks, so it's a good idea to provide several choices. Diet colas, natural juices, water and tea (plain and flavored), coffee—just think about your guests' tastes. Any beverage can be substituted for champagne.

The Fine Art of Seating Arrangements: Who Sits Where?

At most sit-down dinners or formal buffet receptions, it is customary for the bride and groom to determine seating arrangements. Deciding who sits with whom requires tact, consideration, diplomacy, and a sense of fun, so it's wise to begin thinking it over early. You won't be able to complete your plan until you've received most of the guest replies. Ask your reception-site manager for an exact diagram of table placement. Make several photocopies of the diagram so that you can play around with the seating arrangements.

1. **Seating parents.** It is customary to have separate parents' tables, one for the bride's family and close friends and another for the groom's family. It is fine to put both sets together, but this can become unwieldy, as each set generally comes with its own entourage of extended family and friends. When the bride and/or groom's parents have been divorced, however, and all are in attendance, it is usually not a good idea to seat them together. Even if relations between the divorced parents are amicable, the extended family and friends of each make it difficult logistically to seat them all at one table.

2. **The bridal party table.** The bridal party table is often a rectangular table set against one side or end of the room. The bride and groom sit at the center of the long side, facing out so that guests can see them. No one is seated opposite them. The bride sits on the groom's right, with the best man on her right; the maid of honor sits on the groom's left, and the bridesmaids and ushers alternate along the same side of the table. If the group is large, the table can be made into a U-shape, with the bride and groom at the center of the center table. The wedding party's husbands, wives, fiancés/fiancées, and significant others should be seated here, too, if there is room. When the wedding party is large or when the couple wants to seat the attendants with their spouses and significant others, two large round tables may be used to seat the entire bridal party and their partners. In this case, the bride and groom would sit with the maid of honor and best man, their respective partners, and possibly some of the attendants and partners. Children or siblings of the bride or groom who were not in the wedding party may also sit with them.

3. **No bridal party table?** Some couples prefer to wander about and mingle with their guests rather than being seated at a formal table. There should always, however, be a table reserved for the bride and groom and their attendants to sit down and rest. The newlyweds may go to the buffet table just as the other guests do; in some cases, a waiter fills a plate and brings it to them where they are seated. The bridesmaids and ushers need not all sit with the bride and groom at the same time, but all should gather together during the toasts and the cutting of the cake.

4. **Other guest tables.** Deciding where to seat other guests is up to you. Your basic objective is to make each table as congenial as possible. Couples usually try to mix and match—considering guests' interests and personalities.

   - Married, engaged, and steady couples can sit at the same table, but to keep conversation flowing, it's usually best not to put spouses and other committed couples next to each other.

- Seating one stranger at a table where the rest of the guests are close friends can leave the person feeling like the odd man (or woman) out.

- Dining and conversing with people of other generations can be interesting for everyone, so try to vary ages if possible.

- Younger children are usually seated with their parents. But older children and teens often enjoy *not* being with their parents. Take your cues from what you know about a young person's preferences.

- Infirm or disabled guests need special consideration. A person who has difficulty walking may need a table near the entrance or restrooms. A person with impaired sight or hearing might enjoy a place near the bridal table or the band. People in wheelchairs should have easy access to tables.

You can ask some people if they have seating preferences (a guest with a physical disability, for example), but don't make it a general practice. Taking requests will just confuse your seating chart. Trust your instincts and common sense.

WHAT ARE THE PROS AND CONS OF ASSIGNED SEATING?

Q: *My fiancé and I have agreed on everything but this: whether or not to assign seats. Since we're having butlered hors d'oeuvres and food stations instead of a sit-down dinner, I like the idea of not assigning seats (other than the bridal party table). I think it will keep the party fluid and guests mingling. My fiancé has a number of elderly relatives to whom he'd like to offer assigned seating. What do we do?*

A: Here's a compromise: In addition to the bridal party table, have one other assigned-seating table reserved specifically for your elderly relatives. It's not only a way to make them comfortable; it's a way to honor them as well.

5. **Place cards.** Place cards are recommended for seated dinners and formal buffets with more than twenty guests. For small receptions with only a few tables, you can put a card at each guest's place. At larger receptions, tables are usually numbered. The number of each guest's table is then written on his or her card. Delegate someone to arrange the cards in alphabetical order and to place them on a side table at the reception entrance. On entering the reception area or after going through the receiving line, guests pick up their cards. Sometimes, particularly at informal and casual receptions, couples use place cards only at the bridal party and parents' tables, and other guests seat themselves as they wish.

Planning Transportation

TRANSPORTATION AND TRAVEL ARRANGEMENTS

Unless the ceremony and reception are held at your home, getting from one place to another requires planning. It isn't necessary to hire vehicles; you might do nothing more than spruce up the family car or cars. What matters is that everyone involved in the wedding gets where they need to be on time.

In general, the bride's family organizes transportation for the bridal attendants to the wedding and reception. The best man and/or head usher coordinates for the groomsmen and ushers. The best man usually drives the groom to the ceremony site, sometimes drives the newlyweds to the reception, and often organizes transportation for the couple when they leave the reception.

Wedding party members may arrange their own transportation, but they must know scheduled arrival times. If wedding participants drive themselves, you may need to reserve convenient parking for them—even for home weddings. Children in the wedding are usually brought to the ceremony site by their parents; they may go to the reception with the other attendants or the bride's parents, but it's fine if they want to ride with their families.

Working with a limousine service doesn't necessarily mean you must hire stretch limos. You may want less dramatic vehicles that are attractive and roomy enough for the people you will transport. Whatever your preference, begin interviewing reputable rental services as soon as your ceremony and reception sites are confirmed—limousine companies are often booked many months in advance for peak times.

Regardless of how you get to the ceremony and reception, consider the following issues when you choose your transportation:

1. **Determine the number of cars you need.** The traditional complement of hired cars comprises:

   - A car to the ceremony site for the bride and her father or escort (if the bride won't be dressing at the site)

   - Cars from the ceremony to the reception for (1) the bride and groom, (2) the bride's mother or both parents plus any children in the wedding party and/or bridesmaids, and (3) the rest of the bride's attendants

   You'll need more if you provide transportation for special guests, grandparents, and other family members. You may want only one hired car for the bride and groom's drive to the reception.

2. **Interview local transportation services.** Ask their advice on the number and size of cars you will need for your wedding party. Ask if you have a choice in the types of cars. Find out their minimum number of hours and what services are included in the rates. Discuss drivers' attire so that their style of dress will be in keeping with the occasion. If you plan to decorate rented cars, ask about any restrictions.

3. **Confirm directions and driving times.** Drive the route to get the timing down if you have to. When it comes to weddings, it's far better to be early than to keep everyone waiting. When you arrange rentals, be precise about locations. Determine exact times that drivers will be needed, and provide detailed directions to unfamiliar sites.

4. **Make sure the members of the wedding party have transportation home** from the reception site—especially if you will not be using the limousine service to do so. Be sure your attendants know their transportation arrangements. Enlist the best man, the head usher, or reliable relatives to see that every attendant has a safe ride and to stop anyone (attendants and guests) who has overindulged from driving.

5. **Don't try to cram the entire wedding party in with you on the way to the reception.** Even if the car is a huge stretch limo, enjoy the luxury and the romance of having your mate alone with you, if only for a few minutes. This will very likely be the first time you have been alone all day and most probably the last time you will be alone until you leave the reception. Savor the moment.

A PERSONAL TOUCH:

How About a Horse and Carriage?

Maybe you want to arrive at the reception in a Cinderella carriage or a romantic horse-drawn carriage. Perhaps a caravan of taxis is just the thing to set a bright, fun tone for the celebration. The ideas are myriad, from hay wagons to classic vintage cars to motorcycles!

Sometimes, it's necessary to transport guests from parking areas to the ceremony and/or reception site. Vans, buses, trolleys, even golf carts, can do the job. Arrangements to hire these vehicles and other novelty transportation must normally be made well in advance, just as for limos. Pay close attention to the qualifications of drivers. Check with your local municipal authorities about proper licenses for various vehicles and any legal restrictions on the use of public roads.

CHAPTER 16

FLOWERS FOR YOUR WEDDING

Fragrant, lovely, and romantic, flowers are the key decorating elements of the wedding celebration. Flowers not only add visual pleasure and a note of festivity to the proceedings, but they also symbolize the full blooming of new love and a new life. Fresh blooms and greenery—whether cascading from an altar, twined around an arch, spilling over a flower girl's basket, or tucked lovingly into a groom's lapel—represent the flowering of a couple's love.

Many of the traditions of old retain a place in wedding events, long after their origins have been forgotten. For example, the tradition of flowers strewn along the path the bride walks has its roots in ancient times, when a path of flowers and fragrant herbs was thought to keep evil spirits away. Centuries ago, wedding reception halls were decorated with sweet-smelling jasmine to entice angels to attend and bless the event. In a tradition that began in 12th-century Spain, fresh orange blossoms were fashioned into wreaths to crown the heads of brides. Hundreds of years later, England's Queen Victoria would wear fragrant orange blossoms in her hair in her marriage to Prince Albert. Brides who could neither afford nor find fresh blossoms used wax ones; many a wax bridal wreath has become a treasured family heirloom, passed down from generation to generation of brides.

Modern couples may not know the tradition behind the ritual, but they do appreciate the beauty and purity that flowers bring to a wedding celebration. These days, flowers at weddings are used in nearly every aspect of the celebration, from the decoration of church pews to topping the wedding cake. Flowers can be seen everywhere: in the hands of attendants, given to parents, stepparents, and grandparents, in centerpieces, on mantels, wrapped around candles, topping buffet tables, even adorning serving platters. You might even decide to place plants at strategic locations, such as main entryways.

Whether you select flowers for their symbolic meaning, for seasonability, for mix-and-match qualities, for color, size, or fragrance, or simply for aesthetic pleasure, you'll find the process of choosing a delight. Make it a personal quest. Make your wedding flowers an expression of your heart.

How to Choose Your Flowers

You should choose your wedding flowers based on the following factors:

1. **The formality of your wedding.** The more formal the wedding, the more formal the flowers, such as formal bouquets, which are traditionally all white and generally one type of flower.

2. **The time of day.** For an evening wedding, for example, white or brightly colored flowers stand out, especially if the ceremony is held in candlelight.

3. **The colors you and the bridal party will be wearing and the color of table linens.** Some brides actually plan their bridal party colors around the flowers they love.

4. **The season.** Flowers in season not only will be fresher but will last longer and cost less, because they don't have to be shipped from far away.

5. **The interior design of the wedding site and reception site.** A church with a high ceiling, for example, demands taller plants.

6. **The constraints of your budget.** There are many ways to cut costs on flowers, including sharing ceremony flowers with another wedding couple, having friends help you do your own arrangements, using borrowed potted plants, using your ceremony flowers at the reception, and renting plants.

7. **Whether the site is indoors or out.** If you're marrying outdoors, you may need to supplement a blooming spring or summer garden site with only a few flower arrangements here and there and bouquets, boutonnieres, and corsages.

8. **The unifying theme of your wedding.** Are you planning a country-style wedding with baskets overflowing with wildflowers and simple bouquets? Or do you favor a traditional formal celebration and see understated elegance carried throughout from attire to decorating? Do you have a color scheme in mind? Or are you considering all white for flowers and decorations? Will you have accessory themes? Are you making floral choices based as much on fragrance as on color and texture? If you are having a *real* theme wedding—romantic Victorian, for example, Hawaiian luau, fifties-style—you'll want flowers and decorations that match the theme.

Wedding Flowers Checklist

The first thing you should do is draw up a list of all your floral needs. A copy of this list should be presented to the florist at your first meeting.

Determine what, if any, of the following items you would like to have: ribbons, greens, candles, vases, pots, or containers you may also need. The range of floral decorations can go far beyond bridal party bouquets and altar decorations. You may want a plant for each entranceway, flowers to garnish serving platters, flower sprays for candles, bouquets for wedding helpers and grandparents—even a beribboned flower twined around the cake knife. To guide you, the following is a general checklist of floral needs. By no means must you follow this list to the letter: It is simply a guide for you to work from, whether you are collaborating with a florist or floral designer or are planning to do the arrangements yourself.

The Bride and Her Attendants

- Bride's bouquet
- Honor attendant
- Bridesmaids
- Flower girl
- Tossing bouquet
- Floral hair decorations

The Groom and His Attendants

- Groom's boutonniere
- Best man
- Ushers
- Ring bearer

Family Flowers

- Parents and stepparents of the bride
- Parents and stepparents of the groom
- Grandmothers and grandfathers
- Other special guests such as godparents, readers

For the Ceremony

- Entranceway
- Altar
- *Chuppah*
- Pews
- Candles
- Roses for parents, if necessary
- Flowers for the Blessed Virgin
- Aisle runner

For the Reception

- Centerpieces
- Buffet tables
- Cake topper, cake knife
- Cake table
- Mantel, stairway, entranceways
- Place-card table
- Garnish for serving platters
- Restroom arrangements
- Flower petals for tossing

As Gifts

- Party hosts
- Out-of-town guests
- Weekend hosts
- Thank-yous to friends and helpers

Seasonal Flowers

Although the advances of modern technology have resulted in the year-round availability of formerly hard-to-get flowers, you can still cut costs by using seasonal flowers that are in bloom locally. They don't need to be shipped, can be cut close to the time they will be used, and tend to be hardier than blooms forced in a greenhouse, out of season. Following is a list of seasonal flowers:

Springtime Flowers

apple blossoms	iris	larkspur
cherry blossoms	lilacs	peonies
daffodils	lilies	sweet peas
dogwood	lilies of the valley	tulips
forsythia	jonquils	violets

Summertime Flowers

asters	geranium	stock
calla lilies	hydrangea	Queen Anne's lace
dahlias	larkspur	
daisies	roses	

Fall Flowers

asters	dahlias	Shasta daisies
chrysanthemum	marigolds	zinnias

Flowers that are readily available year-round are those that are grown in greenhouses but that are not rare or difficult to grow. These include:

Year-Round Flowers

baby's breath	daisies	orchids
bachelor's button	gardenias	roses
carnations	ivy	stephanotis
delphiniums	lilies	

Floral Themes

There are many ways to use flowers to personalize your wedding. The following are some ideas to make your celebration special and unique:

THE LANGUAGE OF FLOWERS

As you begin making decisions about flowers, you might incorporate those that have special traditional meaning. In the early 1900s, romance was often communicated with flowers. A young man would present a red rose, which symbolized love, to a young woman. She would return a purple pansy, which silently relayed the message "You are in my thoughts." Traditionally, no words were spoken that would commit either party during this courtship, so knowing the language of flowers was of paramount importance if an accord was to be reached. Today it is a charming idea to select flowers, and even herbs, that convey special floral messages between the bride and the groom.

acacia—friendship
agrimony—gratitude
ambrosia—love returned
anemone—expectation
apple blossoms—hope
aster—elegance
azalea—temperance
baby's breath—innocence
bay laurel—glory
calla lily—beauty
camellia—loveliness
carnation—devotion
chrysanthemum—abundance
daffodil—regard
daisy—gentleness
forget-me-not—remembrance
freesia—innocence
gardenia—purity
heather—future fortune
heliotrope—devotion

ivy—fidelity
larkspur—laughter
laurel—peace
lilac—humility
lily—majesty
lily of the valley—happiness
myrtle—remembrance
orange blossom—purity
orchid—rare beauty
parsley—beginnings
peony—bashfulness
Queen Anne's lace—trust
rose—love
rosemary—remembrance
sage—immortality
stephanotis—marital happiness
thyme—courage
tulip—passion
violet—modesty
zinnia—affection

THE LANGUAGE OF COLOR

Colors have meaning in many cultures. You may want to develop your floral color scheme around a particular color for its symbolic meaning.

- **Red or fuchsia.** The color of love in China and India.

- **Green.** The ancient color of fertility. A color symbolizing luck to modern-day Italians and Irish.

- **Red and yellow.** The marriage colors of Egypt, Asia, and Russia.

- **Blue/turquoise.** Attached to wedding ceremonies in Western countries (". . . something borrowed, something blue").

- **Purple.** Represented wealth in ancient Greece. The classical color of the soul.

- **Blue and gold.** Reinforces power, dignity, and rank.

BIRTH MONTH FLOWERS

Another special way to personalize and add meaning to floral choices is to combine the traditional birth month flowers of the bride and groom.

Month	Flower	Month	Flower
January	carnation	July	larkspur
February	violet	August	gladiola
March	jonquil	September	aster
April	sweet pea	October	calendula
May	lily of the valley	November	chrysanthemum
June	rose	December	narcissus

FRAGRANT FLOWERS AND HERBS

A popular trend is including fragrance in your overall wedding theme, using flowers, herbs, and greenery not just for their visual appeal but for their perfume.

bay laurel	lily of the valley
carnations	magnolia blossoms
freesia	mint
gardenias	narcissus
hyacinth	roses, especially old-fashioned or tea roses
jasmine	stephanotis
lavender	violets
lilacs	wisteria

Selecting the Florist for You

In starting your search for the right florist for you, ask for recommendations from friends, local caterers, or local nurseries. A florist who is closely affiliated with nurseries or wholesalers can often get good prices on flowers and plants in bulk. If you are holding your celebration in a hotel or reception hall, get the names of florists who have worked on wedding celebrations there. Some florists may be contracted to do arrangements for hotels and reception halls on a regular basis—in that case, you can view their work firsthand. When you have some names and are ready to interview people, always make an appointment. It is unrealistic and discourteous to think you can walk in, unexpected, and snare the florist's undivided attention.

At the first meeting, there is nothing wrong with saying up front that you aren't ready to sign a contract, but that you are looking for someone with whom you can work. It is very important to find someone that you feel comfortable with. Use the following criteria in your search for a florist:

A QUESTION FOR PEGGY:

FLORISTS VERSUS FLORAL DESIGNERS?

Q: *What is the difference between florists and floral designers?*

A: In the last few years, "floral designers" have become popular. Floral designers, unlike florists, generally do not work out of a shop and are particularly versed in creative, nontraditional themes. Floral designers can create a unifying look for your entire wedding, integrating not only flowers into the decor but lighting and textiles as well. You'll have to decide whether you want to work with a full-service florist, who can provide soup-to-nuts floral needs in-house, or with a floral designer, who generally creates a design and then executes it by outsourcing jobs. Although many floral designers do not have a shop, they often have a full staff to handle every aspect of the floral plans.

Helping the Florist Help You

Be prepared for your appointment with the florist so that you can both use the time efficiently. The more information you provide and the better your research and planning, the more successful and satisfying your collaboration will be. Here are tips and advice on how you can work with the florist to achieve your goals:

1. **Trust the florist.** Trust helps give your florist the opportunity to be creative and do his or her best work. Pick someone that you will enjoy working with. Your personalities should suit each other. The florist will be executing your vision.

2. **Have some flexibility in choosing your flowers.** A florist is not unlike a chef: When going to the market to purchase the flowers for your floral arrangements, your florist will be most inspired if he or she can use the best flowers available—and the best may be what is in season at that time, not the exotics you've included on your must-have list.

3. **Listen to the florist's advice.** It's the florist's job not only to fulfill your needs and desires but also to advise you on the best ways to make it all happen—and that may entail offering solutions that run counter to your original vision. You may be determined to use columbines in your bouquets and table arrangements, for example, but because of their lack of sturdiness, they may not be the best choice. It is the florist's job to provide you with an informed opinion.

4. **Bring visuals.** Bringing along photographs of floral arrangements you like—and those you don't like—is very helpful. Providing your wedding colors up front is also an excellent way to match fabrics with complementing flowers. Give the florist swatches of your gown and your bridesmaids' gowns, if you have them, or a color wheel with the family of colors you've chosen to work with. Photographs of bridal party attire are helpful, too.

5. **Consider others' preferences.** If you are giving flowers—corsages or nosegays, for example—to special people at the wedding, consider each person's personal preferences and style when making a selection.

6. **Come prepared.** It's a good idea to work up a wedding-flowers checklist before you visit the florist—or at least know what is essential to you and what is not.

7. **Be open to change.** Remember that the floral plan is a work in progress right up until the week of the wedding.

8. **Creativity and compatibility.** Try to find a florist who is willing to embrace your ideas, offer advice and suggestions, show you examples, and agree to your budgetary parameters. Look for a florist who will work with you as a collaborator, but who also offers creative input and advice on ways to do things more efficiently. If, for example, your wedding is small but is located in a large site, ask for recommendations on ways to make it intimate. The florist may do this with greens, flowers, or even decorated screens. You'll want a florist you feel comfortable with.

9. **Wedding experience.** Look for a florist who is experienced in the business of wedding decorating. The florist should be capable of managing all the details, including the timing and the delivery arrangements you require.

10. **Portfolio.** Ask to see the florist's album or portfolio containing photographs or illustrations of previous weddings for which the florist has provided flowers.

11. **Flexibility and range of options.** Discuss your wedding-flowers checklist and the range of options for each item. Determine how many of your ideas, large and small, can be accommodated within your budget. The best florists are happy to suggest alternatives that allow you to achieve your vision and stay within your budget, and you will experience less stress if you remain flexible on floral choices. If on the first pass your wish list results in a budget-busting estimated bill, simply rethink your options. Ask your florist to recommend inexpensive backup choices. Start over with the basics and make a list of your priorities. What is the most important floral expenditure? The bridal bouquet? The reception centerpiece? Can you splurge on these and rely on simple choices for the less important arrangements? If your choices are made with loving care, it won't matter whether you used an expensive or exotic flower to express your joy. The magic of flowers is that there is beauty and elegance in the simplest of forms.

Nuts and Bolts: Questions for the Florist

Be sure to discuss the following once you've committed to a florist:

1. **Discuss your overall reception decor with the florist.** Check with your caterer and cake-maker to coordinate the overall floral design and ensure that the color schemes match. Often wedding cakes are decorated with real flowers and greenery, so that will need to be coordinated as well. If the caterer is providing the table linens, you will need to select colors that complement the floral design, or vice versa. If the florist cannot visit

your ceremony or reception site, provide a sketch of the layout and describe its existing color schemes. You may also want to consult with your officiant or the reception-site manager on the types of decor that work well in the space.

2. **Ask for an item-by-item breakdown of the prices before you sign any contract or agreement.** Confirm your arrangements and ask if there is a deposit. Check whether the contract includes delivery costs and any gratuities. Add confirmation-call reminders to your planner.

3. **Discuss when and where deliveries should take place.** If you have contracted with the florist to deliver and install the floral decorations, you should provide a list of all flower deliveries that need to be made. You'll need to discuss the best place and time to deliver each component of the decor. Where, for example, do you want the bride's and her attendants' flowers delivered: the bride's home if everyone will be dressing there, or directly to the ceremony site? If yours is a morning wedding, will the flowers stay fresh if they are delivered the night before? It is helpful to have the florist label the flowers not just with indications such as "bride's grandmother" but with specifics such as "Allison Jensin, grandmother of the bride." Include dates, times, instructions for access, and accurate names, telephone numbers, and addresses. Copy the information into your planner as well, and mark on your calendar to make a reminder call a day or two before the big day.

4. **Ask whether the florist can take care of the little extras.**

   - If you will be lighting a unity candle, can it be decorated with flowers?

   - Can flower petals to toss be provided by the florist?

   - Special floral gifts for helpers need to be discussed up front. The florist might suggest simple nosegays, corsages, or flower arrangements to be delivered after the wedding day.

   - You may include thank-you flowers for bridal showers. If you know friends will be giving you a shower, flowers delivered before or after as a thank-you can be discussed and ordered at the same time you are ordering your wedding flowers.

   - Flowers for welcoming out-of-town guests staying in hotels or inns can be included in the florist contract. (Be sure to write the cards beforehand and give them to the florist.)

Flowers for the Ceremony

If you are having your ceremony in a church or synagogue, ask the priest, minister, or rabbi to advise you on the types of decorations that work best there and what, if any, limitations there are on floral decorations. The range of options includes ceremony flowers or greenery for the altar or chancel, *chuppah,* pulpit, and candelabra. The ceremony flowers may be as simple or as elaborate as the setting, your budget, and the formality of the ceremony.

IN A CHURCH OR SYNAGOGUE

Traditionally, an arrangement or two of flowers that blends with the bridal party flowers is all you need to provide for your ceremony. Placed on the altar in a church or on the reader's platform in a synagogue, they are lovely to look at when guests arrive, and serve as a background for the ceremony. Candelabra and a standing unity candle can be wound with garlands of greens with a few flowers tucked in. When permitted in a synagogue, the *chuppah,* or canopy, can be decorated with garlands of flowers as well. If your budget permits, you can add more floral focal points.

If a stairway with railings forms the entrance to your ceremony site, you can drape the railings with garlands, leading the way to the door. Double doors at a church entrance could be adorned with floral wreaths, a beautiful welcome to guests.

The ends of pews may be decorated with satin ribbons or ribbons and flowers, marking the path the wedding party will walk. In a very large church or cathedral with soaring ceilings, height can be added to pew decorations with arrangements on standards placed at the ends of every three or four pews, leading to the altar.

In most cases, ceremony flowers must stay at the ceremony site, so keep that in mind. Don't blow your budget on floral arrangements that can't serve double duty at both the ceremony and the reception.

AT HOME, A CLUB, OR A WEDDING FACILITY

Ceremonies that take place outside a church or synagogue can be beautifully decorated. It is a good idea to take photographs of the areas that will be used, thus having a reference when you are planning your decorations. If a sweeping staircase is the site of your processional, you can drape it in floral garlands. If guests are to be seated in rows, facing the altar or *chuppah,* frame the aisle in well-secured standing arrangements, or tie ribbons at the sides of the chairs closest to the aisle. A backdrop of greens and flowers can frame the bride and groom. If a fireplace is the center of the backdrop, it can be filled with greens, and the mantel decorated with green roping or an arrangement of greens or flowers.

An altar may easily be made by covering an ordinary table with a white silk, lace, or damask cloth. Whether or not there is a cross or other religious objects on the altar depends on the service, on your faith, and on the officiating clergy. Often there is simply a kneeling bench for the couple. If there is a railing, it can be covered with greens, and a tall stand holding a flower arrangement at each end of the rail makes a lovely frame for the ceremony. Depending on the size of the room, an aisle runner may be used. If the ceremony site is a club or a historic facility, check to see what elements are available. It is very likely your florist can provide a kneeling bench, stanchions for flowers, and an aisle runner.

Assuming that your reception will be held at the same place, you will want to carry over the same floral theme from the chapel to the reception rooms.

OUTDOORS

You may think that because your ceremony is outdoors, you will have little need to embellish nature. That is often not the case. You may want to add such festive ornamentation as potted plants placed at strategic spots, hanging baskets of flowers that match your color scheme, an arched trellis woven with flowers, or colorful ribbons, streamers, and garlands. If the wedding is at night, candles or Japanese lanterns provide a romantic ambience. In the evening, scents are particularly pungent; you may want to marry in the proximity of a sweet bay bush or night-blooming datura.

Don't forget to formulate a backup plan with the florist in case of inclement weather. Unless your wedding is being held under a tent, you will need to consider a floral design for the backup indoors site. Formulate with the florist a set plan of where the floral arrangements will be situated, and if the site is located at a different address, make sure delivery instructions are changed.

Flowers for the Reception

The options for reception flowers are as unlimited as there are sites. Arrangements can be placed on each dining table, on the place-card table, at serving stations or on buffet tables, and even in restrooms. Flowers can encircle the wedding cake, coil around entranceways and archways, and frame the musicians' bandstand. Pots of beribboned topiary and standards may form a backdrop for the bridal party table.

The two most photographed locations at the reception are the table where the bridal couple is seated and the cake table. Another key focal point for guests is the table where the place cards are located. Consider this when you plan your reception decorations.

How Can Flowers for a Destination Wedding Be Successfully Selected?

Q: *I am having a destination wedding and am doing my planning long-distance. One aspect of the wedding I'd really like to control is the choosing of flowers. How can I ensure a successful floral display from so far away?*

A: One of the most popular wedding trends is marrying in a romantic, exotic locale far from home. Destination weddings are generally planned and coordinated long-distance. What you need to do is to first find a reliable florist. To do so, you can take one of several tacks. You can:

- Inquire about coordinating the flowers and decorations through the wedding site or hotel manager. Many popular destination-wedding resorts offer complete wedding packages that include floral selections.

- Ask your local florist if he or she is affiliated with any florists at the wedding location.

- Find a florist through the network of large floral organizations, such as FTD.

- Check the Internet for lists of florists. One, weddingpages.com/home, includes a city directory of florists and other vendors in many cities in the United States.

The long-distance florist may send or fax sketches of plans and photographs of previous weddings. Ask about local blooms; for a Hawaiian wedding, for example, take advantage of the exotic local flowers.

Centerpieces should be either low enough so that guests can easily see one another when seated or elevated in tall vases so that they are above the diners' heads. Bridesmaids' bouquets can form the floral focus at the bridal party's table or be placed around the cake on a separate table. At an evening wedding, candles or candelabra decorated with greens and simple flowers may serve as centerpieces.

If the reception is held outdoors, you can embellish the setting with the same flowers and plants you used for the outdoor ceremony. Decorations don't have to stop with flowers, however. An evening wedding outdoors may be lit by Japanese lanterns, glittering Christmas lights strung through the trees, or candle luminarias placed on the pathway to the site.

Flowers for the Bride and Her Attendants

The formality and style of your celebration determine the wedding attire and the flowers that complement it. It is helpful to know what is traditional for bridal flowers as you plan. Bouquets, by definition, are simply clusters of flowers, tied together or anchored in a bouquet holder. The shape of the bouquet generally determines the best flowers to use.

Do all the bride's attendants' flowers have to be identical? While they should complement their gowns and echo the style of the bride's bouquet, attendants' bouquets carried in semiformal and informal weddings can be of different flowers, with each bridesmaid carrying a nosegay of her favorite flower in the same hue as those of the other bridesmaids. One difference may be the size of the bouquet, generally determined by the height and size of the attendant. Bridesmaids come in all shapes and sizes, and just as you adapt their gowns to flatter, so can you adapt their flowers. Give their heights to the florist who can customize their bouquets. A six-foot bridesmaid holding a tiny nosegay looks as uncomfortable as a petite bridesmaid struggling with a large cascade.

You can also provide a personal touch by asking each bridesmaid what her favorite flowers are and surprising each with a specially designed bouquet.

THE PERSONAL TOUCH:

BOUQUETS AS DECORATIONS

Q: *Any thoughts on creative ways to display the bridesmaid bouquets at the reception?*

A: Here's a lovely suggestion that's also a cost cutter: Use the attendants' bouquets as floral arrangements on the bridal table, placing them side by side at the top of each place setting, with the flower sides turned out facing the rest of the reception. It's a beautiful way to display the bouquets, which might otherwise be relegated to a side table or tucked away in a safe place. And they serve a dual purpose as a table decoration— one less floral cost.

BOUQUETS

Formal Bouquets

Formal bouquets are traditionally all white, generally of one type of flower or a combination of two or three different flowers, such as roses, gardenias, stephanotis, and lilies of the valley. The flowers can be fashioned into a cascade or a formal bouquet or nosegay and are adorned with satin ribbons, chiffon, or organza. A formal bouquet can also be as simple as a single calla lily or white rose.

Semiformal Bouquets

Usually arm bouquets or nosegays, semiformal bouquets often are colorful bouquets, either a combination of mixed colors or different flowers of the same hue or color scheme, such as pinks or corals. Semiformal bouquets can also be all white but are often touched with color by the addition of softly tinted ribbons.

Informal Bouquets

Informal bouquets can be just as elegant as formal bouquets but offer greater variety in shape and flower choices. An informal bouquet can be a gathering of flowers taped at the stem and tied with ribbons, or something as simple as a cloud of baby's breath.

Bouquets to Toss

If the bride decides she wants her wedding bouquet as a keepsake, she may opt for a "breakaway" bouquet, which allows the bride to keep part of it and separate another part to toss, if bouquet tossing is part of the wedding festivities. Or she can order a completely separate "tossing" bouquet, often similar to but not as elaborate as the one she carries.

A QUESTION FOR PEGGY:

ALTERNATIVES TO BOUQUETS?

Q: *I don't care for formal bouquets, and I don't want my attendants carrying them, either. Can I choose to carry something other than a bouquet, even if everything else about my wedding is traditional?*

A: Neither the bride nor her attendants are restricted to carrying bouquets. They may walk down the aisle carrying a single long-stemmed flower (or two or three). They may wear flowers pinned to their dresses, wrist corsages, pomanders (blossom covered globes held by a loop of ribbon), flower- and ribbon-decorated fans, or flowers attached to a prayer book. Additions to bouquets may be potpourri or tiny bells that sweetly ring as the bridal party walks down the aisle.

FLOWERS FOR THE HAIR AND VEIL

Fresh or wax orange blossoms were once the flowers that crowned the bride's veil, but today an array of flowers is often used, woven into bandeaux or circlets and Juliet caps with veils or worn tucked into a chignon, French twist, or French braid. Flowers can wreath the heads of the bride's attendants, too, or be as simple as a small spray attached to the back of upswept hair. If you want to wear flowers on your veil, make sure they are delivered early enough so that the florist can determine the prettiest look and the most secure way of attaching the flowers to the veil.

BOUQUET SHAPES

The formality and shape of a bouquet go hand in hand. There are four basic bouquet shapes:

Nosegays

Nosegays are circular, densely arranged arrays of flowers, approximately 18 inches in diameter. Within this circle there may be *posies,* which are petite nosegays made of tiny buds, or *tussy-mussies,* another type of small nosegay composed of tiny buds carried in Victorian-period cone-shaped silver holders. Tussy-mussies are often made of flowers that have traditional meanings, true to their Victorian origins. *Biedermeier nosegays* are arranged in rings of flowers, with each ring including only one flower variety. Nosegays can be carried with either long or short gowns.

Arm Bouquets

Arm bouquets are crescent-shaped arrangements, curved slightly to fit on the arm. Because they are larger than nosegays, they are usually best suited to long gowns.

Cascades

A bouquet that cascades is one that gracefully trails blossoms and/or greens from its base. It can be any shape, from a nosegay to tear-shaped, and looks best with a long gown.

Sprays

Sprays are flowers gathered together in a triangular-shaped cluster. Sprays can be carried with either long or short gowns, since they can be of varying sizes.

A QUESTION FOR PEGGY:

HOW CAN THE BRIDAL BOUQUET BE PRESERVED?

Q: *What's a good way to preserve my bridal bouquet?*

A: Many florists now have the technical capacity to freeze-dry flowers—preserving them for all time in much the same state they were in when fresh. You can preserve your bridal bouquet and keep it on display with the freeze-dried method. After the wedding, bridal bouquets are taken apart and each component freeze-dried separately. Then the arrangement is put back together and the bouquet is placed in a glass box, frozen in time and on display for your children—and even your grandchildren—to see.

How to Carry a Bouquet

It simply doesn't look right to have one attendant clutching her bouquet tightly at chest level while another has it dropped below her waist. Usually, a nosegay is held with two hands, centered just below the waist. An arm bouquet is rested along the lower half of one arm, with any falling sprays held in front. Attendants walking on the right side hold their arm bouquets on the right arm with the stems pointing downward to the left, and those on the left hold their flowers on the left arm with stems toward the right.

Experiment with loosely tied bouquets and single flowers—and make sure all the attendants are carrying the flowers the same way. Whatever you do, try not to press the bouquet against your gown, for it can get crushed and mark the gown with pollen.

Flowers for the Groom and His Attendants

Boutonnieres, worn by the groom and his attendants on their left lapels, make for a festive and understated grace note to the men's attire. Subtle and small scale are the key words: The groom and his groomsmen should never appear to be wearing corsages. A boutonniere may be any flower, but it should be a hardy variety that won't wilt or crush easily. Usually, the groom wears a flower that is one also used in his bride's bouquet, and groomsmen wear boutonnieres that complement that of the groom. A small-scale white or ivory rose, lily of the valley, stephanotis, or freesia are equally elegant and may or may not be wired with greens. It's a good idea to order one extra boutonniere for the groom—in case his original is crushed or wilted by the time he arrives at the reception.

Wedding-party boutonnieres are usually delivered to the ceremony site where the groomsmen gather, well before the wedding begins. But if all are dressing in the same location and traveling to the ceremony site together, their boutonnieres can be delivered there instead. Pins are provided by the florist for the groomsmen to use to pin the boutonnieres on their left lapels.

Flowers for Children

If your wedding party includes a flower girl, she may hold a tiny nosegay, a diminutive bouquet, or a small basket of flower petals. Traditionally, fresh rose petals from the flower girl's basket are strewn during the processional. But fresh petals are notoriously slippery, so many brides choose dried flowers instead.

Children are also enchanting carrying hoops decorated in satin and festooned with flowers in the spring and summer or swathed in evergreens in December. An old English tradition, and popular in France, this custom is also practiced today in the South.

Children from a previous marriage of either the bride or the groom who are not participants in the wedding ceremony might receive flowers to wear or hold.

THE PERSONAL TOUCH:

WHEN THE CELEBRATION IS OVER

If you have no plans to use your ceremony and reception flowers again, recycle them! Arrange to have them delivered to area nursing homes and hospitals, local charities, or public buildings such as the town hall. Another choice is to offer to leave them for the next worship service in celebration of your marriage. A wonderful idea is to have a centerpiece from the reception delivered to a loved one who was unable to attend the wedding, accompanied by a note from you.

CHAPTER 17

LET THERE BE MUSIC!

MUSIC ADDS JOY, SOLEMNITY, FUN, and a sense of tradition to a wedding day. It serves as a ceremony cue, as pleasant background to conversation, as a call to dance the night away. The right music helps make a wonderful day even better. In fact, no other single element of your celebration has the power to engage the emotions the way music does.

Fortunately, there are numerous ways for the bride and groom to orchestrate and personalize their wedding music—and few professionals are more enthusiastic than musicians when it comes to talking about what they love.

Music at the Ceremony

If you plan to marry in a house of worship, *check with your officiant about any site restrictions.* More and more churches and synagogues have established specific rules regarding music selections, and it is wise to know them before making plans. Some houses of worship are so strict that such well-known pieces as the "Bridal Chorus" ("Here Comes the Bride"), from Wagner's *Lohengrin,* and Mendelssohn's "Wedding March" are not allowed at all, the reason being that each is a secular, not sacred, piece of music.

Your officiant may refer you to a house music director, who can then review the parameters of the musical choices available to you and provide you with acceptable options. But don't take his or her word for it—you need to *hear* the music before you commit to it. The music director should play samples of traditional and popular choices to help you decide what to use for the prelude, the processional, and the recessional and during the ceremony. You can also find musical CDs that play nothing but wedding favorites. Look for such titles as *The Wedding Album* (RCA/Ariola International) and *The Complete Wedding Album* (Telarc). The following are some guidelines to use when planning your ceremony music:

- **Ask about acoustics.** Your choice of music may not be the best selections for the acoustics of your ceremony site. Ask the officiant or music director what type of music and instruments sound best in the space.

- **Find out if you can use visiting musicians.** If you are indeed allowed to bring in your own musicians, you will need to know whether there are any sound limitations and the types of music that work best in the space. The officiant or music director may even be able to provide the names of musicians who have played in and are familiar with the site.

- **Consider your guests' preferences.** Make sure you don't include any music that might offend some guests' sensibilities. Some guests might consider a popular secular tune disrespectful in a church ceremony. If you are having your ceremony in a house of worship and plan on including hymns to be sung by the entire congregation, keep your guests in mind when making your selections. The more familiar or beloved a hymn, the more participation from your guests—and the more joyful your celebration will be.

- **Consider the services of the house organist.** It makes sense to use the services of the house organist in the church or synagogue where your ceremony will take place. Who knows better than he or she the ins and outs of the organ, the acoustics, and the timing of religious ceremonies? Using the house organist might also save you on costs for ceremony music. If you hire an outside organist, you may have to pay a fee, which is standard practice endorsed by the American Guild of Organists. You must also coordinate it so that the outside organist has access to the organ to practice. Find out times that the church or synagogue will be open and when the organist can have practice time. If your ceremony is at another site, you will need to make the same arrangements.

- **Discuss how and when payment will be made.** If a house of worship provides a bill, the fee for the organist is often included and you can write one check. If not, he or she must be paid directly, either in cash or by check, before or directly after the service. This is traditionally the best man's job, so one possibility is for him to take care of this after he has delivered the groom to the room where he will wait for the ceremony to begin.

- **List the songs and the players.** If you are providing a program for your ceremony, you will want to list the music that is performed during the prelude as well as during the ceremony. Be sure to get the correct names of each piece and add the composer, information that may be of interest to your guests. It is also a good idea to list the names of the musicians. Check and double-check the spelling of everything you include.

The Order of Ceremony Music

When working with the music director or organist, organize your choices into the four basic musical components of your ceremony.

THE PRELUDE

It is a happy beginning indeed when guests arrive at a wedding to the joyful sounds of music. The prelude music should begin at least a half hour before the ceremony starts. It can be played simply by a lone organist or performed by a string quartet; it can showcase the smooth strokes of a harpist or the ethereal trills of a woodwind ensemble.

Sampling of Prelude Music

- Air (Handel)
- Rondo (Mozart)
- "Jesu, Joy of Man's Desiring" (Bach)
- Largo (Handel)
- Concerto No. 1 (from Vivaldi's *The Four Seasons,* "Spring")
- Pavane (Faure)

THE PROCESSIONAL

The processional music begins as the mother of the bride is seated, the groom and his best man enter, and the bride and her father (or other escort) and her attendants are ready to begin their walk. The music can simply be that of an organ or, at a home wedding, a piano. A trumpeter can accompany the organ, adding a joyful and regal note. Music played during the entrance of the bride and her attendants should be joyous and formal at the same time. The same piece can be played throughout the processional; sometimes the bride's entrance is accompanied by a different piece of music.

Sampling of Processional Music

- "The Bridal Chorus" (*Lohengrin*)
- "Wedding March" (from Mendelssohn's *A Midsummer Night's Dream*)
- "The Prince of Denmark's March" (Clarke)

- "Wedding March" (Guilmant)

- Air (Bach)

- Canon in D Major (Pachelbel)

- "Arrival of the Queen of Sheba" (Handel)

- Trumpet Voluntary (Clarke)

- Trumpet Tune (Purcell)

THE CEREMONY

Many couples like having guests participate in the ceremony in the singing of hymns or a favorite song. This brings a communal spirit to the proceedings, especially when the ceremony is a brief one. In addition to one or two hymns, other musical interludes may be added at appropriate places during the ceremony. These can be a vocal, performed by a soloist or a children's choir, or an instrumental, performed on a harp, a trumpet, or a combination of both. Work with your officiant and, if there is one, the music director or organist to determine where in the service music should be placed. Make sure, if soloists are to perform, that practice time with the organist or other instrumentalist is scheduled.

Sampling of Ceremony Music

- "Ave Maria" (Schubert)

- "One Hand, One Heart" (Bernstein and Sondheim)

- "Jesu, Joy of Man's Desiring" (Bach)

- "Joyful, Joyful, We Adore Thee" (Beethoven)

- "The King of Love My Shepherd" (Hinsworth)

- "The Lord's Prayer" (Malotte)

- Biblical Songs (Dvorak)

- Libestraum (Liszt)

- "In Thee Is Joy" (Bach)

THE RECESSIONAL

The music you choose for your recessional should be the most joyous of all. It is a jubilant time, and the music should reflect that jubilation. Often the bell note on the organ or bells in the bell tower are rung to add to the festive ambience. Look for upbeat, joyous music, the kind that will have you and your attendants fairly floating down the aisle and out the door.

Sampling of Recessional Music

- "Ode to Joy" (Beethoven)

- Trumpet Voluntary (Clarke)

- "Wedding March" (from Mendelssohn's *A Midsummer Night's Dream*)

- Trumpet Tune (Purcell)

THE POSTLUDE

Sampling of Postlude Music

- Overture (Handel)

- Rondeau (Mouret)

- "Le Rejouissance" (Handel)

Music at the Reception

Music can make a party, and your reception should be just that: a full-tilt celebration of your nuptial vows. Whether you hire a disc jockey playing recorded music or have the house jumping with a full-fledged swing band, music sets the tone. While budget and personal taste are important considerations, the kind of music and musicians you select depends largely on the time of day your reception is held

BRUNCH, LUNCH, OR TEA RECEPTION

If you are having a brunch, lunch, or afternoon tea reception and no dancing, a single pianist, harpist, or violinist, a string quartet, or taped background music is an appropriate choice. The music you select for such an occasion is meant to be background music, and classical or light romantic selections set the mood for relaxed elegance.

MUSICIAN OR DJ?

Q: *My mother wants us to have live musicians at our wedding, while we've enjoyed weddings where disc jockeys played music. What are the advantages of using a DJ?*

A: First, hear out your mother's reasons for wanting live musicians, and tell her yours for a disc jockey. Cost containment is one compelling reason for working with a DJ; hiring a disc jockey to play music at your reception is typically half the cost of a live band. Plus, a DJ often has a larger playlist that can be expanded upon at your request—playing, for example, specific songs that may not be in the musicians' repertoire. Make sure to see the DJ in action before you make a decision to hire him or her—and take your mother with you when you do. If you decide to use a DJ, have him or her visit the reception space and have a trial run there to test the sound system and the space's acoustics.

Your mother is still hesitant? Do you *really* prefer a DJ? There are ways you can compromise. You could hire a flutist or string trio to play during the cocktail hour and switch gears to a DJ for post-dinner reception dancing.

AFTERNOON COCKTAIL RECEPTION

Guests are mobile at cocktail receptions, moving from table to table, standing and talking. Let your music move with them. This type of reception is the perfect venue for strolling musicians, instrumental combos and quartets, or a single pianist. The music itself should be livelier than that at a tea reception but still never showy or obtrusive. This is not the place to have a vocalist—most guests would feel obliged to stop conversing and give the singer their attention.

DINNER-DANCE RECEPTION

The music for a dinner-dance reception may range from a dance band to a full orchestra to a disc jockey. Remember: The smaller the guest list, the smaller the group. If the guest list and reception space are large, use this handy rule of thumb to help you decide what kind of group to hire: For an orchestra or band, you will need five or six pieces for 150 guests; six or seven pieces for 200 guests; and a full orchestra for 300 guests or more. This is just a general guide—some groups can produce a sound that is bigger than they are.

Helping the Musicians Help with Your Reception

The musicians are an important part of your wedding team. It is the musicians' job to tailor their skills to meet your needs and wishes. You can make that job easier by viewing the relationship as a collaboration working toward a common goal: the success of the occasion. Here are suggestions and advice on ways to make working with musicians a positive experience for all involved:

- Find out first of all whether there are any site restrictions. Coordinate the equipment needs of your musicians with the offerings of the reception site; for example, make sure that amplified musicians will have sufficient outlets and electrical power to play. Ask whether the reception site already has a sound system or piano on the premises.

- Always consider the space. Do not hire an orchestra unless you are going to be in a large space, or you'll risk deafening your guests and making it impossible for them to hear one another. Alternatively, the sound of an unamplified flutist may be lost in a large space, making it appear as if you have no music at all.

- If you're on a budget, find musicians who can do double duty. When your ceremony and reception are small or held at the same location, it is entirely possible to have the same musicians play for both. Select a musician with the ability to play both classical and popular music. The benefit to you: being able to work with just one person to coordinate musical selections.

- If your reception is large and lengthy, you don't necessarily need music the entire time. You can play CDs or have a lone guitarist, pianist, or flutist playing background music during cocktails and dinner, and bring in the band just before dancing begins. Ask the band representative if any of the band members would be willing to perform solo during cocktails and dinner—for a fee, of course.

- If you have hired more than one group, make arrangements for the two to coordinate their performance time. For example, if your reception is five hours long and your band is willing to play for one and a half hours, during which they take two half-hour breaks, the strolling guitarist will need to be on call during those breaks.

- Make arrangements for meals for the musicians. You are expected to feed any members of the band or the DJ at some point during the reception. Talk to your caterer about providing meals not only for the musicians, but also for the photographer, videographer, and any other professionals you have hired. A club or caterer will often give service providers a different meal than your guests or the same meal at half the price.

- Be sure to give the musician a rough idea of the timing of everything—when dancing will start, when the cake will be cut, when toasts will be held.

- Just as you should be specific about the music you want played, it is equally important that you be specific about songs you do not want played. If you absolutely cannot bear to hear "Endless Love" played at your reception, by all means let the musicians know ahead of time.

Let There Be Music!

Selecting the Musicians for You

If you've decided to use musicians, keep in mind that reception bands should be booked many months in advance, so you'll want to start looking for musicians as soon as you're engaged. Word of mouth is often your best resource, so ask everyone you know for recommendations. But don't take their word for it; be sure to listen for yourself. You can do this by seeing the musicians in concert or playing at another wedding; you could ask to attend a practice session. If the band has made a tape or video of their performances, by all means get it. When you start to interview musicians, look for the following qualities:

1. **A varied repertoire.** Remember to look for a varied repertoire, especially if your guest list includes a wide range of ages and styles. Quality and proficiency count, but so does diversity. Have your musicians mix it up, combining upbeat tunes with tender ones. Don't subject your guests to three hours of waltzes or three hours of blasting rock selections.

   Remember, your guest list might very well be comprised of different generations. Make sure that the musicians you hire are capable of moving from one kind of music to another, especially if your reception includes dancing. For an ethnic wedding, you'll need to find musicians who can play traditional ethnic music.

2. **The same band you hired.** Often a variety of interchangeable instrumentalists and vocalists comprise a band, so make sure you get in writing that the group you heard on the tape is the one that will be playing at your wedding.

3. **A well-rounded playlist and savvy pacing.** Often musicians provide a song list of their selections. Having a playlist makes things easy—you and your partner simply check off the music you want to hear. A seasoned reception band will generally offer a large, wide-ranging repertoire and have a good sense of the audience. It is their job to pace the selections and know when to move from waltz to rumba to rock.

THE PERSONAL TOUCH:

Top Ten "First Dance" Songs

1. "The Way You Look Tonight"
2. "Just the Way You Are"
3. "Come Away with Me"
4. "Unforgettable"
5. "Wonderful Tonight"
6. "From This Moment On"
7. "This I Promise You"
8. "Thank You for Loving Me"
9. "Don't Want to Miss a Thing"
10. "All I Ask of You"

---

4. **Flexibility.** You'll want to find experienced wedding musicians who are happy to play special requests. You may want to select songs for special moments, such as music for the bride and groom's first dance, for the bride's dance with her father, and for the parents of the couple. In that case, you should communicate your choices to the musicians in writing.

5. **Tasteful presentation.** Sometimes a bandleader or DJ will also offer to serve as a master of ceremonies. Quite frankly, there is no real reason to have a master of ceremonies at a wedding reception. A good bandleader or DJ knows how to keep things moving without constantly announcing the next song or offering a running banter over the microphone. The only time the bandleader or DJ needs to speak to guests at all is to ask for their silence to allow an officiant to say grace, for example, or a best man to propose his toast. You certainly don't need to be hailed over the microphone as you enter the reception, nor do you need anyone telling jokes that are amplified. And an announcement that a flambée dessert has just come out of the oven is over the top. *Be clear about the behavior you expect from the bandleader or DJ to avoid a misunderstanding.*

Nuts and Bolts: Questions for the Reception Musicians

When interviewing musicians or DJs, make a list of questions to ask and provide any pertinent information. Make sure that the songs you definitely want played will be played. Questions you might ask include:

- How many breaks will be taken, how often, and for how long? (The standard is one per hour, for five to ten minutes.)

- Will taped or synthesized music be provided during breaks?

- What will the band members or DJ wear?

- Are there any other costs not included in the quoted fee, such as travel time and music between breaks?

- Is the band willing to play overtime, and if so, what is the charge? What is their cancellation policy?

> THE PERSONAL TOUCH:
>
> ### MUSICIANS ON A SHOESTRING
>
> Here's a great tip on finding musicians to play at your ceremony and reception. Try the music departments of local colleges or universities, local orchestras—even high-school bands. Amateur musicians from local colleges will be less expensive than professional wedding musicians. Don't hire without hearing them play, however.

- Will the musicians you are contracting be the ones at your reception?

- Will the band (or DJ) take requests from guests at no extra charge?

- Do they sing in any other languages (important for ethnic weddings)?

- Does the band have a playlist? (Most bands know from 200 to 500 songs, from swing to top forty to oldies to ethnic.)

Ask for everything in writing. Understand precisely what you will be getting in return for the price you are paying. Find out how many hours of playing time is contracted, how many breaks the band will take, how overtime hours will be billed, what the required deposit is, when the balance is due, whether a refund is available if you cancel, and any taxes or other charges.

CHAPTER 18

PHOTOGRAPHY AND VIDEOGRAPHY

Your wedding photographs and videotapes are a tangible record of a special time in your lives and a gift for generations hence. That's why choosing the right person for the job is so important. The craft of wedding photography knows no bounds, with styles ranging from classical to artistic to journalistic. When you look for the right photographer for your wedding, consider the style that best articulates your vision.

Before hiring a photographer and/or videographer, couples need to consider several questions. Budget is primary, but almost as important is the type of visual record you prefer. Do you want the traditional album of posed wedding photos, mostly candid shots, or a mix of both? Do you want to record the entire event or just the ceremony or the reception? Do you really want costly videotaping, or are you feeling pressured because "everybody's doing it"?

Be honest as you discuss your feelings. Your goal is to take great pleasure in looking at your wedding album and video for years to come. Ultimately, you should please yourselves, but don't overlook the following practical matters:

Photography: What's Your Style?

Each photographer has his or her own distinct style, which is reflected in the photographer's portfolio of work. Before you choose a photographer, decide on the photographic style you prefer, and then seek out those photographers whose work reflects that style.

1. **Traditional.** A traditional photographer generally treats every image as a posed portrait, even shots you may think of as candid. That doesn't mean that the photographs will appear forced or posed, but that there will likely be few spontaneous "action shots" included in the mix. Traditional wedding photographers look to capture perfect moments with artistry and dignity and generally produce excellent, albeit formulaic, shots of the wedding party, families, and planned events.

2. **Classical.** These photographers specialize in expertly composed, well-lit portraits. They try to keep an unobtrusive presence at the reception in order to set up perfect, classical images. You won't find them mingling or telling the crowd to "look at the camera" to come up with magic moments.

3. **Photojournalistic or reportage.** A wedding photographer who takes a photojournalistic approach is one who considers it is the photographer's job to record events, not stage them. This photographer will take the group shots you want but will also include candid and spontaneous images. There are few formal "grip and grin" roundups of guests smiling for the camera, but this photographer prefers capturing close-ups, spontaneous reactions to events, and sensitive impressions of a wedding led by events and the emotions surrounding them, not posed tableaux orchestrated by the photographer.

4. **Commercial.** These photographers will perfectly capture shots of the centerpieces, cake, flowers, and decor and could be hired just for this purpose, supplemented by another photographer to handle "people pictures." A commercial photographer's sense of style may be more formulaic and less spontaneous than that of a journalistic photographer. Just the same, this type of photographer is a professional and capable of taking magazine-quality images.

5. **Photographic Artist.** Similar to a photojournalist, a photographic artist rarely takes traditional shots but prefers to find artistic ways to photograph elements, people, and events. The photographic artist is adept in the medium of black and white and at producing beautifully composed photos, likely to be less candid than full of drama and artistic beauty.

Selecting the Photographer for You

Once you have agreed on what type and style of photographs will make you the happiest, you can begin seeking a wedding photographer in earnest. When you have some names and are ready to interview people, consider the following criteria in your search for a photographer:

1. **Portfolio.** When you visit a photographer or videographer, always ask to see samples of his or her work. This is the most telling element of a photographer's background. A so-so photographer can't hide behind impressive references. The picture tells it all.

2. **Price and service comparisons.** While your first consideration is your ability to relate to the work the photographer has done in the past, you will need to incorporate price and service comparisons into your decision-making process.

3. **Compatibility.** If you like the photographer's work but don't like the photographer, look elsewhere; your annoyance will show up in your photos. If in a visit to a professional studio you are shown the work of several photographers but prefer the work of one, ask that only that person be assigned to your wedding.

4. **Details indicating quality.** When reviewing a photographer's portfolio, look for clean, sharp images that convey emotion and feeling. Don't be dazzled by special effects or complicated setups. Look for a straightforward style. Keep in mind that you are being shown the photographer's showcase work. The photos won't get any better than that, so be sure you like what you see.

5. **Wedding philosophy.** The one factor that makes the difference between two equally competent professionals is their wedding philosophy. Ask the people you interview how they feel about weddings to try to ascertain if they are truly enthusiastic and dedicated— or if this is just another job.

A QUESTION FOR PEGGY:

WHAT ABOUT THE PHOTOGRAPHY CONTRACT?

Q: *What do I need to consider when working up a contract with a photographer?*

A: When you find the photographer you want and agree to the date and terms, have him or her write up *an itemized cost breakdown,* including in the contract the date, the agreed-upon arrival time, length of shooting period, how many photos/hours of video will be taken, breakdown of package cost and inclusions, extra charges, schedule for reviewing proofs, and delivery of finished album and/or edited video.

Make sure that *price guarantees for additional prints, enlargements, and extra album pages/prints and upgrades* are included in your agreement. Ask whether the photographer offers a *package discount* when you buy extra albums for parents and other relatives. All packages are negotiable to a point. If you'd prefer not to have a finished album from the photographer, choosing to purchase loose photographs instead, discuss your options.

Finally, provide your photographer with a *copy of the sites' photography regulations and restrictions* regarding the use of cameras, flash photography, lights, and tripods. You will also need to provide the names and phone numbers of the ceremony officiant and the reception-site manager so that the photographer can scout out the wedding locations. Otherwise, you can show him or her the sites yourself.

Once your decisions are made, make sure you get an *itemized contract,* providing a complete record of what has been agreed. Be sure to ask the photographer to cover all options in full detail. If you haven't discussed these points during the interview process, this is your last chance. You should have a record of the number of hours, the number of staff (assistants may be needed for a very large wedding), delivery and payment schedules, and the final product such as albums or the number of prints.

HELPING THE PHOTOGRAPHER HELP YOU

How well your photographs and videography turn out is in large part dependent upon your success in conveying your vision and desires to your photographer and videographer. Ultimately, the onus is on you to make sure that your vision is executed and that your vendors do their jobs to the best of their abilities. Here are a few tips on how to make your collaboration with your photographer a smashing success:

1. The most important thing is to trust the photographer—and on the wedding day, let the photographer do what he or she does best. Most people have never worked closely with a photographer and are not that familiar with wedding photography.

2. To trust the photographer, you must first communicate your needs. Make clear exactly the vision you have and type of look you want.

3. It's very helpful to have a list of special people you want photographed ready before the wedding day. It's even more helpful to have ready a guest or a member of the wedding party to direct the photographer to these people and organize group or single portraits. This frees the photographer to concentrate on taking the pictures.

4. It's imperative that all parties agree ahead of time on exactly the style you want. Both time and money can be wasted if you don't settle your differences before the photographer starts shooting.

5. Decide up front if you want traditional photography or what is sometimes called reportage photography—a looser, more journalistic approach. If you decide on a combination of both, be specific about which shots you want done more traditionally and which you want done more photojournalistically.

6. Bringing along samples of photographic styles you like and want to emulate when you meet with the photographer is a great idea, and a big help to the photographer.

7. The more time and thought you put into discerning exactly what you want, the more the results will be personally tailored to you. Scour bridal magazines; look at Sunday wedding announcements; ask your married friends for suggestions or recommendations.

8. Don't feel pressured to do something you're not comfortable with. Some people, for example, find the videotaping of the ceremony intrusive but feel pressured to have it done, because "everybody does it." Remember: This is your record of your wedding, and it's yours to shape as you desire.

9. Let the photographer know at what stage you want to view the photographs. Some photographers like to give their clients a finished photo album, while others prefer to give clients a contact sheet and let clients pick and choose their favorite shots to be printed.

10. Keep in mind that many photographers appreciate the opportunity to be a little creative—and sometimes the results can be the most endearing shots of the wedding.

Nuts and Bolts: Questions for the Photographer

Be prepared: Take a list of questions with you when interviewing photographers. Following are some sample questions:

- If you are planning formal portraits ahead of time, does the photographer have a dressing room in the studio? Is there a "prop" bouquet for you to hold, or do you need to provide one?

- Is a wedding package offered? If so, what does it consist of? For example, does the photographer provide an album for the bride and groom and smaller albums for their parents and perhaps grandparents? Is the package mandatory, or are there options, such as a greater number of prints or additional 8″ × 10″ prints?

- What is the number of photographs in the standard album?

- What is the size and cost of extra albums?

- What does it cost for additions to a package?

- What is the number of pictures to be taken before and during the ceremony and at the reception?

- May the proofs be purchased? Can the negatives be kept? How long does the photographer keep negatives after the wedding (in the event that something happens to the bride and groom's wedding album)?

- How long will the photographer stay at the reception? What is the per-hour fee for overtime?

- Is the photographer familiar with the ceremony and reception sites?

- Are there extra charges for site visitation and/or travel time?

Getting the Photographs You Want

Once you have studied the different styles of wedding photography, you can decide which photographs you want taken in a formal portrait style and which you'd prefer to be captured in candid, natural shots. You'd be wise to select a photographer who does both types of photos well, because you'll probably want some of both. Or, particularly in the case of a very large wedding, you may even use two different photographers: one whose specialty is formal portraits and ceremony shots; the other whose candid style you prefer for the reception. Sometimes, one studio will handle both kinds of photography.

Before signing a contract with a photographer, make a list of the photographs you want and how many copies you think you'll want to give to parents and attendants.

ENGAGEMENT PHOTOGRAPHS

In the past, engagement photographs were typically black-and-white head-and-shoulder shots of the bride alone, taken for publication alongside the engagement announcement. Today, however, the bride and groom frequently appear in engagement portraits together. The portraits are then often framed and given to family members. Whatever you decide on—a photo of you alone or both of you—is fine. It's entirely a personal choice.

Although engagement pictures are now usually taken in color, the photographer will also provide 5″ × 7″ black-and-white prints for you to submit to the newspaper along with your engagement announcement. Find out whether the newspaper prefers glossy or matte prints.

You will likely have the engagement portrait taken before you have begun the search for a wedding photographer. Try to use someone you might consider booking as your wedding photographer. It's a good introduction to the way the photographer works—and an introduction as well to the quality of the work. If you find he or she fits the bill, you'll have a head start on your working relationship.

PORTRAIT PHOTOGRAPHS

The portrait photograph is traditionally the photograph you send in with your newspaper wedding announcement—and it is usually the shot that ends up on the living room wall or perched lovingly atop your parents' piano. Photographers usually shoot a formal portrait in the studio, against seamless paper, in a controlled lighting situation. You may, however, prefer having your picture taken at home or even at the bridal salon on the day of your final fitting.

TIMING FOR PORTRAIT PHOTOGRAPHS

Any formal portrait of the bride that will be submitted to the newspapers is generally taken one to two months before the wedding. In general, newspapers need to have it in their possession anywhere from ten days to three weeks before it runs. This means that your gown and accessories also need to be ready that far in advance.

Because you will want the formal portrait to look as though it were taken on the day of the wedding, you may want to have your hair and makeup done in the style you will wear on your wedding day. To ensure a picture-perfect portrait, make sure that your gown is wrinkle-free, that your headpiece is placed correctly and complements your hairstyle, and that you are wearing the jewelry you plan to wear on your wedding day. You'll want your makeup to be neatly applied. Most important: Sleep well the night before. You want to look and feel well rested—even the most flattering lighting will not hide fatigue or stress.

Today the formal bridal portrait that appears in the newspaper often includes the groom. Make a decision on whether you want a portrait of the two of you together before the wedding. If so, book the portrait appointment at a time that is convenient for both of you, and make sure the groom's attire has been fitted, if necessary.

The formal bridal portrait can also be a lovely gift for parents and grandparents. Ask the photographer for prices on extra 8″ × 10″ prints.

CEREMONY PHOTOGRAPHS

Flash attachments have historically been the bane of every wedding officiant's existence. With the advent of high-speed film and high-tech cameras, the flash is no longer necessary to take quality ceremony photographs. But that doesn't mean that cameras are welcome in every church, chapel, or synogogue. Many officiants will not permit the clicking and whirring of cameras during the ceremony, an occasion they consider sacred. So before you contract with a photographer for ceremony shots, be sure to ask the officiant precisely when photographs are permitted and when they aren't.

If photography is not permitted during the ceremony at all, you can have the photographer take simulated ceremony shots before the wedding or re-create them afterward. If the ceremony photos are to be staged before the wedding begins, they should be taken well before, never as guests are being seated. The photographs should be completed at least an hour before the start time of the ceremony.

If you are having photographs taken between the wedding and the reception, don't think you have to rerun the entire wedding ceremony to get the right shots. Keep it brief! Simply select specific images you want to re-create. Otherwise the process will drag on, and guests will be left with an overload of downtime between the wedding and the reception.

Possible re-created photos might include:

- The bride and her father walking up the aisle

- The bridesmaids, maid of honor, flower girl, and ring bearer walking up the aisle

- The groom and best man turned as they would to watch the bride walk up the aisle

- The bride and groom standing or kneeling at the altar and/or exchanging vows

- The bride and groom with their children

- The entire wedding party as they stand for the ceremony

- The bride and groom kissing

- The bride and groom walking down the aisle after the ceremony

THE PARENTS ASK:
"WHAT'S THE DEAL WITH BLACK AND WHITE?"

Q: *Our daughter is getting married this year, and we have a major disagreement over photography. We would much prefer that the wedding photographs be in color, while my daughter loves the look of black and white. Is one more appropriate than the other?*

A: There is a decided trend toward black-and-white wedding photography, particularly among the burgeoning school of brides and grooms who prefer a more candid, photojournalistic approach. Although black-and-white film is less expensive, it is more expensive to process and print than color. If you want some black-and-white shots, make sure your photographer is skilled in this area. Many brides and grooms hire photographers who are willing to switch back and forth, capturing, for example, the processional in color and the recessional in black and white; this can be the best of both worlds, particularly when it is negotiated as part of the package. To accommodate your preference for color, discuss in detail with the photographer any events you want to be captured in color, and those your daughter wants in black and white. Be mindful that black and white won't preserve the day's colors, but it can confer a timelessness that can add power and beauty to some images.

If there are other special moments or people you want photographed at this time, be sure to delegate a friend to ask these people to stay over after the ceremony. Included could be shots of your grandmothers being ushered to their seats or of the organist or soloist at work.

RECEPTION PHOTOGRAPHS

There are three kinds of reception photographs:

1. Portraits

Posing for pictures with your respective families can get a little complicated these days. If your parents are divorced, it is simply not appropriate to ask them to flank you in a photograph in a semblance of a united family. Instead, a portrait of you with each of them individually is fine— and if they have remarried, have a portrait taken of you with each of them with their spouse. The placing of this photo on your list of portraits can make your parent and stepparent very happy. If enmity toward the new spouse is great, you don't have to do it—just don't try to re-create the family you once were.

Provide in advance your list of "must have" shots to the photographer so that he or she can be thinking about suitable backdrops. Possible formal shots might be:

- The bride alone

- The groom alone

- The bride and groom together

- The bride and her maid or matron of honor

- The bride with her parents (or each parent, plus stepparent, as applicable)

- The groom with his parents (or each parent, plus stepparent, as applicable)

- The groom with his best man

- The bride with her mother

- The bride with her father

- The groom with his mother

- The groom with his father

- The bride and groom with all their attendants

- The bride with her attendants

- The groom with his attendants

- The bride and groom with the bride's family (parents, siblings, aunts, uncles, cousins)

- The bride and groom with the groom's family (parents, siblings, aunts, uncles, cousins)

- The bride and groom with their siblings if they are not all in the wedding party

- The bride with "generations"—her parents and grandparents

- The groom with his parents and grandparents

2. Planned Events

For planned events—both the traditional ones, such as the cake cutting, and those that personalize your wedding—ask an attendant, a close friend, or even the catering manager to direct the photographer to the site of each so that he or she can be thinking in advance about the best way to take the picture. Provide the photographer with a list of events and the approximate times when they will occur. These can include:

- The bride and groom arriving at the reception

- Guests going through the receiving line

- Close-ups of the cake table, centerpieces, and other special decorations

- The best man toasting the bride and groom

- The bride and groom cutting the cake

- The bride and groom feeding each other cake

- The groom toasting the bride

- The bride and groom's first dance

- The bride dancing with her father

- The groom dancing with his mother

- The bride tossing her bouquet

- The groom tossing the bride's garter

- The bride and groom leaving the reception

3. Candid Photographs

Let your photographer know up front the kinds of candid photographs that mean the most to you. If you want shots of every table, let the photographer know so no one is left out. If you don't want table shots but prefer shots of people in action, say so. If you love capturing totally spontaneous moments, again, just let your photographer know in advance. Good candid shots can be breathtaking.

If you want work-in-progress shots, you might book the photographer to start before the wedding begins, taking "getting ready" pictures as you and your wedding party prepare for the ceremony. These shots could include:

- The bride putting on the finishing touches—a necklace or a garter

- The bride's mother helping her with her veil

- The bride kissing her mother good-bye as she prepares to leave for the ceremony

- The bride and her father arriving at the ceremony site

Cameras for the Guests: Providing disposable cameras for guests can be great fun if everyone understands the rules. The idea is for guests to snap other guests in unposed moments and leave the cameras behind for the newlyweds. Problems arise because many guests think they

---

A QUESTION FOR PEGGY:

What If the Photos Don't Turn Out?

Q: Do we have any legal recourse in the event that our photographs or videotapes don't turn out? Are the professionals expected to pay a damage fee, or will they offer to re-create portions of the day?

A: While nothing will replace lost photos or footage, you shouldn't have to pay for someone else's errors or accidents. Make sure your contract clearly delineates not only your right not to pay if work is not delivered but also the return of your deposit and the professional's financial responsibility to pay *you* if he or she doesn't deliver. If the photographer will not agree to the latter, check on industry wedding insurance with your insurance agent to see what coverage is available and at what cost.

In addition, your ceremony and reception sites may require liability insurance of any vendor or service you bring in from the outside. Check early on to see if it is required, and if so, make sure the professionals you hire have liability insurance and proof of insurance to be sent to those who require it.

are supposed to get photos of the couple, and the bride and groom can't take a step without a camera in their faces.

People need instructions, so provide written details with the cameras or have someone make an announcement. Keep the instructions simple and include the location of a collecting place for the cameras if they're not to be left on dining tables. If you're planning a wedding Web page, you might also provide the Internet address.

Videography: What's Your Style?

A wedding video can be a wonderful addition to your collection of memories. It will be there on your first anniversary and it will be there on your twentieth. It provides a wonderful record for your children, capturing like no other medium the mood and the moments of your wedding day.

When reviewing a videographer's work (ask to see tapes of previous weddings), you'll be looking not just for artistic quality but for a personal sensibility that matches your own. Do you want a wedding video that is a lush visual record of a beautiful day in a beautiful setting? Or do you want a video that focuses on telling a story, one that has a point of view? Do you want a videographer who presents a cinematic sensibility? One who is proficient at editing and cutting the film? Is a sense of humor important to you? Are you interested in capturing special little moments and not just the standard orchestrated ones (like cutting the cake and throwing the bouquet)? Consider these criteria when deciding on the style of your video.

VIDEO OPTIONS

While the costs of videotaping a wedding have gone up in the past few years, so have the credentials and professionalism of dedicated, full-time professionals, as well as the quality of the equipment they use. Standard video packages include your entire wedding story, from the time you arrive at the ceremony (or even before, if you wish) until you depart from the reception. Finished tapes are usually one and a half to two hours long, edited from three to five hours of raw footage.

A wedding video usually includes the entire service and all or part of the reception. The final product you receive is generally *an edited color videocassette tape with sound*. The editing is done in a studio, and the edited tape can contain not only scenes from your ceremony and reception but old family photographs, an image of your invitation, interviews with guests, reflections by your parents, and messages for each other. Naturally, the more special effects, music, extra photography, and other elements that are added, the more your tape will cost. To produce this tape, the videographer leaves the camera running throughout the ceremony and reception to gather plenty of raw footage from which to edit and select highlights.

A less expensive option: *a tape edited in-camera.* This makes for a choppier video that lacks continuity and transition from scene to scene, one that doesn't include special effects, interviews, or still photography.

A third option, and the least expensive, is *a wedding-highlights tape.* Usually lasting only about fifteen minutes, a highlights tape is a fast-paced clip-to-clip view of special moments of the day. It makes an ideal gift to send to those who were not present. Sometimes a videographer will provide a highlights tape as an extra to couples who contract for a full tape.

Selecting the Videographer for You

Consider the following criteria in your search for a videographer:

1. **Equipment.** Because video cameras and their locomotive-like high beams can be even more obtrusive than 35 mm cameras, you will want to look for a videographer who has the kind of commercial-grade equipment that requires less lighting.

2. **Style and content.** You'll want a videographer who shares your style and content sensiblity.

3. **Credentials.** Talk to more than one professional, and view any previously made wedding tapes. It's a big investment of your time to preview tapes, but it is worth it to make sure the investment of money you will make will be a good one, for seeing the videographer's work will give you the opportunity to see his or her training, experience, talent, and style.

4. **Details indicating quality,** such as:

   ▪ Steady, not shaky, images

   ▪ Clean, crisp focus

   ▪ Continuity of sound

   ▪ A mix of distant and close-up images

   ▪ Seamless editing from one scene to the next

Nuts and Bolts: Questions for the Videographer

Be prepared: Take a list of questions with you when interviewing videographers. Following are some sample questions:

- Will background music be dubbed on the tape? If so, who selects the music?

- Can credits be added so that the names of the wedding party and others can be listed on the tape?

- How much editing is done? Is the videographer the only person involved in editing the final tape?

- What special effects are usually used, and when can you decide whether you want them?

- What do additional copies cost?

- Are there additional costs for a video portrait of the wedding portrait and other groupings?

- Who keeps the original video footage?

- What happens to the footage if it is the property of the videographer?

- How long is the original kept on file, in case you want to order extra copies?

- Can you buy the original footage, and if so, for how much?

- How soon will you be able to view the original footage?

Getting the Footage You Want

Both your preferences and your budget can determine what you arrange to have taped. Do you want the videographer recording the wedding party getting ready for the ceremony? You and your father arriving at the ceremony? The mothers being seated? Guests arriving? Do you want the ceremony taped, if your officiant permits it, or just the reception? Do you want your guests "interviewed" by the videographer or do you think this will be only an unwelcome intrusion? Looking at the wedding tapes of friends or those provided by the videographer may help you decide exactly what elements of your day you want recorded.

CEREMONY VIDEO

The videotaping of your ceremony must be cleared with your minister, priest, rabbi, or other officiant before you sign any contracts with videographers. Any specific guidelines should be discussed with the videographer, such as the placement of equipment, lighting restrictions, and whether events can be restaged later.

Most churches and synagogues allow videographers to tape from a specific location, either from the side of the altar or the rear of the balcony, to prevent disruption. Lights are generally not allowed, so newer equipment that requires little or no extra lighting is essential. Often a wireless microphone is attached to the groom's lapel so vows can be recorded clearly.

If your ceremony will be taped, meet with your videographer in advance to describe the ceremony plans. You will need to answer such questions as: Will you face each other? Is there a soloist? How many members of your bridal party will there be? Will you have a receiving line at the ceremony site? Will guests shower you with rose petals, bubbles, or birdseed as you leave the ceremony?

RECEPTION VIDEO

First decide what video memories and planned events you want recorded at your reception. Then give the videographer you hire a specific list of events planned for the reception. He or she will need to know whether there will be a receiving line, whether guests will be seated at assigned tables or mingling through the room, whether there will be dancing, and the timing of the toasts, cake cutting, and other festivities.

THE PERSONAL TOUCH:

A LITTLE DISCRETION, PLEASE!

Let your videographer know that as far as you are concerned, discretion is the better part of valor. You are not looking to have intimate conversations recorded by hidden mikes or someone's inebriated behavior captured on film. At the same time, you do want to be able to hear your exchange of vows and the like. Viewing a videographer's previously made tapes can clue you in to whether the microphones will be powerful enough to do the job.

CHAPTER 19

THE WEDDING CAKE

Among the oldest wedding traditions is the cake—almost certainly because wheat and other grains, seeds, and nuts are universal symbols of fertility. The ancient Greeks served sesame seed pies. Small wheat cakes were shared at Roman weddings. Wheat biscuits were broken over the bride's head at early Anglo-Saxon weddings.

In the 1800s, wedding cakes reached their literal high point in Europe and the United States. The cake for the 1871 marriage of Queen Victoria's daughter Princess Louise stood five feet high and weighed almost 225 pounds. The 1947 wedding of Princess Elizabeth and the duke of Edinburgh featured a four-tiered cake—nine feet high, 500 pounds, and decorated with, among other things, sugar replicas of Buckingham Palace and Windsor and Balmoral Castles.

Wedding cakes are still the visual focal point of many receptions. The traditional cake is round or square, multi-tiered, and frosted in white or pale pastels. But there's no real limit on the size, shape, color, and style.

New Trends in Wedding Cakes

ONE CAKE, TWO CAKES . . .

Some couples skip the cake cutting and serve individual cakes to guests. Or, instead of one huge cake, they opt for several smaller cakes in different flavors, shapes, and sizes. At a small wedding, multiple cakes can serve double duty as centerpieces. Guests can travel around the room and sample different cakes. What a great way to mingle and meet other guests!

RED CAKE, BLUE CAKE . . .

Color is everywhere in weddings today, and many couples incorporate color themes into the design of the wedding cake. Colored floral adornments, splashes of colored frosting, even entire confectionery constructions in the same shade of lavender as the bridesmaids' dresses.

CARROT CAKE, CHEESECAKE . . .

White cake is still a popular choice, but more couples are indulging taste buds by selecting cheesecakes, meringues, baked Alaska, chocolate cake, fruit cakes, pound cakes, mousse cakes, or angel food cake.

FAKE CAKE . . .

It's perfectly fine to display a frosted cardboard or foam-core "faux" cake and serve slices of real cake from the kitchen. You can go crazy with an elaborate design and no one has to worry about how to cut a monstrous cake.

NO CAKE?

Some couples chose to have a dessert table in lieu of or in addition to cake. Dessert tables can include a spread of pastries, cookies, fruits, cheeses, mini desserts, and more. Including a couple's favorite treat or a family ethnic specialty is a nice way to add a personal touch.

Cost

The cost of the cake will depend on the quantity required, the cake size, the relative simplicity or elaborateness of the decoration, and who does the baking. A custom-designed, professionally baked cake can cost thousands of dollars. As weddings have become more elaborate, the expenses have increased. Today, the wedding cake can be a significant part of the wedding budget. Costs can be determined as a flat fee or on a per-slice basis, ranging anywhere from $1 to $10 a serving.

Factors to consider when choosing a wedding cake:

- Your budget and the formality of your wedding

- Whether the reception site requires you to use an in-house cake or pay an additional fee to bring one from outside

- Whether your meal includes dessert (if cake is not your only dessert, a simpler, less expensive cake may fit the bill)

Cake Bakers

Your caterer or your reception site may be your best source for information on cakes and bakers. You can use a bakery or grocery bakery department. You may have a favorite restaurant that has a bakery or a master baker who does wedding cakes. Fortunate indeed is the couple with a relative or friend who is a skilled baker and offers to make the cake.

Cake Vocabulary

Don't know the difference between a marzipan paste and a fondant finish? The world of wedding cakes is an extraordinarily varied one. You can choose a cake with a traditional look and an adventurous taste. Inside a classic tiered facade, for example, may be a carrot-cake filling. You can mix textures—combining a tender cake with a smooth filling, for example, or using a hard-finish royal icing over a smooth-finish fondant. You can mix and match flavors: devil's food with hazelnut; German chocolate with French creme; Amaretto with chocolate mousse; fudge truffle with strawberry creme. A good baker will help you choose a texture, filling, and icing that marry nicely.

Here's a primer on some of the terms you may discuss with your baker:

BUTTERCREAM

Cakes iced in buttercream are the best value in terms of price per slice. Buttercream is smooth and creamy, but not too sweet. It takes flavors well; remains soft, so it is easy to cut; and is perfect for finishes like basket weave, swags and swirls, fleur-de-lis, and rosettes. Genuine buttercream is made with real butter, so cakes iced with buttercream need to be kept in a cool place; heat and humidity make it bead, run, and drip. Some bakers counter this effect by adding shortening to the icing to give it a measure of stability. If your cake will be kept cool in an air-conditioned reception room, the added shortening is unnecessary. If you want all-butter icing, ask the baker to forgo shortening altogether.

WHIPPED CREAM

Whipped cream is a light, soft icing that, like buttercream, is temperamental in heat and humidity. A whipped-cream cake must be kept refrigerated until just before it is served. Bakers may also use stabilizers when working with whipped cream. If you don't want stabilizers used, discuss with your baker whether this will affect the appearance of the cake.

FONDANT

Rolled fondant icing is a combination of sugar, corn syrup, gelatin, and usually glycerin. It can be rolled out in sheets and wrapped around each tier of the cake, presenting a smooth frosting with a porcelain-like sheen. It serves as the perfect base for flowers and decorations piped in royal icing (see below) because of its smoothness. A cake iced in fondant cannot be refrigerated, however. While this is not a problem for the cake, it may be for a filling that requires refrigeration.

ROYAL ICING

Soft when it is piped onto a cake, royal icing dries to a hard finish. It is what bakers use for creating latticework, flowers, and beading around the edges of the cake. It is used for decorative touches only, not to ice an entire cake.

SPUN SUGAR, PASTILLAGE, AND MARZIPAN

Finishing touches can be made from any of these decorative icings, all of which are edible. Spun sugar is caramelized sugar that is pulled into strands and quickly formed into bows and other shapes. It melts into a gooey mess in heat and humidity, so it isn't a good choice for a non-air-conditioned room. Pastillage is a paste of sugar, cornstarch, and gelatin that hardens as it dries to a porcelain-like finish. It is used to create realistic-looking flowers and decorations. Marzipan is also a paste, made of ground almonds, sugar, and egg whites. It is sometimes rolled in sheets, like fondant, but it is usually molded into flowers and other decorative shapes and painted with food coloring.

Working with the Baker

Make an appointment to meet with the baker, whether he or she is the baker at the club, the one used by the caterer, or one you find and interview yourself. Ask to review his or her portfolio, to see photographs of the baker's work. You'll want your cake to look good, but looks aren't everything—you'll want it to taste as good as it looks. Most reputable bakers offer tastings of cakes, fillings, and icings. Sample a baker's work before signing a contract.

Be prepared to provide the baker with what he or she needs to know to serve you well. This includes:

- The room decor

- The ceiling height

- The general room temperature

- The linen colors

- The wedding-party colors

- The floral scheme (flower types and colors)

- The formality of your wedding

- The number of guests

- The names and phone numbers of the caterer, florist, and wedding planner, and the site location manager to coordinate delivery

- Very clear directions to the reception site

Be sure that any contract you sign—whether with an outside baker or with a caterer—spells out all the details of your arrangements, including flavors, ingredients, decorations, and of course date and time of delivery. Some reception sites charge an extra cake-cutting fee if your cake is not ordered through them; be sure to ask. Inquire about extra charges for cake stands and pillars and delivery.

BRINGING IN AN OFF-SITE CAKE

If your cake is baked at another site and transported, let the site caterer or manager know when the cake will be delivered. A cake consisting of more than three tiers is generally transported unassembled and is put together and decorated on-site. Find out from the location manager if there is space for the baker to work and the best time to do so.

WHEN TO ORDER

Cake orders are usually placed at least six to eight weeks in advance of the reception—earlier if you want a popular baker during the busiest wedding months. If you're marrying on very short notice, you can get a good-quality cake from a professional bakery or grocery store bakery.

SWEETS AND TREATS, TOO?

Q: *I think it's a good idea to serve another, lighter dessert—a fruit cup, for example, or sorbet—along with the wedding cake. My daughter disagrees, however—she feels that another dessert is an unnecessary added expense. I think there will be people at the reception who will like having the choice—and whose diets may prohibit them from eating rich wedding cake. Is it proper to offer dessert and wedding cake, too?*

A: It's considerate of you to think of your guests' dietary restrictions. It's true: Many weddings serve both cake and another dessert. Sometimes it's a rich dessert and sometimes it's something light and refreshing like fruit. A separate "dessert" or "sweets" table comprised of traditional ethnic goodies or an assortment of desserts is popular in some parts of the country. If you know that a number of your guests would prefer a choice, and the extra cost is not prohibitive, providing a fruit cup or sorbet option is a nice way to personalize the menu.

The Wedding Cake Display

The wedding cake is generally in place and on display when guests enter the reception location. How to display the wedding cake is up to you. The cake table is one of the most photographed spots of the reception, so you'll want to make sure it looks just right. It can be placed on the bridal party table, in the center of a buffet table, or on a small table or cart of its own.

You can decorate the cake table in a variety of ways: with a favorite family tablecloth, your mother's wedding veil over an undercloth, or even the bridesmaid bouquets circling the base of the cake. Another option: a cloth from the caterer with swags caught up by fresh flowers, a design that may be repeated on the cake with similar-looking flowers made of edible icing. You might want to wrap the handle of the cake knife with a ribbon or flowers and place it on the table next to the cake. Or perhaps you have a special cake knife to use, such as a family heirloom. Sometimes the presentation of the cake is an event in itself. The cake is kept hidden in the kitchen until it is time for you to cut it. The lights are lowered, the music stops, and the room becomes hushed. The cake is wheeled into the middle of the room and spotlighted. Then everyone gathers around to witness the cutting of the cake.

The Art of Cutting the Cake

Cutting the wedding cake is a traditional part of the reception. At a sit-down reception, the cake is cut just before dessert is served. At a luncheon, tea, or cocktail reception, it is cut closer to the end of the reception. If the cake has been on display throughout, the bridesmaids simply gather around the bride and groom at the appointed time. Notify the caterer or club manager as to the approximate time you plan to cut your cake so that the kitchen staff can be alerted to remove the cake for serving after the cutting. The photographer should also be alerted in advance in order to set up the shot. Here is the traditional sequence of events in cutting the cake:

- **Cutting the cake.** To start, the bride puts her right hand on the handle of the cake knife and the groom puts his hand over hers. It is easiest if they pierce the bottom tier of the cake with the point of the knife and then carefully make two cuts, removing a small slice onto a plate provided by the caterer in advance, along with two forks.

- **The first bites.** The groom gently feeds the bride the first bite, and she feeds him the second. This tradition is meant to symbolize their commitment to share with and support each other, and as such it is inappropriate for either to stuff the cake into the other's face or to comically offer up too large a bite.

- **The wedding cake kiss.** At this point, the couple generally share a kiss, and the caterer then has the cake whisked away and cut so that guests may be served.

- **Slices for the parents.** A lovely gesture before the cake is taken away is for the bride and groom to cut cake slices for their parents. Tradition has it that the bride serves the groom's parents, and he serves hers.

THE PERSONAL TOUCH:

CAKE TOPPERS

The little plastic bride and groom figurines of old may be the quintessential wedding cake topper, but times—and trends—change. Cake toppers are an art form all their own these days, with pieces created from ceramic, porcelain, handblown glass, clay—even crocheted from yarn. The current fashion in cake toppers is a delicate cascade from the highest tier down of fresh, silk, buttercream, or pastillage flowers and ivy or ribbons—or some combination thereof. Before you invest in a personalized cake topper, consider the entire cake design. A tiny plastic model of the car you drove on your first date, for example, may detract from an elegant-looking cake. Inform your baker of your preferences in advance.

- **Saving the top layer.** Many couples want to save the top layer of the cake for their first anniversary. If the top layer is to be saved, be sure to tell the caterer in advance so that it isn't cut and served to guests.

CAKE CUTTING 101
FOR THE HOME WEDDING

If the wedding is small or at home, you'll want someone in charge of cake cutting once you and your mate have made the traditional first cuts. In this case, it is a good idea to review the art of cake cutting in advance.

About two inches in from the outside, cut all the way around the layer (the cut runs parallel to the outside of the layer, circlelike). Individual slices are cut from this section, and each is lifted onto a cake plate to be served.

Remove each layer and proceed as described above, once the individual slices have been cut to reach the bottom of the being removed (per illustration).

The process continues until the center of each layer is reached.

CHAPTER 20

At the Ceremony

A FTER SO MANY WEEKS AND MONTHS of planning and preparation, *your day* has finally arrived! What couple doesn't look forward to a happy celebration with family and friends? Though there may be a few problems along the way, there's no reason for a glitch here and there to spoil your occasion. In fact, many couples look back on their wedding day and take pleasure and pride in memories of how well they handled things that went awry—hurriedly turning a table arrangement into a bridesmaid's bouquet when the florist's delivery was one short; drafting a friend to stand in when the best man fell ill at the last moment; arriving at the reception in an usher's old VW Beetle because the rented limo broke down on the expressway.

It would be unrealistic to say that your wedding day won't be stressful to some degree. But excessive stress (and venting one's frustrations on others) is often the result of unrealistic expectations of perfection. When couples keep the real meaning of the occasion firmly in mind; put the three C's of consideration, communication, and compromise first; and genuinely appreciate the efforts others make on their behalf, they're likely to achieve a kind of perfection that has little to do with dresses, decorations, and seating arrangements. As the hour approaches, take a deep breath and relax. The day is yours to savor.

Getting Ready

THE BRIDE AND ATTENDANTS GET READY

Dressing: The bride generally dresses at home, although many ceremony sites offer "getting ready" rooms where the bridal party can dress for the wedding. If space permits, the attendants will dress at the bride's home as well. In any case, they should all get together at least an hour before all are scheduled to leave for the ceremony. The bride's mother and honor attendant help the bride with the finishing touches. Sometimes, a professional hairdresser and makeup artist are on hand to help prepare the bridal party for the wedding.

It is the duty of the maid of honor and bridesmaids to check that the bride is wearing something old, something new, something borrowed, something blue. The maid of honor makes sure that an emergency kit of pins, makeup, tape, and other essentials is nearby and ready to go.

Bouquets: If the bride's attendants will all be present at the her house, their bouquets should be delivered there; otherwise, their flowers should go to the gathering place at the ceremony site for the bride and her attendants. Also deliveries should be made for the flower girl's nosegay or basket, the bride's mother's corsage, and the bride's father's boutonniere.

Photographs: Pictures of the bride and her attendants getting ready are taken if desired. The photographer then leaves for the ceremony site to take pictures as the guests arrive and to set up for ceremony shots.

Transportation: The bridesmaids travel together; the bride's mother accompanies them or any children who are in the wedding party and/or the bride's children from a previous marriage. The bride usually rides with her father. If the groom has children from a previous marriage, they would be taken care of by the groom's parents or other family members. The flower girl and ring bearer will ride to the ceremony with the bride's mother if they are not delivered directly to the ceremony by their parents before the ceremony takes place.

THE BEST MAN'S LAST-MINUTE DUTIES

It is the best man who makes sure that all the necessary papers are together and that (if there is no ring bearer) the bride's wedding ring is safe in his pocket. If the couple will be leaving directly from the reception for their honeymoon, the best man should check that all bags have been packed and clothes to change into after the reception have been readied. The best man has also traditionally arranged for the newlyweds' transportation from the reception.

THE GROOM AND BEST MAN GET READY

Dressing: The groom should be dressed and ready to go at least an hour before the ceremony. The groom usually spends the hour or so before he is to leave for the ceremony with his best man.

The groom and his best man should arrive at the ceremony site at least 15 minutes before the hour of the ceremony. Once there, the best man drops the groom off in a private room, such as the vestry or officiant's study, and returns to the sanctuary to retrieve his and the groom's boutonnieres from the head usher. Returning to the groom, he helps him pin on his boutonniere on the left side with the stem down. The best man waits with the groom until the signal comes that the ceremony is about to begin.

Arrival: The ushers should arrive at the ceremony site about an hour before the ceremony is to begin. If a head usher is appointed, it is his duty to make sure that the other ushers have transportation to and from the ceremony.

Flowers: Boutonnieres delivered to the ushers and the bride's father are pinned on the left side with the stem down. Any other boutonnieres—for the groom's father, perhaps, or the couple's grandfathers—are distributed. Ushers are also responsible for presenting corsages to those designated to receive them, such as mothers, grandmothers, and any special friends helping out. The bride has provided a list to the head usher, who then parcels out the tasks among his ushers.

Programs: If a ceremony program has been printed, the ushers are usually responsible for handing them to guests as they seat them; however, this job can also be given to children who are relatives of the bride and groom who do not have another part in the ceremony.

Pew Cards: Some couples choose to enclose pew cards in the invitations of certain special guests. The recipients are usually close relatives, such as grandparents, or others close to the couple or their families (godparents or longtime friends). The pew cards alert the ushers that the recipients are seated in forward pews.

If pew cards have been issued, the ushers should not ask for them but should wait for guests to present them. It should be determined ahead of time if certain ushers will escort particular guests who hold pew cards. If the groom's brother is an usher, for example, he would escort his grandmother and mother, just as the bride's brother would escort his own grandmother and mother.

The Aisle Carpet: Some couples like to have a white carpet rolled up the aisle before the bridal attendants and bride come down the aisle. Some houses of worship have them available as a service, or for a small fee. If not, most florists or limousine services can provide them. The "white carpet" is actually just a pressed-fiber strip, although sometimes canvas runners are still used. (Ask your officiant's advice. Some feel that aisle carpets are a terrible trip hazard.) Confirm when and how it is rolled out and how many ushers are required to place it successfully. It is a good idea, if possible, for the ushers to rehearse this maneuver. The head usher designates which ushers will be responsible for rolling out the aisle carpet and which ones will place and later remove any ribbons along the ends of the pews.

Last-Minute Details: A last-minute check is made by the ushers. If the room is stuffy or hot, they can open windows. They can make sure that pews are clear of papers or other debris. They should familiarize themselves with where a telephone is located, in case of emergency, and where the restrooms are, should a guest ask.

Escorting Guests: The ushers show all guests to their places. They should ask any guests they do not immediately recognize whether they wish to sit on the bride's side (the left) or the groom's side (the right). Just as the reserved pews are divided more or less evenly, so should the rest of the church be divided.

In taking guests to their seats, each usher should offer his crooked right arm for the women guests to hold on to, with their escorts walking behind them. Or the usher may lead the way as the couple follows him to their seats. If a male guest is escorted alone to a seat, the usher should walk on his left. Ushers needn't walk in stony silence when escorting guests down the aisle. They may indeed smile warmly and exchange a few quiet remarks. It's a time of joy and fellowship, and the seating of guests should never be done in absolute silence or with somberness.

Greeting Guests: If the day is warm and the weather good—and if the parents of the couple are so inclined and have arrived early—the parents may want to greet guests for a while outside the ceremony site as guests arrive. Their presence is a welcoming one for guests. They should keep conversations brief and warm, however, so as not to detain everyone outside.

Seating Family

- **Seating parents.** The parents of the bride always sit in the first pew on the left, facing the chancel; the groom's parents, in the first pew on the right. If the church has two aisles, her parents sit on the right of the left aisle (as they enter the church from the back), and his parents sit on the left of the right aisle. This way, they are both seated in the center section of the house of worship.

- **Seating widowed parents.** The widowed parent of either the bride or the groom should not necessarily be expected to sit in lonely splendor at his or her child's wedding. If the parent prefers having someone by his or her side during the ceremony, it is perfectly correct to do so. The guest of the widowed parent does not have to participate in any way, however, such as standing in the receiving line—unless he or she is engaged to the widowed parent or is helping to host the reception. Every effort should be made to treat the companion as an honored guest.

- **Seating parents who are divorced.** When either the bride's or the groom's parents are divorced, it is best to give the ushers specific advance instructions for seating, in the interest of amicability. They most likely would not sit together.

  Unless the bride is estranged from her mother, her mother (and stepfather if her mother has remarried) is seated in the front pew. Members of her mother's immediate family—the bride's grandparents, aunts, and uncles—sit immediately behind her mother (preferably in no more than one or two rows of pews). The bride's father, after escorting his daughter up the aisle and presenting her to her groom, sits in the next pew back, behind the bride's mother's family, with his wife and their family members.

  If there is rancor between divorced parents but the bride has remained close to both, the situation is much more difficult. Perhaps she has lived with her father since the divorce. Maybe her mother is hosting the wedding, either entirely or with the bride's father. Sometimes a bride's father (or mother) has remarried and her other parent resents the ex-partner's spouse. If, for example, the bride's mother strongly resents the new wife, it would be more tactful for the new wife to sit farther back in the church preferably with a friend. In these circumstances, the father might not even attend the reception. Grandparents and other relatives on his side might be excluded entirely, unless the bride has remained close to them.

  Even if the wedding is given by the bride's father, the seating arrangements remain the same. The bride's mother (and her present husband if the bride is comfortable about his being there) sits in the first pew. The bride's father and stepmother sit in the front pew only when the bride is estranged from or not close to her mother or is closer to her stepmother. Ordinarily, the father's family sits in the third or fourth pew, where he joins them after escorting the bride.

  When the groom's parents are divorced, they are seated in the same manner. The groom's mother, accompanied by close members of her family, sits in the first pew (or pews) on the right side of the aisle. The groom's father and family sit in the next pew behind the groom's mother's family.

  Naturally, if the divorce is an amicable one and all are great friends, there is no reason that the bride's or groom's divorced parents cannot share the first pew. It is only when relations are strained or sensitivities great that the etiquette of careful seating need be employed.

- **Seating immediate family.** Behind the front pews, several pews on either side of the center aisle are reserved for the immediate families of the couple. The people who are to sit there may have been sent pew cards to show the usher, or the usher may keep a list of guests to be seated in the first few pews.

WHICH FATHER?

Q: *I have a problem deciding who should walk me down the aisle. Naturally, my father would be the logical choice, but my stepfather helped raise me and is an important part of my life. What do I do?*

A: One of the greatest difficulties for a bride today is choosing between her father and her stepfather as the person to "give her away." It is no easy choice, especially when she is close to both. The most diplomatic decision may be to fall back on tradition and ask her biological father to escort her up the aisle. However, it is acceptable for her to choose her stepfather if she feels she is closer to him. The decision may become cloudy again in the event that her father is paying for the wedding. Some brides take a different route and have their mothers escort them. Others choose to walk alone or to have a brother or uncle do the honors.

It is rare that both fathers escort their daughter, but it's not unheard of—as long as they are friendly and share affection for the bride. Under no circumstances, however, would a bride have her divorced mother and father escort her up the aisle if either has remarried. This would be inappropriate and confusing, not to mention potentially painful or threatening to the new spouses. If they are divorced but have not remarried, it would still be better for the bride to walk with her father and let her mother be seated before the ceremony.

The Ceremony

PLACES, EVERYONE

After the Bride's Mother Has Been Seated: After the bride's mother is taken to her place, no guest may be seated from the center aisle. If guests arrive after the bride's mother is seated, they must stand in the vestibule, go to the balcony, or slip into a pew from the side aisles. The ushers may assist them.

Aisle Runner and Pew Ribbons: Once the mothers are seated, it is time to place the aisle runner, *if* one is being used. Two ushers or junior ushers pick up the runner, place it at the foot of the chancel steps, and carefully draw it back down the length of the aisle. Also, a broad white ribbon may be put in place on either side of the aisle. The folded ribbons should already have been stored at the ends of the last reserved pews. The ushers walk with the ribbons to the back

SHARING THE PEACE

When communion is offered at a Christian wedding, the minister or priest will often ask everyone to reach out and share a message of peace with one another, at the point in the service where the officiant says, "Peace be with you." At this time, and especially if the guests are few in number, the wedding party may move out into the congregation, offering handshakes, hugs, and kisses to guests. It is only a small break in the ceremony, but it gives the bride and groom the opportunity to connect with their guests.

of the church, laying them over the end of each row. The purpose of these ribbons is to allow the guests in the first pews to exit before the other guests do. Therefore, the ribbons should not be removed until the guests in the reserved pews leave. After they are escorted out, the ushers will indicate that the remaining guests should exit, starting at the front.

The Countdown Begins: The bride and her father or escort arrive at the precise moment for the wedding to start, and the procession forms in the vestibule at the back of the sanctuary. As soon as the attendants have taken their places, a signal is given, and the officiant, followed in order by the groom and the best man, enters the church. Many churches have a buzzer system in the vestry or study to announce to the groom and best man that all is ready. In others, the sexton or wedding coordinator goes to the vestry with the message; sometimes the opening bars of the "Wedding March" or another specific piece of music give the signal. In any case, the groom and the best man enter and take their places at the right side of the head of the aisle or, in some churches, at the top of the steps to the chancel. The best man stands to the groom's left and slightly behind him, and they both face the congregation. As soon as they reach their places, the procession begins.

THE TRADITIONAL PROCESSIONAL: CHRISTIAN

SIGNING THE PAPERS

The bride and groom must at some point during the proceedings sign their wedding papers, witnessed by the maid of honor and best man. If this has not been done before the ceremony, then it should be done before they leave for the reception.

1. The ushers lead the procession, walking two by two, the shortest men first. Junior ushers follow the adults.

2. Junior bridesmaids come next.

3. The bridesmaids follow, walking in pairs or singly. The space between each couple or individual should be even and approximately four paces long. The hesitation

step, which used to be very popular, is actually considered awkward and difficult these days. A slow, natural walk is the more graceful.

4. The maid or matron of honor follows the bridesmaids.

5. The ring bearer comes next, followed by the flower girl.

6. The bride enters, escorted by her father (or other special person), her left arm looped through the crook of his (or her) right arm.

   The arrangement of the attendants at the front of the church varies. The ushers may divide and stand on either side, as may the bridesmaids, or the ushers may line up on one side and the bridesmaids on the other. The minister or priest will help determine what looks best during the rehearsal.

- The maid of honor stands to the bride's left and below or behind her.

- The best man remains in the same position, but, because he turned to face the altar as the bride and her father arrived at the steps, he should now be on the groom's right.

Traditional processional for a Christian wedding

- Usually, the flower girl stands next to the maid of honor, while the ring bearer stands next to the best man.

BEST MAN   GROOM   BRIDE   FATHER OF BRIDE   MAID OF HONOR

USHERS   RING BEARER   FLOWER GIRL   BRIDESMAIDS

CLERGYMAN

Christian ceremony, at the altar

THE CEREMONY

1. When the bride reaches the groom's side, she lets go of her father's arm, transfers her flowers to her left arm, and gives her right hand to the groom. He puts it through his left arm, and her hand rests near his elbow. If the bride is not comfortable this way, they may stand hand in hand or merely side by side. The officiant faces them from the front of the sanctuary.

2. In a Christian ceremony, the bride's father remains by her side or a step or two behind until the minister or priest says, "Who will support and bless this marriage?" or "Who represents the families in blessing this marriage?" The bride's father reaches in front of her and puts her right hand into that of the minister or priest and says, "Her mother and I do" or something similar. He then turns and takes his seat.

BEHIND THE TRADITION:

"You May Kiss the Bride"

Why does a wedding ceremony end with a kiss? A kiss was long believed to be the medium for the exchange of spirits, where a part of the bride's soul joined the groom's soul, and vice versa, truly uniting the couple as one. In some cultures, a kiss literally seals the wedding contract, while in others a kiss is not required. Most people just think of it as an expression of love.

3. If there are children from the bride's or groom's previous marriage, the officiant could ask, "Who will support this new family with their love and prayers?" In this instance, the bride, groom, children, and often the guests may answer together.

4. Just before the bride receives her wedding ring, she hands her flowers to her maid of honor. Once the vows have been completed, the bride's bouquet is returned to her.

5. At the conclusion of the ceremony, the officiant may say, "I now pronounce you husband and wife." Some clergypersons are still saying "man and wife." If you prefer, ask to be pronounced as "husband and wife."

6. The bride and groom kiss. In some ceremonies, the officiant announces the new married couple by name.

THE RECESSIONAL

1. The maid or matron of honor hands the bride her bouquet back and straightens the bride's gown and train for her before she starts down the aisle.

2. The flower girl and ring bearer walk together behind the bride and groom, followed by the maid of honor and the best man.

3. The other attendants step forward and recess behind the couple either singly or side by side, depending on their number. They may walk together as they entered: groomsmen with one another and bridesmaids together, or a bridesmaid may walk with an usher. Each member of the wedding party should know how to fall in line, since this recessional will have been practiced during the rehearsal.

Traditional recessional for a Christian wedding

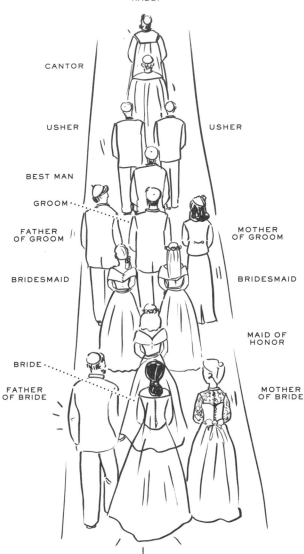

RABBI

CANTOR

USHER   USHER

BEST MAN

GROOM

FATHER
OF GROOM   MOTHER
OF GROOM

BRIDESMAID   BRIDESMAID

MAID OF
HONOR

BRIDE

FATHER
OF BRIDE   MOTHER
OF BRIDE

Jewish processional for a Conservative or Orthodox ceremony

THE JEWISH PROCESSIONAL, CEREMONY, AND RECESSIONAL

1. The processional for a traditional Jewish ceremony is led by the rabbi and the cantor. The groom's attendants—groomsmen, then best man—follow. Then the groom is escorted by his parents—father on the groom's left and mother on the right. They are followed by the bridesmaids, maid of honor, and finally the bride escorted by her parents. The bride's and groom's grandparents may also be included in the procession. They follow the rabbi and cantor and are seated in the front rows as the rest of the party approaches the ceremony area.

2. The bride, groom, their parents (mother to the left, father to the right), honor attendants, and perhaps the rest of the wedding party gather under the *chuppah,* or canopy, and the ceremony begins. (At the rehearsal, the rabbi will help determine how many of the wedding party can be accommodated under the *chuppah.*)

3. The recessional is led by the newlyweds, followed by the bride's parents, groom's parents, attendants (women and men in pairs), and the rabbi and cantor.

Conservative or Orthodox Jewish ceremony under the chuppah

The Celebration Begins

Photographs and Videos: The photographer, who has remained at the back of the sanctuary after taking pictures of the bride's arrival, may now catch the radiant couple as they come down the aisle. The videographer, who may have been taping from the back of the balcony, quickly descends and joins the photographer in catching the wedding party coming down the aisle. The bridal party may then gather for a formal wedding-party portrait. If certain aspects of the ceremony are to be re-created for the photographer, the wedding party waits to the side and reenters the building for pictures to be taken *as quickly as possible.* The guests either wait, taking their cue from the parents, or depart for the reception if it is suggested they do so.

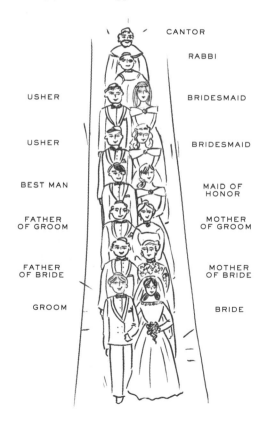

Traditional Recessional for a Jewish ceremony.

Ceremony Receiving Line: If a receiving line is not planned for the reception, the bride and groom, their parents, and the maid of honor (and sometimes the bridesmaids) may form a receiving line and greet guests as they exit the ceremony site. If either the bride or the groom has children, they may want to have them stand in the receiving line, too, as a part of the family.

Bubbles and Rose Petals: Rose petals or bubbles are distributed by someone designated to do so earlier to the guests looking on. Once the photography is completed, the wedding party heads to their waiting cars and is properly showered with rose petals or bubbles by the guests.

Transportation to the Reception Site: Cars taking the wedding party to the reception should be waiting at the entrance of the ceremony site. The bride and groom are helped into the first car by the best man and are the first to leave for the reception. The bride's parents ride together, and the maid or matron of honor and bridesmaids depart in the same cars in which they arrived. The flower girl and ring bearer may travel with their parents or they may ride with either the bride's parents or the bridal attendants.

A QUESTION FOR PEGGY:

Who Cleans Up the Rose Petals?

Q: *I am an officiant for a large church with frequent wedding services. We try to discourage couples from scattering rose petals, or anything for that matter, because of the cleanup involved. Who is responsible for cleaning up after a wedding?*

A: Any couple set on being showered with rose petals or some other celebratory symbol should first ask the officiant if this option is allowed—and if it is, they should then take responsibility for cleanup. Most churches ban guests from throwing anything at the bride and groom as they leave the ceremony for the reception, because cleanup is too costly. So you may want to instill such a policy. Any bride who wants rose petals scattered before or during the processional should keep in mind that petals are notoriously slippery. Instead of rose petals, some couples provide their guests with tiny bottles of bubbles, to blow during the recessional. However, if the bubbles land on the bride's gown, they could stain. Other options include colored streamers or confetti, but the responsibility of cleaning the mess lies squarely with the couple.

Many couples forgo scattering anything, for good reason. Rice is rarely used anymore, even though as a symbol of fertility it is deeply rooted in tradition. Rice can be dangerous for birds and other wildlife, who cannot digest uncooked grains of rice. It is also almost impossible to rake, scoop, or pick up from grass and flower beds.

CHAPTER 21

AT THE RECEPTION

No matter how large or how small, your reception is a celebration, and you and your family are the hosts. You are there to welcome guests, feed them, enjoy their company, and thank them. Let them know how happy and pleased you are that they are there to celebrate with you.

From Here to There

The reception hosts and the bridal couple should get to the reception as soon as possible. This may mean that the parents and perhaps the attendants will precede the newlyweds if photos are taken at the wedding site after the ceremony. Plan the photo session so that the shots including parents, other family members, and attendants are taken first.

If there's a long interval between the arrival of guests and the wedding party, have special helpers at the reception site ready to greet guests, make necessary introductions, and see that guests are offered drinks and hors d'oeuvres. It's nice to have music (live or recorded) to set the mood.

People do expect some delay, but any longer than thirty to forty-five minutes becomes excessive, unless your invitation included a later starting time for the reception. It is not acceptable for the wedding party to disappear, whatever the reason, while reception guests are left to cool their heels and wonder when the reception will begin. If there is any chance of a considerable delay, be sure guests will be served food and drink while they await your arrival.

The Etiquette of the Receiving Line

A receiving line is a traditional way for the wedding party to greet guests, upon their arrival at the reception or after the ceremony before leaving for the reception. Whether you decide to have a receiving line is simply a matter of choice. It is certainly not required.

- **Must there be a receiving line?** No, but it may be a wise choice. A receiving line is an effective way to greet and thank your guests, especially if your wedding is large and you may not have the chance to speak personally with everyone during the course of the day. It is helpful to have a receiving line if there are seventy-five or more guests. If you do not have a receiving line, be sure to greet all of your guests during the reception.

- **When is it best not to have a receiving line?** If the combination of picture taking and receiving line means guests could be left hanging for an hour or more with little to do, do without it. It is worse to leave guests in limbo. Just be sure that you greet each guest at some point during the reception. Also, have the DJ or bandleader introduce the bridal party and the bride's and groom's parents so that guests will know who's who.

- **When do you have a receiving line?** If a receiving line is planned, it can be done at the ceremony site immediately following the service. After the line is completed, the couple takes their formal pictures and then continues on to the reception site. The receiving line can also take place as soon as the couple reaches the reception site—after the wedding party completes the formal photographs at the ceremony site.

- **When should we take the formal photographs?** If taken before the reception starts, keep the session as brief as possible. Organize carefully so that everyone in the photos knows exactly where to go and what pictures will be taken. Other options include taking photos after the receiving line is finished and taking some shots before the receiving line and finishing the photo shoot later during the reception. Work out the timing in

---

A QUESTION FOR PEGGY:

IS THERE GUEST BOOK ETIQUETTE?

Q: What is the proper way to display a guest book for guests to sign at my wedding reception?

A: It is not obligatory to have a guest book at the reception, but it's a nice memento of the occasion and a record of all present. Delegate a friend, a member of the family, or an attendant to stand by the book and remind each guest to sign. Place the book on a table near the reception entrance or at the end of the receiving line. Occasionally, a guest book is placed instead at the entrance to the ceremony, and one of the ushers asks guests to sign it before entering the sanctuary. This is done when there are more guests attending the ceremony than the reception, such as the times an officiant extends to church members an open invitation to the nuptials. If a member of the family or a close friend is supervising the guest book, be sure to present him or her with a boutonniere, corsage, or nosegay to show your appreciation.

advance. Be sure that your photographer and wedding coordinator are aware of the schedule. Do not leave guests in limbo while you pose for endless pictures.

- **Where should the receiving line be?** Decide ahead where you want the receiving line to be. Your clergyperson or club manager will let you know the best location. The ideal location is one that permits guests to have a refreshment while they are waiting their turn or one that flows into the open area where the reception will take place. If you choose the latter, position a waiter at the end of the line with a tray of champagne or other beverages to offer to guests as they make their way to the reception area. To accommodate guests who eat and drink while waiting in line, see that a small table for used glasses, plates, and napkins is placed near the beginning of the line. No food or beverages should be carried through the receiving line.

- **Where to put the cocktail?** Guests shouldn't go through the receiving line with food or drink. Place a table near the beginning of the line for them to deposit glasses, plates, and napkins.

- **Who stands in the receiving line?** The traditional line includes the couple, their parent(s), the maid of honor, and possibly the bridesmaids. The basic order of the line is: the wedding hosts—traditionally the bride's parents (her mother first, then her father)—the groom's mother and father, the bride and groom, the maid or matron of honor, and the bridesmaids. Fathers are not required to stand in line; they might handle other hosting

Receiving line

duties while the line is in place. But if one father participates, the other should as well. In a military wedding, it is protocol for a groom in uniform to stand before his bride. Also, if there is a large number of bridesmaids, they might take turns in the line a few at a time.

If the wedding party is small, the best man and the groom's attendants can be included. Sometimes the children of the couple participate if they are mature enough to stand still and greet people. Ushers, flower girls, and ring bearers are not included, nor are siblings who are not members of the wedding party.

A QUESTION FOR PEGGY:

WHAT TO DO WITH GARRULOUS GUESTS?

Q: *How do I tactfully deal with an excessively talkative guest in a long receiving line?*

A: No one should tie up the line with extended conversation. If a guest is talkative, it is up to the parents or the bride and groom to gently break in and say "We're so glad you're here—let me introduce you to . . ." to help move that person along.

If people other than parents host (the adult children of the bride, for instance, or an aunt and uncle), they are first in the receiving line—before the bride's parents or the couple.

- **Should bridesmaids and children stand in line?** It is perfectly acceptable for bridesmaids to stand in the receiving line, but they don't have to, especially if the line is long. Doing so only prolongs the line and stretches the imaginations of guests thinking up a polite, clever comment for everyone. Young children—flower girls, ring bearers, pages, and train bearers—do not stand in the line, although the children of the bride and groom may be included if they are old enough and want to participate.

- **How should guests pass through the line?** Guests should pass as quickly as possible, pausing only long enough to be greeted by the host and hostess, wish the bride happiness, and congratulate the groom. Close friends and family often accompany their congratulations with a kiss. Otherwise, each person extends a hand to the person in line, who turns to introduce him or her to the next person in line before greeting the next guest. This eliminates the need for guests to have to introduce themselves repeatedly, and makes the process more personal.

- **Where do divorced parents stand?** Divorced parents do not stand in the line together. The parent and stepparent who host the reception or are closest to the bride or groom usually stand in the line. But situations vary so much that you have to work out an arrangement that is the most sensible for your family.

When divorced parents are friendly, it is perfectly acceptable for the bride's mother to have first place regardless of whether she pays the bills—especially if she was the custodial parent and this is agreeable to everyone. But if there is serious discord between parents and stepparents, it may be best to forgo the formal receiving line altogether.

When relations between divorced parents and their current spouses are amicable, they may all be in the line—but separated by the other set(s) of parents to prevent confusion or embarrassment for guests. When all the parents are divorced and remarried, the order can be: (1) bride's mother and stepfather, (2) groom's mother and stepfather, (3) bride's stepmother and father, and (4) groom's stepmother and father. The same alternating order can be followed for single divorced parents. If a widowed or divorced parent is engaged, his or her partner may stand in the line if this is comfortable for everyone.

To avoid a very long line, the different sets of parents might take turns standing in line.

There are so many variables in the case of divorced and remarried parents. Plan early with your parents to determine who stands where. The traditional guideline—the hosts stand first in line—comes in handy for helping to defuse any hurt feelings and questions. And sometimes the fathers circulate among the guests simply to make things easier.

The *full* lineup of all divorced and remarried parents would look something like this:

Bride's mother	Groom's stepmother
Bride's stepfather	Groom's father
Groom's mother	Bride
Groom's stepfather	Groom
Bride's stepmother	Maid or matron of honor (set the bridesmaids free—the line is long enough!)
Bride's father	

Toasts

Toasting the happy couple at the wedding reception is one of the event's most cherished traditions. The customary toasting drink is champagne, but it is fine to toast with water as well.

- **Pouring the champagne.** At a sit-down reception, champagne is poured as soon as everyone is seated. At a cocktail reception where guests are either seated at small tables or standing, it is poured after everyone has gone through the receiving line or after the couple has entered the reception and been introduced. If champagne is not being served, toasts are then made with whatever beverage guests have in front of them, whether water, soft drinks, punch, or juice.

- **Getting the guests' attention.** The best man attracts the attention of the guests, either from his table or from the microphone, and proposes a toast to the bride and groom.

- **Who gives a toast?** The best man gives the first toast. It's perfectly fine for his to be the only one offered. Often, both fathers offer welcome toasts to each other's families and guests or express their happiness at their children's union. The maid or matron of honor and other members of the bridal party may propose toasts, and the groom may toast his bride and new parents-in-law. If any telegrams or messages have been sent, they are read by the best man.

- **Who stands, who sits?** Everyone should rise for the toasts to the newlyweds except the bride and groom, who remain seated. If a toast is directed to the bride only, the groom rises; if it is directed to their parents, both the bride and groom rise. If there is no seating and everyone is standing, including the bride and groom, then the newlyweds simply smile as toasts are made. They do not drink a toast to themselves.

- **When the bride and groom toast.** When making a toast together, the bride and groom do not speak in unison, but rather stand together while one speaks or take turns speaking.

- **How should the bride and groom respond to a toast?** When toasted, the bride and groom do not stand. They smile appreciatively and when the toast is finished acknowledge it with a thank-you.

- **What do you say when toasting?** Wedding toasts are best prepared ahead of time, as you may be more nervous or emotional than you might expect. Keep what you say short and to the point—the spotlight should be on the bride and groom. Comments should be in keeping with the occasion. This is not the time for long stories and humorous anecdotes. Those are more appropriate at the rehearsal dinner. (See also Chapter 10, page 188: "What happens during the dinner?")

There are entire books devoted to the subject of wedding toasts, so do pick one up if you're really struggling with what to say. Don't be intimidated. It's more important for wedding sentiments to be heartfelt than eloquent.

TOASTING TIPS: SHORT AND SWEET!

A wedding reception is not the time for long anecdotes or jokes; those are usually told at the rehearsal dinner the night before or at bachelor or bachelorette parties. Short and sweet: That's what the best man's toast to the newlyweds should be. Here are three recommendations:

- "Please join me in a toast to Mark and Cindy, first written by William Shakespeare: 'Look down you gods and on this couple drop a blessed crown.' May all your days be blessed and crowned with joy and happiness. To Mark and Cindy!" (From William Shakespeare's *The Tempest*)

- A favorite Irish blessing:

  May the wind be always at your back.
  May the road rise up to meet you.
  May the sun shine warm on your face,
  The rains fall soft on your fields.
  Until we meet again, may the Lord
  Hold you in the hollow of his hand.

- A toast sometimes used in Moscow includes this couplet:

  Two birds were sitting in the tree branches vis-à-vis.
  This is to the wind, which rose and joined their lips.

ENGAGEMENT PARTY TOASTS

In days past, a party was often held to announce an engagement. Today, engagement parties are usually a way for friends of the bride and groom to meet their respective families a few months before the big event.

Parents to Couple

- "I [*or* we] propose that we all drink to the health and happiness of Keiran and the woman that he, to our great joy, is adding permanently to our family: Candace Roe."

- "Candace's mother and I have always looked forward to meeting the man she would choose to marry. I have to say we couldn't be happier with her choice—wonderful Keiran Matthews. Please join me in wishing them a long and happy marriage."

Bride and Groom to Future In-Laws

- "Bill and Daphne [*or* Mr. and Mrs. Matthews], I'm so happy you're finally able to meet the friends I've been telling you about. It also gives *them* the chance to get to know *you*—a couple for whom I have the greatest respect and whose family I will be proud to join. Everyone, please join me in toasting Bill and Daphne Matthews!"

- "I remember the first time Candace took me to meet her parents. They quickly bowled me over with their hospitality, good cheer, and great sense of humor. Please join me in toasting two people whom I look forward to having not only as in-laws but also as life-long friends. To Ken and Fiona [*or* Mr. and Mrs. Roe]!"

REHEARSAL DINNER TOASTS

The rehearsal dinner allows any guest present the opportunity to toast the happy couple and others.

Parents to Parents

- "I'd like to ask you to join me in toasting two wonderful people without whom this wedding could never have been possible: the mother and father of our soon-to-be daughter-in-law, Lynne—Mr. and Mrs. Brown."

Parents to Couple

- "I don't need to tell you what a wonderful person Lynne is, but I do want to tell you how happy Brett's mother and I are to welcome her as our new daughter-in-law. Here's to Lynne and Brett!"

Best Man to Groom
- "Alex and I have been friends for what seems like a lifetime now, and I've always noticed what a lucky guy he is. Tonight, all of you can see just what I mean as you look at Amy. Please join me in a toast to both of them. May their lucky numbers keep coming up for the rest of their lives."

WEDDING RECEPTION TOASTS

Traditionally, the best man offers the first toast. Friends should keep their toasts to three or four minutes at the most, which will give family members and other attendants more time to propose their own.

Best Man or Maid or Matron of Honor to Couple
- After a brief speech, the head attendant could propose the toast by saying, "To Rosemary and John—extraordinary individuals in their own right. May they enjoy happiness and prosperity their whole lives long," or "To Rosemary and John—may they always be as happy as they are today."

Groom to Bride, Bride to Groom
- "All my life, I've wondered what the woman I'd marry would be like. In my wildest dreams, I never could have imagined she would be as wonderful as Keisha. Please join me in drinking this first toast to my beautiful bride."

- "I'd like you all to join me in a toast to the man who's just made me the happiest woman in the world. To Michael!"

Parents to Couple
- "We're thrilled you're now a part of our family, and we know that Matt's life will be blessed and enriched by having you as his wife. Matt and Sherry, we wish you health, wealth, and lifelong happiness as you set off on your greatest adventure."

- "As long as I've known Sherry, she's kept the perfect man in her mind's eye. And the first time I met Matt, I knew immediately that she had found him. Kids, you were no doubt meant for each other, and I want to wish you a long and happy life together."

- "Love does not consist in gazing at each other, but in looking outward in the same direction." (Antoine de Saint-Exupéry)

Blessing the Meal

If your reception includes a meal, you might say grace beforehand. Here is a wonderful opportunity to honor a relative or friend by asking him or her to participate. No matter who gives the blessing, you should be sure to ask the person ahead of time, so that he or she can prepare. If you have a DJ or bandleader, ask him or her to request everyone's attention, at which point the person giving the blessing goes to the microphone. If there is no microphone, the best man may call for quiet. Usually the best man makes a brief introduction; the person you've asked offers the blessing; and then the best man thanks the person, signaling to guests that they can begin eating.

A QUESTION FOR PEGGY:

WILL A FAITH-BASED BLESSING MAKE SOME GUESTS UNEASY?

Q: *We're planning our daughter's wedding reception, and a question has come up about saying a blessing before the dinner. Not all guests belong to our faith, so is this appropriate? And if so, whom should we ask to say grace?*

A: A blessing before the wedding meal is certainly appropriate. Guests who are not religious or are of other faiths can simply lower their heads and remain respectfully silent during the blessing.

Dancing

Dancing is often an essential element of the reception. Almost every culture has a tradition of joyous dancing at the wedding celebration. As it was noted in *A Bride's Book of Wedding Traditions,* by Arlene Hamilton Stewart: "Italians do the tarantella; Irish dance a jig; Scots do the Highland fling; Greeks join hands in a chain dance they call the *kalamatianos;* and the Jewish people dance circles around the bride and groom in their famous dance, the *hora.*"

While there are many types of dances and a wide variety of customs, here a few general guidelines for dancing at the wedding reception:

- **When does the dancing start?** If there is dancing, it follows dessert at a seated dinner, but at a buffet reception, it might start after the receiving line or photo session. At an afternoon reception when the meal is served later, guests might dance before the bridal party goes to their table.

- **Who dances first?** The bride and groom dance the first dance while guests watch and applaud.

- **What is the second dance?** In some locations, there is a traditional "second dance." For the second musical number, the father of the bride dances with the bride, and the groom dances with his mother. Then the groom's father might dance with the bride and the groom with his new mother-in-law, or, the groom might dance with the maid or matron of honor, and the bride with the best man. At this point, other guests usually join them on the dance floor. The "second dance" is completely optional. Some couples prefer not to have it.

- **When do the bride and her father dance?** If there is no prearranged "second dance," at some point during the dancing, the bride and her father usually have a special dance of their own. The groom and his mother may do the same. The bride and groom may want to select special songs in advance for their respective parents. The bride and her father may either dance the entire song alone, or be joined by the bride's mother who dances with the groom and the groom's father who cuts in on the bride's father to dance with the bride. They may change partners halfway through the song and join their respective spouses, and the other guests may join them on the dance floor.

- **Stepparents and blended families.** When family relationships are more complicated, everyone can join the couple after their first dance. The newlyweds should then make a point to dance with all parents and stepparents at some time during the reception.

Closing Activities

Traditionally, guests would wait for the bride and groom to make their grand departure before leaving. But today it's much more likely that the bridal couple will see their guests off and then continue the celebration. There are other closing activities that guests may wait to witness before taking their departure, such as:

CUTTING THE CAKE

At a seated dinner, the cake is cut just before dessert is served. At buffets or passed-tray receptions, the cake cutting usually takes place nearer the end of the reception. When the couple and their attendants gather at the cake, guests know that the time has arrived. Be sure to give your caterer or site manager and your photographer an approximate time for the cutting. (See also Chapter 19, pages 344–345: "The Art of Cutting the Cake.")

THROWING THE GARTER

In some communities, it is traditional for the bride to wear an ornamental garter just below her knee, so the groom can remove it easily and tastefully without fanfare. For this event, the best man and the ushers gather, and the groom throws the garter over his shoulder. According to tradition, the man who catches the garter will be the next to marry. The throwing of the garter should never be done in a tasteless manner, with the groom fondling the bride's leg for all to see, for example. This can be embarrassing, for the participants and for the guests.

TOSSING THE BOUQUET

Traditionally, just before the couple leaves the reception, the bride or her maid or matron of honor gathers the bridesmaids and all single women guests together, often at the foot of a stairs, in the center of the dance floor, or by the door. The bride then turns her back and throws over her shoulder her bouquet or a facsimile of it (called a "tossing bouquet"), if she wants to keep and preserve her original bouquet. Tradition has it that whoever catches the bouquet—who gets to keep it, by the way—will be the next one married.

Both throwing the garter and tossing the bouquet are completely optional activities. Decide in advance whether or not you plan on including these traditions, so that your DJ or bandleader will be prepared.

AND YOU'RE OFF!

The bride and groom may leave in their bridal finery or change into "going away" clothes. If they decide to change at the site, the maid or matron of honor and the best man generally attend the bride and groom in their separate changing rooms and collect the wedding clothing. At some point, parents and relatives join them for a good-bye.

When the newlyweds are ready to go, the attendants form a farewell line and are joined by the guests. The couple is often showered with rose petals, confetti, or the like, as they dash to their departure vehicle, which may have been decorated by the ushers with "Just Married" written in shaving cream or some other (hopefully) biodegradable and easy-to-clean medium.

CHAPTER 22

AFTER the WEDDING: FROM THIS DAY FORWARD

It's your responsibility to make sure post-wedding loose ends are taken care of, so that they don't become a burden to anyone else while you are away on your honeymoon. These duties include making arrangements for gift deliveries and delegating rental returns, the mailing of wedding announcements, and the storage of wedding clothes. It goes without saying that if you are leaving your children behind or if you have pets that will need to be cared for, you will have to make arrangements in advance. Many of these duties can be delegated to members of the wedding party and friends and relatives.

Storing Wedding Attire

You will want to take as much care with your wedding clothing after the event as you did before. Here are some practical ways to store your wedding attire so that it will stay fresh and wrinkle-free for years to come:

- **Wedding gown.** Have an attendant or relative hang your gown up as soon as you take it off. Get it to a professional cleaner who specializes in wedding gowns, particularly in the event of spots or champagne spills. The cleaners will then clean and store the gown in a sealed box or container. Store the box or container on a high shelf in a closet or in the attic.

- **Headdress.** Any headdress not attached to a veil should be cleaned professionally and placed in a hatbox.

- **Train and veil.** Have each cleaned professionally with the wedding gown and stored in the same manner.

- **Gloves.** Launder cotton gloves. Wrap in tissue in a box and keep in a drawer. Have kid or leather cleaned professionally.

- **Shoes.** For cloth shoes, sponge with a cloth and a mild detergent; when dry, put them away in tissue in a box. For leather shoes, polish and store. If tough grass stains are on shoes, have them cleaned professionally, no matter what the fabric.

- **Bouquet.** If your freezer is large enough, store your bouquet inside until you return from your honeymoon. When you return, have it freeze-dried by a florist or dry it yourself by hanging it upside down in a dry place.

Thank-Yous

Ideally, you have kept up with your thank-you notes throughout the pre-wedding period. You will most likely be inundated with more gifts, however, upon your return from your honeymoon—and thus have a whole new batch of thank-you notes to pen. Remember: Grooms write thank-you notes these days, too, so make writing them a shared task. (See also Chapter 8, pages 162–166: "The Importance of 'Thank You.'") It's a nice touch to send your parents a thank-you note and a gift, perhaps a souvenir picked out on your honeymoon travels. Don't forget to thank your attendants for being in your wedding when you're thanking them for their gifts.

Selecting Wedding Pictures

One of the things you should set up with your photographer and videographer before the wedding day is a date to view and select wedding photos and videos. Both you and your mate should be present to select photographs; often other family members are included as well.

Once you've made your selections, you will want to decide the quantity to be printed of each photograph, their order in photo albums, and how many albums you will want to order, to present to family later.

A QUESTION FOR PEGGY:

WHAT'S THE BEST WAY TO ENSURE RENTAL ATTIRE IS RETURNED?

Q: *Who is responsible for returning rental attire after the wedding?*

A: You can designate the best man, parents, or someone else who is reliable to see to the return of the tuxes and any other rentals that have been used. Just make sure you have supplied your helpers with all the information they might need (rental agreement, hours of operation of the rental establishment). Also, be sure to thank any after-the-big-day helpers, just as you have thanked all of your helpers before these final tasks.

PHOTO GIFT LIST

☐ Bride and groom	Bridal party
☐ Bride's parents	☐ Best man
☐ Groom's parents	☐ Maid/Matron of honor
☐ Bride's grandparents	☐ Bridesmaids
☐ Groom's grandparents	☐ Ushers
☐ Other relatives	☐ Flower girl
☐ Special friends	☐ Ring bearer

Make sure the wedding negatives are stored in a safe place. You may want to have them scanned onto a disk or printed on a CD-ROM for safekeeping.

Peggy Post's Top Ten Honeymoon Tips

The honeymoon is the romantic interlude bridging your past and future lives. It's the time to revel in your nuptial bliss and recuperate from the hectic planning and activities of the weeks and months before the wedding—and from the big day itself. Here are some tips to help make the honeymoon live up to the romantic myth—and create an experience that you'll both look back on fondly for years to come.

1. **Tap into the tradition.** In the Middle Ages, mead, a fermented drink made with honey (the symbol of fertility, health, and life), was drunk by the bride and groom for thirty days—the cycle of the moon. During this period, the couple stayed hidden from their parents and friends, the mead no doubt loosening their inhibitions and getting the marriage off to an auspicious start. Even if you have been together for quite some time, you can enrich your getaway by tapping into the traditional spirit of the honeymoon as a period of treasured communion between the couple—a time like no other. Note: You certainly do not need to drink mead, or other alcoholic beverages!

2. **Plan together.** Both of you should be involved in planning the honeymoon. That includes doing the research, meeting with a travel agent, and making reservations. Discuss what type of honeymoon experience you want. A lazy beach retreat? A tour of a European country? A week of sky and scuba diving? Make sure you are in agreement. If you dream of biking in Italy, but he's visualizing cocktails by the pool, aim for something in the middle.

3. **Plan ahead.** The honeymoon, for many couples, is a top-priority decision—with good reason! Some couples make all of their other wedding decisions around their honeymoon plans. Make the preliminary decisions as early as possible, such as the honeymoon date, location, transportation, accommodations, and length of stay.

4. **Set a honeymoon budget.** Honeymoons need to be planned in advance for budgetary reasons as well. It is all too easy to get caught up in the frenzy of planning the wedding and reception, only to find you don't have the funds you need for the honeymoon you've dreamed of. So don't forget to add up all of the expected (and unexpected) costs of the honeymoon. Beyond transportation and lodging, the honeymoon budget should also include meals, transfers, souvenirs, sightseeing and sports-related costs, tips, taxes, and the little luxuries, like a massage or poolside charges for lounge chairs and towels.

5. **If you have children, plan for them and your honeymoon.** Many couples marrying for the second time bring children into the marriage. Remarriage can be unsettling for kids, especially for young children who are dependent on their parent. They may feel that they are being abandoned or will become less important in your life. If your

kids feel threatened by your marriage, you may rightly be concerned about leaving them immediately after the wedding to go on a honeymoon. This is a clear conflict, as you and your new spouse may be eager—and certainly deserve—to share some private time together.

Some couples decide to take their kids on the honeymoon with them, making the trip a family vacation. This is fine—as long as you and your mate are enthusiastic and in complete agreement about this. Others find ways to divide their honeymoon, with the first part a time for the two of them alone and the second part a trip as a new family. This gives your children something to look forward to during the few days you are away from them.

Or you could plan a special kids' party after you get home from the honeymoon. If you do decide to take a honeymoon away from your kids, think of ways to remember them while you are gone. Call often and send plenty of postcards or e-mails. You can even make videotapes or audiotapes to mail overnight to your children, describing your vacation spot and sending your love.

6. **Take care of the caretakers.** As a matter of security as well as courtesy and common sense, leave a written schedule of your trip, including telephone numbers, with the people who maintain your home, take care of pets, water plants, or pick up mail. The same, of course, applies if you have children and you're leaving them with a relative or other caregiver. Be sure to give your parents or other close relatives copies of your schedule, as well. Take with you on your honeymoon the phone numbers of any caretakers. Leave written instructions for feeding pets, giving medications, or watering plants. Be sure to stock up on food and the like so that caretakers are not obligated to spend money on supplies. Don't forget to write thank-you notes and perhaps even purchase small gifts for those people who took care of things while you were away.

7. **Don't neglect post-wedding tasks.** Take care of postwedding loose ends so that they don't burden anyone else while you are away on your honeymoon. It's fine to delegate tasks to others; just make the arrangements ahead of time. These jobs could include dealing with rental returns, keeping an eye out for wedding gift deliveries, mailing your wedding announcements, and delivering your wedding gown to storage.

8. **Plan for wedding announcements.** If you're sending wedding announcements, it's a good idea to have them addressed and stamped before the wedding, either by you or someone helping you. Ideally, they should go into the mail soon after your wedding day. Traditionally announcements are mailed the day after the wedding, but that's no longer necessary. Mailing announcements anytime a few days—or even weeks—after your big day is fine. Ask a friend or relative to mail your announcements if you would like them sent during the time you're away on your honeymoon.

9. **Set aside time to talk.** It's easy for couples who are swept up in countless pre-wedding details and duties to become somewhat myopic about preparing for life after the wedding. Make sure to set aside time during the honeymoon to discuss ways to make the transition to married life go smoothly. For example, the realities of keeping a household budget and dividing household chores are something you'll need to discuss. Talk about how you plan to communicate in general, making sure you are both committed to open communication. It helps enormously to commit from the start to a certain flexibility and willingness to compromise—and to stick to it. It's a lifelong pledge.

10. **Pamper, indulge, relax!** This should be a once-in-a-lifetime event for the two of you. So don't be afraid to splurge on a few extras. It could be his and hers massages at the hotel spa—or supplies for giving each other spa treatments in the privacy of your own room. Other possibilities: a sunset sail if you're near a beach, or an extravagant meal of lobster tails and filet mignon. Whatever the indulgence—enjoy! This is a special time.

The Two of You: Life After the Honeymoon

Many newlyweds returning from their honeymoon will be living together for the first time. As part of making the transition from "me" to "we," below are some considerations to decide on together:

Start with the practical details. It's a good idea to have made any *financial and name-change arrangements* before your wedding day (see also Chapter 3, pages 53–55: "Name Changes"), particularly if you will be sharing a bank account. Discuss the *division of household duties:* Who will be responsible for keeping a household budget, for example, or buying groceries or cleaning the house? Even though you may plan to share household duties, you may quickly discover that one of you naturally falls into the role of cook or cleaner, or that each of you has a distinct preference in household chores. Whatever you do, try to keep the balance of duties equal. There are also adjustments to be made for differing styles: He wants all the counters clear, for example, and you don't mind a little clutter. The key words here are *flexibility* and *communication.*

Other little sticking points you and your spouse should discuss include:

- Which side of the bed to sleep on.

- Closet and drawer space.

- Making sure each of you has a sacred private place.

- How much and what to watch on television, and clicker control.

- Music volume.

- Privacy boundaries, such as always knocking before entering an occupied bathroom.

- Your policies on drop-ins, such as in-laws popping in without calling first.

- The pros and cons of pets. It would be a big disappointment to count on sharing a pet with your loved one, only to find out after the fact that he or she is simply not interested in having the responsibility.

Finally, continue to affirm your mutual commitment to *open communication*. If something is making either of you increasingly unhappy or irritated, you'll want to feel free to express that unhappiness in an open forum—and the sooner you deal with a problem, the less time it has to fester into resentment. Do so sensitively, however, without playing the "blame game." At the same time, you should both promise to listen open-mindedly to any complaints the other may have. When conflicts arise, as they inevitably will, it is a great help to have practiced your communication skills in many small ways, and to have built mutual trust in your willingness to listen, be flexible, and compromise.

THE PERSONAL TOUCH

THE POST-WEDDING GET-TOGETHER

A post-wedding party, hosted by the newlyweds, is a great excuse for reuniting with loved ones and close friends to remember and celebrate a shared momentous event. Whether held a month or six months after the wedding, the gathering of the wedding party and family and close friends can also be an occasion to view wedding videos and photo albums. It can be the most casual of affairs but can also be a chance to show loved ones your new home, wedding gifts, and entertaining skills as a couple.

Best Advice from Newly Married Brides and Grooms

I asked recently married brides and grooms to share their pearls of wisdom—what's the best advice they could offer to someone just beginning to plan their wedding? Here's what they had to say:

"The best advice I'd give to a bride and groom is to relax and focus on the real meaning of their big day. Have fun with the planning! Don't get too caught up in all the little details or obsess about decisions to be made. Remind yourself that the whole purpose of the day is to celebrate your love and the beginning of your lives together. . . . There will inevitably be something that will go wrong or not be exactly as you wanted it, but your guests will never notice, and (hopefully!) you'll be too blissfully happy on the big day to care."—Sally

"I think it's important to do what you want, while bearing in mind the sentiments and preferences of your families. Take advice graciously, but ultimately make your own decisions. You will be inundated with advice (both solicited and unsolicited!), which can become confusing."—Jennifer

"One thing that I think is still so important yet often overlooked is the thank-you note! A lot of people, especially those who have large weddings, just don't get around to sending out thank-you notes anymore. After an occasion where you are on the receiving end of so much generosity and well-wishing, it is the least you can do, and I think it says a lot about you whether you do or don't!"—Sally

"I would invite everyone. I was so scared of going over numbers, I didn't invite everyone I wanted, and in the end, I missed having some great friends there. Don't forget to eat! I ate at my wedding and it was great!"—Lisa

Anniversaries

Anniversaries are special milestones, honoring your commitment to each other, past and future. Your first anniversary is full of special traditions, such as sharing a bit of the wedding cake that has been frozen for the occasion. Here is a list of traditional gifts given to couples on each subsequent anniversary of their wedding vows:

1.	Paper or plastics	14.	Ivory
2.	Calico or cotton	15.	Crystal or glass
3.	Leather or simulated leather	20.	China
4.	Silk or synthetic material	25.	Silver
5.	Wood	30.	Pearls
6.	Iron	35.	Coral and jade
7.	Copper or wool	40.	Ruby
8.	Electric appliances	45.	Sapphire
9.	Pottery	50.	Gold
10.	Tin or aluminum	55.	Emerald
11.	Steel	60.	Diamond
12.	Linen (table, bed)	70.	Diamond
13.	Lace	75.	Diamond

Renewal of Vows

Traditionally, couples who reaffirm their vows do so on a big milestone anniversary, such as the twenty-fifth, but the celebration can occur on any anniversary. This practice is becoming more and more popular as a way for couples to celebrate earlier anniversaries. It's a way to recommit to each other publicly or to have the no-holds-barred celebration they may have missed out on the first time. A large party will usually suffice—as it may have to, given that some clergy will not perform a duplicate of the first wedding ceremony. Most, however, will conduct a simple reaffirmation of vows. The ceremony can occur during a regular Sabbath service or at a separate time. The form of the service varies, depending on the wishes of the officiant and the couple, and the tenets of the place of worship. The couple may be joined by any members of the original wedding party, plus their children. The ceremony is generally followed by a celebratory party.

Baker's Tips for an Anniversary Cake

It's a special tradition to freeze part of your wedding cake and eat it on your first anniversary. Often the top tier of the wedding cake is saved and frozen. Some tips to keep in mind if you want to take part in this tradition:

- Some icings hold up better in the freezer than others; ask your baker for suggestions if you are planning to save some wedding cake to eat on your first anniversary.

- Many couples choose to freeze only one piece of cake and eat the pretty top layer at the reception.

- Some couples don't like the idea of eating a year-old, possibly freezer-burned cake, preferring to take it out of the freezer and share it on their one-month anniversary.

- If you go the one-year-in-the-freezer route, freeze the cake (or delegate someone to do this) as soon as possible after the reception. Ideally, it should be placed in plastic wrap and then aluminum foil.

Index

(contracts *continued*)
musicians, 318, 320
photographers, 324, 327, 332
postnuptial, 56
premarital/prenuptial, 56–57, 247
wedding reception, 271–72
co-officiant, 197, 203
Episcopal, 202
Jewish, 208
Roman Catholic, 201
corsage
children and encore weddings, 245
delivery, 300, 349
groom gifts, 68
honorary attendants, 86
honor attendants, 265
usher distribution of, 350
counseling. *See* premarital counseling
coupe de marriage, 224, 227
court clerk, as officiant, 50
court records, 48
court train, 253
crest, wedding invitation, 106
crowning
Eastern Orthodox, 205, 223
Greek tradition, 228
cultural customs, xxiii, 222–32
adaptation of, 223
color, 225–26, 296
dancing, 228, 229, 231, 232, 371
engagement gifts, 155
wedding attire, 251
wedding financial responsibility, 39
wedding-gift giving, 148
wedding personalization, 198
wedding program explanations, 143, 222, 225
See also ethnic customs
cummerbund, 262, 266
cutaways, 29, 261

dancing
bride with father, 372
Greek tradition, 228
Irish tradition, 229
Italian tradition, 231
Mexican tradition, 228
Scottish tradition, 232
second dance, 372
wedding couple first dance, 32, 67, 318, 331, 371

wedding photos of, 331
wedding reception, 30, 67, 83, 270, 318, 331, 371–72
death
fiancé/fiancée, 18, 155
premarital/prenuptial agreements, 56, 247
See also deceased parents; widows and widowers
death certificate, remarriage and, 48
deceased parents
engagement announcements, 8
honoring of, 198
wedding invitation wording, 116, 118
Defense of Marriage Act (1996), 52
delegating duties, xix
deputy city clerk, as officiant, 50
designated drivers, 287
dessert table, 339, 343
destination weddings, xxii, 35–36
attendant obligations, 79
backup plan, 36
belated receptions, 189
date and time, 27
expenses, 35, 79, 91
flowers, 303
guests, xxii, 35–36, 90, 91
legal/medical requirements, 36, 53
outside United States, 53
save-the-date notices, 91, 143
style, 35
diamond basics, 12
dinner jackets, 30
direct deposit, name change, 58
disabled guests, 271, 275, 285
disclosure
financial, 56–57
health conditions, 49
Disney World, weddings at, 27
disposable cameras, 332–33
divorce, xxi
diplomacy, 15
documentation, xix, 48–49
engaged couple parent meeting, 6
engagement announcement, 3, 7–8, 9
ex-spouses. *See* ex-spouses
former in-laws, 243
premarital/prenuptial agreements, 56, 247

religious concerns, 51, 201, 202, 208
wedding invitation wording, 117, 121–22, 123
wedding photos, 330
wedding receiving line, 365–66
wedding rings and gifts, 236
wedding seating, xxi, 284, 352
DJs, wedding reception, 373
bridal party introduction, 363
decorum, 319
meal for, 281, 317
selection of, 32, 315, 319–20
site concerns, 272
documentation
baptismal record, 47
beneficiary changes, 58, 380
birth certificate, xix, 47
court records, 48
diamond certification, 12
divorce, xix, 48–49
driver's license, xix, 47
employment certificate, 48
foreign nationals, 51
health certificates, 49, 53
immigration records, 48
life insurance policies, 47
marriage certificate, 49, 55, 82, 83
marriage license, 47, 49, 53, 55, 67
naturalization records, 48
passport, 36, 47, 53
school records, 48
service contracts. *See* contracts
visas, 36, 51
weddings outside United States, 53
domestic partnership legalities, 52
double weddings
ceremony and service, 218
invitation wording, 127
dowry, 17, 38, 226
dress and grooming. *See* wedding attire
drinks. *See* alcoholic drinks; beverages
driver's license, xix, 47
drunkenness
designated drivers, 287
liability, 272

Eastern Orthodox weddings, 205
Egyptian traditions, 39, 296

(wedding ceremony *continued*)
Unitarian-Universalist, 213, 215
video of, 193, 196, 336
vows, 63, 192, 197, 209, 215,
216
witnesses, 51, 53, 82, 83, 217,
354
Wedding Channel (Web site), 65,
150, 173
wedding consultants, 22, 24–26
caterers and, 269, 280
commitment ceremonies, 34
cost, 25–26
destination weddings, 36
qualities, 25
role, 24–25
wedding ceremony location,
194
wedding rehearsal, 186
weddings outside U.S., 53
wedding flowers, 290–308
allergies, 292
birth month and, 296
bouquets, 32, 82, 186, 228, 292,
300, 303, 304–7, 331, 349,
357, 373
boutonnieres, 67, 68, 86, 216,
245, 262, 265, 266, 292, 307,
349, 350
centerpieces, 100, 293, 303, 308,
331
ceremony site, 193, 194, 195,
196, 291, 293, 301–2
checklist, 292–93, 298
chuppah, 196, 208, 293,
301
color, 291, 296, 298, 299–300
corsages, 68, 86, 245, 265, 300,
349, 350
delivery of, 300, 307, 349
destination weddings, 303
disposition of, 196, 308
encore weddings, 245
floral designers, 297
florists, 32, 196, 272, 292,
297–300, 303
flower girl, 84, 260, 292, 307,
349
fragrance, 296–97, 302
hair decorations, 292, 306
herbs, 296–97
Hindu weddings, 212
maid/matron of honor duties,
81
military protocol, 216, 266

orange blossoms, 227, 230, 290,
306
petal toss, 195, 300, 307, 360
remarriage, 245
seasonal, 294
selection of, 291
Sikh weddings, 213
symbolic meaning, 295
traditions, 228, 290, 295
usher distribution of, 350
wax, 290, 306
wedding attendants, 291, 292,
300, 307, 349
wedding reception, 272, 291,
293, 302–3
wreath headdress, 255, 290
wedding gifts, 148–66
acknowledgment of, 153, 166,
169
belated receptions, 190
bride and groom exchange, 32,
66, 157
broken/damaged, 161
broken engagements, 16, 154,
161–62
charitable, 151
from coworker, 163
death of fiancé/fiancée, 155
delivery acknowledgement, 153
delivery of, 105, 139, 153, 154,
376, 379
display of, 160–61
duplicate, 161
exchange/return of, 161–62,
166
expected, 98, 141, 152
from/to attendants, 32, 40, 41,
81, 82, 156–57, 183, 185, 188
gift cards, 154, 160
heirlooms as, 257
invitation don'ts, 141, 243
invitation exception, 98, 152
money as, 151, 153, 160–61,
164, 166, 231
monogrammed, 154, 158–59
opening of, 152
pre-wedding events, 176. *See
also specific events*
record-keeping, 93, 105, 153,
154
registry. *See* gift registries
remarriage, 141, 148, 149, 152,
234, 236, 243–44
return after breakup, 154
same-sex unions, 101

spending for, 153
thank-you note deadline, 162
thank-you note do's and don'ts,
153, 154, 161, 166, 236, 377
thank-you note examples,
165–66
thank-you note recipients,
163–64
thank-you note stationery, 145,
163
timing of, 153
unwanted, 161, 166
wedding announcements and,
96, 98, 128, 150, 157
wedding insurance, 58, 160
for wedding party, 156–57, 188
wedding gown, 250–53
appropriateness of, 253
belated receptions, 189
bustles, 253
classic silhouettes, 252–53
encore brides, 234
fabric and styles, 251
fabric swatches, xix, 298
heirloom, 256
order timing, 250
rented/borrowed, 253
storage of, 376, 379
trains, 253, 376
21st-century trends, xxii
type of wedding, 250
undergarments, 251, 256
See also veils and headdresses
wedding guests, 88–101
A and B lists, 90, 93
activities for, 68, 97–98, 136
attire of, xxii, 29–31
ceremony, 88–89, 204
ceremony seating, 83, 218, 350,
351–52
children as, 90, 94–95, 130–31,
134, 141, 272, 277, 285
civil marriage blessing, 217
computer file backup, 172
contact information, 93
destination weddings, xxii,
35–36, 90, 91
disabled/infirm, xvii, 100, 271,
275, 285
disposable cameras for, 332–33
elderly, xvii, 81, 100, 275
encore weddings, 90, 242–43
etiquette for, 98–100
expenses, 41, 95
ex-spouses as, 242

formal wedding flowers, 291, 304

wedding gown, 250

women wedding guests, xxii

white tie, 261, 264

white tie wedding, 30, 141

widows and widowers

child's engagement announcement, 8

child's wedding invitation, 116

child's wedding receiving line, 365

child's wedding seating, 351

former in-laws, 243

wedding invitation wording for, 121–22

wedding ring, 236

See also remarriage

wills, 58

wine

wedding reception, 283

wedding shared cup, 224

witnesses

civil ceremony, 217

marriage certificate, 82, 83, 354

religious restrictions, 76

wedding ceremony, 51, 53, 82, 83, 354

weddings outside U.S., 53

work associates, as wedding guests, 92, 141

EMILY POST

JAMES MONTGOMERY FLAGG

Emily Post 1873 to 1960

Emily Post began her career as a writer at the age of thirty-one. Her romantic stories of European and American society were serialized in *Vanity Fair, Collier's, McCall's,* and other popular magazines. Many were also successfully published in book form.

Upon its publication in 1922, her book *Etiquette* topped the nonfiction bestseller list, and the phrase "according to Emily Post" soon entered our language as the last word on the subject of social conduct. Mrs. Post, who as a girl had been told that well-bred women should not work, was suddenly a pioneering American career woman. Her numerous books, a syndicated newspaper column, and a regular network radio program made Emily Post a figure of national stature and importance throughout the rest of her life.

"Good manners reflect something from inside—an innate sense of consideration for others and respect for self."—Emily Post